A SPIRITUAL AUTO

A Spiritual Autopsy
OF SCIENCE AND RELIGION

Kelly Mitchell

Red Pill Press

Published by
Red Pill Press
10020–100 Ave.
Grande Prairie, AB
T8V 0V3

Printed in Canada

ISBN: 978-1-897244-68-5

Table of Contents

Author's Foreword

Feedback presents an author with a strange insight. The book you wrote seems different from the book the other person read. They draw unintended themes – which are probably there. The question – which is the real book – is meaningless. Both are and neither.

The original title for this work was *Buddha Is an Atheist*, and the current title was the subtitle. My background as both Buddhist and atheist made me notice an enormous hole in the atheism debate. Buddhism is a religion without God. This puts it in a unique position to comment.

During my research on atheism, the book changed. What was intended as further illumination of a world without God became a critique of new atheism and its hypocrisy. This new atheism holds a trivialized view of religion and a blind worship of mainstream science. It aims to negate the one and proclaim the other as absolute truth. Skepticism is totally redefined to mean that only science is true and science always is true. This faith-based rewiring of skepticism automatically believes any mainstream scientific pronouncement and automatically rejects any non-science idea. It is very far from genuine skepticism and very close to holy awe.

The arguments against religion consistently suffer from improper rhetoric. The straw man fallacy is a favorite. Religion is what atheists say – proponents are ignored. Religious arguments are cherry-picked for the most absurd or extreme. If members are racist, violent, or distrustful of education, that view is falsely implied to extend to all religious persons. Because certain areas of the country are poorly educated and religious, the *cum hoc ergo propter hoc* fallacy is invoked to claim that religious views cause poor education, even though many religious people are very well educated. Appeal to fear claims that Muslims will swarm over the peace-loving West and a Clash of Civilizations is inevitable. Since 'all terrorists are devoutly religious,' the false conversion fallacy explains, all devoutly religious persons are terrorists. A critique of science must be wrong, the genetic fallacy points out, because a Christian thought it up. With practice, the stream of rhetorical errors becomes easy to spot. Seeing which are intentional or accidental is more problematic.

The complete dismissal of religion by skeptics is disheartening. To my mind, skepticism is not a weapon, but a friendly and direct question. Another title briefly considered was *The Sword*

That Cuts Itself. Skepticism should question its own assumptions. It was once a humble, but vigorous discipline, reveling in uncertainty. That is the essence of the cause. No certainty about the world can be attained, even the existence of physical objects. Modern skepticism claims that mainstream science is absolutely and always correct and everything else is wrong or irrelevant. This is not proper skepticism. True skepticism is the subject of this book. Listen to contrary evidence with an open mind. Question everything, especially your deepest beliefs.

Recently, science became an atheist sacrament. You are not allowed to doubt it and still call yourself 'atheist.' But studying expert literature in scientific fields, I found disagreement to be the rule even among the most strongly believed theories. There is probably no scientific theory that is universally believed by experts in the field itself. However, we are presented with consensus views and haughtily informed they are the truth and not to be questioned by us – we're not 'scientists.' Curiously, the consensus view is often the more profitable one. The horrors of global warming, for example, have increased funding by 10,000%. Advocates, however, have an extremely superficial view of the science. So it is with most theories.

The skeptic magnifies poor ethics and flawed understanding in any religious context, and ignores them in any scientific context. Medical science may be the worst offender. For example, Morris Fishbein was 25-year head of the American Medical Association (which still licenses all doctors) and editor of its prestigious journal. He was also convicted of racketeering. Such simple facts should properly lead to questioning of the establishment line – but for some reason we never hear them. Ignoring evidence is not proper skepticism – it is merely hypocrisy stealing the name. And it is the modern methodology of 'skepticism.'

The word 'spiritual' in the context of the title means the search for truth. In this philosophy, religion and science are both an outgrowth of that quest. Spirituality can certainly have other meanings. The point here is not to dispute those or make some final definition of the term. It's intended as a working definition – a lens to analyze science and monotheistic religion. The hope is to bring them together – not as a Hegelian dialectic where thesis and antithesis become synthesis, but by realizing they flow from a common stream. Instead of synthesizing ideas, it cuts away complexity. A single source emerges. In some sense, this is the notion of the autopsy – a critical analysis, a getting to the bones.

An autopsy suggests death and that is the idea here – science and religion have died. They have forsaken their purity and been co-opted by profit motive, ego, and lust for power. Whatever exists now is something different which has taken the names science or religion. Endless base motives long ago destroyed the higher form of these broad human endeavors. Of course, it is only an analogy. The point is not to abuse it, but to use it as a guiding metaphor. A book covering this much ground needs some type of handle. In this case, death is the loss of ideals, integrity, and even simple kindness. The degradation of our civilization has seen all nobility disappear from even the greatest human achievements. Science and religion have vacated their essence and left us with rot. Of course, there still exist pockets of virtue – but these take effort to find. They should not be ignored. This book is not about forcing evidence into a pre-ordained conclusion. All my beliefs changed in the research. I only report what I found.

The cover image is a *kila* – a three-bladed ritual dagger used in Tibetan Buddhism. The kila is based on the premise of wrathful compassion – compassion without fear. This compassion can look at the worst in the world and see that basic goodness is ever-present. It cannot be destroyed. The kila cuts away the three emotional obscurations – grasping, hatred, and ignorance. They obscure the truth. The kila also cuts away non-emotional obscurations – incorrect views about reality. Most people want to know the truth. No one likes the pain of conflicted emotion. No one wants delusion. The kila is a contemplative symbol used to cut through internal noise and confusion. It is a scepter proclaiming rulership of one's own mind.

The book is not hierarchical. The sections do not build one upon the next, but each one stands more or less on its own. While there is encouragement to read the entire text, there is no harm in picking out the most appealing sections.

The reader will quickly notice a strong movement against the mainstream body of Western opinion. Probably every section disputes mainstream thought and decisively so. The book is not my set of opinions – everything is based upon research from experts in each field. It is more or less a set of alternative expert theories – references are provided. The particular areas covered here seemed sorely compromised in the mainstream. Alternative ideas or critiques were superior in evidence and logic. They had abundant substantiation to refute the accepted theories. The point of the book is to demonstrate that the mainstream body of belief in our culture is not true simply because of broad acceptance. People are encouraged to question their most deeply held views, especially as arisen from social agreement rather than examination of contradictory sources. Most conventional belief is based on the simple fear of being different.

The journey of writing this book was a difficult one. The strangest part was how deeply the book rewrote me. I am not happier for it. I doubt that reading it will make you so. But I hope that it gives a greater degree of mental freedom, more willingness to question common 'knowledge', and powerful tools to rest in uncertainty with dignity and courage. I know it will not give anyone peace, but I hope it shows the way. Genuine peace cannot arise from ignoring the hard truths of the world. That is a superficial version. Actual peace only comes after looking at the ugliest aspects of reality and accepting them, even as one works to make this a better place.

If you come to believe these things in a different way (and I ask only that you look with an open mind), intense despair may occur. Fear may come, too. But on the other side of despair may be great joy. Freedom is the opposite of security. It can be frightening. And even though this time in human history may seem terrible, we don't know but that 10 or 100 years gone may see the brightest period in our growth. We may become worthy of the unfathomable bounty we've received living in the modern age, and just living at all. We cannot know what the future will bring. But if we don't try, then we cannot possibly leave anything good behind. And if we do try sincerely, something good will come of it. The best instruction I ever received was a short maxim, written in my heart by a very wise soul. Never give up, he said. Never, ever, give up.

—June 4, 2012

Part I

Science

Introduction

Things are not as they seem…
—The Buddha

Despite contrary claims, the all-seeing eye of science has less than perfect vision. In fact, it's legally blind. The beginnings of life remain veiled and we can't say for certain that it even began on Earth. Evolutionary explanations for altruism are tail-chasing convolutions, while causes for dreaming, kissing, adolescence and superstition stay stubbornly inscrutable. No one can explain the origin of the universe. The meaning of its existence is likewise unknown. The question of why there is something rather than nothing is a closed and locked door. The binding of galaxies and the continued acceleration of the universe are mysteries filled by symbolically stated voids. And beyond these supercilious mock-ups, there is only silence. Weather prediction is a dream, free will is anybody's guess, and the cosmological constant is astrophysics' favorite theoretical shuttlecock. Quantum mechanics is results without a theory. Physics can only scratch its wooly old head about the massless particle and chemistry answers with a shoulder shrug about protein folding. The attempt to integrate quantum gravity has created the impossible rabbit hole called string theory and there is no explanation of gravity's underlying form except for waves that cannot be found. We don't know why we age and the theory of everything recedes further every day. Are we alone in the universe? Science has no answer. We lack all understanding of how the eye turns light into images or how the brain comprehends anything. The disappearance of the honeybees is a critical concern for us all – we eat plants that need pollinating. Science cannot help, and may even be the cause. Chemotherapy kills more than it cures, yet in its fumbling quest for a cure, mainstream science ignores the obvious – processed foods, sedentary lifestyle, lack of sunlight and ubiquitous chemicals cause most cancer. The looming energy crisis is bearing down like a freight train on our modern world – the laboratory provides no alternative to fossil fuels that can avert a serious collapse.

Science has abandoned questions of meaning. Attempted answers are astounding in their triviality. Researchers have zero observations about the soul, the spirit, or the animus of life. These are empirical dead letters. There is no scientific reason for moral behavior or any notion where the seat of decency lies. The mind in all its glory is irreconcilable with marginal maps of neuro-chemical activity. They solemnly assert that humanity is a haphazard mischance. Scores of 'non-believers' solemnly agree, nodding their heads in united assent. Such is the conviction of these new atheists, a conviction put forth with the subtly veiled implication that most of humanity simply lacks the courage to accept it. There is no need for proof when something is so evident.

"Science is not a unique, omnipotent force that will by itself make a better world," Bryan Appleyard writes. "It is not a truth about the world that renders all other truths obsolete. It is not on the verge of explaining life, the universe, and everything. Its past achievements have not proved unambiguously good. The benefits have not been free and we should not be deluded by those benefits into thinking that science can provide salvation for the human predicament."[1]

In spite of vast areas of unknowns, science blocks its own progress. *Scientific American*, the US Army and most scientists of the day disbelieved in powered flight despite the testimony of numerous eyewitnesses and photographs of the Wright brothers in action. It is the hymn of science – people cannot know anything, only scientists can. When will they listen to us and quit trusting their own eyes? A John Hopkins astronomy professor published an article proving scientifically that flight was impossible. A few weeks later Kittyhawk humiliated the skeptic.

Here is a list of ridiculed or suppressed discovery, now vindicated – continental drift, ion chemistry, meteorites, transistors, the television camera, black holes, DNA, bioelectricity, blood circulation, non-Euclidean geometry, sterilization, lasers, conservation of energy, powered flight, neurogenesis (new neurons), Ohm's law, germ theory, medical hand-washing, Doppler effect, and the electric current. After 32 years of ridicule, Barbara McClintock won the Nobel Prize for gene-transposition. Even child abuse was medically dismissed as unscientific.

Among the foremost scientific axioms today is that of physicalism. The world is made up entirely of little particles and anything appearing beyond it is merely an epiphenomenon. 'Epiphenomenon' is a semi-slurred concept meaning, according to Wikipedia, "a secondary phenomenon that occurs alongside or in parallel to a primary phenomenon." This has no legitimate meaning. It is impossible to establish primary versus secondary phenomena. In terms of mind, it means that mental phenomena are incidental to physical phenomena. Thoughts and emotions cannot ever, under any circumstances, affect the physical world.

But the idea defies our every experience. Thus it demands far better evidence than so far we have.

By implication, epiphenomena do not really exist – they arise in dependence on the 'real' phenomena, the physical. Love, hate, fear and happiness – they are not real. Only chairs and tables, neurons and (more or less) quarks are real. Some might disagree – nothing is real; the word has no meaning.

It is a logical puzzle – words are representations of other things. Linus Pauling, the only person ever to win two solo Nobel prizes, said, "All consistent thinkers conclude that pure logic is incapable of constructing a link between sense perceptions and concepts." Even if it has a provisional existence as a word, 'real' cannot represent that which it attempts to. This abandoned question is enormous. What indeed is 'real?' It must be the brain, we are told, while the mind must be an epiphenomenon. Why? Because the experts say so. A skeptical hand raises. One problem with such logic is that *all* phenomena arise in dependence on other phenomena. That is their nature. In that spirit of enquiry, let's examine the structure of modern science.

One of the more unsettling testaments to science lies in North Carolina – the eugenics display at Winston Salem University. 7,600 women, mostly black, as young as 14, were sterilized against their knowledge and will. The program ran in many other states, even liberal California, from the 1920s until the '70s. The logic came straight from Darwinism – culling the unfit. It led to the holocaust. The Nazi eugenics program attempted to 'evolve' humanity. This inescapable truth is cleanly ignored by the New Atheists, who go to great lengths to prosecute Catholicism for its support of the Nazi state. But the sword cuts both ways. Did the Catholics design the V-2 rockets for bombing England? Did the Muslims invent Zyklon-B to gas Jews? Did the Protestants develop the computer system to catalogue inferior peoples? Or does science shoulder its own sins?

Eugenics didn't even end there. 60,000 US citizens had been sterilized in the name of eugenics by 1960.[2] Eight million people were sterilized in India in 1976 alone. In the late '80s, a US government investigation showed that approximately 44% of Brazilian women between 14 and 55 had been sterilized.[3] Sterilization of people for 'unfitness' is a program of evolution. Science bears the moral burden. And eugenics is alive and well.

It's a long-standing presumption that science is (except for the atomic bomb) benign. Counterproofs would choke a supercomputer. Jacobins in the 1790s created a cult of reason. Trying to destroy Christianity, they descended into violence, killing half a million people in France. In 2004, the *Journal of Pediatrics* claimed that injecting mercury improved behavior in children. President Clinton apologized in 1994 for forty years of radiation testing on unsuspecting people. Vioxx killed 60,000.

Skepticism is proper, but nowadays, improperly understood. A number of principles seem to have gone missing from the philosophy of science. Indeed, the very idea of science philosophy has vanished. Without a sound epistemological and procedural scrutiny, we cannot evaluate the direction, value, and integrity of science. It's much too powerful a force to run unchecked. Part 1 of this book seeks to re-invigorate these lost principles. Also, it counters the trend attempting to fuse science and atheism into a single unit. The following principles should mainly be common sense:

- Science is accessible to anyone who can read and maintain concentration.
- Science cannot and does not have all answers. It has limits.
- Everything is open to question – the root of true skepticism.
- Science and religion are not implicitly at odds. Not all scientists are atheists or even materialists.
- All preprogrammed views (e.g. 'scientific outlook') obscure reality.
- All people have metaphysical (unproven, unprovable, and unevidenced) beliefs.
- Zealots of rationality have sacrificed the greatest virtue of science: creativity.
- Science does great harm.
- Logic cannot prove empirical truths.
- Logic cannot perceive intuitive truths and assumes their non-existence.
- Reality contains logical paradoxes.
- To refute a theory it is not necessary to have another theory. These are two distinct functions which have become erroneously conflated.
- An atheist is not required to accept any scientific supposition.
- Atheism has a single, simple definition – not believing in any god. An atheist can have 'metaphysical' beliefs.
- Both science and religion are outgrowths of an underlying spiritual essence. (Spirituality as defined here is the quest to understand reality and one's relationship to it.)

When Richard Feynman tried and failed to reduce a principle to freshman physics, he said, "that means we don't understand it." Incomprehensibility equals incorrect theory. Any intelligent person can comprehend valid science. It's a radical notion, but it's true. In fact, it's necessary.

There are different methods. People should challenge all a priori (before evidence) beliefs. For example, 'mind does not exist.' The belief has no evidence, only the tautology that mind has no physical form and the unexamined assumption that only physical forms exist. Science is stuffed with a priori assumptions leaning on the flimsiest evidence. 'DNA is the sole factor in heredity.' 'The universe began from an infinitely dense zero-size point 13 billion years ago.' 'A simple RNA virus causes 20 different diseases.' The discerning skeptic will uproot these without fear of dirty hands or barking dogmatists.

One should also challenge the evidentiary ideas science holds. Taking a creationist stance against evolution won't make much headway, but any idea is attackable within the dominion of science. In fact, most scientific ideas are hotly debated, but the debate gets no airplay. It's a primary reason for this book. Science needs to go back in the box as one of our best tools and get off our backs as master. There are other ways to look at reality, each of them valid. It is not their failure that science is unable to test them. It is the failure of science. The noise of this crowd is wrong. Nothing can be all things.

Several fallacies hide in the belief that 'scientists' can make a superior judgment of a theory than non-scientists. The idea presumes that scientists have always properly educated themselves on the theory and that non-scientists are incapable of understanding it. Both are blatantly incorrect, even foolish. Typically, a small group has put together their studies and most 'scientists' have faith in confirmations from potentially compromised authorities such as NIH and NSF. To put it succinctly, if a scientist has not studied a phenomenon, his opinion is worth less than a studied 'non-scientist.' If they are outside of their field, then their opinion is no better than a layman's.

The attempt to exclude non-scientists from debates begs the question of what makes someone a scientist. Is it accomplishments? This would take out anyone beginning their career or who invested their career in a disproved field. But disproving one's hypothesis is supposedly the hallmark of good science. This conundrum has led to the delusion that one is only a scientist with a proper degree. However, according to a 1995 NSF study, 334,000 (10%) people working in Science and Engineering jobs have no S&E degree.

Many non-degreed scientists have made enormous contributions. Here is a tiny sample: Philo Farnsworth first conceived of a working television and held 300 patents. Gregor Mendel, a monk, fathered genetic law. Joseph Priestley discovered oxygen. Dean Kamen invented the Segway and a kidney dialysis machine. Jobs and Wozniak dropped out of college. Nikola Tesla left in his third year, then gave us alternating current. With no degree, Michael Faraday invented the electric motor and founded electromagnetic technology. R.A. Fessenden built the first power plant at Niagara Falls. Henry Ford quit high school. Ben Franklin's formal education ended when he was 10. Bill Gates and Paul Allen dropped out of college. Jane Goodall accomplished her groundbreaking work before college. Oliver Heaviside, high school dropout, reduced Maxwell's equations from 20 to 4 – a major achievement. Soichiro Honda, founder of Honda motors, quit school with the sentiment that a movie ticket was more valuable than a diploma. Richard Leakey, world-famous paleontologist, had no college degree. Thomas Edison, Humphry Davy, Alexander Graham Bell had only honorary degrees after their accomplishments. Frank Lloyd Wright created a school of architecture without studying the discipline. And Charles Darwin, atheist icon, had an ironic degree in theology.

Which brings up another point – atheism is not the same as science. The new atheist thought police are out of bounds. Being an atheist does not require one to fetishize science. Nor does being a scientist require one to be an atheist. Only when the new atheists realize this will they earn a place at the table of civilized discourse. Until then, they remain a dogmatic fringe shouting down their many opponents. They falsely feel that only science can disprove God. But by simply looking, anyone can see that God is not there.

Much of science is gibberish. Karl Popper believed that philosophy of science was meant to "save the sciences from an obscurantist faith in the expert's special skill, personal knowledge and authority."[4] It's a desperately needed sentiment. Obscurantism is the landmine of modern science. The door has an implied ban on novices – 'you don't understand, therefore we're correct.' It's an absurd position, of course, and the sources are threefold: pride of domain, job security, and salvage operations. The last needs explanation. Failing theories are routinely salvaged by complexity. It's not a deliberate deviance – it's more a gradual accretion of auxiliary hypotheses to cover flaws. At some point, the complexity becomes too great for comprehension. But any expert who admits to not understanding is excluded. So experts have to 'understand' even if they don't. No one can admit that the theory makes no sense. Obscurantism is a serious, unacknowledged problem for science.

The ideal that science is the only possible understanding of reality is called Scientism. Some call it prejudice and it sends at least one mixed message: Scientific illiteracy is a terrible thing, but we must defer to the experts in all matters of science. The first attitude is reasonable, the second is dangerous.

Scientific literacy has three forms – standard, alternative and hidden. The standard form, literacy of consensus, understands the mainstream theories and blankly agrees. The alternative form, literacy of skepticism, understands the mainstream theories and allows itself to disagree. An important point – to disagree, it's not necessary to provide an alternative idea. Despite the common picture, science is not composed of universally accepted theories. All theories exist under rigorous contention – only thus are they meaningful. This book aims to present this second view – the backside of science. Mostly because somebody needs to; otherwise we are trapped in the sleep of consensus.

The hidden form of literacy is the process of creation/ discovery of 'knowledge'. Science is indifferent to its greatest concern – the brute validity of theory. Theory is not reality. This critical point is simply lost today. Theory is a set of abstract symbols interpreted by the mind. It is a description. Reality is our manifest experience. Just as the word 'bread' cannot satisfy hunger, so theory and reality have no actual link save the human mind.

This book does not delve deeply into consensus views – it is about the alternative and the hidden. Science, it can be shown, has not objectively mapped out reality. And it has lost track of its own substance. It has not put to rest all possible opposition. There is enormous dissent, but it gets no publicity. This is not an attempt to unfairly weight the issues. They already lie so heavily on the consensus beam that we must rebalance the scales. Suppressed voices point out problems. A censored premise is not a refuted premise. Mainstream views are easy to find; alternative views are not. More practically, due to the volume of material, consensus views are not detailed here. The book would be overlong. Many readers will be familiar in any event.

This text is not meant to be anti-science. Science is among humanity's great achievements. Splendid service comes from the noble ideology at its base. The question is whether it lives up to that ideology and how many more splendid acts await. Smaller human elements of greed and ego have co-opted the purer interests of the discipline. A string of self-evident successes have puffed up the overall ego. It can, according to its cheerleaders, do no wrong.

One thing receives the most gushing praise – the scientific method. But there is no such thing. If we examine the history of scientific inquiry, we see that it differs dramatically from its former incarnation. In fact, it has had many incarnations – twenty years ago and two hundred before that. That consistent change can be tracked back to the beginnings of science. As an example, the telescope and the microscope changed inquiry forever. As did numberless other tools. The methods to discover Relativity were visualization and a pencil. Those to develop the presumptive theories of neuroscience were completely different. Darwin had his methods, Fermi his. Great science is not constrained by the smaller ideas of proper method. Great science invents method because new arenas of study demand it.

For the Greeks, reason, analogy, and debate were the principal features. Today, the evidentiary basis and experimentation are the most prominently cited. It could be argued that mathematical structures are the real basis. Or computer models. In the 17th Century, science was called natural philosophy. Such philosophers dealt with the depth and breadth of nature. They left us a beautiful legacy and advanced human understanding by great strides. Now it has become so large and complex that compartmentalization is the rule. The smaller the unit of study, the more 'Scientist' one is. Each investigator has the tiniest tranche of focus.

Isaac Newton was the head of the Royal Academy of Sciences. Through rigorous investigations, he developed coherent, verifiable mathematics of the orbits of celestial bodies, explained the foreground of gravity (though not the underlying mechanism), invented calculus, and ran the Royal Mint. In short, he was a man of massive talents and broad fields of inquiry. Albert Einstein worked primarily in thought experiments such as the famous elevator in free fall – experiencing weightlessness though in a gravitational field. These men revolutionized science precisely because they did not accept the previous assumptions.

Lesser scientists conduct their queries via the scientific method, great scientists invent method to test their queries. Similar advances can still be made in inquiry. They should be. But we must respect the guiding ideas of the titans. Great minds create great science. They revolutionize. Mediocre minds investigate the details, and all too often, hold back the great. Dogmatism claims to be skepticism.

Science has thrown over our religion and trappings of culture, but it doesn't address the concerns that those things addressed. We live in a void. Science can't help. Awkwardness at approaching profundity is a legacy of science.

The atheist–religious debate, from the atheist perspective, separates the seeker of knowledge from the religious naïve believer. The scientist is a stalwart of truth, while the religious person is a corrupted leader, a deluded liberal go-along, or a fundamentalist fanatic. Religion is revelation; science is investigation. Unfortunately, this picture is wrong.

The General Relativity field equations came through a thought experiment. Like many discoveries, it was a Revelation. Expressing the universe, the equations are a mind of God. It was given to a single person. Only the elect can understand it. Functioning as prophets, they interpret it for our benefit. The analogy is not meant to make science into a religion by fiat; it shows that common strains exist in these disciplines. Human tendencies aim to discover meaning – whether called 'religious' or 'scientific.'

The new atheism, we are told, is 'science.' We must also accept other postulates – science as absolute virtue; rationality as the only means to truth; all metaphysical propositions are inherently bankrupt; there can be no mind existent beyond the brain; all religion is ipso facto flawed; religion stems from evolutionary psychology processes; the Western democratic ideal is the proper and true approach; the secular Western approach is superior to all other approaches; Islam is irrational, barbaric, and anti-scientific; war is an unfortunate necessity to protect us from terrorists; pre-emptive military strikes are sadly required to hit 'them' first; civilian casualties are unavoidable; our innocents are more important than their innocents; all Christian fundamentalists are raving lunatics; and evolution is inarguable. In addition, there are a number of optional specific theses: the universe is deterministic, religion comes from a God module or a sociological need for explanation of natural phenomena, liberal theologies are as culpable as fundamentalist theologies by not speaking out against them, and religion and science are in a titanic battle. We must accept the entire first set and one or more of the optional set to be a 'proper' atheist. But in the words of Mark Twain – it just ain't so. Atheism has but one criterion – no belief in God.

For new atheists, reason is a new god supplanting the Christian myth. Many Christians claim that science is merely another religion. Sadly, this infantile argument is true.

Wisdom of Knowledge

Rest in the nowhere to rest
—Trungpa Rinpoche

There are limits to knowledge. Kurt Gödel's first incompleteness theorem proved there will always be valid propositions impossible to prove. By the second incompleteness theorem, inbuilt paradoxes hide in axiomatic systems and such systems cannot self-verify. This problem has less formal variations. "Nobody wants to face the consequences of Gödel," said Gregory Chaitin, PhD in mathematics. In some domains, Chaitan showed, most things cannot be calculated. "They want to go ahead as if formal logic can prove everything. The obvious consequence of his work is that logic is a failure."[5]

Science philosopher Michael Polanyi echoed this. The mechanistic (Laplacean) framework and its 'unbridled detailing' prevent perception of higher-order realities. For example, focusing exclusively on the constituent atoms of a body voids out the comprehensive person. "No inanimate object is ever fully determined by the laws of physics and chemistry."[6]

There are limits to certainty. Georg Cantor, widely held as one of the greatest mathematicians of all time, worked on infinity sets. By invoking and proving irresolvable paradoxes, he forever undermined the certainty of mathematics. Trying to solve these was his life's work, the continuum hypothesis. Failing and rejected by his peers, he died in an asylum.

Ludwig Boltzmann made a similar creation for physics – the arrow of time. Entropy, or increasing disorder of a closed system, became the second law of thermodynamics. Few doubt this principle. (One physicist we will meet took a Nobel Prize for contravening it.) Entropy went against the old idea of an orderly and predictable universe. Boltzmann was outcast by his fellow scientists on ideological grounds. There was no proof against his work, only hostility to his ideas. He hanged himself.

When Alan Turing created a computer to simplify Gödel's theorem, he found something odd. A computer, being a logical system, would be unable to solve certain problems. Further, there was no way to know which problems these were beforehand. This created a stunning quandary for logicians. Before, provable (but unproven) and unprovable problems were thought logically separable. Turing showed they weren't. He showed that machines have limits humans do not. We instinctively know when to give up. Turing, the father of computers, showed that the brain is not a computer.*

Turing was convicted in 1952 for homosexuality and forced to take estrogen. After growing breasts, he became mentally unstable and ate a cyanide apple. When he died, Gödel took over his work trying to show that logic didn't lead to truth. Gödel also tried to fulfill Cantor's continuum hypothesis. Failing, he went mad and starved himself to death.

Gödel is probably the greatest logician of all time. He also fiercely believed that intuition could lead to mathematical and logical truths. He trapped himself in a quandary of his own discovery. He could never prove that thing he found most important in the human mind – intuition. Proof is a logical function. Intuition is not subject to it.

Still, the incompleteness theorem stands. Mathematics, therefore, has a limited ability to express the world. The importance for science and math is crucial. No one has overturned Gödel's theorem – it's elegant, it's concise, it's 'bulletproof.' There are limits to knowledge. The scientific goal of explaining all natural laws will never happen.

Logical systems have inbuilt paradoxes. Still science relies on logic or rationality to prove everything that it asserts. Gödel's attempt to logically prove a supra-logical proposition is the same trap faced by science. The materialists have thus given up on the supra-logical, claiming that anything beyond logic cannot be real. But Gödel's theorem shows this is incorrect – valid realities lie past the pale of logic. Science must accept this before it can escape its current trap. But to do so, the scientific community must operate in uncertainty.

Science has reduced to functionality. It is true because it works – its sole proof. But there are many examples of utility being wrong. Surveyors and sailors both use Earth-centered astronomy. The Bohr model of the atom still works marvelously for chemistry. Computer models routinely use falsifications – bogus premises to get useful results.[7] Polynesians' extremely accurate weather prediction used sky-gazing – the gods controlled the weather. Accurate results can come from flawed explanations – utility is not veracity.

We can heat our water in a humming box, watch images on another box, fly through the air in a winged box, and speak to someone in Asia on a ringing box. We can even live underwater. But functionality is not truth. Bacteria and cockroaches can adapt to any environment, but that does not make them true any more

* He seemed to also believe the opposite – he thought an intelligent machine could be made.

than dinosaurs are false. It makes them versatile. The confusion underwrites all popular faith in science – results measure truth. This is wrong.

Science has many other problems: Excessive reliance on experts leading to uncritical public acceptance; fraud; incompetence; non-reproducibility; faith in science as absolute truth; groupthink; corporate control; flawed peer review system held as the ultimate validation; career fear; career ambition; social pressures; greed; magical thinking; hero worship; political pressures; desire for fame; publish-or-die mentality; faith in medical propositions; corporate subterfuge; radical rejection of holism and intuition; contempt for traditional wisdoms; overweening faith in mathematics as underpinning reality and logic as structuring reality; trust in rationality as the only and best means to truth; overt rejection of all metaphysical propositions; covert acceptance of numerous metaphysical propositions; cultish indoctrination; conceiving a machinelike orderly universe against all evidence; rejection of radical ideas; ruthless contempt for truly innovative thinkers; punishing cruelty against differences of opinion; tendency to directed perception; faith in objectivity and causality (metaphysical ideas); woeful ignorance of epistemology and science philosophy; naïve trust in the mechanism of science; rule by entrenched committees; secret governance by corporations; illusion of independence; increasing fractionalization of 'knowledge;' control by moneyed interests; pretense that emotionality is absent from science; belief that the central body of scientific theory cannot be mistaken; gratuitous hostility to novice presentations; faith that the proper way to change things in science is the agonizing process of being attacked for one's opinions; foolish belief that shy scientists can and should endure this to prove their theory; faith that true theories will emerge through this process based on rational argument rather than warfare, connections, or charisma; lack of insight into the sensitive character of genius leading to silence over the most profound ideas; myth of superiority; self-righteousness; secret desire to maintain the ignorance of the masses to feel superior; simultaneously bemoaning scientific illiteracy; lockout – whereby experts have the only key to certain knowledge; an insistence on relying on people with letters after their name; pre-emptive proclamation of consensus to clinch victory for a view; emergence of consensus by force and subterfuge; creation of public belief through repetition rather than explanation; and a default assumption that those who disagree with the mainstream view are crazy. One could extend such a list to an entire book. Like all our projects, science is a symphony of human weakness.

It is time for science to grow up, or to put it less pejoratively, to expand its domain. It is also time to reintegrate. By severe prejudice, science only operates in the realm of extension – if it cannot be measured, it does not exist. Codifying the human genome, for example, provided the best validation of evolution. Quantitative differences rise to absolutes; qualitative differences vanish. It is a self-sealing construct, arrogantly excluding all other modes of seeing. To get beyond this pale knowledge, this 'extreme rationalism' as Einstein called it, is a difficult proposition.

Knowing and understanding are different. Kim Peek, the 'Rain Man' savant, memorized almost every word of Shakespeare – he would shout the correct line to actors in the theater. He knew Shakespeare better than anyone alive, but he clearly did not understand it. Science has become a sort of Kim Peek – vast knowledge but little understanding.

The Indeterminate Multiverse

What happens to your fist when you open your hand?
—Zen koan

Genius can be stupid. Inventing his scale, Anders Celsius put freezing at 100 and boiling at 0. Great scientists can be crazy. Before leading the 50,000-man Manhattan Project, Oppenheimer tried to poison his tutor. Great thinkers aren't always benevolent. Werner Heisenberg chose to lead Nazi efforts to develop the atomic bomb.

It's good to challenge any principle in science. Because language has a built-in imprecision, it's even necessary. The Earth, we say, revolves around the sun. But this is untrue in a precise way. To demonstrate, look at a binary star – star B a kilogram lighter than A. Does B orbit A? No, they are in mutual revolution. There is no precise weight ratio at which one orbits the other. The impossibility of proper expression mounts – they do not orbit each other, but a gravitational point between them. Of course, we can never find such a thing. A point is a dimensionless locator, but a location without dimension cannot exist.

One could say that physics cannot be expressed in spoken language – it requires math. Fair enough, but we still lack a means to ground the math in the reality. No matter how it is expressed, there is no ψ, no Δ, no number 2 anywhere in physical reality. Symbols and signs are radically divorced from phenomena. This brute fact science has never come to terms with, thus many believe equations are objective truth. But there are no equations in the physical realm. To posit them as underlying is to posit a *meta*-physical reality – equations are not physical things. Of course, most physicists have little problem with a metaphysical reality – it's a quick walk from quantum theory.

The desire for objective truth leads every science to prostrate before mathematics. Sociology has game theory, biology has evolutionary arithmetic, physics long ago placed math as the crown on its head. Math is the validating and binding factor for all sciences. Having no empirical contradictions, only math can 'prove' something. So every discipline strives to represent itself so. Materialist science exists under this paradoxical claim: the entire world is reducible to matter and energy, which are in turn reducible to math. The concept is a self-contradiction.

If we decide that equations are the underlying fabric, then science must answer how they got there. If they are mere descriptors, then we are unable to find physical laws. We are not in contact with forces; we only describe behaviors. If the equations are there, guiding the universe, why? Who created this insensate god? Some physicists have an answer – the blatantly metaphysical, unfalsifiable multiple universe theory. Most atheists likewise believe we are narrowing in on the truth. But this is an empty house. There is no means for understanding why natural laws are there, or even if they truly exist.

In spite of this failure, physics restricts alternate views. Aristotelian physics held that objects behaved according to their innate properties. Newton created the 'laws of physics' revolution – now that is the only plausible 'reality'. These laws state that there is a hidden system pervading the universe, manifest everywhere without exception. It is a mystical interpretation. No one has ever seen 'gravity,' only its effect. No one has ever seen a physical 'law,' only an interpretation of it. What physical form could such a thing possibly have?

The laws of physics are supernatural. Super means above or transcending. Supernatural means beyond nature. The laws of physics dictate nature, but are in themselves beyond it. Nature cannot act on these laws – they are unchangeable. There is also no explanation of how or why these laws came to be. Their origin is supernatural – unexplainable by science.

Likewise, metaphysics means beyond the physical. Laws of physics have no material manifestation – they suffuse and control 'physical' reality without physical form. If they were physical, they would be separable from other physical forms – thus not universal. But then they would not be laws of physics. Any orderly materialism is, by definition, impossible. The laws of physics are metaphysical and supernatural.

Physics is not even the linear progress commonly believed. Aristotle said that a vacuum was not possible. He said that objects define the space. Later, a vacuum became possible. Now, through a quantum sleight of hand, virtual particles saturate the vacuum. We've gone back to Aristotle. Newton's void is no more.

In 1901, Max Planck created the constant *h*, the quanta of quantum physics. Electrons do not move from one orbit to another. Absorbing a quantum, they vanish and reappear. Planck was not pursuing this as underlying principle. He came in through the back door as so much science does. Concocting a shorthand solution, only later did he realize the enormity of the implications – reality is not continuous. It is a series of cuts. Quantum denies the common-sense application of classical science. It is irrational. The decay of a radioactive particle cannot be determined, for example. The timing has no reason. In fact, an observed radioactive particle will not decay. At a very deep level, quantum disputes causality. It defies scientific explanation – therefore it is supernatural by scientific definition. But it is proven to occur. Science has proven the supernatural – only a few scientists vocally deny it.

QM forever changed the world. The pursuit of science now stands on shaky ground. Solid reality is undermined. We are still early in the transition and most people, scientists or no, have not internalized it. The order that seems apparent around us was once based on an orderly microscopic world. But quantum physics, which is 'objectively random,' has destroyed that project. Objective randomness can be experimentally shown and experimentally contradicted. Two single-source photons can be sent in opposite directions. It is provably random whether one passes a polarizer at angle x, but if it does, then the other always will. Two random processes cannot get the same result – yet they do. Quantum mechanics introduces a situation where logic "cannot build a chain of reasoning," according to physicist Anton Zelinger. This entanglement can extend to infinite objects. "The old notions cannot solve the problems of quantum physics. The information is not carried separately by the particles. There is strong evidence that there is no hidden causality, but there is a connection."[8]

Nils Bohr said "No phenomenon is a phenomenon until it is an observed phenomenon." His well-accepted school believes there can be no objective picture of reality. Our models, assumptions and ideas are completely separate from any underlying reality. Quantum models of the atom are mere utilitarian fictions. His only truth is a quantum flux, indescribable in any way.

After QM, we have a set of inescapable issues: Wave particle duality destroys the concrete identity of phenomena. Definitive randomness of events upends determinism. Entanglement demonstrates an atemporal connectivity and demands a bottom-up restructure of our entire worldview. Non-locality mocks the reductionist approach, virtually shouting that we are missing the holistic nature. The transition to macroscopic effects makes our experience an illusion. And the measurement problem terminates objectivity. These are some of the many consequences of QM that have yet to enter our zeitgeist, although the man on the street intuits it better than the average book-writing scientist.

Physics labors under a *Star Trek* mentality, the vapid consequence to the success of exotic theories. It's too exciting, weird and groovy to ever find anything normal again. It has to be far out. A physicist working on plain old classical stuff may as well be the janitor.

Questionable 'laws' have become fashionable for another reason – a discredited one. Under a tenet of logical positivism, scientists must 'beware' of common sense. Nowadays, the standard is to reject it. Virtually every principle now flies in the teeth of common sense. A heretic who loves the discipline might suggest reintroducing everyday insight. Under that guideline, let's see if modern physics passes the Ben Franklin test.

Dark Ideas

Hypotheses have no place in experimental philosophy.
—Isaac Newton

In 2006, a NASA spokesman announced that the Bullet Cluster had caused a deep lensing of light, proving that 96% of the universe was invisible. The Dark Matter agenda was set. This hidden universe ties together cosmic space with the submicroscopic of particles, fields, unaccountable linkages, binding and repelling factors, and modes of engagement in the nebulous mess called particle physics. Spinons, fermions, quarks, antiquarks, neutralinos, gravitons, charm, holons, spin, W- W+ and Z bosons, leptons, and anti-particles appear and disappear in portions of a nano-second. There are hundreds.

Dr. Murray Gellman, as part of his feud with Richard Feynman, wanted to make sense of the huge number of particles flying out of quantum labs. So he invented quarks. They can never be seen because they only exist with other quarks. This allows everything to be made of either quarks or electrons. Heisenberg called them 'absurd.'

A fundamental particle has no internal substructure. This self-contradiction means a particle so small there is no actual particle. Explanations are off-putting. "A pion (+) is an up quark and a down anitiquark," the *Particle Adventure* website explains. "The antiparticle of a meson just has its quark and antiquark switched, so an antipion (-) is a down quark and an up antiquark. The kaon (K-) meson lives much longer than most mesons. It was called 'strange.'"[9]

It goes on and on, allegedly explaining this esoteric realm to the laity. Many particles 'exist' for a tiny fraction of a second and are represented as lines and curls on a computer drawing. There are also a number of 'inferred' particles that can't be detected even on these million-dollar cartoons. Z particles and neutrinos must be there because of momentum changes. There are even hypothetical particles. Supersymmetry theoretically brings together gravity with other basic forces. It posits an opposite, massive 'shadow force-carrier particle' for every fundamental particle and an opposite 'shadow matter particle' for every force carrier. These have never been detected, but field leaders never doubt they exist. A skeptic might call them supernatural.

One of the problems is that the fundamental particle, the quark, is not directly observable. The theory states that the force holding quarks actually increases with distance. No other such paradoxical force has ever been observed. Another problem: quarks were theoretically shown to have identical states and location, which violates a fundamental quantum tenet. So they invented a new property, color, to distinguish the quarks. All of these properties are theorized, not observed in any way. In order to explain these different things, more and more particles are theorized. This leads to the root difficulty – why are there so many particles hypothesized and why are so few seen? Part of the difficulty is that all forces are associated with some particle – the graviton, for example.

Some physicists say the electron (and any quantum phenomenon) is an illusion, albeit a practical one – it explains things. However, the experimental results are radically separate from the actual concept. Quantum theory explicitly denies the idea that these phenomena are definitively particles – they are defined as wave-particle duality, neither one nor the other. Particle physics philosophically disagrees with quantum theory. The discipline lacks a grammar – all it has are nouns. The ideas are self-contradictory – like a fat thin person, a massless particle defies possibility and good sense. Nils Bohr reversed the particle physics argument: "Everything we call real is made of things we cannot call real."

Welcome to the 'particle zoo.' Excepting medical science, more money is spent on particle physics than all other sciences combined. If it sounds like Dr. Suess on the holodeck, then the ultimate Cat in the Hat is the WIMP. Weakly Interacting Massive Particles are the target candidates for dark matter. These hypothetical entities come in a variety of flavors – the neutralino is the reigning champion. Tens of billions have been spent looking, but this DM has never been directly detected. The expense creates a 'theory momentum' – it can't be dropped now. But why do so many physicists insist it exists?

The answer is galactic rotation curves. (See figure 1, next page.) Mercury orbits very quickly lest it fall into the sun. Pluto goes very slowly or it would fly away. Galaxies are different. Outer stars move at the same velocity as inner stars. They should be going much slower. In 1974, Dr. Vera Rubin showed that

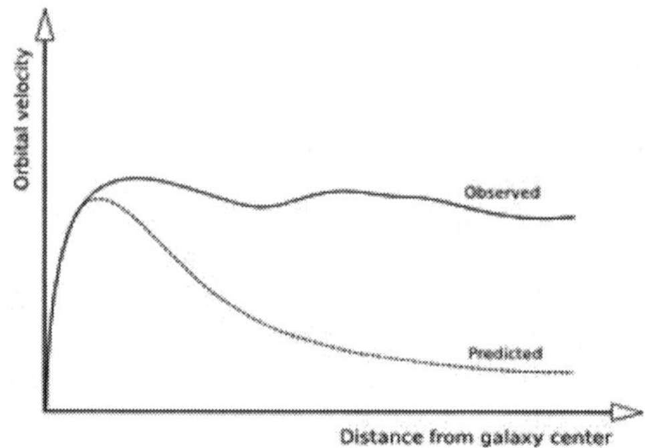

Figure 1: Galaxy rotation curve velocity vs. distance from galactic center.

galaxies don't spin like they should. At the same time, Professors James Peeble and Jerry Ostriker looked into matter quantities in the universe. Computer models of the Milky Way dissolved. Like Dr. Rubin, they needed more matter – a lot. Physics was standing in a hole. To save the theory of gravity, they posited dark matter.

The solution dated from the '30s. Fritz Zwicky, one of the most irascible astronomers ever, had performed the same calculations 40 years before and proved amounts of matter were insufficient. Because of his personality, no one paid attention. (In science, personality and position are critical factors.)

It's ironic. In 1906, Hugo von Seeliger theorized dark matter particles near the sun to explain Mercury's precession. Einsteinian gravity dispelled DM and has now reintroduced it on a galactic scale.

Dark matter has a contradictory nature. It is posited to be smoothly distributed in voids to account for homogeneity, but is collected in galactic halos for gravitation effects. If DM is smoothly distributed throughout space, it would have no effect on objects – the gravity would average to zero in any direction. (It would still have a relativistic effect on the curvature of space.) Without the universal smoothing, however, galaxies should move at twice the observed rate.

Dark matter has many forms. The baryonic (normal) form is dust, dead stars, and any normal matter that eludes telescopic vision. This type is verified. Non-baryonic DM does not interact with baryonic matter in any way except gravity. It can never be seen, is not made of atoms, and can pass through all atomic material. DM must exist, it is said, because it is needed by other physics.

Massive resources have gone to detecting dark matter. Dust-free, sterilized labs house specially designed technology, super-sensitive to all movement, deep in the Earth, even under the ocean. After sixteen years, not a single particle has been detected. Dark matter is meant to be everywhere. "They will stop," professor Mordehai Milgrom said, "when the money runs out." A dark matter skeptic, Milgrom believes the laws of gravity need a going-over.

In 1999, the mystery deepened. Saul Perlmutter investigated the question of whether the universe would keep expanding or collapse. In a surprising finding, he claimed the universe was not only expanding, it was speeding up – which gravitational theory cannot account for. It began about 7GY (billion years) ago when the slowing reversed. The amount of energy causing the expansion was exactly equal to the missing quantity needed by the Big Bang to make space flat. (More on this concept later.) Dark energy has properties not applicable to normal energy. As the universe expands, the amount of dark energy expands with it. A form of magic, some skeptical cosmologists say. It's also leading to a revival of the retired ether theory – the vacuum is not empty. The result is the standard model of cosmology. 4.6% matter we can detect, 22% dark matter no one can find, and 73% dark energy no one can comprehend.

Cosmological contrarians are not silent. "One of the worst determined constants of nature is Newton's gravitational constant," John Moffat explains. It's well determined for the planets, but because it's weak, it's impossible to analyze in microscopic distances. For these, gravity is not even meaningful compared to the nuclear forces – billions of times stronger. It is also not established for galactic distances, hence the dark matter problem.[10]

The longest standing member of the Hubble telescope's science committee, Michael Disney, is an utter skeptic of the standard model. Professor Carlos Frenk made computer simulations of the universe with the proportions of elements. He claims to have proven the standard model. Disney's answer is that cosmology has become a religion. Anybody can manipulate a model, but it doesn't prove the laws of physics. The original DM founder, Professor Peebles, is quite skeptical of the computer model as well.

They have practical objections. Dispersion velocities in globular clusters obey Newtonian dynamics – clusters can have no DM. But DM must exist in all galaxies by its uniform distribution. Proponents claim all the DM has been 'stripped away,' but have no mechanism for that. Dark matter would have to be located in a massive, roughly spherical halo enshrouding each galaxy, but there is no reason for it to do so. Dark matter should clump since it is gravitational.

More sensible explanations, based on observation, may suffice. Warm plasma has been found in massively greater quantities, enough to threaten the need for dark matter.[11] Many more white dwarfs discovered add to this.[12] Other theories of gravity have been proposed. They account for observation, but are dismissed as being contrary to the standard model.

DM may be the new Vulcan. The planet Vulcan, circling inside the orbit of Mercury, was once believed to cause the precession in Mercury's perihelion. Urbain Jean-Joseph Leverrier predicted the existence of Vulcan in 1889. Having predicted Neptune earlier, he was assumed correct. For decades, Vulcan was a real planet for astronomers. Then came Albert Einstein.

There's more strangeness – dark flow. A number of galaxies are heading to a central point and possibly vanishing. The observations don't fit the standard model. It's led to a proposal to change the speed of light. The multiverse theory is also invoked to explain dark flow. It's not been incorporated into the standard model, but the data is well regarded by the mainstream. But the strangest idea of all now sounds ordinary, the raison d'être of all other astrophysical strangeness: the Big Bang.

Beginnings and Imaginings

Asked the origin of the universe, the Buddha remained silent.
—oral tradition

"The beginning scenario in big-bang theory is indistinguishable from a miracle," physicist John Hartnett said. It's also quite fast. Reading like hard science fiction, the six most important events in the history of the universe happen in less than a trillionth of a second. The BB timeline starts with the Planck epoch. At 10^{-43} seconds, it is the shortest quantum interval of time. By presumption, during this time the four forces of physics are united. Next, the Grand Unification epoch ends at 10^{-36} seconds. Gravity separates from the other forces. The electroweak epoch extends to 10^{-12} seconds and includes several parts. The strong force separates from the electronuclear force. The inflationary epoch lasts up to 10^{-32} seconds. This hypothetical bare instant of time saves BB theory. While expanding the initial universe at many times the speed of light, inflation smoothes out the universe, making it flat, homogeneous, isotropic, and free of magnetic monopoles. It also lays microscopic seeds which later become galaxies. It is a robust quintillionth of a quintillionth of a second.

Next is reheating. The potential energy created by the 'inflaton field' turns into a superheated plasma of subatomic particles – quarks and electrons. A major problem for BB theory, baryogenesis, follows. Matter is created without balancing quantities of anti-matter – a theoretical impossibility. Between one picosecond (trillionth) and one micro-second (millionth) is the quark epoch, when everything is quarks and gluons.

So far the model is completely speculative – supernatural, if we're honest. After this point, standard model physicists claim to understand the process very well. Between one millisecond up to one second, quarks form into hadrons – protons and neutrons. In the lepton epoch, most of the hadrons and anti-hadrons annihilate each other. The temperature rapidly falls. Up to ten seconds, the leptons – electrons and neutrinos – annihilate each other with anti-leptons. From ten seconds to 377,000 years, we have the photon epoch. Photon energy dominates the universe. Nucleosynthesis, the formation of atomic nuclei, occurs at the beginning, from 3 to 20 minutes post BB. Because the nuclei are separated from electrons, photons cannot move about freely. At 377,000 years, the universe cools enough so the electrons bind into hydrogen and helium atoms. With photons able to move freely, the universe becomes transparent and the Cosmic Microwave Background Radiation (CMB) is set free.

The dark ages, dominated by a dense hydrogen fog, continues until between 150 and 800 million years. This period was shortened when the Hubble telescope found a galaxy 600 million years post BB. Up to a billion years quasars form. Towards the end come stars and galaxies. Later are galactic clusters, then superclusters, then walls and filaments – structures hundreds of millions of light years in size. A billion light years away, the Sloan Great Wall, at 1.37GLY (billion light years) across is the largest structure ever found.

Big Bang theory happened, in part, from a mistake over the General Theory of Relativity. GR assumed space was non-Euclidean. It sounds complex, but non-Euclidean geometry is a fact of our world. Longitude lines cross the equator at right angles, thus they are parallel. They also meet at the poles. Parallel lines intersect – a non-Euclidean postulate. Earth is 'closed' – bounded in space, but without edges. Maybe space, under gravity's thumb, could have similar properties.

Einstein proposed a static, finite universe, but this would gravitationally collapse to the center. The rotating universe could save it, but as Einstein pointed out, rotation is measured against something else. The universe cannot rotate against something else because it is all there is. Rotation also needs a central point, but that defies relativistic space-time. Einstein thought the field equations mandated a closed universe, but that would require rotational velocities faster than light. These observations, combined with the Hubble redshift, created the expanding universe idea.

In 1927, Monseigneur George-Henri LeMaitre theorized the first singularity. The law of increasing entropy requires that the universe began at low entropy. Since entropy is increasing, the quanta in the universe must be increasing as well. If we reverse that, it must decrease eventually to a single particle of zero radius – the primeval atom. Lemaitre called it the cosmic egg; skeptic (and atheist) Fred Hoyle facetiously named it the Big Bang.

In the 1950s George Gamow formalized BB theory. By setting a single variable, he was able to accurately predict the proportions of elements in the universe. This gave the theory legs until Hoyle proved that the elements were produced inside of stars and through supernovas. If the elements were produced by the BB as theorized and by the stars as demonstrated, there should be double the amounts of the heavier elements than are observed. For a time, the theory subsided.

Then the cosmic microwave background radiation predicted an ambient microwave temperature of 30 Kelvin. When Bell Labs discovered the CMB, the astronomy community overwhelmingly called it BB proof, ignoring the temperature difference. The detected CMB was only 3.5K – an energy prediction off by a thousand times. But never mind, the BB arrived with a bang. By the 1970s, it was received wisdom in cosmology.

The community divided into theorists fighting over mathematical mechanisms. Few assumed the idea wrong. Part of the problem was a big decrease in funding. Experimentation, which is expensive, declined and low-cost theoretical mathematics prevailed. The theory had no reliance on data. The thought-style overwhelmed contrarian views. Anyone who dissented became an opposition to the careers of mainstream cosmologists. Mavericks were cut from the herd. The Big Bang had to be real – everyone mostly, sort of believed it.

Redshift

The greatest obstacle in science is the illusion of knowledge.
—Daniel J. Boorstin

The BB comes from one set of observations, one theory, and one philosophical question. The last, Olbers' paradox, wonders why an infinite space-and-time universe with infinite stars is not filled with infinite light. The theory is General Relativity which mandates an expanding or contracting universe, not a stable one. The set of observations come from unsung astronomer Vesto Slipher – Edwin Hubble's assistant. Slipher noticed that some stars were too red. He postulated redshift due to Dopplering, a movement away from us. The movement stretches the wavelength, lowering the color. After exhaustive number-crunching, Slipher's boss formalized the relation as Hubble's law.

This law is complicated. It has many forms and many adjustable parameters. In the beginning, though, it was simple: v=cz. Velocity is the speed of light times the redshift. At z=1 or more, objects go ftl – faster than light. Since telescopes back then couldn't see distant objects, this was not a problem. They thought the universe couldn't be that big. Nowadays, we have objects that would be traveling 8 times ftl. The special relativity version forced this to stay under c, but the general relativity version did not. It is common to speak of distant galaxies moving ftl away from us. Even BB dissenters don't object to this, however. The theory is that space is expanding at these speeds, not that the objects are moving through space.

It leads to bizarre paradoxes, such as light moving towards us but getting further away. At least until the expanding Hubble Sphere, our zone where space expands less than light speed, passes the light and it starts to gain ground.

Leaving aside Einsteinian brain-scramblers, the name redshift is a misnomer based on the visible part of the electromagnetic (EM) spectrum. ELF-shifting is better since the entire spectrum moves to the extremely low frequency end.* All spectral analyses of cosmic objects demonstrate a distinct pattern of absorption lines – blank spots in the spectrum. In most objects these gaps are shifted to the left – they have longer wavelengths. Therefore the entire spectrum must be shifted to the left. Near and intermediate objects can be distance-determined by a variety of independent means. Mostly, distance correlates to the amount of spectral shifting – near objects are the same as the sun. In gen-

* A true redshift would cause radio waves to shorten.

eral, redshifts increase with faintness, reinforcing the distance hypothesis. This gives a tool for gauging enormous distance.

Redshifts can occur by other means than Doppler, but with signatures which are not found. This leads to two hypotheses. Redshift now occurs, in standard cosmology, by wavelength expansion from light traveling through expanding space. The second hypothesis is an unknown cosmological principle.

Slipher's original theory was Doppler effect, but current theory is space expansion. They are quite distinct, and there is no corroborating proof for this mechanism. It's a typical occurrence in science – explanation creep. One proven mechanism fails in the particular case and becomes, inexplicably, another process which lacks experimental verification, but leads to the same conclusion. This is exactly the case with relativistic redshifting. For a few such reasons, it has formidable dissenters.

Edwin Hubble was a superb scientist. He died a skeptic of his own expansion principle. According to his 1937 lecture, looking at EM as waves leads to the velocity-shift, or expansion, hypothesis. But looking from quantum theory offers a different perspective – "light loses energy in proportion to the distance it travels through space." This is tautological – redshifting is loss of energy. Photons, however, could lose the energy – the 'tired light' hypothesis.

The critique that there is no known mechanism can be deflected – there is no known mechanism for the Big Bang. A recent theory suggests that plasma, which is everywhere, draws energy from the light. It's also possible that, à la thermodynamics, light gives energy to the medium it passes through.

Hubble calculated the age of the universe at 1.5GY.* Though this sounds strange now – the current age of the universe is not well agreed in standard cosmology. It's had a tendency to get a bit younger this decade. A more open universe might be 11GY and a slightly closed one would be about 14GY. Hubble listed several objections to the velocity-shift interpretation: the universe is too small and too young. Also, the matter to keep the universe together, by general relativity, is not there – a prescient critique of dark matter. "The ever-expanding model suggests a forced interpretation of the data. [Without] velocity-shifts, the picture is simple and plausible."[13] Hubble preferred observational to theoretical cosmology. To him, velocity-shifting was sensible, but contradicted the universe he saw – infinite in time and space, transparent, and without invisible matter.

* G=billion.

The debate is ongoing and plenty of evidence contradicts velocity-shifting. Even the sun redshifts from center to fringe, a phenomenon unaccountable by velocity-shifting. A few astronomers showed that some 'black holes' were actually high-redshift quasars – objects which put the lie to the test. The larger the redshift (z), the further away an object is supposed to be. A z of 1 would be 10 times the distance of a z of .1. The inverse square law says that, at that distance, it would be 100 times fainter. But quasars average the same brightness independent of redshift. A quasar ten times away is thus deemed 100 times brighter. So for quasars, brightness as a measure of distance is uncorrelated with redshift as a measure of distance. To solve this, BB theory introduces 'evolution' – all quasars lose energy over cosmic time scales, so all older ones, being further away, appear exponentially brighter than all younger ones. But they have to be exactly correlated to lose brightness logarithmically, which is impossible.[14] Evidence is forced to fit theory.

Astrophysicist Halton Arp analyzes photos of quasars interacting with galaxies by ejection and streaming matter. Thus they must be at the same distance, but the quasars have vastly higher redshifts than the galaxies. Some quasars are clearly visible in front of galaxies with lower redshift. Applying Hubble's Law, we have a visibly closer quasar which, by expansion theory, must be further away. Hands wave and the problem vanishes, another common sin of science – using statistical analysis to get rid of anomalies. But the quasars are there.

Other theories exist. The Compton effect – electron/neutrino 'friction' – could explain intrinsic redshift. Some say it would cause blurring by scattering. However, there are unblurred, but dimmed, Hubble-shots of objects behind dust clouds. The light intensities don't support the idea well, however. C.F. Gallo presented an energy loss of light based on thermodynamic principles. As light travels through a cooler medium, it sheds energy.* Gravity could also cause redshifts. Because resources are only available for BB research, the theories languish. When Halton Arp dissented from BB theory, he was banned from the use of the telescope.

It's a critical point. Under expansion theory, redshift is inviolable. It means objects are far away and their light is stretched. But the anomalies prove other mechanisms for redshift exist. Therefore, the redshift of distant objects does not prove they are moving away. Proper science should invite uncertainty. It

* This energy also adds to the ambient temperature, creating the 3K CMB.

should attack theory relentlessly, trying to disprove it. But this seldom happens.

Because of the equation v=cz, any redshift above 1 gives a speed above that of light. There are thus three different velocity measures – linear (as above), General Relativistic, and speed of light maximum – the slowest. Anything beyond 11GLY moves away from us faster than light, according to the linear formula. Anything redshifted past 1.46 exceeds the speed of light, according to the GR formula.

There is a scientific principle called corroboration. It means that a firm theory requires two distinct lines of evidence. BB does not fulfill this. The primary piece of evidence is the redshift hypothesized expansion of the universe. A few scientists tracked this in reverse, deciding it must have come from a singularity in the past. But the expanding universe has never been corroborated. It's only backing is the redshift. Critics claim this is not enough to prove the BB.

Although expansion has become Church of Science dogma, it at least makes sense. The Big Bang does not. The entire universe began from a seed a trillion times smaller than a proton. It could be created with 'a single gram of matter.' The premise is absurd. It could still be true – quantum mechanics is – but it demands far more skepticism than it has received. Absurdity may not be a problem for BB theorists, but other things are.

Isotropy, monopoles, and the exploding vacuum

Disregard authority whenever the observations disagree with it.
—Richard Feynman

If a theory predicts an infinity or a singularity, a rule says, the theory is breaking down – BB theory is entirely based on a singularity. The theory has three openly acknowledged problems: Horizon, flatness, and magnetic monopoles. Because information cannot exceed the speed of light, there is a limit, the particle horizon, on the distance for causal interactions – heat transfer in this case. However, the uncertainty principle demands that irregularities appear in the temperature of the universe. They aren't there – the universe is a uniform 2.7K. But until BB +377,000 years, photons were trapped – information exchange could not begin until then. It doesn't leave time enough to equalize the temperature – by a factor of 10^{88}.

Flatness is two problems. Omega (Ω) is the ratio of the universe's density to the amount of matter needed to 'close' the universe – making the space-time curvature 'spherical.' The initial value of the constant Ω must be 1 in order to have a flat universe. If it differed by less than 1 part in 10^{40}, then the universe would have vaporized or collapsed immediately. This Ω that was .999 (to forty places) created an idealized symmetry for the hypothetical universe. Though theoretically beautiful, the odds against it are more than a quadrillion^2 to 1. It's called the fine-tuning problem.

There is also an observational flatness problem – the currently observed matter density is less than 5% of the required – the BB universe should have vaporized. For this reason, the theory needs dark matter and dark energy to round out the matter-energy imbalance. Neither has been directly confirmed.

Magnetic monopoles are theoretical magnets with only one pole. The separation of forces in the first epochs should have produced enough magnetic monopoles to dominate the universe. None has been found.

Inflation was invented to solve the big three problems. In the beginning, the nuclear force breaks away from the electroweak, causing a phase transition, like water into steam. This unleashes the vacuum energy, giving gravity a repulsion effect. For 10^{-35} seconds, the universe goes from about a centimeter to vastly larger than anything we can observe today – billions of light years. It then settles into the more normative BB expansion.

Quantum fluctuations "become frozen in time and imprint themselves on the surface of last scattering through the process of space-time expansion," physicist John Moffat explains. "Classical matter was present in the original soup, but inflation vacuumed it away, emptying out the universe by diluting the matter to almost nothing. After inflation, matter and energy had to be reinstated to produce our present universe," pretty close to magic. An even worse problem – "the potential energy associated with the inflation must be almost constant for a long time, an unnatural fine-tuning, canceling large numbers to many decimal places. It is the Achilles heel of inflation theory." Even Hawking and Collins said, "The initial assumptions make inflation virtually impossible."[15]

The cosmological constant, the power to drive this expansion, comes from 'the most successful theory in physics.' But even the amazingly useful QED theory makes absurd predictions – the enormous energy density in the vacuum, so big that the universe should be a curved sphere the size of New York. So the vacuum energy 'disappeared' after causing inflation. The theory also predicts an infinite mass for an electron. We get a neat mathematical subterfuge called 'renormalization,' wherein the infinity is subtracted and the measured value is re-added. The theory then works perfectly, but they don't know why. With these errors, there is a problem with the theory. Because it's successful in practical applications, electronics and so forth, the theoretical problems are ignored. So we lose the infinite mass which doesn't help and dredge up the 'worst prediction in history' to save inflation.

In the first two epochs, before inflation, the expansion allows heat to equalize throughout the tiny universe. Inflation massively expands the homogeneity, solving the horizon problem. Inflation also stretches out any initial curvature, like a tennis ball becoming Earth-sized, so that it appears flat. Inflation dilutes the magnetic monopoles to a vanishingly small ratio, as well. But as Martin Rees explains, "skeptics might not be impressed by a theoretical argument explaining the absence of a hypothetical particle."[16] By solving all three problems, it became the favored son of BB theory. Of course, inflation has its problems, which accounts for the bewildering versions of it.

There is no mechanism to halt it, for one thing. Inflation theories mostly have 'eternal' inflation – it's still going on, but not here. The inflating universe is in a time-stop mode. That part is immeasurably larger than the rest of the universe. As space inflates, observers fly outside of each other's light cone. There are thus three areas of space – the inflating, the normal, and the observable universe.

Inflation predicts a flat universe. It has to because that's one of its reasons for existence. Unfortunately, it requires a combination of dark matter and energy to keep the universe together. This proof of inflation is circular – finding a flat universe, it claims that dark matter/energy must exist, therefore the flat universe prediction is correct. Of course, dark matter has the advantage of accounting for galaxy rotation curves, too. Dark energy accounts for the recently assumed 'acceleration' of the universe. When added together with the known matter, they add up to the critical density needed to flatten the universe. It is a nice symmetry with another theory and lends badly needed credence to inflation.

Space moves faster than light in inflation. One critique is that it violates special relativity. It's true, but general relativity trumps special relativity. Space can expand ftl, but objects can't move through it ftl. (Nobody said relativity was simple.) It does lead to one uneasy problem – to produce inflation, the inflaton particle must travel ftl.

Inflation has many models, e.g. Hartle-Hawking, chaotic, brane inflation, string-gas cosmology, and ekpyrotic universe. When bubble inflation failed to create radiation, Andre Linde created slow roll inflation. He's also made chaotic inflation, which extends eternally in the past. It's an ironic use of inflation theory. Invented to support a clear beginning to the universe, it now negates any beginning. The theory has come unglued, attacking its own origin. Even Stephen Hawking put out a no-boundary proposal – inflation without a Big Bang. The paradox is that inflation was meant to solve BB problems – that's its only real task. The problems don't exist in other theories. Without BB, inflation is just straps without a boot.

In an eternal/infinite or a plasma universe, thermal equilibrium, magnetic monopoles, flatness, isotropy, and homogeneity explain themselves. Inflation theory now approaches insensibility – "the discovery of flux compactifications opens the way for reconciling inflation and string theory. Brane inflation suggests that inflation arises through d-Branes. The compactified geometry, usually towards a stack of anti-d-Branes…"[17] and so on.

In 1994, skeptic Fred Hoyle wryly noted that his Steady State equations were exactly the same as those of new inflation. The theorists were surprised.

Cosmic Background vs Galactic Walls

A foolish faith in authority is the worst enemy of truth.
—Albert Einstein

In 1964, Penzias and Wilson found the Cosmic Microwave Background Radiation (CMB), predicted by George Gamow as a BB consequence. The CMB is a low energy, at 2.7 Kelvin and a whopping redshift of 1100, that pervades the universe. (See figure 2, next page.) Before the measurement, estimates were all over – 50K, 28K, 7K. The CMB itself could be from any number of sources. The reason it's now cited as proof is the black body radiation curve.

A black body is black, like it sounds, and absorbs all EM energy that hits it, then re-emits it perfectly, with no reflected or transmitted light. The emission forms a curve. The peak wavelength gets shorter (higher energy) with higher temperature. A human body, for instance, emits 9500nm light – infrared, but the curve is ragged. There are no detected ideal black bodies in the universe, so the pattern is cited as proof that the radiation came from the reionization period after the BB. It has an awesome name – the surface of last scattering – telescopes cannot see further back in space-time. The photons, from the time the universe became transparent, have lost energy to the expansion of space via redshifting – hence the low microwave frequency.

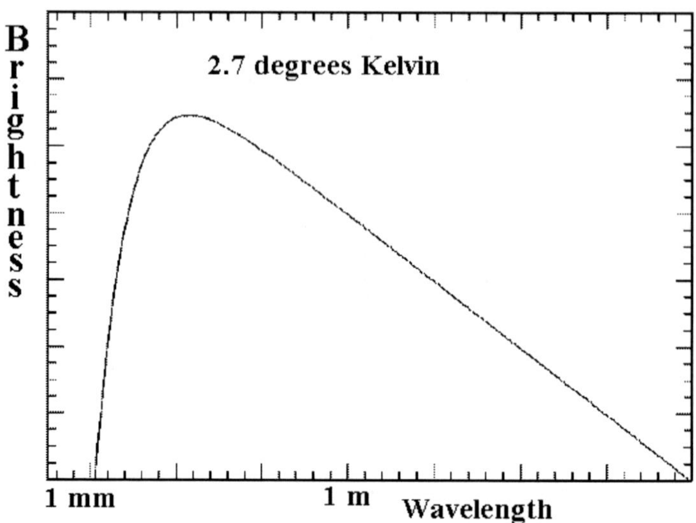

Figure 2. Spectrum of cosmic microwave background radiation

It's not perfect evidence. The 2006 WMAP data should have had 'shadows' from nearby x-ray galaxy clusters, since the CMB is further away than they are. The shadows weren't there, indicating the CMB measured was in front, thus newer. But it's supposed to be the oldest phenomenon in the universe.[18] Enormous foreground radiation makes it difficult to sort out the faint CMB. Gerrit Verschuur, a noted astronomer, was pilloried for saying the data was from nearby hydrogen clouds mistaken for CMB.[19]

A second prediction is anisotropy of the CMB. When the WMAP probe found 1 part in 100,000 variations in CMB temperature, most people paid no attention to what Stephen Hawking called "the most important discovery of the century, if not of all time."[20] However, they used a stunning 7 adjustable parameters not measurable by any means,[21] giving enormous latitude to fit theory to data. Earlier WMAP observations don't fit the theory, but these disagreeable measures are discarded as 'anomalies.' Of course, any theory predicts tiny variations – that's just the nature of things. Also, the WMAP 'cold spot' puts a major kink in the theory – it's many times larger in variation than theory allows.

In 2010, there were 8 major experiments ongoing to measure the anisotropy. With this investment of money for projects assuming BB cosmology, it seems little wonder that they would find faint signal data inside of such enormous noise to support BB.

"There is no explanation at all of the microwave background in the Big Bang theory," Hoyle said in 2001. The model doesn't predict the observed X-ray, ultraviolet or infrared backgrounds. Galaxies, being in front of the CMB, should decrease its signal, but observations show the reverse.[22]

The 2.7K temperature of space is easily predictable in any cosmology. In 1926, Arthur Eddington predicted 3.18K based on heating by ambient light. BB predicted 30K and hailed the results as a proof.

BB theory also has quite a few ignored problems. "The vacuum energy density is at least 120 orders of magnitude smaller than the naive quantum estimate," one vocal Big Bang proponent writes, "so there must be a very effective suppression mechanism at work."[23] Even with such a monstrous error, Dr. Wright never considers that the underlying theory is wrong – he invents a 'suppression mechanism.' This faith in theory over evidence may be the worst problem with BB cosmology. It leads to distortions which overlook the many practical problems.

In 1986, Dr. Brent Tully discovered galactic supercluster complexes. These formations require matter to have moved 270 million light years. Galaxies never move faster than 1000 km/sec. In 20 billion years, that amounts to 65 million light years of movement. Tully has verified cosmological objects requiring 80 billion years to form. Since then, the Hubble found the Sloan Great Wall and the Eridanus Supervoid, objects which would take 400 hundred billion years under ideal assumptions. The Supervoid, according to one theory, is a 'quantum entanglement with another universe.' Even the most lenient computer simulations have voids no bigger than 35 megaparsecs[24] – one-fifth Eridanus.[25]

The oldest object is a galaxy formed at 500 million years post BB. Considering the epoch of re-ionization lasted until four hundred million years, nothing could have begun to form until then. This leaves a paltry hundred million years for galaxy formation (from quantum fluctuations) – wildly insufficient. The discovery of very old objects caused revisions. In 2007, the theory had galaxy formation beginning at 500m years. Certain globular clusters, at 16GY, appear older than the universe. These difficulties have been ignored for 20 years.

Galaxy formation is one of Hawking's unsolved problems. "We have no direct evidence of how galaxies were formed,"

NASA scientists said in 1998. "We don't understand star formation at a fundamental level," Harvard astrophysics professor Abraham Loeb said.[26] If the universe is composed of galaxies, planets and stars, according to physicist John Hartnett, then BB theory does not address the origin of the universe.

Major rifts exist between the theory and observation. Except the CMB, no BB predictions have panned out. It doesn't coherently account for the origin of galaxies. The rift between homogeneity of CMB and the observed lumpiness of galaxies is poorly explained. For all its beauty, the unified force is not remotely falsifiable. Exquisite math explains a lot, but it's all internal to the model. Regardless, it's hailed as proof of cosmological theories, perhaps because Nobelist Paul Dirac once said, "it is more important to have beauty in one's equations than to have them fit experiment."[27]

A circular argument posits a model proven by its own assumptions. Alarming numbers of never-seen particles are proposed by the marriage between cosmology and particle physics. The Higgs field apparently gives birth to 10^{143} baby universes per cubic centimeter every second.

Our galaxy could only have rotated about 55 times since the Big Bang, not long enough to attain its spiral shape. Even very distant, hence close to BB, galaxies show spiral formations. And they aren't packed together as a smaller universe should indicate. Many galaxies are colliding – ours is headed that way. This shouldn't happen with the ftl expansion of space in BB theory.

Even the singularity idea underlying the theory is unsubstantiated. "The belief in black holes is entirely circumstantial," John Moffat writes, "but we see what we believe."[28] It takes a near infinitude of time for something to fall into a black hole due to relativistic distortions. It is theoretically impossible for a 10G solar mass black hole to form in under a billion years. They've never been proven, only suggested by plasma velocities near the center of galaxies – 1500 km/sec. This enormous velocity is offered as evidence for massive gravitational fields, but in 1989, the University of Arizona showed that stars in the same area moved at 70 km/sec or less. Gravity would require the same orbital velocity to keep them out of the alleged black hole. Therefore it doesn't exist. Plasma theorists posit electromagnetic forces, shown in the laboratory, as the mechanism for the plasma velocity. They only need theoretical scale-up, and claim it is shown in observation of cosmic phenomena. The standard model ignores electromagnetic force.

Type-III stars have no metal. In BB theory, earlier stars had no metal – it didn't exist until supernovae created it. But the oldest stars are not Type III. In fact, no Type-III stars have ever been seen. But everything in the furthest reaches should be. We do see light of many galaxies from the dark ages – when the universe was filled with hydrogen – which we should not see.

And nothing yet addresses the baryogenesis problem. Since matter and anti-matter are created in equal amounts, the BB needs some way to get rid of all the anti-matter. Theorists posit a decay of positrons (anti-matter electrons) into protons by combining with other particles. This means that protons must decay over time. According to BB theory, the half-life is 10^{30} years. Watching water-filled uranium mines, no decay was observed at even 100 times that amount. They rewrote the theory so that decay time is too long to experimentally confirm.

"Currently," Eric Lerner writes, "there are at least eight known contradictions between theory and observation: the abundances of ^{4}He, ^{3}He, and ^{7}Li are too low; there is too much dispersion in the high-z value of Deuterium abundances; the halo white dwarfs would have produced too much helium; the voids are far too large and old; there is a complete lack of evidence for the existence of cold dark matter; and there is evidence for absorption of long wavelength radiation in the IGM. Yet in no cases are these contradiction viewed as reasons for questioning the Big Bang theory."[29]

Hannes Alfvèn won a Nobel for plasma physics. He objected to big bang theory. Cosmology, he critiqued, begins with a mathematical, mythological basis. It works from the beginning through theory. Science should work the opposite way – by observation and tracking back as far as possible, saying only what can be legitimately said. It's not that theory and math are irrelevant, but they should follow observation rather than lead. The evolution of the cosmos should not be a radical mystery of inexplicable processes that cannot be shown. It should be available in the ongoing actions. No one has seen something come from nothing. We cannot theoretically extrapolate that occurrence in the past. It has no direct evidence.[30]

It's important to bring up a previous point. In order to object to a theory, it is not necessary to introduce an alternative theory. Any theory should stand or fall on its merit, not as a competition with a 'better' theory. It's certainly not disallowed to compare different theories, but a theory is not proven wrong only by a better theory. It is wrong in and of itself. This is a big problem in science – incorrect theories hang on until a better theory comes along.

A general problem applies – theory and observation tend to split over time. An idealized, Platonic, mathematical structure predominates over empirical evidence. Scientists are so overwhelmed by the beauty of equations that they force reality to fit them. They confirm sexy theory on minute evidence.

Einstein made one of the most damaging assumptions. He assumed a homogenous universe in contradiction to empirical evidence, leading to three deleterious effects. Because it's a simplifying premise, homogeneity became the basic structure, but it seems untrue. The laws may be homogeneous, but the universe is galaxies with huge empty swathes. The Beijing Astronomical Observatory published evidence contradicting homogeneity – mass density increases with distance. At 30 million light-years, density is only 10% of critical, but at 300 million, it approaches 90%.[31] Partly, homogeneity is just easier to deal with, but mainly the theory was accepted because of Einstein's outsized authority. This created a second problem, a precedent of contraindicated theory based on expert mandate. If Einstein said it, we have to believe it.

Unfortunately, another prediction has problems: the relative proportions of matter such as helium, lithium, and deuterium. Without dark matter, the proportion of elements holds up. With the matter added in, the big bang prediction for these proportions falls apart. They become much smaller percentages compared to the dark matter total. But the dark matter is essential to maintain homogenous matter distribution. In other words, homogeneity and this proportion of elements directly conflict. They cannot both be valid, but both have to be valid for the theory.

The Future Universe

The opposite of a trivial truth is false;
the opposite of a profound truth is also true.
—Nils Bohr

"The distinction between past, present, and future," Einstein said, "is an illusion, albeit a persistent one." This strikes to the heart of a fundamental flaw in physics – time-reversibility. According to physics, past and future are not meaningful distinctions. Reactions occurring one way can occur in reverse. This is directly contradicted by the second law of thermodynamics – entropy increases with time. Thus time has a direction. Einstein was wrong.

These two principles – mechanical reversibility of processes and increasing entropy – are fundamental to physics. Yet they cannot both be true. It's called Loschmidt's paradox. If physics accepts two mutually exclusive principles, it is committed to a logical falsehood. Every hard science has similar problems. As Ilya Prigogine said, "The epoch of certainties is over."[32]

Prigogine won the Nobel Prize for reconstructing thermodynamics. He claims that time is indeed not reversible, but shows that the 'law' of entropy is not a law at all. Entropy decreases in many situations. "Irreversibility is the mechanism that brings order out of chaos."[33] According to Prigogine, while it's true that gases separated in a bottle will mix, the phenomenon is not scale invariant. It's false on a cosmic size. As we get vaster, the universe finds itself in a more orderly state, rather than a disorderly one.

This is basic observation. Light from the furthest, hence oldest, objects shows higher entropy than closer objects. In other words, stars, planets, and galaxies come into being over time rather than dissipate. They display far more structure than much older quasars which have more structure than plasma clouds. These ancient structures are so entropic as to have free moving electrons. Only theoretical rumblings claim this order will one day dissipate. The universe is a closed system, yet it is increasing in orderliness. As example, if we fill an entire galaxy with two gases, they will mix, but will contract under gravity. Even a slight rotation will rapidly increase to maintain the average velocity as it shrinks. It will develop a stable rotation which will evolve into stars and planets. (Without rotation, it will heat up.)

The increasing entropy theory says that the apparent order is counteracted by a 'dimpling' or disordering of the gravitational field. But this defines entropy as orderly matter with disordered fields. It's a mathematical trick to save the theory. If high-profile experts say it is so, it must be so. It makes no difference that it defies observation. Mathematics rules. In short, the decay of the universe into blanket homogeneity is contradicted by what we can see. We have increased flow of energy, more complex structures (including life), and increasing velocities of evolution.

Prigogine dissects Boltzmann's theory that disorder always increases. "In the world we are familiar with, equilibrium is a rare and precarious state."[34] It is true for highly entropic situations, but a high degree of order tends to increase over time, provided it has enough internal flow of energy to do so. And order can emerge spontaneously from tiny fluctuations.

It can be shown that energy flows have increased over time. Quasars, which are very old, emit thousands of times the energy of galaxies, but are a light year across. Thus their energy density is thousands of times less than that of a star. Stars are much newer. Each second, quasars have 1 millionth of an erg per cubic centimeter. Stars have a thousand. Life has 30,000 ergs/sec/cc.

We have more energy density than the sun. The sun is so hot because it is so massive and gravity holds the force in over time.[35]

In looking at particles, quantum theory claims that events are reversible. Prigogine countered that time is irreversible here, too. "Irreversibility cannot emerge magically in going from one level to another." The error is in the assumption of reproducibility in reverse. But if space is continuous, rather than quantized, then it is impossible to obtain the infinite precision needed to reverse a quantum operation. This is because space is infinitely divisible, so one can never find the exact position and momentum. It is not a limitation of experiment or technology; it is an absolute. If something is infinitely divisible, perfect precision is unattainable. Tiny errors accumulate over space and time, leading to extreme differences in results – chaos theory. After 20 million years, for example, planetary orbits are no longer predictable.

There are a number of 'Rodney Dangerfield' theories – they get no respect from the funding establishment. Any BB alternative has the burden of proof for three things: the Hubble expansion, the amount of lighter elements (helium and deuterium), and the CMB. Alfvén, Eric Lerner, and others have proposed a plasma cosmology. Plasma is ubiquitous in the universe. It's also agreed that it is the basic material for formation of celestial objects. According to these theorists, no big bang is necessary. The force of electromagnetism is necessary, but this force is erroneously discounted in cosmological theories.

Plasma is superheated gases. Because of the heat, electrons move freely from atom to atom. This creates enormous electromagnetic forces. These can be shown to scale up from laboratory to solar to galactic to supergalactic levels. As the plasma interacts, it creates twisted filaments, extremely powerful. There is plenty of laboratory verification. The filaments create enough electromagnetic force to bind and draw in increasing amounts of matter. Eventually, this forms, according to theory, quasars, stars, and other formations. The cosmology has no beginning, but the time-scale is trillions of years.

The uniformity of the CMB seemingly wouldn't be there, because galaxies would be the source of energy. However, if the universe is that old, then the radiation would have been absorbed and re-emitted throughout the universe for hundreds of billions of years, smoothing the effect.

The Hubble expansion is more difficult. Nobel Laureate Paul Dirac has one of several competing theories for this, but the plasma theory suggests that matter and anti-matter exist in equal quantities. The predominance of matter is an enormous problem for big bang theory – the two should be theoretically equal. According to plasma cosmology, gravity and electromagnetic forces automatically separate matter and anti-matter on large scales. We have entire anti-matter galaxies and plasma clouds. When anti-matter and matter formations collide, they create an explosive force in a narrow band, blowing each other apart. The process takes a few million years. If this happened after a large-scale contraction of the visible universe, the ongoing explosion could have lasted a hundred million years. The intense gravitational force worked against the explosive force, prolonging the event.* The ongoing interaction rippled out through the universe, pushing everything apart.[36]

The theory is not a slam-dunk. It has problems, but it shows the big bang is not the only possible answer to the Hubble shift. Because Alfvén is a plasma physicist, his papers were automatically rejected by astrophysics journals as being off-topic. They were accepted by plasma physics journals. In polls, plasma physicists are far more likely to reject the big bang theory than cosmologists. This is largely due to the radical specialization in sciences. As each field develops its theories over decades, specialists are highly reluctant to admit their life's work was an error. Therefore, they reject what contradicts it.

Infinite Chaos

Being empty in essence, everything is interconnected.
—Sanggye Chodrak

There are more than a hundred scientists today for every one 50 years ago. The proliferation of exotic theory is in part due to this – all these researchers need a career. The simple problems have been solved, so elaborate ones are made up in an unconscious group process.

Bosons, for example, are massless particles – a patent contradiction – that mediate forces between matter particles. To deal with these, string theory requires 26 dimensions. In three decades, this theory has no testable predictions and no means of falsification. On the other hand, the addition of the word 'super' has gotten the media and legions of grad students involved. The theory is failing. A recent scramble has tried to exempt it from the normal testable guidelines of science. Thousands of bright minds have vanished in the string theory vacuum. This blind

* This theory suggests we only see a small corner of the universe.

fumbling has led us into an untenable system of beliefs. Future ages will mock us just as we mock the past.

Contradicting the BB is the quickest path to losing funding. The NIH and NSF members who allocate funds unanimously support it. Their career is invested in it. All astronomers who want money toe the line. For better or worse, BBT has revived any number of old ideas. The ether belongs to dark matter. Michelson and Morley dispelled it originally with their parallel-perpendicular light experiment. When light traveled the same velocity in both directions, ether couldn't have been affecting it and thus couldn't exist. With virtual particles and dark matter, it's returned. George Louis le-Sage ascribed gravity to corpuscles. Later discredited, the theory is now revived as the graviton. We are told that science is marching into a brave new dawn, understanding the world. It isn't really true.

This book is meant to provide arguments against this tyranny of small intent. The line of attack seeks a profound atheism versus the trivia of new atheism, the on-offness of its truth value and the yawning pretension of its scientism. New atheism pushes us to absolute agreement with mainstream theories. But there are signs these theories are wrong.

The laws of physics affect the world, but not the reverse. This indicates "a degenerate theory beyond which a more symmetric action lies. [Perhaps] the law too evolves and is subject to change by what happens in the world. Since the world is quantum, the law has a quantum nature. It can never be completely known or written down."[37] We know far too little to stumble into the flawed argument that since we don't have a better explanation the current one has to be right.

Relativity, physicist David Finkelstein claims, has been adapted to the point that Einstein would no longer agree. [38] Attempting to rewrite fundamental attitudes of science, Finkelstein wants to move away from states/properties to operations/actions. An electron, for example, has no size and therefore cannot have shape or location. Every electron is the same – no two can ever be distinguished. This ineffable and deep symmetry opens a doorway to an interconnected reality. For now, it's beyond us, but if we restructure our approach, then one day we might enter.

Fraud

Scientists in the United States are forced to produce results, which sometimes warps their sense of ethics.
—Luc Montagnier, 2008 Nobel Prize Winner

In revelations from January of 2010, MIT professor Jonathon Gruber took undisclosed payments from the Department of Health and Human Services, then posed as an independent researcher. He toured the country and wrote articles, arguing for the health care plan. The administration used the man's platform and credentials as 'independent' scientific evidence that its plan would work.[39]

Scientific fraud, it's commonly believed, is nonexistent or at least so slight that it's a non-problem. However, experts in fraud repeatedly find that, the more they investigate, the more certain they are that misconduct is very widespread. As self-regulating institutions – banking, stock market, medicine, the Church, the law – are increasingly shown as corrupt, so it is with science. It nonetheless insists on self-regulation, even in spite of external funding. This funding, however, can and does dictate the direction of scientific inquiry. Along with this, science has exploded into a massive arena with thousands of sub-disciplines. Funding requirements pressure researchers to find new discoveries. The same pressures delimit ethical constraints. Results are required. The complexity makes systems of checks and balances impossible to maintain. Fraud is burgeoning, but on a positive note, it is still considered a major disgrace, so much that the extent is denied. Most scientists caught in fraud will have a difficult career.

A logic of cover-up causes the 'statesmen' of science to guard its reputation. Thus when a large-scale case of fraud occurs, they quickly pronounce it an aberration. The problem, they say, is not systemic. They probably believe this, but the evidence points in the other direction. Of course, not all scientists are corrupt; far from it. Corruption is not an on-off situation in any event. It is a scale. The rigorous standards of science may be impossible to live up to as the examples of even the most important scientists – Newton, Pasteur, and even Darwin – show. At any rate, there is a long-standing mistake that science is above such tawdry approaches.

Charles Babbage developed a toolbox for examining scientific fraud. Categories were hoaxing, forging (fabrication), trimming (falsification), and cooking. Hoaxing is not much of an issue now, but Piltdown man, which fooled paleontology for 40 years, shows science to be vulnerable. Fabrication is made-up studies to put forth a pre-ordained idea. Falsification is trimming outlying data that weakens the scientific case. The last type, cooking (cherry-picking) means to take numerous observations and use the ones that support the case. Alternatively, two methods may produce differing results, so the 'better' method prevails. We can add to Babbage's list bare assertions (claims without evidence) and deliberate misinterpretation.

Classic science has numerous cases of high-profile misconduct. It's a bit unfair, because they are being measured by standards that didn't exist. The names are stunning – Newton, Pasteur, Millikan, Freud, and Cyril Burt.

It is uncontested that Newton falsified data. He altered observations for lunar orbits, equinox precessions, and the speed of sound to conform them to theoretical expectations. The defense is that Newton was correct, but this is a slippery slope. It opens the door to legitimate falsification for a 'true' theory based on instinct – which is exactly what Newton did. This defense is still used today. It's called the genius defense.

Millikan's oil drop experiments established the value of *e*, an electron's charge. Many say he cherry-picked data. Even the best analysis shows inexplicable exclusions. Many analysts use Millikan to argue for scientific intuition, or proper exclusion of data, focusing on good data and discarding what 'feels' wrong. Others point to him and claim scientific misconduct in even the most rigorous of scientists and one of the most important experiments in history.

Pasteur is far worse. His claim to have 'rendered a large number of dogs immune [to rabies] after being bitten' was a lie. His notebooks, secret for a century, showed that 16 or fewer were immune while ten died – no better than an unvaccinated group. Pasteur used no controls, and thus had no valid statistical grounding to claim a legitimate vaccine. Gerald Geison's biography of him observes that the greatest scientists cull data. If they have 'bad runs' they will trim the official record. Marginal experiments become central results through slight manipulations. The legitimate focus of research is truncated, altered, or sanitized to arrive at a theoretical expectation.

Ernst Haeckel forged a number of evolutionary drawings. These deluded biologists for half a century 'proving' ontology recapitulates phylogeny – the idea that a fetus develops through the stages of lower animal kingdoms. His fakery wasn't found until the '90s. He left out many details and redrew scales to fit the thesis. His drawings were used as the principle theoretical basis. Haeckel's law is no longer accepted, but still holds sway in popular belief.

Sigmund Freud is the poster child for scientific misconduct – it defines his career. He seldom used evidence for his theories. When Wilhelm Fliess told him the nose and genitals were connected, he sent a woman for sinus surgery. After a ghastly infection, the woman was disfigured. Ida Bauer, a young woman, was sexually harassed by a family friend. Disbelieved, she was forced into Freud's care. By his diagnosis, she was secretly in love with the friend and her bedwetting showed that she masturbated, of which Freud disapproved. She denied masturbation. Her revulsion at a forced kiss from the friend proved she had been vaginally stimulated by it. Her strong wish that her family end the friendship with Herr K demonstrated a homosexual love for her mother. All of Freud's cases bear similar traits. The more outlandish his theories, the more people lined up to buy them. Freud ruled psychology for decades and still bears an outsized influence.

Cyril Burt showed a strong correlation between I.Q. in twins. His theories became the basis for evolutionary psychology. Among other unsavory ideas, he showed that blacks were 'less intelligent.' Twenty years later, researchers pointed out total fabrication – at three decimal places, Burt's correlations were absurdly high. The discrepancies were obvious all along, but no one ever looked.[40]

Among the problems, 'hot' theories like this infiltrate the popular thinking. They become part of the society and exert leverage on both common and scientific thinking even after they are discredited. Sometimes more so by the attention received.

All research, being essentially contingent on previous research, has an in-built problem with fraud. It becomes incumbent on the author of a paper to verify all work on which the paper relies. This can become an endless situation, extending back to Newton or Darwin – obviously not workable. The unfortunate result is that certain research is based on faulty, sometimes fraudulent premises.

There are thousands of documented cases of scientific fraud. Most modern cases, except plagiarism, demonstrate group complicity. Though typically committed by individuals, it is covered up by groups. The pattern indicates an ignoring of fraud in order to complete the research. John Darsee published hundreds of papers, creating revolutionary bases for science and evolutionary biology. His exposure showed fabrication in virtually every paper. Interestingly, almost all his papers were co-authored. By some standards, a co-author is responsible for all material in a paper.* It calls into question how he managed to get away with such egregious errors – in one paper a 17 year old had an 8-year-old son. Other subjects were dead, then later alive again. Summaries and main texts had differing, even mutually exclusive, data sets. Stewart and Feder investigated Darsee on their own recognizance. They showed 39 errors in one paper, and up to 19 co-authors on papers with at least 10 errors. In 1993, Stewart and Feder were forcefully transferred to unrelated jobs.[41] Some saw it as retaliation for their successful analyses of misconduct.

94 papers published by Herrman and Brach had fabricated data. The case is significant – it provided a catalyst for other cases to be exposed. Inge Czaja and her chief Richard Walden confessed to fraud on 30 papers. The fabrication lasted for 6 years. They were caught only when they published in important journals.

Notably, the cases exposed tend toward serial fraud – a career pattern. Isolated cases or subdued patterns seem to go undetected indefinitely. If it is not egregious, overt, and high profile, it might remain uncontested. When discovered, behavior patterns typically reach back years or decades. Discovery happens by chance. No structure of prevention or detection exists – the peer review system does not detect fraud.[42] Fraud occurs under the eye of the most ethical senior scientists. They may be the least likely to catch it because their high standards make them unsuspecting. Often they develop a paternal relationship and cannot bear the thought.

One indication of fraud is Herculean output. Darsee published every ten days. Yet this goes unremarked by publishing in different disciplines or excused by 'genius.' Because of the amount of papers, these people exert disproportionate influence. Without normal restrictions, their discoveries are more revolutionary.

Fraud can come from the highest ground. Dr. Hendrik Schön of the prestigious Bell Labs announced a major breakthrough – electrical current delivered through a single molecule. He zeroed in on the goal over 30 months with increasingly remarkable discoveries. A Princeton physicist named Lydia Sohn uncovered the deceit. Bell Labs moved quickly to isolate the scientist, claiming it was his work alone. But there is reason for suspicion. That Schön was able to do this for so long speaks poorly of either quality control or of ethical standards. Bell is a very careful and highly regarded lab. Science is far more competitive than people

* This criteria can, and should, be contested on papers with hundreds of co-authors – particle accelerators, for instance. In smaller papers with two or three authors, the principle applies.

realize – it's more than possible that they turned a blind eye to a rising star.

These examples lead to a more serious question. Not how many fraudsters go undetected, but how much institutional fraud is ongoing. Beyond that, how systemic is it? The difference is one wherein a company has a culture of fraud. Systemic fraud is far worse – a group of companies commit regulatory capture, taking over the watchdog government bodies.

The phenomenon of regulatory capture is demonstrated by the biotech industry. Michael Taylor was an attorney representing the biotech industry until a new FDA position was created in 1991 – Deputy Commissioner for policy. He then worked as a biotech VP and is now US Food Safety Czar. In 1992, the FDA neutered its authority on Genetically Modified Organisms, calling them safe on the manufacturer's say-so alone. To this day, the FDA requires no safety evaluation of GM foods. Margaret Miller was an industry executive who became Deputy Director of Human Safety and Consultative Services, where she reviewed and signed off on her own report (on rGBH safety) written previously at the company. Examples abound.

The GMO debate (Jeffrey Smith's book *Seeds of Deception* covers the debate and the dangers of GM foods) highlights several rampant scientific malpractices. The industry organizations state that Bt-toxin (produced by GM corn to kill insects) is destroyed by digestion – a verified deception. This commits the fallacy of bald assertion (statement without evidence) and ignoring valid evidence. Further, the test data and procedures are completed by the companies and withheld, even from the regulators. The studies thus cannot be replicated or even analyzed for flaws – a grave, but common scientific error. Almost all tests are concluded in a very short time (two weeks), nullifying any claims about long-term, cumulative effects. The data is deliberately misinterpreted to make such claims. Multiple tests are done, changing parameters until desired results are achieved – cherry-picking and forcing.

Suppression of negative findings is commonplace. In the most noted case, Dr. Arpad Pusztai documented severe effects from GM potatoes and was fired within days. One lesson is obvious to an alert citizen – industries that self-regulate will, more often than not, choose profit over public safety. Conflicts of interest are usually easy to identify.

Stephen Lock gives talks on fraud. Afterwards, multiple audience members tell him of incidents they have witnessed. "Physicians concerned with or in drug companies seem to be particularly cynical."[43] In a November, 2010 guilty plea, Maria Carmen

Palazzo falsified records and psychiatric diagnoses for Paxil under a GlaxoSmithKline study. Paid $5000 per child enrolled, Palazzo knew that few, if any, of the children suffered from the diseases under investigation. Glaxo is defending against charges of concealed evidence that Paxil increases the risk of suicide in children. The company also paid out $1 billion for birth defects from Paxil.[44]

According to Drummond Rennie, just the accusation of fraud can destroy the career of accuser and accused.[45] It can create divisions, stop research, cause media blow-ups, and diminish confidence in science. Scientists are not willing to admit the depth of the problem. An informal survey of 29 medical institutions showed that only 3 had a system for investigating misconduct. The resistance to admitting it and the newness of the field make fraud investigation a poorly developed field. Serious researchers are concerned that the 'self-correcting mechanism' no longer functions.

An interesting omission in fraud investigation is deliberate misinterpretation. It is far less difficult to do than people might suppose. Raw data differs sharply from conclusions. The editor of the *Lancet* studied the source data for a number of scientific papers. He found "evidence of self-censored criticism, obscured views about the meaning of research findings, incomplete, confused and sometimes biased assessment of the implications of a study, inconsistency in publishing evaluations, especially regarding weaknesses... Probing beneath the published report, one will find a hidden research paper that reveals the true diversity of opinion among contributors about the meaning of their research findings."[46] In other words, there is great contention among research teams, but that is smoothed out of published papers. One might call this fraudulent exclusion of dissenting opinion.

A primary difficulty in fraud detection – most investigations are not replicated. Brain damage, natural disasters, astronomical events and so forth are beyond the ethical or practical scope. People would rather do original work than replication work. Thus it only happens with major finds and sometimes not even then. HIV, for example, has never been re-isolated as per Gallo/Montaigner (a very strange story in the next chapter). Publication is the primary M.O. of career advancement, but replication studies don't get published for obvious reasons, so few people do them.

Moreover, primary funding refuses to pay for replication of expensive research. The vast majority of scientific papers go uncontested and unconfirmed. "The modern biomedical research system is structured to prevent replication, not to ensure it," *The New England Journal of Medicine* (*NEJM*) reported. "It appears impossible to obtain funding for studies that are largely duplicative."[47] In short, there is little motive or means for replication work, so it seldom happens.

The decline effect also plagues science, a recent problem. When first compelling results are published, they cannot be replicated even though the original results hold up to scrutiny. Often, it's the same researcher who cannot replicate. It's happened again and again. Many researchers, victimized by the effect, are distressed. Biologist Michal Jennions believes it comes from publication bias – the desire to publish positive results. Richard Palmer thinks it stems largely from selection bias. Analyzing a number of experiments across a broad range of disciplines, he found major statistical skewing toward confirmatory results – cherry picking the data. "Selective reporting is everywhere in science."[48]

A severe negative consequence comes when new work is built upon previous unverified research. A slow accretion creates an increasingly complex structure. But if the basic research is flawed or fraudulent, there can be a disincentive to retroactively disprove theory and question whole fields. Careers would become meaningless and money would be lost.

It's also difficult even to redo complex experiments. There is intuition/ judgment/ impossibility in the mixing of reagents, use of biological materials, and even strains of mice that cannot be rediscovered.[49] In short, replication of studies is cited as a hallmark of good science, but it seldom occurs.

The system actually works to conceal fraud. "In most medical institutions in Britain," Stephen Lock wrote, "the whistleblower would have been hounded out of their job."[50] People who expose it are often victimized.

MIT researcher Thereza Imanishi-Kari went through Congressional hearings for fraud. A post-doc assistant in Imanishi-Kari's lab discovered the claims of an important paper had never been experimentally verified. All attempts had failed. The assistant didn't accuse fraud, but merely insisted on a retraction or correction of the paper. She endured ten years of torment for her efforts. The evidence was irrefutable. David Baltimore, overall project head, wrote that the paper had in fact made false claims, but paradoxically backed Imanishi-Kari and held to the paper's validity.[51] A decade-long imbroglio resulted in Congressional hearings. The interesting lesson is the entrenched quality of parties in violation of standard scientific procedures. In order to defend the paper, all they needed to do was prove the experiment valid by standard replication. They refused. As Howard Timmon, a scientist with sterling credentials and integrity said, "when an experiment is challenged, no matter who it is challenged by, it is your responsibility to check. That is an iron-clad rule of science." Imanishi-Kari eventually received a strained not-guilty verdict.

Baltimore could have simply retracted the paper. Instead, he claimed people were unable to understand the research. He used his Nobel Laureate credentials as evidence for the paper's validity in lieu of the research. To dodge critics, he refocused the intent of the paper in an ongoing fashion. Consequent validation of a study, he claimed, was the important criterion rather than validation before publication. He created a 'climate of emergency,' in which science battled official regulation.[52]

One of Imanishi-Kari's former mentors called it a typical scientific problem that such researchers are addicted to and erect structures of complexity. Over-complexity may indicate lack of confidence in basic assumptions.

Research shows that when an incident of fraud is brought before an administration, the response is inappropriate. The standard instinct is to downplay the issue and move it elsewhere. Scientists are not good at conflict. Fraud threatens relationships, workplace, career, and the thought-style of faith in scientific integrity.

A 2009 meta-analysis (the first of its kind) of fabrication and falsification of data, done via self-reporting, revealed that 14.2% of scientists admitted they had seen colleagues commit falsification (and 72% for other forms of scientific misconduct). Questionable practices were admitted to by 33% of scientists. They admitted more frequently to having altered results to gain a desired outcome than to recording knowingly false results, a difference of degree, not kind, and a subjective measure, at that. The meta-analysis results were believed to be lower than actuals, due to the sensitivity (as in career-destroying nature) of the questions.[53]

One third of those surveyed indirectly admitted to falsification by "dropping data points on a gut feeling" or "changing the design, methodology or results of a study in response to pressures from a funding source."[54] Because of the difference between self-reporting and collegial reporting, fabrication and falsification almost certainly exceed previous estimates.

If a laboratory's continued funding relies on particular results, then an employee is unlikely to report fabrication or falsification.* Other problems exist, too. Previous belief sets skew results.

---

* Medical / pharmacological sciences had the highest levels of misconduct.

Scientists can have big egos and want to prove a pet theory. Often they've spent years investigating something. If the research reveals their career might have been a waste of time, then personal considerations will exert pressure on behavior. The mistakes can easily be unintentional, a subconscious finger on the scale.

The meta-analysis suggests the problem is larger than the raw data reveals. No international association exists to investigate charges. An ad-hoc structure for one rests on entrenched conflicts of interest. Any allegations must be self-investigated by the very organization they are brought against. There is no system.

Massive incentives exist for cover-up and ignoring. If a whistleblower reports something and it is judged to be a false allegation, their career is finished. Even if the accusations bear out, he is seen as a troublemaker, blocking further advancement. There is no incentive to expose data fabrication and a lot of incentive to suppress evidence.

In a depressing example, the Cantekin affair demonstrates repeated high-profile conflicts of interest, confidentiality breaches, funding source disclosure failures, and reviewer bias. Dr. Cantekin, who objected to the endorsement of Amoxicillin and other expensive antibiotics in an industry-funded study he participated in, pointed out that the data showed no difference in reinfection between controls and trials at eight weeks. The data did show a slight improvement in trials at four weeks, but Cantekin said this was not enough to recommend antibiotics considering the negative effects and zero long-term benefit. He was isolated, his salary frozen, his offices randomly moved, and when offered a settlement, he refused. He wanted the study rescinded in the public interest. After fifteen years, his position was vindicated by research, but his career never recovered. If he had known the consequences, he said, he would not have come forward.[55]

Scientific misconduct, according to Caltech's David Goodstein, has several motives – career pressure, laziness, money, ease of getting away with it, and ideology. The last two need explanation. The enormous amount of data precludes verification of most studies. As to ideology, some people think that getting societal results (e.g. global warming, investigated later) is more important than presenting accurate data.

The evidence is extensive. A UC, San Francisco study of postdocs showed 17% would exclude or concoct data to obtain a better outcome.[56] One study showed that 50% of biostatisticians (who are well-trained to spot flaws) reported witnessing deceptive research during the previous decade.[57] Researchers with advanced training in perceiving scientific misconduct are no less likely to engage in it.[58] A number of studies indicate that funding severely influences biomedical research.[59],[60] One fraud study showed 22 of 26 cases were 'medical or related to medical purposes.'[61]

A science journal found 1% of images were improperly manipulated. In customary data audits, the FDA found faults in 10-20% of research, with an assessment of 2% of experimental investigators culpable for "serious scientific misconduct."[62] The paper mentions other examples and cautions that these estimates "significantly underestimate" the problem. Whistleblowers are rare, fabrication and falsification are extremely difficult to detect, and, when detected, a facility may have a disincentive against external reporting, as it would tarnish their image. One 'non-systematic review' approximated serious misconduct at 1% of research.

Ushma Neill, executive editor of a prominent peer-reviewed journal, wrote, "The numerous cases of scientific misconduct that have crossed my desk in the past year leave me disappointed, disenchanted, and disillusioned."[63]

Hippocrates Betrayed

By means of injections, drugs and chemicals,
the population could be induced to bear whatever
its scientific masters may decide to be for its good.[64]
—Bertrand Russell

In 1963, Los Angeles doctors went on strike and the death rate immediately declined. Today it's worse. The US medical system is now the number-one cause of death. In 2000, it was third. Unnecessary antibiotics, improper diagnosis, needless surgery, bedsores, and lethal side effects of pharmaceuticals killed 780,000 people in 2007.[65] The system, critics say, suffers under bad ideas.

In one gruesome example, the standard in neo-natal surgery for four decades was no anesthetic. Babies were given curare, a paralytic, on the untenable belief that infants cannot feel pain. Many thousands endured agonizing procedures including open heart and brain surgery. It is nothing less than torture of infants, if we are honest. The AMA endorsed the practice. In 1987, a mother crammed some common sense into the system, by pointing out that infants *actually feel pain*.

Our mental health is also under assault from mistaken authority. A 1972 experiment sent sane people into psychiatric hospitals with one made-up complaint – they mentally heard the word 'thud.' All 8 were admitted as schizophrenics and forcibly held despite normal behavior, even telling doctors the 'thud' was an invention for an experiment. They were made to take anti-psychotics and only by agreeing they were ill were they allowed to 'get better.' David Rosenhan caused an uproar when he published the results in *Science*.[66] The hospitals challenged him to send more impostors, claiming they would detect them. 41 were detected. No one was sent.

In response, psychiatrists created a computer database for auto-diagnosis. In statistical tests, the system immediately diagnosed half the population as mentally ill. That system is the current standard, growing out of control. *DSM-IV* had 25% more mental disorders than III. Lead authors of the *DSM-III* and *IV* have even teamed up opposing the DSM-5.* They believe it will lead to the "wholesale imperial medicalization of normality," a virtual pharmaceutical takeover.

Other areas are no better. The allopathic success rate for cancer is "appalling," according to tumor specialist Dr. Ulrich Abel

* They dropped the Roman numerals.

at the end of his multi-year research on the subject. *NCI* journal reports the lymphoma treatment successes to be a lie and worse – chemo patients were fourteen times more likely to contract leukemia and six times more likely to contract bone and joint cancers.[67] "Most cancer patients in this country die of chemotherapy," Alan Levin, M.D. said.[68] The great promise of genetic analysis turns out to be irrelevant to the prediction of cancer and all other diseases.[69] Still companies continue this highly profitable business.

Malpractice is not even new. Jonas Salk experimented on senile subjects – he could not have obtained their consent. In 1973, pharma confessed that it used prisoners because they were cheaper than chimps.

The United States has dropped to 49th in life expectancy. The annual US death toll from pharmaceuticals is 200,000.[70] The industry pushes drugs for 'healthy-eating disorder.' A vast pharmacopeia – including antibiotics, anti-convulsants, mood stabilizers and sex hormones – are in the drinking water supplies of at least 41 million Americans.[71]

600 scientists, including Nobel Laureaute for neurology Dr. Arvid Carlsson, have petitioned Congress to ban fluoride. The Associated Press reported that excess fluoride can lead to "crippling bone abnormalities."[72] Bob Carlton, former EPA scientist, called it a mistake from the beginning. NIH and CDC found it actually damages teeth. It can cause arthritis and disrupt the thyroid. The senior toxicologist at the EPA leveled serious accusations about doctored reports on lab rats who acquired bone and liver cancer from fluoride. He was fired for whistleblowing. Most countries have blocked it, but it's still added to drinking water in the US. Water supply fluoride is not medical grade – it is labeled toxic waste for shipping. A product of phosphate mining, it killed livestock from indiscriminate dumping and was banned. Now it's a commodity we drink every day. In January, 2011, the CDC finally acknowledged fluoride poisoning in children – and lowered the permissible amount. Soon after, a hazmat team had to clean up a spill at a water plant when a spilled chemical "ate holes in the concrete." The chemical was fluoride.

Health science watchdogs are not acting in the public interest. The EPA raised the 'safe' limit of radiation by 3000 times when Fukushima dumped 20 million gallons of radioactive water into the Pacific. "Under the updated [guidelines] a single glass of water could give a lifetime's permissible exposure."[73] Canada, during the worst nuclear emergency in world history, turned off radiation monitors because of "low levels of radiation detected."[74]

John Ioannidis showed, in the *Journal of the American Medical Association*, that 41% of the most highly quoted replicated studies were proved false. Mainstream medicine commits dangerous quackery as readily as anyone else. As recently as 1922, doctors officially recommended mercury inhalation therapy for syphilis, in spite of massive evidence of extreme toxicity. Even later, they prescribed heroin and cigarettes – apparently the latter are good for teeth. Everyone hopes the system is past such lunacy now. Let's look at some evidence from around the world.

Genetic Epidemic

I feel pain but I cannot cry.
—Tito Mukhopadhyay

For 60 years, one country legally mandated injecting a known neurotoxin into its most vulnerable populace – infants. Consequent with that practice, it has seen a terrible disorder. The injections increased. The amount of the substance increased. The age decreased. From two years, it slid under a year, then six and two months. Finally, infants were injected with this neurotoxin at 6 times the adult dosage on the day they were born. Four more times by their first birthday, they received additional injections up to 125 times the adult limit. The disease became an epidemic. Official government bodies deny, attributing the disease entirely to genetic factors. These were never found. The injection manufacturers engineered laws to protect them from liability.

The government medical authority (CDC), a military organization, held a secret conference with industry leaders to protect financial interests. Information massage seemed the first line of attack. "You can look at this data," the lead analyst said, "and turn it around." When their studies found no link, they forbid independent researchers access to the data. Their studies could not be analyzed for fraud.

Parents with affected children were outraged. They demanded accountability and were stonewalled. The party line ridiculed their belief that "it was a bad idea to inject an extremely neural toxic compound into a day old infant."[75] Few are aware the debate ever occurred – it went mostly unreported in the media. The substance is still being injected into the general populace on an aggressive agenda. The disease is autism. The chemical is mercury. The country is the United States of America.

In the 1920s, Eli Lilly, the head of the company by the same name, created a 49% organic mercury compound now called thimerosal. The only testing it received was injection into 22 terminal meningitis patients. A few weeks later, all were dead. As no toxic effects were documented, the drug was pronounced harmless and released. This is the benchmark test for its safety to this day. Thimerosal has never been tested by the FDA.

There are independent studies. One paper commonly cited as proof of safety showed the death of half the rabbits injected. Numerous studies date to the '30s correlating thimerosal with retardation and severe mental disturbance in children. Over the years, Lilly received a slew of reports on thimerosal dangers. All were ignored. In 1972, they were sent an article – clinical merthiolate (thimerosal) in vaccines caused six deaths. In 1999, Lilly printed Material Safety Document Sheets for workers – "thimerosal can cause nervous system and reproductive effects, fetal changes, mercury poisoning. Exposure in children may cause mild to severe mental retardation. Hazardous substance. Toxic waste disposal."[76]

Mercury poisoning has a long history. 'Mad as a hatter' is a truism – hatters worked with mercury. In 1972, a number of Iraqi children were accidentally fed methyl mercury-treated grain intended for seed. The children developed difficulties with speech, memory and attentiveness. Early in the twentieth century, topical mercury in some products caused acrodynia, or pink disease. The symptoms are initial loss of cheer, aggression, unresponsiveness, hitting, biting, self-abuse, and repetition of phrases.[77] The industry that put out these products – mercurochrome, teething powder, calamine lotion – lobbied hard against the theory that mercury caused the damage. It took years for general acceptance. When mercury was removed, acrodynia vanished.

In one case study, a man was accidentally given a massive dose of thimerosal. Days later, he could no longer speak. He withdrew socially and soon began arm-flapping, a hallmark of autism.[78] Infants known to have mercury exposure exhibit a very high rate of difficulty with speech and comprehension. They are often intolerant of noise and touch, with muddled senses. They are highly sensitive or totally desensitized to pain. They are socially withdrawn, obsessive–compulsive and cannot understand abstract concepts.[79]

In the late 1930s, thimerosal was added to vaccines. 1943 saw the first recorded case of autism. Diagnoses average 4 years of age. Japan introduced it in 1945 and saw its first autism case a few years later. England introduced it in the 1950s and had its first cases within five years.

Thimerosal vaccines are, by definition, toxic waste. Over 200 parts per billion of mercury qualifies – thimerosal vaccines have 250 times that. For decades, repeated DTP injections gave children 100mcgs of thimerosal. Then the amount soared. In 1988, the HiB vaccine added 25 mcgs to the schedule. In 1991, Hep-B* appeared with 12.5 mcgs. With repetitions, children received a total of 237.† One day's injections might be 62.5mcgs, or 120 times the FDA toxic limit for an average 2-month old.

The FDA, in 1982, called for the removal of mercury from all over-the-counter topical products and said that mercury was "no better than water at protecting mice from fatal streptococcal infections." It fails as a preservative; its only reason for being in vaccines. Out of twenty mercury compounds, this panel felt thimerosal was the most toxic.[80] As one of the parents said, "they knew it was too toxic to rub on the skin, but they injected it into infants."[81]

In 1999, the FDA's viral products director sent an internal email about the compound: "conversion of the percentage of thimerosal to actual micrograms of mercury involves 9th grade algebra. Why didn't the CDC and the advisory bodies do these calculations while rapidly expanding the childhood immunization schedule?"[82]

CDC researcher Thomas Verstraeten put out an internal study linking mercury with autism. The data led to a secret June, 2000 meeting of government and industry officials at Simpsonwood Conference Center in Norcross, GA. Verstraeten showed an autism increase from 1/2500 to 1/166 children since thimerosal-vaccines had seriously increased. The CDC later claimed Verstraeten's work had been lost and could not be replicated. Then they contracted the Institute of Medicine with orders to "rule out" any link between thimerosal and autism.

In 2001, the National Institute for Environmental Health Sciences said that thimerosal "emits highly toxic fumes of mercury, sodium oxide, and silver oxides." They advised lab workers to remove clothing and evacuate in the event of a spill. Unswayed,

Pediatrician Eric Fombonne published a paper claiming there was no environmental evidence for autism. The increase was due to higher public profile and superior diagnostic standards.[83] The study, Dr. David Ayoub pointed out, linked vaccination rates from one city with autism rates from another. Pediatrics

---

* Children get this, according to a manufacturer, "because a vaccination strategy limited to high-risk individuals has failed." (Miller, 7 reasons).

† RhoD and flu shots given to pregnant women create additional prenatal exposure.

refused to publish Ayoub's response because Fombonne "did not wish to answer."

More and more activists and autism groups began to support the mercury hypothesis. Researchers found that Russia had banned thimerosal, naming it a potent neurotoxin. Lynn Redwood, R.N., mother of an autistic child and firm believer in the vaccine system, was skeptical of the mercury hypothesis. Looking at the evidence, she became convinced and started Safe Minds, an anti-thimerosal group.

At a 2000 autism conference, SafeMinds and other groups requested a number of studies be conducted by the NIH: electromagnetic brain imaging to detect mercury, thimerosal variability in vaccine batches, an EEG comparison between mercury-poisoned and autistic subjects, an epidemiological study between non-vaccinated (Amish) and fully vaccinated children, animal toxicological studies with bolus doses given to mice or monkeys. No official body has ever conducted any of these studies.

On June 21, 2000, the CDC announced it had found "statistically significant associations between thimerosal and neurodevelopmental disorders."* Autism was found to occur at 1.69 times the frequency with doses above versus below 62.5 mcgs. The baseline of 1 fell within the 95% confidence interval.† They drew battle lines – the results for autism were not statistically significant. When Verstraeten announced his results, he also announced being hired earlier that day by pharma giant GlaxoSmithKline.

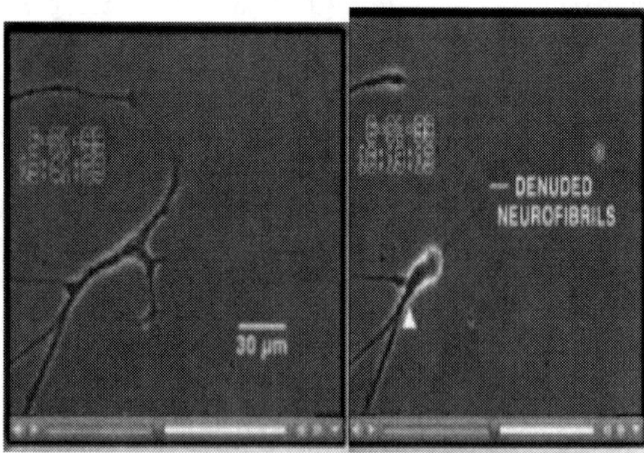

Figure 3. Neuron exposed to mercury (*Neuroreport* 12:4 [2001]).

* 16% of US children have a diagnosed learning disability.

† A confidence interval is the probability for a specific measurement to lie within a range of values.

A video from University of Calgary labs soon caused an uproar. In it, a mere .001mcg of mercury visibly causes "direct degeneration of brain neurons" with "visual evidence that mercury produces a molecular lesion of the brain."[84] (See figure 3, previous page.) Though worth watching, the brief film is disturbing.*

The EPA lowered the infant exposure limit. The commonly injected single-day exposure – 62.5mcgs – is about 500 times their limit. Although the EPA is concerned about mercury exposure to pregnant women and children from power plants and fish, the CDC's vaccine program vigorously promotes injecting more than 500 times the limit into two-month-old babies.

The hazard to infants is far greater because they are still developing. Mercury stops cell division and migration, bonds with DNA and blocks essential protein creation. High single (bolus) doses of mercury increase harm. They body cannot excrete a high dose and incorporates most. Severe cases may result from massive doses. Being extremely dense, mercury settles to the bottom of a multi-dose vial and could end up largely in one injection. An infant can thus get many times the 'normal' amount of mercury.

Long-time mercury researcher Boyd Haley, U. of Kentucky, showed that vaccines with mercury were between 10 and 100 times more toxic than those without.[87] Later, he isolated groups of nerve cells in vitro. Controls almost all lived for 24 hours. Aluminum killed 10%. Antibiotics killed 20%. Thimerosal killed 70%. All three combined killed 90%. Stunningly, thimerosal and testosterone caused a hundredfold increase in the death velocity. *All neurons died in minutes*. Autism is 4 times as prevalent in males as females.†

Autistic children, Haley later found, have very low concentrations of mercury in hair samples. Non-autistics have 3.63 ppm; autistics .47. It correlates strongly with severe autism being the lowest. Autistics, they hypothesize, cannot properly excrete mercury through normal systems (like hair), so it remains in the body tissues.

The first CDC study on vaccines/autism[88] looked at one- and three-month exposure, even though vaccines were routinely given at four, six, and twelve months. The study simplistically divided the children between those above and below the limit of .1 mcg/kg/day. With no analysis of mercury quantity injected per visit, the study came to the easy conclusion that there was no negative effect. The report averaged out the mercury doses by the calendar days – this brought the exposure below acceptable

* Google 'How Mercury causes brain neuron degeneration, Calgary.'

† Both genders create testosterone and estrogen – it is the proportions that differ.

limits. It is a heinous toxicological flaw – as if there were no difference between taking two Tylenol per day for two months and taking 120 at once. One will kill you.

They assigned the task of conducting the study to a junior pediatrician, Dr. Ball. When asked about the illegitimate methodology, she replied, "I don't know. I'm not a toxicologist. I'm a pediatrician. *I just did what they told me to do.*"[89] The parents asked for a recall of the vaccines. Dr. Egan said they couldn't because it would open them up to litigation from the pharmaceutical industry.

Official clinical/lab experiments do not exist. The few cited studies are abstracted from other experiments. All clinical studies are from independent and university sources. All are consistent with mercury causing autism. For example, a large international team gave weight-adjusted vaccines to macaques. Compared to controls, they developed autistic symptoms.[90]

Another study led to the career casualty of Dr. Horning. She injected mice with body-weight comparable levels of ethylmercury as in vaccine schedules. The mice developed clear autistic symptoms such as excessive partner grooming to the point of wearing through the skull and killing them. The videos were volatile, especially with parents who saw the same symptoms in their children. Her NIH funding was cancelled.

Some unusual case studies linked Gulf War syndrome with mercury by vaccination. Frank Schmuck received an astonishing 800mcgs in military vaccines.[*] Severely compromised, he underwent chelation therapy and returned to normality.

Every few years a new study 'definitively disproves' the mercury-autism hypothesis. A 2009 study based in Italy claimed no correlation between autism and mercury. According to the paper itself, no thimerosal-free children were studied – it was only between 62.5mcg and 137.5mcg receivers. *Only one child with autism was in the study* – making any conclusion irrelevant. It was conducted by telephone. The entire sample size was only 1700 children. Italian children receive far lower amounts of thimerosal than US children and have a far lower autism rate.

Pediatrics published an article citing several strikes against the thimerosal idea: they discounted the epidemic theory, claiming that superior diagnostics, public services and referrals accounted for the autism increase. No study showed that autism was subsequent to a mass mercury contamination. It claimed pink disease and autism symptoms differed significantly – pink disease

[*] Still lower by body weight than most infants receive.

includes sores, hypertension, poor coordination and slurred speech.[91] The paper had no peer review.

The SafeMinds rebuttal was rejected as failing peer review. SafeMinds responded: The theory of better diagnostic standards was hypothetical and unresearched. *Pediatrics* omitted the Fukushima case in Japan (see below). Autism was a novel form of mercury poisoning coming as it did from direct injection. Mercury poisoning does not have a single set of symptoms. Different known mercury diseases such as Minimata and pink disease have widely divergent symptoms – mercury is well-known for this property. They also pointed to overlaps: arm-flapping and motor coordination difficulties.

Autism and mercury poisoning have sixteen different comparative categories including psychiatric, physical, linguistic, motor skills, cognitive, behavioral, gastrointestinal, neurological, biochemical, and immunological. Several hundred autistic characteristics correlate at 99% with mercury poisoning – the two are virtually indistinguishable. Symptoms include a number of specific and unusual traits. Here is a random sample – OCD, Dysarthia, 4-to-1 male preference, abnormal sensations, jerky movements, toe-walking, self-injury, cerebral palsy, incontinence, anorexia, glutathione deficiency, mitochondrial disruption, microcephaly, epinephrine and glutamate elevation, demyelization of neurons, seizures and epileptic EEGs.

The United States has the highest number of mandated vaccines of any country in the world and places 34th for under 5 mortality. The vaccine schedule for children aged 5 and under has tripled in 25 years. With 3 to 12 times the rate of any other country, the US is the autism epicenter. The rate has risen from 1/2500 to 1/166. Folding in ASD (Autism Spectrum Disorder), it breaks the 1/100 mark. 1/50 male children has ASD. The official theorists dig in – it is not an epidemic because it is genetic. Genetic epidemics are impossible.

Epidemiology studies the movement of disease. It is statistical – thus easily manipulated. To discuss the epidemiology in light of vaccination, one fact is salient – the US gives (by law) three times the vaccine injections of almost any other country in the world – 36 before five years of age*. It also has three times the autism rate of the second place country – Japan. Four times the third – France, five times Finland, six times Israel, and fifteen times that of the favored country for epidemiological studies – Denmark. Note that no third-world countries appear. They have

* France is the exception with 17.

had no autism and minimal vaccinations – until recently. Thimerosal was banned by Russia in 1980 and later in Japan, Scandinavia, Denmark, Austria, and Great Britain.

Interesting epidemiological evidence comes from Japan: children born in 1966 near Fukushima-ken suffered a 1000% increase in the autism rate. There was a large mercury spill in the area that year.

Mark Blaxill is a professional statistical analyst with an autistic daughter. Initially skeptical, he came to believe the mercury hypothesis after examining the data. Over the years, he has been the primary analyst exposing the methodological errors in the various studies. He noted several problems with the CDC's first study, which found a 1.69 correlation. The diagnostic age was capped at three years even though the average diagnostic age for autism is 4.4 years. At least half, and probably far more, of the autistic children had not been diagnosed. The data used from the California HMO showed a far lower rate of autism than the national average. They only used HMO-diagnosed children, although most children are diagnosed by specialists and few at an HMO. Moreover, follow-up diagnoses were ignored – children initially diagnosed with one disorder, such as ADD, were not included as autistic even when their diagnosis was later amended to include autism. These 'errors' eliminated up to 90% of the autistic children.

But it wasn't all. The study was cut off before six months of age, thus ignoring additional exposures of up to 62.5 mcgs of thimerosal. 70% of the children were excluded based on perinatal or congenital disorders without explanation. Pervasive developmental disorder not otherwise specified (PDD-NOS) and Asperger's syndromes, although autistic spectrum disorders, were not included. The planned phase-2 segment was not conducted. It was substituted with Harvard HMO, a far smaller set of records. The HMO was in receivership for bankruptcy and under investigation for poor record keeping. The small sample size made for a much larger 95% confidence interval. This means that the correlation between autism and mercury could be far higher, without being called statistically significant. The HMO was a strange choice for an epidemiological study for another reason. The CDC owns the Vaccine Safety Datalink, the largest and most thorough vaccine database in the world. There is no legitimate reason to use records from a badly managed, small HMO.

In one of the long-standing criticisms of all CDC, NIH, and other studies, no outside researchers are allowed access to the data. Independent confirmation guards honest science. The CDC contends the restriction safeguards health records, even though identifying data could be redacted and non-disclosure penalties put in place.

A withheld study came out, showing a 2.48 association of autism with over 62.5 mcgs.[92] In March of 2000, Verstraeten wrote an email, obtained through a Freedom of Information filing, with the heading "It just won't go away." He showed a correlation of 5.0 – meaning 5 times the likelihood – between premature infants who received 200mcgs versus 100mcgs. He called the finding "very extreme."

Mark and David Geier did a study using the public VAERS database and found a mercury-autism correlation of 6 between a group of children given DTAP vaccine with thimerosal versus a group given DTAP without. They wanted access to the far more thorough Vaccine Safety Datalink of the CDC.

The Geiers, professional epidemiologists, gained a very limited access to the VSD after years of exhaustive paperwork. It seems they were sabotaged. They were required to use a proprietary computer code and had to pay a programmer to learn it. They were not given consecutive days, but had to come up, flying the programmer in, multiple times. They were locked out of the ancient computer when they arrived. A sympathetic monitor, assigned to watch over their every move, furtively helped them log-in, telling them about an autistic relative.* They compared groups receiving DTAP with and without thimerosal. The former group had 27 times the autism prevalence. Their follow-up study was rendered impossible by failed equipment and bureaucratic obstacles.

A Danish study showed that a number of years after mercury was removed autism climbed from 10 to 181 cases per year. The authors admitted they "may have spuriously increased the apparent number of autism cases."[93] No peer reviews were allowed.

Blaxill's response to the study was published elsewhere: The cohort size was as low as 10 cases per year – rendering the study meaningless by any epidemiological standards. They changed the inclusion criteria mid-study without explanation. They only counted inpatients until 1995 when they added outpatients. The early years omitted the Copenhagen clinic, which processes 20% of all Danish cases. Third, Denmark changed its autism criteria and pushed diagnoses of autism by educating health care workers. The study thus compared differing data sets. In any event, Denmark had one of the lowest autism rates in the world both

* On the second visit, their aging computer crashed. Their printouts came in a locked room and no one could be found with the key.

before *and after* thimerosal was removed. It's fraudulent to compare a tiny sample from a country with the least significant autistic rate to a large country with a raging epidemic. There is no valid reason to conduct a study on small numbers with California's excellent record system awaiting discovery. These official epidemiological studies were repeatedly from foreign countries where children received less than a third of the US mercury exposures.

The Denmark report is still cited by uncritical doctors to disprove the mercury hypothesis. The American Academy of Family Practice and the American Association of Pediatricians calls it an excellent study. Information is missing. Poul Thorsen was the lead researcher. Although he wrote papers proving the efficacy of vaccines, Thorsen was a psychiatrist with no medical research credentials. He disappeared with $2 million of research funds – the money for that very study. He faces serious fraud charges. An investigation found falsification of documents and fraudulent payroll schemes. Autism groups demand the CDC reinvestigate the studies. They refuse and still cite them as valid.[94]

In a study of the unvaccinated Amish, Dan Olmstead found 4 cases out of 23,000 children. The national rate predicts 138. Three were documentably vaccinated and one was adopted from China without definitive records. Vaccination would be a normal procedure.

"Why isn't the CDC putting their money into a reasonable hypothesis?" Boyd Haley asked. "There doesn't seem to be any money to search for an alternative cause. Only more money for doing studies to deny that thimerosal is the cause... I'm a full professor of biochemistry. I failed to convince this highly regarded medical committee that it was a bad idea to inject an extremely neural toxic compound into a day old infant. This does not reflect well on our society or American medicine."[95]

In the secret meeting at Simpsonwood – parents excluded – CDC officials met with pharmaceutical executives to discuss thimerosal and autism. "What if the lawyers get hold of this?" the notes read. "There's not a scientist in the world who can refute these findings." They were also "not in favor of expressing a preference for a particular vaccine without thimerosal for fear of alienating the other manufacturers and disrupting a free market economy." According to Blaxill, Simpsonwood showed a definite desire to 'diminish the signal' by any means available. The information needed to be concealed, conflicts of interest were readily apparent, and there were a number of errors and omissions in the recommended methodology.[96]

Verstraaten said at the Simpsonwood Conference, "some children are not old enough to be diagnosed, so the crude incidence rates are probably very much lower than what you would expect." He also discussed the 2-3 times higher incidence in premature babies due to low birth weight upon receiving thimerosal. "The bottom line is – *our signal will simply not go away*." At the meeting, Dr. Weil rated the likelihood 4 of 6 that thimerosal was implicated. "You are across the line," another member threatened. "You are across the line toward the strong."

Politics came in big. Lobbyists said that if thimerosal lawsuits against companies came to fruition, it would hamper their ability to make bioterror vaccines. They wanted litigation protection. Families were forced into the Federal VICP – Vaccine Injury Compensation Program.* They would not be allowed to opt out and pursue direct litigation against manufacturers. Families with a grievance more than three years old would not even be allowed that option – thousands had no legal recourse. Senator Bill Frist pushed through two provisions preventing lawsuits. Then a Homeland Securities Act rider removed all rights to litigate over the injection of thimerosal – specifically protecting Eli Lilly. Every member of Congress denied responsibility for the rider.

Mitchell Daniels, senior vice-president of corporate marketing for Eli Lilly, was named president of the Homeland Security and National Security councils. These posts have wide bioterror vaccine latitude. Lilly CEO Sidney Taurel got a post on the Homeland Security Council.

Congressional hearings revealed biases. The pharma lobby, in exchange for money it spends, receives rapid licensing of pharmaceuticals, decreased regulatory oversight, protection from lawsuits, and mandated product use. It is the only industry bequeathed with mandatory use and litigation immunity. The taxpayer-funded CDC has spent $300 billion promoting vaccines and under $1 billion testing them.[97] CDC board member Margaret Reynolds, it was disclosed, receives money from every vaccine manufacturer. "The CDC has dedicated significant funding to epidemiology while starving funding for clinical and biological research," said Congressman Weldon. "The IOM bases their conclusion on five epidemiology studies conducted by researchers with an interest in not finding an association, all of which have shortcomings and all of which the IOM declares would miss an association if it were in a genetically susceptible subset of children."[98] Later, CDC members left the room before independent studies were presented.[99]

* VICP is funded by a vaccine surtax – no industry liability.

In November of 2002, the Department of Health and Human Services tried to permanently seal any records relating to thimerosal toxicity under criminal penalties. They wanted all previously released documents to be found and destroyed. Any evidence presented in vaccine court would be inadmissible in civil court.

Bradstreet and Holmes demonstrated that autistic children accumulated far more mercury than non-autistics. The Geiers found high correlations in the VSD and VAERS databases between thimerosal and autism. Blaxill correlated autism rates with thimerosal in California. Horning showed autistic tendencies in mercury-injected mice. Calgary showed mercury destroying neurons in real time. And still Dr. Steve Cocchi expresses the official position on the mercury-autism connection as "junk science and disinformation put forth by charlatans."[100]

At the same time, the *Lancet* published a study claiming that ethyl-mercury was removed from the blood rapidly after injection.[101] Based on this study, the WHO recommended that thimerosal remain in vaccines sent throughout the world. Blaxill objected to the study – it counted only 33 children. The time of blood draw was a month after peak mercury. The author had ties to Lilly and grants from 11 pharma companies. As has been known for decades, mercury leaves the blood for other tissues quickly. And the brain preferentially absorbs mercury 6 times greater than other tissues. A simple test for mercury-autism link would be to test the tissues of children with autism to determine if they are holding onto mercury. The test has never been done by any official body.

The FDA vaccine advisory panel recommends approval and licensing of new vaccines. ACIP, for the CDC, decides which vaccines go to the childhood immunization schedule. Numerous members of both bodies have received speaking honoraria, travel moneys, research grants and other awards from drug companies. Several own vaccine patents and pharmaceutical stock. In one meeting, more than half the members were either not there or abstained. Five temporary voting members licensed the product. ACIP members are routinely granted conflict-of-interest waivers to participate in voting.[102] "The FDA science agenda lacks a coherent structure and vision as well as effective coordination and prioritization," an internal inquiry later concluded. "The FDA cannot fulfill its mission."[103]

In 2004, the Institue of Occupational Medicine (IOM) published a large epidemiological study concluding that there was no connection. Gayle Castle, VP of Infectious Diseases for Eli Lilly, sits on the IOM governing council. The chair for this study,

Dr. Merrick McCormack, said, "the CDC wants us to declare that these things are pretty safe. We're not ever going to come down that autism is a true side effect." The result "Walt [Dr. Orenstein] wants" would be to find "inadequate evidence to accept or reject a causal relation."[104] Announcing the study, the IOM "declared the case closed." Trampling the principles of science, they recommended blocking any further research into the hypothesis.

There were more developments. Dallas TV reporter Valerie William conducted a hard-hitting expose of thimerosal. Told to stop the investigation, she was soon fired. A house government reform committee report stated, "thimerosal used as a preservative in vaccines is directly related to the autism epidemic." The parents contacted the office of special counsel, a politically insulated office, which began investigating the claims.

The CDC got a new director, Julie Gerberding. Weldon spoke to her privately, saying, "you took the mercury out of vaccines and you're stopping the collection of data immediately afterward. Wouldn't you want to collect that data and know whether there's a trend downward?" She said he had a good point and would get back to him. She never did.[105] In 2008, Merck hired her to head their vaccine division.

Eventually, a bombshell leaked from the CDC. An earlier Verstraeten study compared children receiving 25 mcgs and 0 mcgs by 1-month age.[106] The secret 'generation zero' study revealed an average risk of 11.3 times the likelihood for autism with thimerosal. The high end of the range was 47 times the control rate.*

The CDC's official position remains: 1) Mercury is highly neuro-toxic. 2) The safe exposure limit is .1 mcgs/kg. 3) Mercury has been repeatedly injected into millions of infants at 62.5-mcg doses. 4) This is good medical practice and cannot have caused serious harm.

The story is not over. The CDC has since moved its database into private hands. The Brighton collaboration is offshore, immune to FOIA requests and subpoeanas. The public will never have access to these taxpayer-funded records. August 26, 2004, California voted to remove thimerosal given to infants and pregnant women. Without comment, the UK Department of Health banned thimerosal from DTP. A few months later, a mass recall averted the most drastic health emergency in decades. Over a million doses of Fluvirin were contaminated with the often fatal Serratia bacteria. Fluvirin contained mercury. Thimerosal cannot even perform its stated function – to keep vaccines sterile.

---

* The CDC studies showed a significant correlation with the same parameters for nine neuro-developmental disorders.

The FDA suggested, with no enforcement or penalties, that thimerosal be removed from vaccines. Manufacturers quit making it, but the multi-year supply remained in circulation. Merck, in fact, put thimerosal in vaccines for two years after claiming it had removed them.[107] Meanwhile, the Bush administration blocked attempts to litigate over products approved by the FDA, saying victims had no recourse to claims.

The flu vaccine still has thimerosal at many times the limit for fetal development – it is pushed on pregnant women. Merck and GlaxoSmithKline began aggressively marketing thimerosal vaccines in third-world countries about 1999. On August 11, 2004, China reported a catastrophic rise in autism rates from 0 to 1.8 million. Autism was never seen in developing countries prior to mass vaccination.

Lifetime care is $5 to $10 million per autistic. California has seen a 1000% rise in rates – crippling its medical system. The problem is worsening as numerous autistic children become adults. The proof "that vaccines in mercury has no relation is an absolute lie," Russell Blaylock, M.D. says. "And they know it."[108] Indeed, in 2007, the courts found in favor of Hannah Polling – vaccine mercury had caused her autism.

The burden of proof is backwards. The people presenting their concerns have said that injecting mercury into children might cause harm. They are required to prove that it is harmful. Normally, in injecting substances into children (or anyone), the manufacturer is required to prove the substance is safe. It's an odd point to have to make – our children's safety should have the highest priority. Mercury should not be injected into children. The debate would be ludicrous if the consequences were not so grave.

It is simple and clear. Either our government watchdogs do not understand or they are protecting the pharmaceutical companies. In regulatory capture, an industry gets its people in control of the watchdog organizations and sets its own rules.

One uneasy possibility arises from this. Due to the enormous body of evidence and prior knowledge that injecting mercury is harmful, some officials at FDA and CDC probably already knew the dangers. Certainly vaccine manufacturers did. It is obvious enough. Most officials probably missed it, but some deliberately allowed it. Some people, somewhere, made a deliberate choice to inject mercury into hundreds of millions of babies. And wrapped in the mantle of science, it's still happening – in fact, it's spreading across the world.

The Straightjacket of Science

To grasp the basis of phenomena in logic may be impossible.
— Schroedinger

In the beginning, any theory changes rapidly. Over time, it becomes more complex and interconnected. At this point, the set of elaborations, connections, specialized ideas and fundamental concepts is so tightly woven that it cannot be disentangled. At all stages, it has a living quality – being born, growing, being sick or well, and dying. Without research and new formulations, it withers. It is not static. Nor is it built as a pre-planned, organized structure. Theories emerge as slow-motion accident. They change, as well – a later theory normally appears wildly different from its early manifestations.

The creation of science is a poorly understood process. The best analyses are distorted by others or ignored entirely. In 1935, Ludwig Fleck, a prominent Jewish German microbiologist, wrote a monograph called *Genesis and Development of a Scientific Fact.* He published it in Sweden – Jews weren't allowed to publish in Germany. Fleck also published and spoke widely on serology, the new science of blood testing. He was a pioneer in the field. *Genesis and Development* uses Fleck's expertise on syphilis as a deeply probed example.

The modern scientific notions of the disease fused from a mishmash of previous ideas – "the ethical mystical disease entity of carnal scourge" and "an empirical therapeutic disease entity." Though the two notions are logically exclusive, they became joined to the temporary definitions of the day. Some of the earliest causes of syphilis included astrology and punishment by God for carnality. "The sign of Scorpio explained why the genitals would be attacked." These preceding beliefs created the basis of the 'scientific' theory of sexual transmission. It was not based on evidence.

In this nutshell version of syphilology, a number of 'thought communities' believed in tainted blood: the religious subset called it the carnal scourge. Medical practice related it to leprosy and dermatological disorders. Medieval pathologists connected it to mercury poisoning. The idea existed for hundreds of years to test the blood. When it happened, the reigning champion of medical ideas, germ theory, looked to bacterial causes.

Syphilis is notably pleomorphic – many forms. Any disease or symptom not clearly known was thrown into the 'syphilis' basket. Some physicians stated that syphilis did not exist – it was too vaguely defined. The first recognizably scientific modern theory was based on the idea of 'bad' blood – an acidic fluid producing changes in the humors. This idea never left – but it did change form to the bacteria. Endless experiments and tests trying to prove this blood connection failed. Finally, the Wasserman reaction, from poor initial results, achieved 70-80% accuracy (which means little – verification by symptoms is inaccurate for syphilis.) Based on this test, which does not directly find bacteria, the bacteria equals syphilis theory became fact.[109] The modern AIDS-theory, as we will see, has stunning parallels to syphilis-theory.

Fleck, an expert in the Wasserman technique, argued that the serological foundation followed no rules of science and could not be explained by any expert. Scientific ideas, in fact, seldom arise from evidence. They arise and are modified from previous thought styles.

Thought styles emerge in a chaotic manner from many non-scientific influences – the individuals involved, the society, neighboring thought styles, and products created. They range from a conversation to a seminar up to a thought community – an insular Baptist church or a specialized research facility. Each has its own language and modes of thinking and each arrives at its own conclusions, subsequently called 'facts.' The longer these swim in the milieu, the more they are accepted.

Within a thought collective, the large share of knowledge is organized, verified, utile, and obvious to all the individuals. Foreign systems of thought seem fraught with paradox, unverifiable, inutile, supernatural or ad hoc. Each group will look at other groups that way and the further the groups are apart, the more will the differences appear bizarre.

As increasing relations (facts) establish themselves, the system solidifies. Contravailing opinions have less and less chance for a decent hearing. Differing opinions must be carefully crafted and delivered by 'experts.' They must exhibit large conformity with prevailing theories, disagreeing only on specific points. Radical theories are summarily dismissed. In this regard, science is no different from any other thought style.

The stages of research for theories follow certain rules. "1) A contradiction to the system appears unthinkable. 2) What does not fit remains unseen. 3) If noticed, it is kept secret or 4) laborious efforts are made to explain an exception in terms that do not contradict the system. 5) Crisis – despite legitimate claims of contradictory views, one tends to see, describe or illustrate circumstances which corroborate current views and thereby give them substance."[110] We should unpack these principles.

Number 1: The unthinkability of contradictions relies on a metaphysical premise: an objective reality lies beneath the subjective haze we interpret. However, there exists no formalized correspondence between ideas and evidence. Evidence is interpreted in line with pre-existing concepts. Kant's imperceptible reality was necessary, Fleck said, "otherwise we would be landed in the absurd conclusion that there is appearance without anything that appears."* This underlying reality which cannot be found must be axiomatic, another word for 'taken on faith,' or metaphysical. Underlying reality is therefore not scientific.

Number 2: Each theory has an evolution. At first, all the evidence seems to support theory. Later, all the evidence goes against it. Another way to put this – to perceive a particular causal linkage, numerous others must be reinterpreted, ignored, or theoretically minimized. Every idea comes at the expense of a dozen others.

Number 3: Every discipline has a number of contraindicative evidence points. The specialists all know them, but they don't publish them in the popular literature. Thus emerges a 'solid front.' It is often taboo to even speak of them. They are smoothed over into the thought style, making it feel coherent.

Number 4: The evidence against becomes overwhelming. Towers of Babel are constructed to retrofit data into existing theory. The community defends the theory against all onslaughts. The resulting system becomes blockaded and highly stylized. Ideas cutting against fundamental assumptions and hidden structures are ridiculed, ignored, or bluntly stated as false. They are not disproved.

Number 5: Crisis. The extension of theory manufactures exorbitant fictions. They are sophisticated and increasingly technical reworkings of previous ideas to 'save the theory.' The effects are pathological. Due to publicity, a meme under assault ironically reifies in the public imagination as the proof degrades. This 'obvious truth' becomes further conditionality for thought styles. It diminishes creativity. Any scientific question is formulated within the thought style – a directed answer is already implied in each question.

Though the styles become cemented in basic assumptions, they slowly and inevitably change. Ideas move from person to person, group to group, society to society. As it moves, personal biases add and subtract, altering the idea. Because of emotional and ambitious investment in projects, sociological baggage is thrown on the train. Science, despite contrary beliefs, is rife with competitiveness, favoritisms, antagonisms, high-handed pronouncements, theft of ideas, propaganda, and plagiarism. These

* Fleck has, of course, nailed a Buddhist principle called emptiness – there is appearance without anything that appears.

inobvious traits infuse into the theory itself, affecting the style of thought and the discipline. Such small, unauthored changes create a different theory, not acknowledged as such.

Thought Styles

With our thoughts, we make the world.
— Siddhartha

Thought style is the way one views phenomena – the hallmarks are channeled understanding and directed observation. The tendency to integrate each new observation within the pre-existing thought style minimizes conflicts and reinforces sustaining notions. Groups produce social reinforcement to sustain thought styles.

Synergy of thinking creates a shared mood which quickly can be discovered or found missing. It is the seed of genuine communication. If it fails, the individuals disagree. Any collective form of their process aborts. For harmony, all thoughts, without regard to logical sense or content, tend to uphold the thought style. They reinforce the collective view and provide only the subtlest alteration. Expert solidarity plays off public opinion to form an ossified background of solid 'fact.' The time an idea remains in a collective, regardless of the level of examination, determines its certainty. (The big bang makes a good example.) The public accepts this certainty because of distance from expertise. Experts must know.

The structure as such fades into the background. Invisible, it exerts a more powerful force and becomes the only possible mode. Other forms seem alien, silly, bizarre, even insane. Thought communities appear virtually everywhere – military branches, politics, athletics, religion, families, towns, companies, and friendships. The tighter the area of technical focus, the more solidity its style exhibits. Special jargon enhances the effect – nobody questions these terms. As jargon leaks to the outer circles, it creates a sense of holy awe among the uninitiated, especially in physics – think singularities, dark matter, and quarks. Metaphoric language is borrowed with war as a favorite source.

Different collectives can communicate only through shared thought traits – distances in theme, substance and style reflect communication difficulties they will experience. At enough distance, each seems like impenetrable noise to the other. They require common features to establish a ground of communication. Foreign groups seem to have no fixed theoretical structure. If it exists, it will appear without solid foundation. The manner of thought will appear supernatural. The areas of investigation will seem to be senseless. Buzzwords such as 'delusion' and 'rationality' or 'infidel' and 'faithful' pervade the group, reinforcing ramparts against assault.

Porosity is the measure of openness to new ideas. How sharply does a group delineate its facts as proven? How willing is it to allow non-established experts to critically examine? Does it lecture or dialogue? Does it promote otherness or inclusiveness? Is there a subtle or gross condescension from experts or a sense of curiosity about outside opinions? Closed systems are always wrong because they proclaim exclusive truth. Open systems are always right by acknowledging the relative nature of human understanding. "Talent hits a target no one else can hit," Shopenhauer said. "Genius hits a target no one else can see." The degree of openness directly measures the degree of truth value. Openness is a powerful scientific virtue – severely lacking these days.

Words are a special case. A thought collective shapes a term in its own way, collecting connotations. The words 'power' or 'law' mean different things to a physicist, an imam, a congressman, or a priest. As words move across collectives, they can subtly alter or radically diverge even to 'the destruction of all sense.' More porous collectives have more opportunities by infiltration of unusual ideas. New stylistic devices, new language, and new truths come about. Cross-pollination is the most helpful tool for any collective to avoid stagnation. However, communication entails alteration. There are no pure statements – only interpretations of words. When communication occurs inside a collective, it reinforces and supports the stylistic devices. Cross-collectively, it generates helpful differences. Dialogue is essential – new atheism gets an 'F' here. An inability to bring this into practice disallows legitimate understanding of knowledge and blocks opportunities for organic growth.

Theories need ventilation for meaning and for taking root. Without feedback, theories lack characteristics of both truth and falsity. Like string theory, they become impenetrable esoterica. A small coterie of experts strives or pretends to understand. The best in the world don't know what they are talking about. They create ever more elaborate structures on a pinhead of futility. Such a theory is easily defended – it cannot even be understood. This happens more than one might think.

When old modes of thought wither, the most faithfully held concepts extend into the new structure. Disease theory moved from invading spirits to pathogenic miasma (bad blood) to infectious agents. Each stylized answer holds total sway until supplanted. It then becomes ridiculous in retrospect. All ideas must conform to the reigning notions in a discipline. Truth thus has two manifestations – the historical (now gone) perception and the current restriction on thinking. Facts exist only in the thought collective.

Facts have several traits. They align with the goal of the collective. A resistance to counterfactual thinking exists as internal compulsion. The fact must take tangible shape. The expression of the fact must conform to the thought style. All community facts thus relate to all other facts.

As new discoveries come about, they are integrated by subtle changes in the overall structure. In spite of this perpetual reworking, an older discipline rests in fixity and obdurateness. The picture of conceptual knowledge cognitively links to some 'intrinsic reality' beyond the network. The longer a collective exists, the more it moves from creativity and inspiration to practical engagement. Inspiration then reduces to a codified, socially acceptable level. Most disciplines exist in this state.

This principle of exclusion whittles down observational tendencies. Highly focused systems offer no allowance for wide-ranging questions. If such concerns are noticed, they seem unimportant or nonsensical. The culture rejects and accepts proper areas of study. Intolerance becomes radicalized as antithetical ideas appear.[†] Experts control the debate.

To be an expert, one must carry those strictures of expertise in the discipline – it becomes enormously difficult, even impossible, to think outside the bounds of expertise. Fleck's case in point – what virologist, microbiologist, pathologist, or medical practitioner in any area could speak against the germ theory of disease?

Germ theory is based on an attack-and-defend philosophy. "This results in conflict taken to be the essence of disease. The whole of immunology is permeated with such primitive origins of war. *The idea originated in the myth of disease-causing demons that attack man.*" Defeating the evil spirits/disease agent "is still taught today. But not a single experimental proof exists that could force an unbiased observer to adopt such an idea...The disease demon haunted the birth of modern concepts of infection and forced itself on researchers irrespective of all rational considerations."[111] There are a number of non-infectious epidemics – diabetes, for example.

---

[*] One restriction was alchemy – the monarchy feared losing its gold monopoly. Alchemists worked in secret.

[†] The scientific studies on reincarnation by Ian Stevenson are a good case study.

All scientific and diagnostic procedures incorporate a technical and laboratory style of perception. Phenomena are reduced to components. Holistic, empathic, or intuitive understanding is incomprehensible. A universal category error in science assumes that theories are 'true' or 'false.' The more relevant view is utility and explanatory power.

The notion of thought style does not refer to an existent phenomenon. It is more a group process. Thought styles are necessary – conceptual formulations cannot exist in a vacuum. The trick is to see through them. They are characterized by restrictions on thinking and the active engagement of a view, or mode of perception, to the exclusion of all others. "The analytical field thus rests upon the thought style. In its absence, the truth also vanishes."[112]

The Wasserman reaction exemplifies the developing thought style. A terrible initial correspondence rate moved to a much higher one. The mysterious process was not reproducible. None of the team was able to articulate how they transformed one test into the other. The relation between the reaction and syphilis is established by the success rate between a positive result and manifestation of symptoms. No empirical evidence links the test to the bacteria.* The system can be gamed to come to predetermined results in the absence of other verification. If serology is the only mode of proof, then what is really proven? Results also come from teams, and when these teams are shuffled, the correspondences change enormously, even with no loss of experience. Serology is subjective.

Many discoveries follow a similar pattern – beginning from erroneous hypotheses, they pass through a phase of non-reproducible experiments. When the important results emerge, no one can really explain it. Moreover, money talks and politics blusters. As a carnal scourge, syphilis was an ethical disease. Despite its low death rate compared to TB, funds poured in because of a high profile. A constant pressure to produce results came from ambition, acclaim, and national egos. Each country wanted to win the race.

In later stages, complexity, sophistication, and detail minimize differences between experts' opinions. Thought constraints choke off novelty. As the theoretical edifice becomes larger and denser, research becomes constricted. Experiments become stylized and clever, proving nuances, but they are plugged exactly into the pre-existing framework and can no longer run against it.

* As we will see, the trend has worsened considerably. Serology is now fraudulent, according to some critics.

Cross-cultural communication requires seeing constraints upon thought. Otherwise, true communication is impossible. This pernicious blindness and channeling can be unlocked. Methods include studying the principles of epistemology, contemplating thought collectives, applying contrary ideas to particular situations, deliberately violating the collective's principles, and non-judgmentally exploring alien or contradictory styles. The thought collective says this is not proper. A true scientist will do it anyway. Great scientists feel this as a demand; mediocre ones feel the opposite. Curiosity about other modes of thought rather than innate hostility or contempt befits the scientist.

Fleck strenuously objects to pompous notions of scientific thinking. For many, rational thought diminishes other styles as if we have now found the 'proper' mode of thought. The ideas claimed are thus, ipso facto, true. Such an approach is an obstacle to a legitimate study of science. He asks the pertinent and very spiritual question, "would it not be possible to manage entirely without something fixed? Both thinking and facts are changeable, if only because changes in thinking manifest themselves in changed facts."[113]

Circles of Authority

In the beginner's mind are many possibilities,
in the expert's mind are few.
— Suzuki Roshi

Larger, established thought communities, whether religious, political, or scientific create circles of expertise. Important distinctions emerge between expert and populace. Expertise has different circles, but no area is dominant. Even popular science is not beneath research science. At the research level, specialized experts form 'journal science,' a jumble of notes and experiments without clear theoretical formulation. Over the years and decades, journal science is analyzed, culled, and has theories projected onto it. These are published and broadcast to the general experts. After digestion, it's repackaged without contention and distributed to the educated laity. Disagreements, nuances of interpretation and the general chaos of research are gone. Supporting evidence is seldom seen and contradicting evidence never. It is simply presented to the masses as rote fact.

Journal science has the following traits: it's between 3 and 15 years ahead of and seldom agrees with popular science. It is contradictory and fragmented. The more generalized experts functioning as intermediary streamline the information, consciously editing for sensibility and subconsciously for acceptability. In a capital system, public opinion flows back to the center, especially over the bridge of money. What the public wants, they buy. They talk about it. The jargon of such a field enters popular language and the thought style becomes 'locked in' by general public acceptance. Finally, the cost and complexity of research makes the scientist a vassal of the NIH and other large funding sources.

The expense of research allows institutions that attain lucrative results to quickly dominate and decide the scientific direction. Consequently, these institutions gain hegemony over the thought style, creating the public view in a more or less conscious manner. Larger organizations have a vested interest in doing so – by cultural ownership of the technology of understanding, an establishment can guide public perception to a predetermined, typically profitable, end. The pharmaceutical industry is notorious for this.

In journal science, many hypotheses are discussed, discarded, judged and experimented on. It is also the source of accidental discoveries. Journal science happens among small, isolated teams, though cross-fertilization occurs somewhat with other experts. Mostly, however, they draw on vademucum or handbook science (which we'll get to), for their research bases. Each of these many horses pulls the general cart of expertise in different directions and it's never certain which way it will lurch off to next. More depends on good publicity of results, remuneration for research, pre-determined agendas of profit, and force and persuasion of personalities than on specific facts of research or ability to penetrate 'reality.' Money is king and utility its law. Journal science also seeks to integrate into handbook science – it seeks validation and is not research for its own sake. This constricts the types of research and thinking for researchers.

What emerges for the written record are the journals of these teams. It does not resemble our picture of science. A heap of notes, suppositions, and cagily written possibilities, nothing appears definite or cohesive. It is only coherent insofar as it seeks to find a place in the formalized, vademecum science.

Vademecum is the main body of science where scientific nonspecialists can discover a field. It is a "critical synopsis in an organized system," characterized by impersonality and self-existence of knowledge. Journal science, by contrast, is highly personalized because of eccentricities in notes and style. Journal science is provisional, handbook science is 'factual.' The journal scientists need the consent of the collective to properly assert findings. The signal is the use of 'we' instead of 'I' – the rhetoric of objectivity. In such publications, a style of false erudition fumbles for authority.

In this sense, science is democratic, needing communal validation. By irony, the examination comes not from content but conformity – so long as the ideas fit accepted theory, they will be incorporated. Scientific findings are confirmed by extensions of consensual norms, not by contradictions to norms. Independent validity is a non-issue – the peer review section will expose all this and more. It takes extreme personality, will, and oratorical powers to push through an unpopular idea. It also takes powerful allies, weak enemies, and careful navigation of political terrain – hardly the common image of science. The history of science is littered with personal and political conflicts.

Vademecum science is a mosaic built by collective selection and rejection of journal science hypotheses. Selected avenues will consequently set parameters and close doors for future research. When theories clash, what emerges takes a form different from any of the sources.

For the vademecum, various struggling and copious journal notes are edited, redacted, suppressed, elevated, discarded, altered, shaped, and related to other areas. This is the fixed idea, what is regarded as 'Science' proper. Mutual accord validates ideas as the greater range of experts comment on each other's work. Seldom are experiments repeated, though numerous variations occur.

The movement from journal to vademecum science has characteristic phases. First, a concept attaches on the data, then is reformulated for the generalized expert. A different sense of the idea forms simultaneous with a change in the initial question. Initial questions seldom relate to final conclusions. (A problem remains the same throughout research only because of a preordained agenda or over-raked ground.) Next, layers of cumulative adjacent research secrete meaning and force onto the hypothesis, subtly altering it. Finally, it seats itself in the proper scientific view. It takes on a formulated theoretical framework with strictures against alternative understanding. The more idiosyncratic and prominent a thought style is and the less it seeks synchrony with prevailing theory, the more difficult of a time it will have.

The status of provisional research becomes accepted fact by a mysterious process of collective agreement. If a hypothesis conforms to collective assumptions, stylized formulations and general worldview, it is generally regarded as true. Repackaged, it fits neatly into the mainstream body of science. Thus the coherent vademecum of a specialty comes to light by consensus. It's like sausage – if you like it, don't ask how it's made.

Textbook science has a different function – it initiates students; it creates 'experts.' Presenting a streamlined body of technical theory, it impresses the thought style into the student. It is impossible to become an expert without adopting the thought style – a lockout for contravailing ideas. Creativity is barred. Students are programmed.

Popular science is very powerful. It sets social moods and beliefs. Scientists studying a field distant from their own will tend toward popular science because handbook science will be overly technical. Unfortunately, popular science is grossly divergent from handbook science. Bald assertions are the norm (science has found that…) and there is no supporting evidence. Popular science simplifies, harmonizes and vivifies. Fascinating, slick graphics abound. Ideas are pictorial and set in concrete. Lack of the debates, the jerky evolution of ideas, and research counterfactuals allows popular science to show a well-rounded, complete, unified theory. It's dumbed down, then reified to absolute truth. This type of science creates public opinion. It's not written by scientists, but journalists subjected to corporate, institutional and monetary interests. Journalists have editorial agendas to present a tidy package rather than the actual messy smorgasbord of maybes and contradictions.

All directed communications move vaguely toward the public. Aiming at comprehensibility, they simplify through pictures. The effect of unity is fictional. The faith in simplified, graphical, matter-of-fact ideas suffuses the culture, and circles back to infect the mind of the expert. He then seeks to shape ideas in this way.

The narrative of discovery is streamlined: hypothesis leads to experiment to fact to confirmed replication of experiment. It looks so clean and orderly, the powerful advance of science. It is anything but. The particular experience of researchers is abundant constraints, difficulties and hostile opinions. Tidy stories conceal the crucial distinction between research and theory. Stories present these two as identical when they are absolutely not. All research results must be interpreted. But these narratives read as if the ideas were an underlying reality found by research rather than a data set interpreted by consensus. By making all other formulations seem impossible, theory becomes found reality rather than interpretation of data. Most popular narratives read as if the theory emerged fully formed without debate – never the case.

The central power of imagery in popular science cannot be overstated. Irrespective of matching the theory, pictures become reality. Ironically, because of pithy explanatory power, vivid graphics return to the expert domain, supplanting the more detailed, substantive and vigorous theory, which they only vaguely resemble. The pictorial representation of general relativity, for example, shows the Earth following a sensuously shaped grid around the 'curved' space of the sun – as if this had anything to do with relativity. As if an immateriality such as space-time could be 'curved.' It's not made of particles. What could curving mean to something without physical substance? Yet the shorthand image, initially intended as a guide to frame the mind, becomes the explanation in toto. These images carry a felt sense, an almost passionate vividness that overleaps logical contradictions and speaks to a different part of the mind. Well-constructed images step around objections. They take on a quality so 'obvious,' it's almost sacred. It would be a sin to contradict it.

Because of the communal approach, ideas roam from collective to collective to popular science to academic settings and return to the origin. Meanings accrete all along the way. The product is a moving 'syncretion' from many sources. Moving around and gathering research points, it becomes holy writ without a writer. These changes mean that the resultant theory is never truly tested. Changes in form, idea, and meaning distance the result from the original. Even slight changes in interpretation have enormous scientific implications. More or less validly expressed journal science ideas which appear as possibilities aggregate out of a dialogue in motion into a handbook theory where they appear as certainties. Because of burgeoning complexity, almost all contemporary theories follow this pattern.

Fleck gives an example from his own field. "The etiological concept of disease entity is not derived directly from individual journals. Emerging originally from exoteric or popular ideas outside the collective, it gradually acquired significance in esoteric communication of thought and basic concepts of vademecum bacteriology. It could be attained only through a directed selection of individual investigations and a directed compilation. But once part of the vademecum, it is taught and generally used. It forms the keystone of a system and thus exerts a constraint on thinking."[114]

A body of evidence concerning syphilology validates his claim. Through directed selection and compilation, journal science was mined for supporting research. All contradictory research was ignored. Syphilis can only be defined by the Spirochaeta pallida bacteria – it cannot be defined symptomatically. It becomes impossible for the expert to formulate a hypothesis under an alternative theoretical framework, such as chi theory. It becomes embarrassing to even suggest the concept.

Concepts fusing from all these sources – popular imagination, generalized expertise, cross-disciplinary fertilization, historical precedent, and society – imprison the expert. The impulse for 'directed perception' has a definitive shape. Contradicting research stops and supporting research doubles up. The expert suffers cognitive dissonance. He knows vademecum is the party line, but research has moved on and often disagrees. He may know promising avenues, but cannot say 'we have found thus and thus,' because it conflicts with formal theory. The initial 'signal of resistance' has become a strict limit on thought – train tracks for the diagnostician to travel.

The process carries a number of expert assumptions limiting free inquiry. Expert observations only come after studied practice and training. The skill to perceive specialized forms destroys the ability to perceive antithetical forms. The discipline thins the totality of characteristics to what it recognizes as valid. We see what we are trained to see and nothing else.

A scientific fact thus has several stages. An initial signal of resistance to certain ideas turns into a thought restriction culminating in a unified perception of reality – called a 'fact.' The aim of any empirical discipline is to generate a field of facts. This emphasis on facts and their applicability runs against objectivity – it presupposes facts awaiting discovery and the need to use them for human ends. Though this trait is not always present, it generates a strong push to validate the discipline from popular culture – the 'what have you done for me lately' mentality. A science that brings no rewards will receive no attention – or money.

The springboard of this 'reward' is hidden. Modern science adores the notion of conquering nature. Each bit of recalcitrant understanding is brought to heel, then placed within the theory. The unity of purpose creates a utility of results and further demonstrates a definitive belief of a separate, substantive reality being studied. A fundamental disconnect exists from this reality, however. There is no connection, the great physicist Linus Pauling said, between observation and idea.

Collectivist Science

To kill an error is as good a service as establishing a new truth.
—Charles Darwin

Science as collective has specific characteristics. 1) A mechanical mindset conceives the universe – the driving goal is a Grand Unified Theory. Currently, a realization glimmers that science is moving away from that, coming up with many theories in all directions. Furthermore, each solution creates additional questions, almost as a law of discovery. The long-standing sanctity of idealized postulates is mercifully fading – objectivity, precision, clear thought, rationality – these are holy ideals. When the implications of Gödel and quantum theory finally burst through the psyche, if that happens, there may be room for a more powerful and inclusive thought style in science.

2) The scientist feels as if he is pursuing a sacred endeavor, contributing his small part to the great glory of human knowledge. An idolatry of the past, Darwin, Newton, Galileo, Einstein and so forth, creates paragons of rationality. (Perhaps Newton's Christian beliefs and alchemy obsession put the lie to that.)

3) Science is portrayed as an emergent and novel tradition. Nothing like science has ever occurred before. It is impossible to top it. Nothing can ever overcome the lofty ideals of science. The scientific method is repeatedly confirmed as the best, only, and unfailing means to truth.

4) Peer review is volleyed about as proof of any hypothesis. 5) Research and specialization fatigue abound. Scientists often feel trivial because their area of research is so narrow. Secretly, they yearn for the great days when scientists roamed through all disciplines – when that was not only permissible, but expected.

These factors combine to a 'readiness for directed perception,' a subordination of the individual to the collective will. Another consequent is the objectivization of theory – it becomes real, existent truth unto itself. This reification happens in motion as the theory travels from journal to vademecum to academia to other disciplines to popular science and back home. A central concept, such as HIV or climate change, takes on extraordinary connotations of meaning – scientific, sociological, ethical, and political. Further, these meanings, though appearing fixed, constantly change, affecting the scientific definitions. As more debate and contention arises around fixed theories, jargon and obscurantism come to defend the theory – we see all this in the AIDS domain. If it can't be understood, the idea is, it must be so advanced that it's correct. The logic fails utterly, but the method works to sustain a flailing theory. It happens all the time.

Obscurantism also eliminates the vast majority, even general experts, from the debate. Only the specialist can survive. Becoming discouraged or bored, the public retires and accepts the verdict delivered by popular sources, never questioning the bias of *Time* magazine. A pictorial lexicography inserts itself for understanding, then becomes, like the periodic table, the central fact. By hyper-specialization, the resultant terminology becomes inert, a gargantuan block of stone. Though shades of meaning creep in around the edges, the formal interpretation becomes rigid and absolutely true.

Beyond this is the sacrament of mathematics. Every discipline strives for mathematical expression – even evolution. An unconscious powerful motive desires the eruption of startling clarity. A push to button down the framework seeks a requisite ocean of data. An increasing web of meaning relates all facts to each other. Faith strengthens that the discipline is, bit by bit, hunting down genuine reality.

Reality, alas, may not be coherent, cohesive or comprehensible. To assume it is requires a metaphysical stance – it cannot be proved. Reality, from this angle, has no inherent substance. It is not even a matter of consensual agreement like a fact or theory. Reality is the embedded consequences of scientific assumptions. The wetness of water is a metaphor. The question 'which way is up?' illustrates the deception.

The strand of perception of visible light is one billionth of the electromagnetic spectrum. The image symbolizes scientific objectivity – the subjective defines the objective. But objective reality must be beyond all definition – it simply is. Every attempt to discover the objective is a subjective interpretation. By necessity, any attempt includes and excludes certain data – it cannot include unknown information. Science relies on this objective reality as the final test, casting aside the subjective. But it is caught in this paradox. Even in communal decisions, 'objective reality' is a subjective construct.

Knowledge is not a rote understanding of facts – it is a system of thought. It is not rooted in reality; it is rooted in concepts. Example after example shows that original hypotheses, observations, and problem formulations lead, in different hands, to different conclusions, even category jumps. Research is colored by moods and structured by expert habits. First observations are seldom reproducible. The problem of understanding what is first observed leads in random directions. The resulting artifice veers from the initial intent.

Knowledge must be known, hence it must have a knower. A knower is an individual – a subject. It is impossible for a non-subject to know anything. Hence, all knowledge is subjective. Objective knowledge is impossible by definition. But knowledge, by definition, is an understanding of objective truth. The terms objective and subjective are mutually exclusive, yet knowledge must be both. The very idea of knowledge is inherently nonsensical.

This epistemology disturbs most people – they simply reject it. It takes away the secure ground of 'knowing the truth.' But truth cannot be formulated according to the blind assumptions of science. It does not reside in numbers, words, logical formulations, or any theory whatsoever. Truth is neither a concept nor a non-concept. It cannot be subject to relative strictures and remain truth. Whatever it is, it defies all description. It is neither rational nor irrational. It cannot be found – there is no thing to find. It cannot be lost because if true in any meaningful way, it must be everywhere so. If there is such a thing as objective truth, it cannot be grasped by subjective mind for the very fact that that mind is caught within the iron reality of the limitations of consciousness. Human truth is collective agreement. Science is not special in this regard – truth has meaning only when ensconced in a particular thought style.

Past scientific thought styles appear as madness – we can scarce believe anyone validated Ptolemaic cycles or caloric. Yet the ideas were logical and at each point, the entire community felt the same way about all those before them. They felt that their modern community brought them out of the dark ages, just our age believes. No generation believes it is living in error. We do not have any proof that we have solved all these problems, that any of our theories cannot be overturned. In the future, it will look as if we have been imprisoned.

A true revolution would reveal our delusion. We could move from 'discovering facts' to using theories as tools. A theory does not have to be true to be useful. We should shift from believing we know to knowing we believe.

Deceptive Immunity

My wife is not going to immunize our kids.
—Dr. Oz[115]

On September 15, 2010, twin 9-month-old girls received a measles vaccine in Ghaziabad, India. After the first began vomiting, the doctor insisted it was a normal reaction and vaccinated the second against the father's wishes. Within an hour, both were dead.

Other vaccines are dangerous, too. Japan stopped use of Hib and pneumococcus in March, 2011 after a string of infant deaths. 2000 US babies died after getting the same injection and the CDC called any concerns "foolish."[116] The flu vaccine, by manufacturers' own admission, is only 1% effective – worse than a placebo. In 2009-10, 50% of pregnant women received the H1N1 vaccine. A subsequent 700% nationwide rise in miscarriages was, according to the CDC, not related. However, the VAERS database catalogues hundreds of miscarriages within days and even hours of vaccination.[117]

Dr. Maurice Hilleman is probably the most celebrated vaccinologist in the 20th century. He developed Merck's MMR vaccine and led the department for decades. "Vaccines," he said, "have to be considered the bargain basement technology for the 20th century."[118] Dr. J. Anthony Morris was Chief Vaccine Control Officer at the US Federal Drug Admininistration. "There is a great deal of evidence," he said, "to prove that immunization of children does more harm than good."[119] These are odd statements, considering the reputation of vaccines – didn't they stop all the terrible epidemics? When we dig, the evidence is not so clear.

The basic idea – a vaccine gives the body a chance to develop antibodies in response to an attenuated virus – has never been proved. It seems true. Where did pertussis, polio and mumps go, if not for vaccines? It's so logical. Strangely, though, all of these diseases saw a 90% decline in mortality before the vaccines were introduced.

Vaccines are unusual potions. Here's a list of common ingredients – Formaldehyde, aluminum hydroxide, aluminum phosphate, ammonium sulfate, calf serum, fetal rhesus monkey lung cells, monkey kidney cells, chick embryo, fetal bovine serum, washed sheep red blood cells, casein (from pig pancreas), ethylene glycol (antifreeze), neomycin/streptomycin (antibiotics), organic mercury, and diploid cells (from aborted human fetal tissue).[120]

Few people would eat such a stew, but most don't think about injecting it directly into the body. Vaccines are forced through live animal tissues to attenuate the virus. After picking up foreign proteins and viruses, it is restrengthened with adjuvants or anti-body boosters – aluminum hydroxide, formaldehyde, mercury derivatives, streptomyicyn among them. Any number of studies shows all of these substances can cause brain damage, cancer and autoimmune disorders. Yet infants are injected with thousands of times the daily adult limit. The mass of foreign proteins and viruses can't be screened out. Both are among the most harmful of substances. All animal venoms, for example, are proteins.

The history is dubious. Edward Jenner, father of mass vaccination, led a checkered life. With certain evidence that cowpox conveyed no smallpox immunity and 30,000 British Pounds for his venture, he worked to suppress the data. He never received medical training, and his life's work was roundly discredited as a failure in preventing disease. In fact, he caused innumerable deaths.

Early on, Jenner vaccinated eight-year-old James Phipps with cowpox. A few months later, he inoculated the boy with smallpox. "No effect was produced," he wrote. On this one experiment, Jenner claimed his vaccine would "forever secure a person from smallpox." The government made vaccination compulsory. Phipps and Jenner's own son were both vaccinated 20 times. Both died of tuberculosis by 21. In spite of this, his vaccination theories laid the foundation for the ones still in effect today. He even introduced re-vaccination (now called boosters) because the first shots failed immunity.[121]

It's widely believed that vaccination came from the modern theory of antibodies. The reverse is true. Ancient Hindus used cowpox to vaccinate against smallpox.[122] Other ancient societies did similar things. The origins, by scientific standards, are superstition. Though never proven effective, modern scientists looked for a reason why this 'worked.' Antibodies, though none had yet been found, were born.

Scientists, by the way, do this in almost every field – take a theory and leap over key critical components of evidence. The 'evidence' comes in the form of artist's renditions. Nowadays, it's computer graphics. And the forms look great – they bypass the critical faculty. Visual media is different psychological terrain from the rational evidence based on words.

Compulsory vaccination in 1853 England preceded a smallpox epidemic. People refused the vaccine and the epidemic ended. 1871 saw the highest vaccination rates in the world – 125,000 vaccinated Germans died of the disease. Examples are endless. A London recorder wrote, "St. James Picadilly – 145 of 155 smallpox cases were vaccinated."

"In the 1940s smallpox vaccination ceased and with it smallpox," Dr. H.M. Shelton said. In 1929, India ceased vaccination and enjoyed an immediate decline while Mexico, with forced vaccinations, had up to 8 times the rate.[123]

Of course, smallpox is archaic technology. What about more recent vaccines? Without vaccines, declines for measles (94%), scarlet fever (97%) and whooping cough (91%) exceed diptheria (89%) with a vaccine. (See table 1.) In the late '30s Germany began vaccinating for diptheria and endured an immediate epidemic of 150,000 in 1939. Without vaccines, Norway had 50 cases.[124] The following chart needs one comment – no vaccine for typhoid or scarlet fever has ever been made. (See figure 4.)

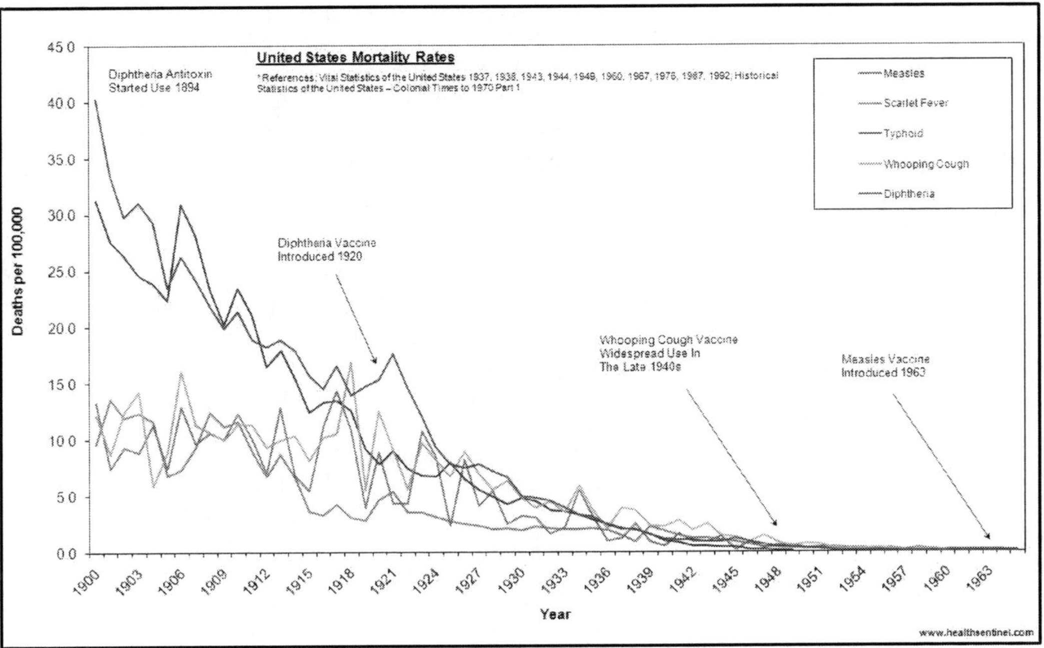

Figure 4.

20-yr periods	Measles	Scarlet fever	Pertussis	Diptheria-vaccinated
1861–1880	1,062	1,973	1,344	932
1881–1900	1,149	585	1,104	838
1900–1920	877	197	684	504
1921–1940	297	50	294	293
1941–1948	62	69	121	105

Table 1. Decline of unvaccinated diseases – England/Wales Deaths per 100k – children 5–15

The automobile may have done more to eliminate diseases than vaccinations – horse offal vanished. Vaccination skeptics cite improvements in sanitation, nutrition, vitamins, and hygiene as primary causes for disease decline.

Did vaccines improve later? A mumps outbreak happened in February of 2010 – 88% had been vaccinated for mumps.[125] Versus natural immunity, vaccines provide only a temporary and lower level, if any.

In outbreaks, diseases occur in the same percentage for vaccinated as for unvaccinated – directly contradicting immunization. Vaccines are held to be about 90% effective. But in even the worst epidemic, only 10% of the population contracts a disease. In other words, non-vaccination is also 90% effective. The statistics for flu vaccine are not released. We are never told, for example, that half the people get vaccinated and only 10% of flu victims were vaccinated. It could be 85%, though, and the fact that the CDC do not publish such an easy statistic to track is questionable.

Even if useless, do they cause harm? On average, 13,000 adverse vaccine reactions are reported every year. The FDA said 90% go unreported, meaning there are 130,000 cases. They include permanent brain damage and hundreds of deaths. FDA commissioner David Kessler said, "only about one percent of serious incidents are reported to the FDA." This gives a number above a million. The government does not investigate any VAERS reports.[126] Families must prove a causal link to win a suit in vaccine court, and over $2 billion dollars have been paid for vaccine injuries. According to the courts, vaccines cause plenty of harm.

One aboriginal study from the '70s showed a death rate up to 50% of all children in some areas after the introduction of mass vaccination. The study author linked the high rate to an already weakened system due to malnutrition unable to survive the assault of vaccines. When the doctor gave Vitamin C simultaneous with vaccines, the death rate dropped to zero.[127]

Senior CDC epidemiologist Dr. William Atkinson said, "In some large [measles] outbreaks...over 95% of cases have a history of vaccination."[128] Atypical measles, occurring only in the vaccinated, kills 13% of patients. In 1978, the mandatory vaccine for school attendance program preceded an immediate 3-fold increase in whooping cough.* The unvaccinated Amish population had zero cases of measles from 1970 to 1988. Polio

---

* Dead whooping cough cause the disease as it is toxin mediated.

vaccines are well-known to cause outbreaks.* Even the inventor, Jonas Salk, testified before Congress that almost all polio outbreaks since 1961 were due to the oral vaccine. Indeed, Massachusetts had a 642% increase in polio one year after introducing the vaccine.

In 1975 Japan ceased vaccinating children under 2 years and enjoyed a drop from 17th in infant mortality to lowest in the world. They reinstated the policy of 3-months-old vaccinations and infant mortality reverted. The malaria vaccine is clinically established as causing recurrent psychosis for ten years. This is called a 'side effect.' The *Journal of the American Medical Association* reported that pertussis-vaccinated children had five times the asthma rate.

Sudden Infant Death Syndrome is eight times more likely within 72 hours of a DTP shot. Dr. William Torch, Univeristy of Nevada Medical School, studied 103 SIDS cases. 4 died within 12 hours of vaccination, 9 within 24 hours, 28 within 3 days, and 78 within three weeks. Dr. Vera Scheibner showed an enormous increase in cessation and abnormally shallow breathing immediately after DTP vaccination. "Vaccination," she said, "is the single most prevalent and preventable cause of infant deaths."[129]

The typical time test for a vaccine is about two weeks – no long-term consequences are tested. The vaccine registry now requires every person to be vaccinated. Parental failure to comply can result in forced vaccination and charges of child abuse.

Are pharmaceutical companies acting in the best interests of their clients or their shareholders? Experimental vaccines are forced on servicemen for profit to the industry. Paul Offit wrote *Vaccines: What Every Parent Should Know*, a rabidly pro-vaccine book. Merck vaccine division endorsed it, bought 20,000 copies and gave them to doctors' offices. Merck gave $350,000 in grants to Offit's partner. Offit holds the patent for Merck's rotavirus vaccine, as well, garnering royalties from its use. Dr. Offit is on the CDC's advisory committee for immunization. The committee is charged with promotion of vaccines and overseeing their administration. They recommend vaccines that are mandatory for school attendance. According to Dr. Offit, "[we] did more harm than good in ... allowing the parent to be fully informed."[130]

* A redefinition of polio caused a steep decline after the introduction of the vaccine – any mild paralysis in one arm changed to 60 days thereof, eliminating 80% of polio diagnoses.

The American Association of Pediatrics, 100% pro-vaccine, receives about half a million dollars per year from Merck alone.[131] Current recommendation by the CDC is 50 injections for sixteen diseases by 18. It is a quadrupling of the 1970s schedule. There are no studies comparing the overall health of vaccinated versus unvaccinated children. "In the absence of facts," Dr. Jay Gordon wrote, "doctors and others are trying to frighten people into vaccinating,"[132]

Louis Cooper, M.D. said, "I don't know any rational person who could truly be anti-vaccine because the results are so profound." This is a typical statement of scientism – if one is against a practitioner's belief, then the person is irrational. According to Dr. Robert Sears, no vaccine study has had a large enough control group to have any meaning. It's commonly said that unvaccinated children put other children at risk. The logic is contradictory – if vaccinations confer immunity, there is no risk. The 90% unvaccinated Principe school, for example, has never had an outbreak of any vaccine-preventable disease.

Of course, pharmaceutical malfeasance is not limited to vaccines. First, let's look at the profits. One example suffices – the markup for Xanax is 569,000%. The total market is in the billions.

The revolving door between regulators and industry spins at a blur. Daniel Troy, for example, was chief council for the FDA. Prior to that, his law firm advocated for pharma and tobacco, regulated by the FDA. Barbara Lowe Fisher, President of the National Vaccine Information Center, claims the Pharmaceutical Industry "unduly influenced the World Health Organization to declare a highest level, world-wide pandemic influenza emergency in order to give these companies tremendous profits selling this [swine-flu] vaccine to governments." The EU is investigating. The profits were $7 billion and the governments want to return the unused vaccine. The companies refuse, stating contractual obligations.

The FDA commissioned, then suppressed, a report written about the suicide danger of SSRI drugs – anti-depressants. Knowing the dangers, they approved VIOXX. The drug soon caused 160,00 heart attacks and upwards of 60,000 deaths. Dr. David Graham, an FDA official, testified in Congress, calling VIOXX "a profound regulatory failure." Senior FDA officials pressured the *Lancet* when Graham tried to publish an article on VIOXX, even accusing him of scientific misconduct. (It's a classic whistleblower fate – kill the messenger.) Both safety data and the number of deaths due to VIOXX and other drugs are withheld. Apparently, they are trade secrets.

Pharmaceutical companies, *USA Today* reported, sponsor the coursework in medical schools. This makes their sales rise.[133] Key Opinion Leaders are doctors paid up to $3,000 per lecture ($400/hr consulting fees, $200/hr clinical trial fees) to give talks about a disease/treatment at industry-sponsored conferences. Their performance is tracked by sophisticated software showing relative increases in prescriptions after a presentation. Good sales lead to more engagements and higher commissions.

A dark fog of this influence pervades society. Two drug company lobbyists exist for every legislator. Pharmaceutical companies track prescriptions by doctors, who receive an endless stream of gifts. Starting in the '80s, research money and control came more and more from industry. Often the researchers do not get access to the data for their own study and the data is never available for independent confirmation. Medical journals and patient advocacy websites are owned and operated by industry. Articles are frequently ghost written with a famous doctor's name attached. Pharmaceutical corporations, not the journals, pay the doctors.

90% of studies now funded by drug companies find a positive result – five times better odds than in previous decades. Half of those who set up testing guidelines have overt financial ties to pharmaceutical companies. Drug companies fund about 70% of continuing medical education for doctors to retain licenses. They spend $20 billion or $30,000 per doctor marketing to doctors. Once drugs are approved, they can be recommended for any condition, and often are. Companies strive to find new conditions for drugs. Drug companies write disease definitions for the Physicians' Desk Reference and rewrite old conditions to broaden the patient base.[134]

Lilly's Serifem, for example, costs three times Prozac. They are chemically identical. The patent was set to expire, but due to a clause in the law, a new use extends the patent. Pharma has created an industry around the discovery of new application for old drugs. Feminine premenstrual anxiety syndrome, social anxiety disorder, restless leg, and other syndromes like premenstrual dysphoric disorder are 'fabricated conditions for the purpose of profits.'

Only positive trials of these drugs are published. Then, when 'testing' fails, the FDA does not report all the deaths. Independent studies are difficult to non-existent. When *NEJM*, for example, wanted an antidepressant study, it could not find a single expert who was not paid by drug companies.

These issues in medical science are not anomalous. This is science. Contrary to the benevolent image, science frequently kills. Knowingly or not, research suggests it has created an epidemic of autism. Science may not call for holy wars, but, some say, it is the vassal of a ruthless corporate system.

The strangest disease

Do no harm.
—Hippocratic Oath

In 2007, AIDS killed 28 Canadians, 73 Germans, and 15,000 Americans. It is 60 times more lethal in the United States.[135] For this and many other reasons, AIDS is the most anomalous medical condition in history. Out of millions, HIV is the only pathogen whose antibodies do not confer immunity. It violates virtually every principle of infectious disease. And yet it remains a dreaded threat – the cash cow of the pharmaceutical and medical research industries. More money has been spent researching the condition than any other, including cancer. They still can't figure out how HIV kills. But then, not everyone agrees that it does.

Rebecca Culshaw received her doctoral degree in 2002 for constructing mathematical models associated with HIV. After several years of lab work in the field, she realized that the central argument that HIV causes AIDS was incorrect. For starters, the incidence of HIV in the US has remained steady since 1985 at one million. (See figure 5.) This does not fit the pattern of spread

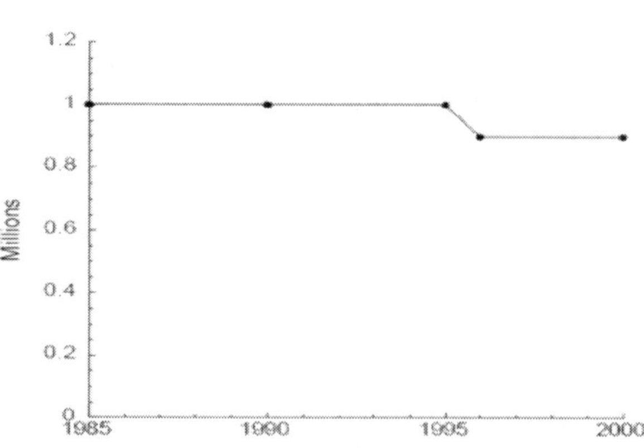

Figure 5.

of an infectious disease. According to Farr's Law – when a new epidemic enters a population, the virus will spread exponentially, but if it's long established, it remains stable – HIV has been around 200 years or more. AIDS remained in the initial risk groups – therefore it is non-infectious by simple epidemiological understanding. Culshaw signed an unusual petition.

The Scientific Reappraisal of the HIV/AIDS Hypothesis was signed by thirty, then hundreds, then thousands of doctors and medical scientists, including Nobel Prize winners. One of these, biochemist Kary Mullis, claims that HIV does not cause AIDS. More astonishing – HIV may not even exist. The voluminous evidence is not difficult to understand.

In terms of AIDS research, three names stand out: Robert Gallo, Luc Montaigner, and Peter Duesberg. "Gallo's walls," one reporter writes, "were adorned with framed blow-ups of awards and articles about him. Prosperity, publicity and no-holds barred competition were the themes. The laboratories were large and busy...Gallo had repeatedly distorted and exaggerated the significance of his results. In the most naked way, he was bucking for a Nobel Prize. He was in the habit of telephoning opponents late at night and talking at them unstoppably for an hour or more."[136]

Both Montaigner and Gallo were credited with the discovery of HIV, but the less ambitious Montaigner grabbed the 2008 Nobel Prize for it. The record includes a scandal and vitriolic accusation. Gallo's sample came, allegedly by misappropriation, from the Pasteur Institute. It was Montaigner's. The presidents of both the United States and France stepped in to end the conflict. Gallo is certain of the HIV/AIDS hypothesis. Montaigner less so. "HIV," he said, "may be benign."[137]

Peter Duesberg rejects any notion that HIV causes AIDS. A molecular biology professor, Duesberg was the foremost researcher in retrovirology. Even Robert Gallo agreed. "Peter Duesberg knows more about retroviruses than any man alive."[138] He put together the first map of the retrovirus genetic structure. The youngest ever member of the National Academy of Science, he received five NIH outstanding investigator grants. Before rejecting the HIV/AIDS hypothesis, Duesberg was never denied a grant. Despite 25 applications, he has never received another. He has been disinvited from scientific assemblies and refused publication in scientific journals. Sir John Maddox, editor of *Nature* magazine, denied the standard right of reply to Professor Duesberg. "They took him out," said a colleague at UC-Berkeley.[139]

As part of a planned series in the '80s, *Science* magazine published a short debate between Duesberg and Gallo. After the first, all future debates were cancelled. "He doesn't believe HIV causes the disease," Gallo later said. "I can't win that debate. Rational people learn not to debate such things."[140] No rebuttal of Duesberg's detailed assault on the hypothesis has ever appeared in the peer-reviewed literature. Duesberg issued another lengthy multi-point refutation of the HIV/AIDS theory in 1988. Gallo agreed to respond, but never did. Now Gallo's stance is a refusal to debate with 'AIDS denialists.'

In this time frame, Gallo lost the credit for discovering HIV. He was investigated for fraud and theft by Congressional Committee, the NIH (his employer), and the Dept. of Health Office of Research Integrity. He was charged with poor recordkeeping, lack of primary data, erroneous conclusions, falsifications, absence of assay data in developing the HIV test, and blocking access to data for external replication. The Secret Service investigated him for data tampering, but the Attorney General said the statute of limitations had expired. The Inspector General reported that the experiments had probably never been done. The 1994 Congressional Report concluded the 1984 experiment was totally flawed and HIV had never been isolated. Gallo won the World Health award in 2001 for his work.

Duesberg has declared his willingness to be publicly injected with HIV.[141] His conditions are an agreement by both parties to abide by the results as scientifically conclusive and wide public exposure for his theory. The mainstream community refused to set terms.

Numerous qualified professionals do not subscribe to HIV/AIDS. Dr. Rodney Richards helped develop the first HIV antibody tests. He claims that HIV has never been properly isolated and that these tests measure an excess of antibodies to many conditions. David Rasnick, a PhD in biochemistry, holds several patents on protease inhibitors, widely in use for current treatment. Rasnick rejects the HIV/AIDS hypothesis and laments the fact that AIDS research has dropped clinical standards to the point of outright fraud.[142] Even Gallo said there is no connection between HIV and Kaposi's Sarcoma, the most common homosexual AIDS-defining disease. "All those original papers Gallo wrote on HIV have been found fraudulent," Duesberg said.

More than five thousand researchers signed the Durbin declaration supporting the HIV/AIDS hypothesis. Unfortunately, one sentence in the solicitation undermines its credibility: 'Many of you will say that HIV/AIDS is not your area, but by now you have heard enough of the arguments."[143,144] So, what are the arguments?

Gallo's 1984 paper showed positive HIV detection in 26 out of 72 AIDS patients.[145] If HIV is the sole cause of AIDS, the result is impossible. A sole cause must be in all cases. Gallo said the low percentage was due to "sample contamination." They were, in fact, contaminated with mold. Amazingly, even this contamination did not invalidate the theory. This seminal flawed experiment upon which the theory rests has never been replicated.

One of the common skeptical questions is why so little HIV is found in the blood of AIDS patients. If it is even found at all, it is many orders of magnitude less than other infectious diseases. The question was answered by *Time* magazine's 1996 Man of the Year, David Ho. Ho claimed to have found high viral loads by a novel testing procedure. It's still quoted as the answer, even though both sides of the debate have refuted Ho's paper. The treatment plan of Ho is still used – HAART, or Highly Active Anti Retroviral Therapy. "HIV researchers know the Ho/Wei papers are wrong," Culshaw writes, "yet they continue along the clinical path charted by the papers. They know that the quantitative use of PCR [polymerase chain reaction] has never been validated, yet they continue to use viral load to make clinical decisions. They know that the history of HIV/AIDS is littered with documented cases of fraud, incompetence and poor-quality research, yet they find it almost impossible to imagine that this could be happening at the present moment. They know their predictions have never panned out, yet they keep inventing mysterious mechanisms for HIV pathogenesis. They know many therapies of the past are now acknowledged to be mistakes ... yet they never imagine that their current therapies ... might one day be acknowledged as mistakes themselves."[146]

AIDS is a syndrome, not a disease. The distinction is critical. A syndrome is a basket defined by commonly associated symptoms. A disease is the underlying factor of a group of symptoms. The difference is marked in the case of AIDS – it is defined by laboratory results in conjunction with one of many 'AIDS-defining' diseases. Among these are such varied conditions as pneumonia, diarrhea, candidiasis, dementia, and tuberculosis. The official definition says that it causes thirty different diseases when present, and when absent, the original causes create the disease. This artificiality forces a correlation by defining away non-correlated cases.

However, a solitary pathogen cannot account for thirty different diseases, especially when many of them pre-exist AIDS by 2000 years. HIV cannot cause dementia, for example, because HIV depends on cell division. Neurons do not divide.

Symptoms do not distinguish an AIDS-defining disease from AIDS. AIDS with TB is physically identical to TB alone. The sole difference is a blood test. Though AIDS is defined by the diseases, it is diagnosed only through lab results – the HIV test and CD4+ T-cell count. Again, AIDS is unique in such a clinical profile.

Though AIDS has no particularized symptoms, the definition expanded after naming HIV as the cause. According to Culshaw, "This is contrary to all logic and counter to the reasoning that underlies the existence of clinical syndromes in the first place."[147] Syndromes narrow down the symptoms so that an actual condition can be more clearly identified. Most syndromes are defined by a grouping of symptoms, but in the case of AIDS, one can have no symptoms and be diagnosed as having the condition through a positive test.*

In 1993, the addition of the low T-cell count to the AIDS diagnosis immediately doubled the number of AIDS patients. The criterion is questionable – it is not used in most other countries. T-cell counts fluctuate enormously by time of day, after a meal or intense exercise, and between different persons. The best athletes have AIDS levels of T cells. They have vigorous red blood cell ratios to carry oxygen and less need for T cells in the bloodstream because they don't get sick. But with a low T-cell count (below 200) and an HIV-positive test, then one permanently has AIDS – there is no possibility of remission.† AIDS is the only condition from which one can never, by definition, recover. T-cell counts can go to the moon with HIV-negative tests, and they have, but the diagnosis remains. The upshot is that a person can receive a death sentence without a single clinical symptom. They are then subjected to a debilitating round of medical treatments that are often lethal.

HIV supposedly destroys CD4+ T cells, but Doctor Zvi Grossman, a mainstream researcher, said that none of the hypothesized mechanisms is valid.[148] One theory is "remote programmed 'suicidal' mechanisms. A hypothetical genetic

* It's also argued that the diagnosis of cervical cancer as an AIDS defining illness is politically motivated – it balances the male/female statistics.

† Once a person has been diagnosed class four, they can never return to class three or better. No disease has ever been categorized as irrecoverable. Only AIDS has this as part of the definition. According to Luc Montaigner, "AIDS does not inevitably lead to death."

mutation, which many Caucasian Europeans lack, but most Africans have. Gay men also seem to possess these receptors, as do intravenous drug users and transfusion recipients."[149] The theories change rapidly, indicative of flawed basic assumptions. This leads to a paradox where the community points to the enormous body of research as vindication for the baseline hypothesis, but speaks of theories a few years old as being out of date. The studies must thus be simultaneously correct and incorrect – a logical impossibility.

HIV occurs in concentrations lower, by several orders of magnitude, than any disease ever. If it resulted in 1:1 death rate of T cells even the most anemic system would easily replace the cells. Each viral cell would have to kill thousands of T cells – an absurd proposition. Experiments contradict it. In vitro T cells receive no AIDS medications and are exposed to thousands of times the HIV concentrations as the bodily cells are. *Yet they never die.*[150]

A virus almost always causes a disease within 1 to 2 months. After that, the host destroys it or vice versa. The 10-to-15-year stated latency of HIV is an utter anomaly. If HIV leads to AIDS 50% of the time (the minimal prediction) then the 1.5% annual conversion from inactive HIV to active AIDS equals a 30-to-65-year latency. In other words, since 1.5 of every 100 HIV positives develops AIDS each year, then for half of all HIV positives, it will take 30 years. HIV alone is thus insufficient to cause AIDS. Slow viruses are impossible because they need to regenerate at a rate faster than the body replicates cells.[151]

Professor Stefan Lanka, a German virologist, says that the connection between the virus and the condition is not established. He believes, along with most dissenters, that AIDS in gay men is due to heavy antibiotic use. From numerous sexual infections, they have constantly upgraded the potency of antibiotics. This harms the immune system. Further insults are caused by the use of amyl nitrate, an intoxicant which suppresses the immune system. The inhalant is strongly linked to Kaposi's sarcoma, an AIDS-defining illness only found in gay men.[152]

Retroviruses do not kill T cells, yet part of the AIDS diagnosis is a T-cell deficiency. Retroviruses do not cause diseases and there is no pertinent reason for them to do so. There has never been another acute retrovirus in humans. Retroviruses 'ride' on cells by reverse transcriptase – injecting their RNA for replication when the cell divides. Cytocidal viruses like influenza, by contrast, destroy cells. HIV is the only retrovirus ever thought to destroy cells. A retrovirus that kills host cells *cannot replicate*, thus it would disappear immediately.

HIV, such as it is, is extremely simple. It is practically identical to all other retroviruses and has only three genes. It uses all three to replicate. It has no genetic mechanism to cause AIDS or any disease. It is far too simple to account for the extreme latency periods, the priming of T cells for later destruction, or for the multitude of diseases ascribed to it. It is also too simple to selectively inflict most Westerners with pneumonia or Kaposi's Sarcoma and most Africans with fever, slim disease, and diarrhea.[153]

Gallo earlier had failed to prove retroviral causes of cancer and Alzheimers. He first blamed HLTV-1 for cancer, then for AIDS. (Later it was renamed.)[154] Etienne De Harven, Professor Emeritus of Pathology, said that the failed attempt to find retroviral causes for cancer led to a shift. In order to save the field, the researchers built a case for retroviral AIDS.[155] At a press conference the Department of Health endorsed the HIV hypothesis before anything was peer-reviewed – a preemptive strike, and a form of scientific misconduct. As Gallo said, "We would need to convince the academic community as totally, as widely, and as quickly as possible."[156]

HIV has claimed more research funding than any disease in history, yet its etiology remains without consensus, even in the mainstream.* Sexual transmission, for example, has never been demonstrated. It is assumed due to the promiscuity of gay men. Even the statistics appear rigged. In many places, any HIV-positive's death is attributed to AIDS. In Massachusetts, if an HIV-positive falls from a cliff – officially AIDS got him.

The proof of science is an ability to predict. In italics are predictions from 20-25 years ago: *HIV will spread rapidly throughout the population* – it never happened. *By 1990, 1 in 5 heterosexuals could be dead of AIDS (1987). A cure and a vaccine will be available by 1986. AIDS will not be present in the HIV negative* – in the first tests, Gallo found that only 36% of AIDS patients had HIV. Later 4000 more were verified. One study published in the *European Journal of Epidemiology* found that 40% of 465 patients with clinical AIDS tested HIV-negative.[157] HIV-free AIDS was renamed ICL in 1993 to sweep away the problem.

AIDS will develop within 1 to 5 years – there are many untreated HIV-positives who, after 20 years, have not developed AIDS. In fact, of the first five cases of AIDS, three survived. *HIV drugs stop*

* Dr. David Rasnick publicly questioned a lecturer about HIV paradoxes. The lecturer responded, "the non-infectious particles are pathogenic." An equivalent claim from geography might be, "the Earth is flat."

AIDS – medicated HIV positives die at 5 times the rate – 8% per annum versus unmedicated at 1.5%. *Prostitution and pornography industries will be decimated by AIDS* – these groups have no higher infection rate than any other.

The theory is consistently wrong. Places with high HIV do not have high AIDS. No cases of AIDS after HIV infection from accidental needle sticks have been documented.[158] Increased breast-feeding lowers the percentage of HIV-positive babies from HIV positive mothers.[159] A multi-year study of partners, one positive and one negative, showed zero cases of infection.[160] Numerous studies show condoms are ineffective against HIV – indicating it is not sexually transmitted.[161] Normal infectious disease increases the infection rate with medical personnel, but with AIDS there is a decrease from the general population. 95% of HIV-positive individuals never contract AIDS. HIV has no specific disease – unlike all other pathogenic microbes.

The Army tested for HIV in 1984, finding a 50/50 male-female ratio. The sample size makes it valid for the general population. However, 90% of AIDS patients are male. In Africa, AIDS is 50/50. This makes the HIV/AIDS hypothesis absurd. The demographic is incoherent – these are different problems.

Four general criteria, asthenia (weakness), diarrhea for thirty days, high fever and 10% weight loss over two months are sufficient to diagnose an African with AIDS. No test is necessary; few are given. Many have been so diagnosed and left to die by their community. They are barely fed. If this definition of AIDS sounds like another condition, that's because it is – malnourishment. Undernourished people have weakened immune systems. Antibiotic-resistant tuberculosis and malaria are raging in Africa, along with other diseases. So are parasitic infections. These conditions have all the following symptoms – asthenia, diarrhea, fever, and weight loss.

African AIDS is not exponential, self-limiting (reduced by herd immunity), or bell-curved. It is the first infectious disease ever to defy any, much less all, of these normative criteria. It is also highly non-specific in being defined by 30 different possible conditions. Only 3% of African HIV-positives have AIDS.

The rampant AIDS epidemic in Africa is not supported by real world data. The World Health Organization has no official AIDS numbers, only estimates and projections. In 2008, UNAIDS announced they had been overestimating AIDS cases by millions. In Benin, where they practice voodoo medicine, deaths in AIDS patients are below two percent, far less than the Western mortality rate. In Zaire from 1985-88, 3 million HIV-positives were reported. There were only 335 cases of AIDS.[162]

The WHO database reveals no change in total number of AIDS cases from 2003-2006. The database shows fewer than 3 million reported cases of AIDS in 2003, yet the computer models* show between 24 and 48 million.[163]

According to Montaigner, the discoverer of HIV, malnutrition weakens the immunity of Africans diagnosed with AIDS and they suffer from malaria, TB, and other infections. A lot of it stems from bad water. He also said that HIV is not the sole cause of AIDS and might even be of secondary importance. "Our [healthy] immune system," he said, "will get rid of the virus within a few weeks."

Perhaps the most egregious anomaly is the mode of infection. In Africa, heterosexual sex transmits AIDS. HIV has never infected the Western heterosexual population via sexual transmission. Any anecdotal cases are too few to have statistical relevance. A virus cannot restrict such a vector based on geography.

Though used as the industry standard, HIV tests were never intended as diagnostic tools. They were intended to test for safety of the blood supply. AIDS is diagnosed purely on serology or blood testing.† Three factors are used: antibodies, T-cell count, and viral load.

In order to test serology on a disease, three criteria are essential: standardization, particularity, and reproducibility. HIV tests fail on all three. Apparently the FDA agrees. *No HIV test has ever been approved for the diagnosis of HIV*. The test manufacturers themselves acknowledge it. "The Amplicor HIV-1 monitor test is not intended to be used as a screening test for HIV, nor a diagnostic test to confirm the presence of HIV infection."[164] Every test contains a similar statement.

There are four AIDS/HIV tests. Elisa and Western Blot test for HIV antibodies. Elisa is non-confirmatory, but is used to screen out negative results. Its original purpose was to discard tainted blood – where a better-safe-than-sorry policy makes sense. For diagnosis, the opposite is true because of the stigma and aggressiveness of the treatment. Yet it is still used. Western Blot is confirmatory, but other conditions – leprosy, TB, recent vaccination and pregnancy, for example – often give false positives. Opponents point out that no single test is considered confirmatory because of non-specificity. It takes a series of these tests, each positive, to diagnosis HIV. No other infectious

---

* Computer models are an easily abused method of hopping-up weak theories – we shall see them throughout this book.

† It is defined by the 30 diseases, but not diagnosed by them – in the West, at lest.

condition requires this as standard procedure. If any single test is not conclusive, a series of them is not either – it is merely an attempt at probability abrogation. But the statistics can kill.

Western Blot is the gold standard for AIDS tests. But in one of the more bizarre twists, the test measures antibodies. Antibody tests with any other disease show a prior infection of the body. Further, they demonstrate immunity – the antibodies show the disease is gone. Strong antibody presence means you cannot contract a disease – except in the case of HIV. There is no explanation for the anomaly.

Dr. Robert Giraldo ran HIV tests on undiluted blood.* 100% of the random samples were HIV positive. Almost all were negative when run in the standard, diluted way.[165] The message is undeniable – the tested antibodies are not specific to HIV. If they were, they could not exist in non-HIV-positive blood.

The Western Blot measures ten bands of protein antibodies. An interpretation is required to determine the limit – how much of the protein qualifies as indicating infection. This is flawed – antibodies are either there or not. They cannot indicate pathology by being above a certain quantity. And all people show all the HIV antibodies – in a below-threshold amount. The original test showed a 30% positive rate for the general population – these limits were adjusted to give a predetermined infection rate.

The criteria differ from country to country and by sexual preference. In Australia, four (out of ten) positive bands are required to be diagnosed with AIDS. In Africa, it only takes two. In 1990s America, a single band would earn a gay man the diagnosis, but not a straight man. In 1992, Britain canceled the Western Blot for unreliability. People of African descent are 800% more likely to test positive than Caucasians. The Western Blot test has created identical results in dogs as in humans, but dogs are not diagnosed with HIV.[166]

The antibody tests are determined positive at a certain cut-off level. If one's antibody count is over that level, HIV is presumed to be present. The idea of being positive or negative based on a graduated scale is a direct contradiction.

Many of the proteins are contested even within the HIV/AIDS acceptance community. P32 is a common human protein, yet is still used as a diagnostic sample. Gp41, a part of cellular actin, suffuses the body and has no specificity. P24 occurs in 24% of donated blood.[167] P24 has been found in high concentration for non-HIV-positives and absent in AIDS patients. In other words –

* Normal dilution is 50X for an HIV test – no dilution or less than 1:4 for most serology tests.

this HIV-defining antibody is not correlated in any way with the virus. If HIV-specific antibodies exist, then a single antibody should be sufficient to prove that. Also, if the antibodies are specific, HIV-positive blood should have a reaction on all the proteins rather than just a few.

The PCR viral load test, also confirmatory, tests for fragments of HIV nucleus by massively amplifying them. It is typically used to track disease progression. The test does loosely correlate with progression of the disease, however, two viral load tests on a single sample give widely different results. It fails as science because it is not reproducible. Kary Mullis, the Nobel Laureate inventor of the underlying PCR technique, condemns the viral load test as worthless for all but making money.

The tests have a stunning failure hidden in the '99% success rate.' At first blush, one false negative out of 100 sounds pretty good. But the false positives give the lie to success. Bayle's law – the lower the prevalence, the greater the error – reveals a gross problem. With the infection rate at .4%, a 1% false-positive rate gives a hundred false positives to forty true positives. In other words, 7 of 10 HIV diagnoses are false positives.* African children, for example, frequently test positive though their mothers are negative – a near impossibility.[168]

Again, HIV is the most anomalous condition in history. It does not conform to germ theory, antibody theory, or normative serological procedures. It produces an enormous range of diseases from a single retrovirus. It is the first retrovirus to ever cause harm. It is the only disease where antibodies register pathology instead of immunity. And it fails Koch's postulates. Other diseases, such as beriberi and scurvy, were originally thought to be infectious, but failing a single one of Koch's criteria is a normally a deathblow to a medical theory, so other causes were sought and found.

As Duesberg showed, the HIV/AIDS hypothesis fails all four of Koch's postulates: 1) the agent must be found in all cases of the disease. 2) It must be isolatable from the host and grow in pure culture. 3) It must reproduce the same disease when injected into a susceptible host. 4) It must be found present in the newly infected host. Against postulate 1, in 4000 documented AIDS cases, there was no discernible HIV. In the 'isolated' HIV samples, the virus does not normally grow in culture. It arguably passes postulate two but needs to be 're-activated' to replicate, another HIV-only feature. The original chimps violate three and

---

* Another way to understand the math is to use a 100,000 person sample. 400 are infected; 99,600 are not. The 400 will have 396 positive tests. The 99600 will have 996 false positives.

four: 250 chimps were injected with HIV in 1984, leading to a funny problem in AIDS research – what to do with monkeys who won't die when they should. Due to strong genetic similarities, trials with chimpanzees are the highest standard of animal testing. In all other viral contamination, the chimps contract the disease. Yet none of these 250 ever contracted AIDS.[169]

Perhaps the answer to all these paradoxes is money. Until 1994, Robert Gallo received royalties for every test. And the pharmaceutical industry receives a lot more – plus the windfall from the 'treatment' for AIDS.

According to many dissenters, HIV is an unconfirmed postulate – it fails to fulfill rigorous scientific criteria. Normally, tests are measured against the gold standard of viral isolation – "the microbe isolated in pure form and shown to consistently and specifically generate only those antibodies."[170] The alternative camp, Professor Eleni Papadopoulos-Eleopoulos, for example, strongly disputes the claim that HIV has been isolated. Even Montaigner, in 1997, stated that he had not isolated HIV in 1983, nor had Gallo.

By standard medical procedure, researchers attempted to isolate the virus. In spite of ubiquitous artists' renditions and computer graphic depictions, no actual image of the virus exists. (See figure 6.) It's never been found. Electron microscopes have rendered clear images of many other viruses. HIV has only been inferred from high antibody concentrations.

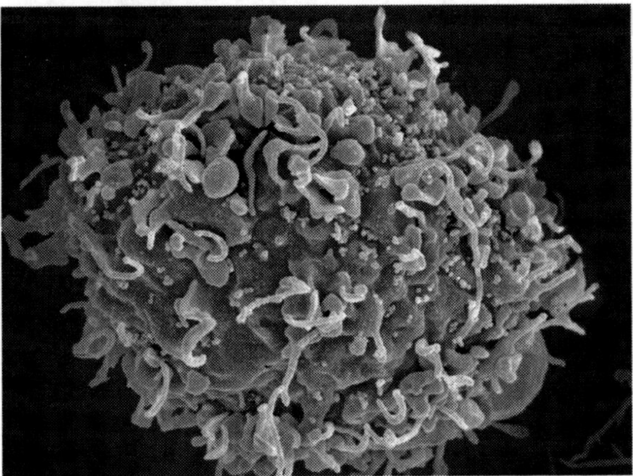

Figure 6: HIV (computer enhanced graphic)

The dissenting camp point out that an endogenous (coming from inside) retrovirus, of which there are many, cannot be distinguished from an exogenous retrovirus. HIV, if it exists, could well be a harmless endogenous retrovirus. The retrovirus has never been isolated from a patient, pathology Professor Etienne De Harven claims, even though it should be possible in all patients. None of the particles in an isolated sample have ever been shown to be HIV, or even a retrovirus.

It has certainly not been isolated by the traditional means of electron micrograph – there is no visible record of commonly appearing, *replicating* HIV-viruses. Bits and pieces of retroviral particles are called isolation, but this is not standard viral isolation of a full and distinct virus. The body hosts millions of retroviruses. Dissenting experts say the samples are non-distinct. They could be any retrovirus. For example, the different RNA genomes in given samples of HIV can vary by 40%. The difference between humans and chimps is only two percent – and they're different species. In these later 'isolations,' the HIV particles do not even have proper dimensions for retroviruses. They are too large, extremely variable, lacking in retroviral spikes, not rounded, and without a dense core. They are floating in excess cellular material – thus not isolated.[171] Moreover, *identical particles* are present in the non-infected controls.[172] (See figures 7 & 8.)

I repeat, we did not purify.
—Luc Montaigner, 1997

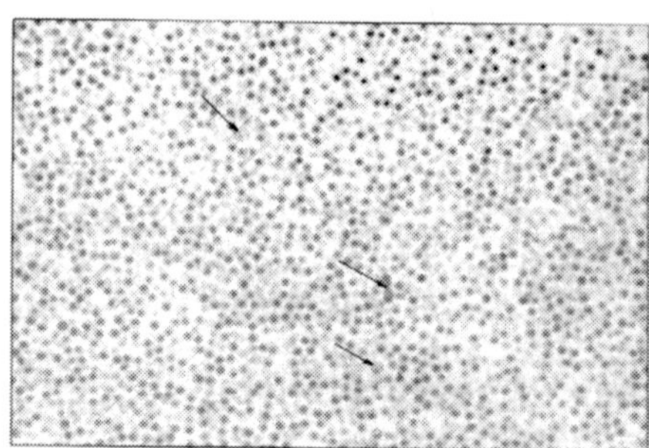

Figure 7: Isolation of Friend virus. (AltHeal.org)

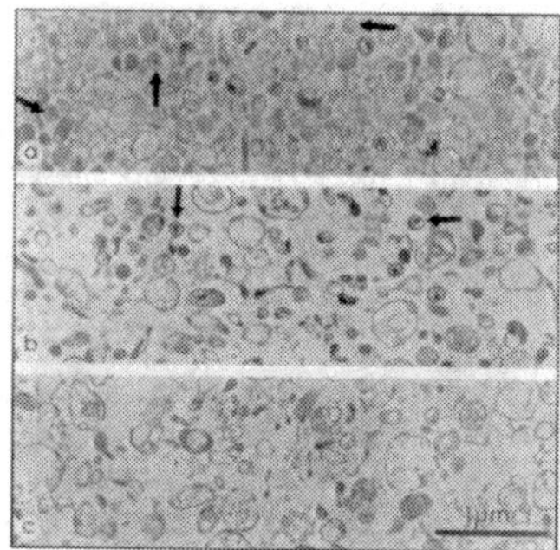

Figure 8: First 'isolated' HIV virus. (Pasteur Institute)

This modified isolation consists of "certain chemical reactions indicating phenomena consistent with HIV have been observed."[173] The logic is circular: If, in certain patients, chemical signatures are observed, it indicates the presence of an infectious agent. Therefore, if those chemical reactions can be reproduced, the agent is assumed to be there. The proof presupposes what it intends to demonstrate. The infectious agent itself is never found.

The existence of HIV (though not the pathogenic factor) could be resolved on a number of grounds, especially an HIV isolation experiment proposed by dissenters. For a paltry sum of HIV-level research money, they can isolate HIV or show isolation to be impossible. The establishment refuses to perform the experiment. Isolation is simple and inexpensive, but no AIDS patient has ever been shown to have HIV in their blood by viral isolation.

HIV-testing, however, is a misdemeanor compared to the profitable treatment regimen. Sadly, some doctors are unethical enough to blatantly commit HIV fraud. Six medical professionals, led by Dr. Roberto Rodriguez, were convicted in 2009 of falsely diagnosing people with HIV and billing millions of dollars to Medicare.[174]

AIDS medications themselves have never been tested in placebo-controlled clinical trials. AZT, the first one, is the sole exception. And even then the placebo controls were abandoned mid-trial for various reasons. AZT costs $5/bottle to make and is sold for $500. It is probably the most toxic drug treatment therapy since the mercury suppository. The AZT trials are deeply fraudulent and plagued by incompetence.[175] Many of the latest rounds of drugs have never been clinically tested *at all*. A field test is ongoing, unmonitored, and probably at great human cost. No meaningful studies show an effective treatment of AIDS. HIV-positives on the latest meds die at about 7% per year. The global death rate for all HIV positives, treated and untreated, is below 2%. Taking the drugs makes death 4 times as likely. Liver failure has always been the foremost cause of death among AIDS patients. It has never been an AIDS-defining disease, but it demonstrably results from prolonged exposure to almost all retroviral medications.

Antibiotics such as AZT are so strong that, as it says in the package, prolonged usage will cause AIDS-like symptoms. The reason is simple – they attack the immune system as vigorously as any infection. In other words, the treatment causes AIDS. The course of treatment destroys the genetic material and the energy-producing mitochondria in the cells. The patient loses all energy.

From the Treatment Guidelines, the side effects of AZT (now called Retrovir) include bone marrow suppression, intestinal intolerance, liver damage, lipid metabolism disturbances, severe damage to mitochondria, risk of diabetes, and flesh decay. These effects are common. California lists it as a carcinogen, yet it is still a preferred treatment for pregnant women, children, and Africans. The Sigma AZT label reads "Toxic. Toxic by inhalation, in contact with skin and if swallowed. Targets organs, blood, and bone marrow. Wear suitable protective clothing." The medical practitioner requires protective clothing against a substance injected into infants.

Pregnancy creates high antibodies and leads to many false positives. The medical situation is human rights abuse. Pregnant women who test HIV-positive are pressured to abort. Women are forced into C-sections. Breastfeeding is illegal in many places. An HIV-positive pregnant woman can be compelled into the regimen. These questionable chemotherapies are compulsory for the newborns as well.[176] Worse, AZT use in pregnant women causes numerous birth defects. Most of the drugs are not approved for children, so they receive AZT – proven to be the worst.[*]

The Concorde study showed a 25% increase in death rates for patients receiving early treatment. The Darby study, published in *Nature,* revealed a 1000% increase in mortality for hemophiliacs given AZT.[177] Although its toxicity is well-established and not in dispute, AZT is now widely disseminated in Africa, funded by NGO's and donations from non-profits like the Gates foundation. We need to ask why. It cannot be the cost, because Vitamin A is more effective. So is clean water.

The introduction of the T-cell criteria in 1993 increased the number of healthy AIDS patients, leading to a sharp decline in the death rate. New retroviral therapies were lauded as the cause although they were introduced two years after the decline. Ironically, almost all HIV meds decrease T-cell counts. As most dissenters and even the package inserts agree – these drugs cause AIDS.

Marcia Angell, former editor of *NEJM,* describes a situation where medical professors lost income and grant money. The pharmaceutical industry stepped in with funding in exchange for support of new drugs.[178] In the eighties, three years was 'lightning speed' for new drug approval. Now, seven days is not unheard of. Six weeks is about average. The rapidly approved protease inhibitor Crixivan costs $6800 per year. In the official report from the company, "the relevance of changes in viral load have not been established." There is no reference to any effect on the progress of the disease or chances of survival. Crixivan

---

[*] AZT was rejected as cancer therapy in the '60s as being too toxic.

tested out as having no benefit at all. It became the standard of care. "At least half of the AIDS cases in the 1990s," Dr. Rasnick said, "are a direct result of the antiretroviral therapies themselves." Though slower acting than the first anti-retrovirals, protease inhibitors are possibly even worse. The body often cannot discharge them and they cause diabetes, kidney failure, liver failure, and "two new conditions every month."[179]

The history of the drug testing reads like a Nazi experiment. The NIH tested AZT and other anti-retrovirals on New York City orphans and foster children, against their will. Some were forced by stomach tube. 25 children died during the trials and another 80 afterwards.[180] The untreated, HIV-positive orphans consistently recovered through better nutrition and normative medical care, according to the medical body itself.

In a 2006 *Harper's* article, Celia Farber detailed the case of Nevirapine. Attempting to cover up a wrongful death due to the drug, the doctors called it 'accelerated AIDS.' The trials for the drug, mostly conducted on pregnant Ugandan women, erupted in a scandal. Farber documents staggering incompetence and subterfuge. Though now approved, Nevirapine is 'alarmingly toxic.' Canada rejected the drug application twice. A group attacked the Harper's article, demanding an apology, a rejection of Farber's conclusions, the editor's resignations, and an endorsement of Nevirapine. Harper's refused on all counts. There was no lawsuit. Ms. Farber, however, was blackballed from journalism for two years.

Farber put it best – even if the dissenters are wrong, the Duesberg situation alone shows the politics masquerading as medical science. The mainstream has a "reflexive hostility to ideas that challenge the dominant paradigm." Scientists live and die by the approval of the massive web of government and industry boards that control funding approval. "Nobody is safe," one NIH researcher told her. Professor Strohman at Berkeley notes that success only comes from following consensus. "Science has totally capitulated to corporate interests."[181] It's well documented that pharmaceutical companies finance and even operate non-profit AIDS organizations. These organizations are all behind the HIV/AIDS hypothesis. And they all endorse the meds.

Tens of billions of dollars of AIDS research has been conducted. At least the money has been spent. All tests have one thing in common – they begin with the assumption that HIV causes AIDS and seek to find out how. It's never been established; each theory falls apart in a few years. No money goes toward a mainstream investigation into any other hypothesis.

Dr. Harvey Bially challenged Dr. John Moore to debate the AIDS hypothesis. Moore replied, "It would give him a credibility he does not merit. The science community does not debate with AIDS denialists. It treats them with the contempt they deserve." Considering the petition for reappraisal was signed by thousands (and growing) of medical researchers and doctors, including many prominent experts on virology, immunology, and pathology, it is presumptuous of Moore to exclude these people from the 'science community.' The language is ad hominem and has little to do with the proper language and approach of research. That this is considered a scientific position is disturbing. Scientists with legitimate concerns, nothing to gain, and reputation and career to lose, are stated to be outside the debate because they do not agree with the mainstream view. The worst thing is the normality – it's the way science is done. When billions of dollars are up for grabs, the safeguards against corruption must be formidable. Unfortunately, at least for AIDS, they appear fictitious.

The Wall Street Journal reported that the CDC deliberately falsified the sexual transmissibility of HIV in order to gain public support for funding.[182] Indeed,

> the NIH, CDC, Medical Research Council and WHO are terrorizing hundreds of millions of people around the world by their reckless and absurd policy of equating sex with death... putting these organizations in an impossible situation. It would be intolerably embarrassing for them to admit at this late date that they are wrong, that AIDS is not sexually transmitted. [It] could destroy these organizations. [They] not only maintain but actually compound their errors, which adds to the fear, suffering, and misery of the world — the antithesis of their reason for being.[183]
>
> —Dr. David Rasnick, PhD, Biochemist,
> Developer of protease inhibitors,
> University of California

Mainstream science is now backed into a corner. It has validated the HIV/AIDS hypothesis for decades. Many have died, and if this dissenting group is correct, most have died from the medications. The death rate alone of medicated versus unmedicated virtually proves it. It is a credibility issue for science itself. Our civilization may be approaching a crisis point where a number of strongly held, critical assumptions crumble. As more and more of society loses faith in science, capitalism, and the façade of US democracy, the consequences grow uncertain. One thing is certain – the loss of faith will be global.

Falsifiability and Arrogance

Every scientific statement must remain tentative forever.
—Karl Popper

A.J. Ayer was one of the chief proponents of logical positivism, a noble, but ultimately failed attempt to establish an objective theory of science. Logical positivists created a blend of empiricism and rational mathematical deduction. The primary criterion for a theory was verifiability. They came to the radical conclusion that a theory was 'cognitively meaningful' only if it can be demonstrated as true or false. It was designed to eliminate metaphysics, ethics, theology and all other such statements not only from science but from sensibility. The Vienna Circle, as they were called, believed their approach to be a higher order of meaning. They even created a special language.

Positivism gives rise to scientism, the idea that science possesses the sole voice of truth. The scientific method, we often hear, is the 'best of all possible methods for determining truth.' Scientism is an ideological formulation – it is not verifiable. Positivism is a metaphysical assumption that undercuts itself.

Philosophically, logical positivism is essentially dead. In the 1970s Ayer said, "I suppose the most important defect was that nearly all of it was false."[184] Unfortunately, it crept in the back door and is fully re-animated. Objectivity is a central claim under the new atheist banner. Scientism includes an overweaning faith in the power of science to answer all questions, the dismissal of social sciences (unless they can be rendered mathematically), faith in the omnipotence of scientific understanding, a belief that such knowledge is the only true knowledge, and a demand that all other disciplines debate on science's terms rather than its own.

Sir Karl Popper is probably the most referenced analyst of the scientific process. He strongly argued against dogma and did not want his method to be used in that way. Sadly, it has been. Falsifiability has become a dogmatic dividing line between science and non-science. He wanted to establish criteria for what functioned as scientific and what did not, but he was *agnostic to value*. The point cannot be overestimated. "Purely metaphysical ideas have been of the greatest importance for cosmology."[185]

Popper's theories are seriously abused. Logical positivists, he said, have "an anxiety to annihilate metaphysics, [but they] annihilate natural science along with it."[186] Absolute theories about reality are not genuine concepts. They miss the mark because any formulated idea rests on other formulated ideas, not on experience. There is always a gap between experience and formulation. This is Popper's demarcation problem – the lack of clear distinction between science and metaphysics. And it is where his theories are grossly misrepresented. With no clear division, both areas deserve equal status. In other words, any universal law, idea, or principle of science has a metaphysical – untestable, unfalsifiable – component hidden within. To destroy metaphysics is to destroy science.

Popper's idea of falsification is inextricably linked with this notion. Falsification merely states that an idea must have a means of disproof for science to analyze it. It is value-neutral. In the dance between theory and experiment, theory opens new doors of knowledge and experiment closes the door on pointless theories. This is why falsifiability is so critical. But non-falsifiability does not mean an idea is wrong – it only means it cannot be proven wrong. The overlooked distinction is enormous.

Almost all science philosophers have at least this one truth in common – human contexts cannot be removed from theoretical constructs. No theory can exist independently of a human (or its creators) point of view and no theory can escape unintended uses. Most people, for example, use falsifiability to heap scorn on 'metaphysics.' Popper hated this and said so very clearly. It was his principle argument with his foes – the logical positivists. Falsifiability was a means to turn metaphysical ideas into testable science – *and nothing more*. "Instead of eradicating metaphysics from the empirical sciences, positivism leads to the invasion of metaphysics into the scientific realm."[187] He adamantly opposed getting rid of metaphysics or using it derogatorily. To the contrary – he upheld it as a wonderful breeding ground for hypotheses which could slowly be formulated in scientific terms and give rise to testable ideas. All non-falsifiable ideas are metaphysical – neo-positivism says – hence they are wrong. Karl Popper, father of modern epistemology, said the opposite. Ideas can, indeed must, arise from the fertile ground of metaphysics. Science must then derive a means of testing them. Further, a la Gödel, science must utilize concepts it can never prove.

Popper defines the central principle of causality as the idea that any occurrence is causally explicable and thus deductively predictable. This divides into two methods – the conceptual explanation (scientific logic) and the extant reality, wherein "the world is governed by strict laws. The assertion is not falsifiable…I shall neither adopt nor reject the principle of causality. *I exclude it as metaphysical from the sphere of science."*[188] But without causality assumed, science has no meaning.

It's a scathing critique. Popper's idea of falsifiability is probably the most often invoked to validate an idea as scientific. Most people using this logic separate the world into science/ truth/ reality and non-science/ bogus/ irrelevant. Popper unequivocally states that the entire scientific enterprise of natural laws giving rise to particular events is a causal explanation and that causality is a metaphysical assumption. The entirety of science is thus founded on metaphysics.

It gets much worse. The problem of the empirical basis results from a trilemma. We must accept theory dogmatically (unscientifically), or justify it in one of two ways. Theory can be grounded in other statements but since each statement needs validation, we have an infinite regress. The third option is psychologism or justification by sensory experience, but this leads to subjectivism. Moreover, it "demands immediate experience as justification for belief. But any concept or idea goes well past what can be personally and definitively seen. We must accept almost all of science *on faith*. The empirical basis has nothing absolute about it. The bold structure of science's theories rises above a swamp."[189]

This is the problem of the empirical basis – how to connect statements to experience. "In demanding objectivity for scientific statements, we deprive ourselves of any logical means by which we might have hoped to reduce the truth of scientific statements to our experiences."[190] It is a paradox that objectivity could arise from subjectivity. The best we can attain is 'intersubjective testability.' Yet the hypotheses from this always rely on other hypotheses and assumptions. This leads to an intractable problem – science cannot provide absolute statements. It is incapable of expressing objective reality. Likewise, "every discovery contains an irrational element or creative intuition."[191] As Einstein said, "there is no logical path leading to universal laws. They can only be reached by intuition."[192]

Positivists "fail to notice that whenever they believe they have discovered a fact, they have only proposed a convention, hence the convention is liable to turn into a dogma."[193] Our measurements, for example, are unreal. If human time is a real measure, then time travel is simple, an hour lasts a day, and a day is 48 hours. Stand east of the international dateline at midnight. Wait until 11:59 – 24 hours later – then cross westward. It will be the beginning of the same day and you will be able to spend 24 more hours on the same day. A calendar day exists for 48 hours, but a day is only 24 hours long. Our way of marking time measures nothing absolute.

Popper also guns down scientific logic. The problem of induction (general laws drawn from specific data) asks where and when inductive inferences are valid. The principle of induction claims to validate empirical science. However, induction itself has no empirical basis. It is therefore a self-defeating concept. It must be a universal principle, but it needs other universals (which need their own universals) to give it credibility. It becomes an infinite regress – no fundamental ground can be found.

This all-important method is therefore metaphysical. If induction were ipso facto falsifiable, then any theory arrived at through induction and later falsified would also falsify induction. Thus every new advance would falsify induction. Instead we have an a priori (metaphysical) principle of induction that cannot be falsified. Again, science requires metaphysics for any movement.

Simplicity is another important criterion. For Popper simplicity means high testability. A theory should be relentlessly attackable on as many fronts as possible. For this reason, auxiliary hypotheses should be sharply limited – they always seek to defend the theory by workarounds. For the same reason, axioms should be minimized. Simplicity amounts to a "high level of universality."[194] But again and again, complexity creeps in to defend failing theories.

His warning about the current corruption of science is prescient. We should not "issue prohibitions that draw limits to the possibilities of research."[195] The NIH, CDC and others have done exactly that under suspicious circumstances. "It is always possible to find some way of evading falsification by ad hoc hypotheses or definitions. It is even possible without logical inconsistency to simply refuse to acknowledge any falsifying experience."[196] This has become the virtual leitmotif of 21st century science – baldly asserting a lack of evidence. When an absence of evidence is cited, it is almost always a lie – the evidence is typically so overwhelming it must be denied completely.

Popper's most important criteria was not falsifiability, but its cousin consistency.[197] A theory has to be logically coherent, otherwise it self-refutes. Of course, consistency is not a provable reality. "Scientific method [has a] metaphysical faith in the existence of regularities in our world – the immutability of natural processes. It is a metaphysical idea that natural laws are invariant with respect to space and time and have no exceptions."[198]

"Science is not a system of certain or well-established statements, nor is it a system which steadily advances toward a state of finality. Our science is not knowledge: it can never claim to have attained truth or even a substitute for it, such as probability. Every scientific statement must remain tentative forever."[199]

Life: Simplicity vs. Complexity

Starting with ether, electrons and other physical machinery, we cannot reach conscious man.
—Sir Arthur Eddington

Richard Milton's *Neo-Darwinism: Time to Reconsider* earned him the erroneous label 'secret creationist' and censorship from the *New York Times*. The great fallacy of hard-core Darwinian theorists echoes the words of George Bush, "If you're not with us then you're with the [creationists]." Nowhere is debate more intense than in this arena. Neo-Darwinists claim to be scientific while Intelligent Design fights a valiant battle for the title. Only one can win. But the entire debate ignores a critical possibility: what if both are wrong?

Perhaps the most objectionable aspect of evolution is dogmatic faith in the current theory. 'Evolution is a fact,' we read. 'Evolution is True,' a book title tells us. While there is little doubt that all life is interconnected, there is every reason to doubt our understanding of the many processes involved. An astoundingly complex set of organisms, molecules, reproductive styles, chemical reactions, migration patterns, societies, fossil records and communication systems is summed in a sound-bite. Biology has levered an obvious truth – life flows from other life – into an unobvious one "Life began with one primitive species, perhaps a self-replicating molecule. It then branched out, throwing off many diverse species. The mechanism for most, but not all, change is natural selection."[200] It's easy to grasp and, from a vague initial truth, lulls the mind into gullible acceptance. Gross simplification, a type of distortion, is a valuable tool in gaining public acceptance for the theory.

In short, we are pretending to understand. This is a bait-n-switch: because evolution is true, we can fully explain it. Evolution *is* true, the contrarian argues, but the current theory is massively incomplete. We know a tiny fraction of what is happening. We need to quit pretending we understand, because that blocks creative approaches. If we 'know,' then anything challenging our knowledge must be wrong. All good science begins, like Darwin, as rogue science. All good science challenges the status quo. When it becomes the dominant theory, it is never the same.

The atheist–Christian debate was once cosmological before it was about evolution. Pope Pius XIIth caused a serious row when he proclaimed the Big Bang as proof of God. Times change.

Recently, an atheist reviewer called an evolution book, "much more than the latest volley in our culture war."[201] This idea of war is part of the underlying and almost sinister problem. Aggression, we are repeatedly told, is necessary. We need to fight. The metaphor appears as distortion in the scientific process. As that book aptly demonstrates, it is no longer possible in the popular venue to discuss evolution per se. Evolution contra creationism is now the only legitimate framework. ID is hooted down as veiled creationism. Battle lines are drawn.

The beautiful purity of evolutionary theory suffers. No longer can evolution be put forth. It must battle creationism. It cannot be shown as it is – much well-established evidence with an aging theory under scrutiny, question and change. It must be stated as a fact; indeed, the aforementioned book states that evolution is a fact six times in the preface alone. Such flag-waving should have no place in science. A believer in evolution might become a skeptic because proponents 'doth protest too much.'

Evolution has characteristics of most other theories. Beginning with valid evidence, it creates valid hypotheses. Valid means explanatory power – it rides the data well. Like all theories, it encounters situations which don't fit. The theory must adapt and the theory has done well. But because of a constant pressure to always be true, to defend at all costs, there is now both rigidity and a tendency to theorize on little evidence. As Jerry Coyne says, "there is an increasing (and disturbing) tendency of psychologists, biologists and philosophers to Darwinize every human behavior."[202] It's called evolutionary psychology, and it may be the bane of evolutionary theory. A corollary tendency theorizes all outlying data into the theory, even if it doesn't match, because 'evolution is a fact.'

The evolutionist story says only the truth should be taught in the classroom. The creationists say that Darwinism destroys morality. But who owns the curriculum? One could envision a more balanced approach – debate them. Teach critical thinking and trust children to master it. Demand it, in fact.

One author, who claims his 'book is necessary,' mentions some variation of the phrase 'evolution is a fact' 19 times in the first chapter. "Evolution is a fact, beyond reasonable doubt, beyond serious doubt, beyond sane, informed, intelligent doubt, beyond doubt, evolution is a fact. The evidence is as strong as the Holocaust…It didn't have to be true, but it is...Evolution is a fact… No reputable scientist disputes and no unbiased reader will close the book doubting it."[203] He mentions creationism over 200 times.

This hostile rejection of God as a tenet of evolution backs the dogmatists into a corner. Any implication of non-physical influence is automatically and without warrant equated with the Judeo-Christian God. It is a principal objection of the book you hold. But materialism trips over the starting gate – what is space but the absence of all material and therefore an immaterial phenomenon?

In a common scientific error, a popular 1970s theory presumes what it sets out to prove. The basic premise – all alleles (genetic variations) are inherently interested in survival. Alleles program an organism's behavior into organisms so as to ensure their own continuation by replication. Any allele failing to properly program its organism will not survive. The premise is tautological – a genetic variation without means of continuing will not continue. Though it doesn't feel that way, we are "robot vehicles blindly programmed to preserve genes."[204] Altruism is repeatedly invoked as a misunderstanding of self-interest. "[T]his must be why altruism by parents towards their young is so common. ... so an animal may be pre-programmed in such a way that it behaves *as if* it had made a complicated calculation."[205] It must be – who can argue with those words? Never mind that such a gene has never been found.

These replicator molecules constructed survival machines (called animals) for themselves to out-compete other molecules. The details of how survival machines emerged are fuzzy, but it has something to do with protein barriers. How they learned to make these is equally fuzzy. The confusing part is that a repeated attribution of consciousness to these molecules is a short-hand for gene behavior. The genes "program the body ... the albino gene should be quite happy ..."[206]

Unbelievably complicated explanations occur when the shorthand is expanded. For example, genes develop 'learning systems' called brains in order to ensure their own survival. It's unclear how genes would choose to build a learning system without choosing to do so. It does make intuitive sense and here is the problem. The shorthand of the conscious gene is graspable. It 'works.' The long-hand is cumbersome, counter-intuitive, and has gaps that fade it into obscurantism. It is a card-house of justification.

We have genes that "invented many ... techniques of human engineering,"[207] followed by a multi-page genetic-math thesis on how a gene might evolve to save ten cousins, but not five. The genes have "conscious aims, [but] we could translate our sloppy language back into respectable terms if we wanted."[208] "[G]enes might 'recognize' their copies in other individuals."[209] The theory still controls the popular science version of evolution and strongly influences the academic version.

Evolution is claimed falsifiable, hence scientific, hence verified. But Popper clearly stated that theories can never be verified. That is the meaning of falsifiability. Biology mouths the platitude of falsifiability, but behaves by the rule of verifiability. This tendency undercuts the validity of science more than anything else – it smells of distinct hypocrisy to the informed student of science philosophy. Thus we have a strong theory like evolution – life flows from one form to another. The idea is almost certain. With all this evidence, we think we can let our guard down and not be rigorous about trying to falsify. But this allows new pieces to free-ride on the more generalized, validated theory. Thus, every trait is interpreted as a survival adaptation under natural selection's empire.

Scientists no longer truly attempt to falsify. No one wants to disprove their theory – it's an emotional blockage. Some try, and scrupulous scientists spend their career proving themselves wrong. More ambitious scientists publish with far less evidence and sloppy procedures. Making a name, their theory folds-in to the meta-theory, in this case, inheritance by random mutation.

"[I]nheritance of acquired characteristics doesn't happen,"[210] the world's most prominent zoologist writes. Experiments disagree. Experts have no lock on scientific understanding. Gregor Mendel's work was ignored because he was not a recognized scientist. Then it was misunderstood. Now it's the basis of genetic theory. Combined with natural selection, it's called the Modern Synthesis of Evolution. That theory is in trouble.

Modern Synthesis

Science is the belief in the ignorance of the experts.
—Richard Feynman

Charles Darwin didn't discover evolution – his grandfather Erasmus told him about it. In 1635, Swedish botanist Carl Linnaeus developed a natural classification system. His graphic system of taxonomy offers visual evidence of relatedness. And if things are related, then that is evolution. Darwin contributed astounding evidence from the Beagle voyage and the almighty mechanism of natural selection. In summary: a common ancestor evolved gradually by random mutation of genes acted on by natural selection (NS) to form new species. NS is helped by sexual selection and genetic drift.

August Weismann, in the 1890s, elevated natural selection to the solitary role it has occupied for so long. What is thought of as evolution in the popular parlance is closer to the Weismann theory. He thought the germ-line (egg and sperm) were generationally stable. The only road to change was altering the germ-line. At the time his ideas were deemed overly restrictive. People favored keeping Lamarckian (acquired-transmissible) traits from Darwin's original theory. (That's right – Darwin was not a neo-Darwinist). In 1900, Hugo Devries introduced mutation, setting the stage. Thomas Hunt Morgan put genes front and center. Combined with the monk Gregor Mendel's work, the Modern Synthesis (MS) emerged. Here, genes are definitively in the cell nucleus. No hereditary action comes from the cytoplasm – the cell medium. In 1911, Wilhelm Johannsen codified it: "Heredity may then be defined as *the presence of identical genes in ancestors and descendants.*"[211] By the MS, germ-lines transmit heredity, and their individual molecular structures in the nucleus chromosomes are called genes. Sexual reproduction creates alleles – slight differences in genes. When these accumulate, more significant phenotype (physical) changes happen. In 1937, evolution was defined as a change in the genetic composition of populations.[212] At the time, European biologists claimed the cytoplasm could carry heredity, but were ignored.

Neo-Darwinism is presented as a fait accompli, but most people accept or reject it with no knowledge of the full evidence: the fossil record, homologous (similar) structures, embryonic similarities, geographical distribution, and genetic make-up. Combine this with discoveries like plasticity, gene networks, and horizontal gene transfer and there's abundant evidence to create various theories of life's processes – for example rapid evolution or directed mutation.

The Modern Synthesis brought together genetics with natural selection. It theorizes evolution through genes, characteristics, and populations. Darwin focused on organisms and speciation. The thought style shift is significant. It is a different theory. According to the MS, an organism undergoes random mutation. Mutations that create survival advantage will propagate. Survival of the fittest is a misnomer. The opaque phrase 'differential reproductive advantage' is more accurate. When a mutation allows more offspring, the gene gains dominance. This genetic heritage drives the animal.

Evolution doesn't properly explain the mechanism. DNA reproduces RNA which makes proteins. These build the animal and sustain it, but the process is shrouded in a hundred layers of fog. No understanding of DNA to organism construction exists, only that amino acids link into protein chains.

This chemical monologue might be a dialogue. Sexual selection already demonstrates this in a gross, external manner. Females choose males based on traits. Often these are non-adaptive, like the disadvantageous peacock's tail. The species is evolving itself.

Supposedly, it's unidirectional – the gene has a profound, almost total, effect on the animal, pushing it down the highway of life, but the genetic changes are random – either acausal or causal without directed focus. The animal has no effect on the DNA. Any directed force to cause mutations is labeled 'supernatural.' This is untrue. If a force can guide these changes, then it is by definition natural. But materialist dogma blocks all such research.

The reverse direction – organism affecting DNA – has never been investigated. Recent mavericks have actually found evidence of it, but still we are assured, "there is no will involved, no conscious striving."[213] None has been found because it is forbidden to look.

To combat such ideas, evolutionists say there would be an obviously directed focus – a goal. The critique is confused – a force can move in a general direction with no precise goal. The animal drives are the direction – survival, reproduction and so forth. In other words, a species could subconsciously evolve itself. All we need is a bi-directionality to genetic mechanism. The idea is no more mystical than acausal mutation.

At the University of Rochester, Barry Hall eliminated a gene that created enzymes to digest sugars in e. coli. Within a generation, the species modified another gene to the purpose. A survival instinct should be investigated as a directed adaptional focus to get food. It makes as much sense as the consistent 'lucky break.' Interestingly, when Hall deleted the new gene, the bacteria were unable to evolve a second time even for thousands of generations. One explanation is a limited evolutionary capacity, which is really a tautology.

Like other fields, theorizing becomes prominent in the face of outlying data. Two studies suggest that females pick males with superior DNA – the preferred theory. But this ignores hundreds of studies which show the opposite.[214] The impetus to believe chooses data preferentially which then pushes into the popular science. Negative evidence is culled by these pre-set beliefs.

The MS has a number of problems. For example, the definition of species is among the most problematic and debated issues in evolution. The working definition is a population reproductively isolated. The definition is neither precise nor firmly stated. Does reproductive isolation occur geographically? Fish splitting at an estuary would be immediately different species. Biologically, it is when animals have no preference for mating with each other. Of course, the male sage grouse happily mates with cow manure. Bacteria, and many larger organisms, asexually reproduce – rendering the definition senseless.

Evolution is said to be directionless, but there is a consistent move from simplicity to complexity. Today's evolutionary biology operates with numerous concepts that were not part of the original Synthesis theory. Since their retrospective inclusion into the well-defined classical framework is impossible, propositions for a new and expanded theoretical synthesis are on the rise.

The most fundamental aspect is failing. When one variable in a theory acts on a second, but the second cannot act on the first, it is called asymmetry. Asymmetry signals a degenerate theory. Relativity corrected this for physics – now space and time affect each other. The problem still exists in evolution. DNA is a one-way street.

Darwin originally believed in acquired transmissible traits. In other words, an organism could gain an ability or characteristic after birth and pass it on to its progeny. Other theorists took the postulate out using Occam's razor. They acted in haste. The razor is not an absolute.

William of Ockam, a monk, proposed that of the two hypotheses, the one with fewer assumptions is probably correct. Mathematically, this means that a probability of 90% (one assumption) is more likely than 90% X 90%=81% (two assumptions). With no way to gauge probabilities, this works well enough, but if we have a single assumption of 70% and two of 90%, then the two assumptions, hence more complexity, are favorable. Otherwise God, being the ultimate in simple hypotheses, would always be right.

Though an excellent principle, the tool is not infallible. Complex realities are forced into simplified explanations. It also has an unfortunate tendency to cut away parallel causes. In this case, the razor cuts away anything beyond random mutation filtered through natural selection by mistakenly assuming that simplicity is the whole truth. Evolution does occur through other means, such as sexual selection. There is no reason to assume that we now have in place all valid avenues of evolution. Life is extraordinarily adaptable and complex – it may have evolved other methods of evolution. Experiments strongly suggest so, but the old guard dismisses it, clinging to a preconceived, streamlined agenda.

The human genome is only 1.5 times that of fruit flies, and only 6 times that of E. coli. The additional variation did not come strictly from our genes.[215] The idea that genes completely determine us and we will be able to manipulate them to set children's traits is called genetic astrology. The original predictions called for genes to directly affect traits. Though most biologists know this is wrong, it has entered the popular imagination so forcefully that it's entrenched. It's strong enough that many high school teachers still discuss it and popular magazines still promote it. Biotech companies make a lot of money on new parents off this incorrect idea.

Most of the exciting research in genetics is funded by biotech companies. There are cancer scares, hopes of immortality through cloning, and desire to design children. Such large economic interests are dictating the research direction and making a promissory materialism they will be unable to fulfill. Still, biology is catching up to the reality of different inheritance systems. What's been known in the cutting edge of research is filtering into mainstream science. It might take decades for it to enter popular science.

Despite the loud claims of genes for particular traits, there is only a mild correspondence. Most traits appear without a gene and vice versa. In only a small percentage of diseases (e.g. sickle cell anemia) is there a direct genetic relation. In one experiment, scientists knocked out a plant gene proven responsible for a particular trait. Nothing changed in the phenotype – the organism possessed a mechanism of compensating for the missing gene. In many cases, exact genes lead to differing phenotypes and differing genes produce identical phenotypes. Genes simply do not equal traits. John Ioannidis analyzed 432 claims of genetic disease correspondence. Only one had any validity.

The myth is shown in its most negative way in the cholesterol scare. Four alleles (A,B,C,D) predict heart disease, with D being the strongest. This gene predicts it most strongly with *low* cholesterol. So those with highest risk (allele D) who try to lower their cholesterol are increasing their risk of heart attack.

Junk DNA was once a popular idea – obsolete genes that just stayed around because natural selection quit using them but didn't throw them away. It's looking like that idea was wide of the mark. The DNA does something, but no one knows what. Most DNA functions are still unknown. So far, all they know is that it transcribes mRNA which in turn makes the multitude of proteins constructing the body.

Likewise, the MS encounters a number of real-world contradictions. There is no record of a 'spontaneous inheritable genetic mutation' that caused a differing physical trait. To be clear, there have been numerous cases where plants and animals are specifically bred to enhance specific traits. All mutations (as opposed to genetic variations) observed thus far have been negative, mostly fatal. Animal breeding is incapable of creating a new species. It either exhausts variety or hits a sterile offspring. A necessary component to 'prove' evolution, a genetic mutation resulting in a new species, has not been verified.

Morris Goodman at Michigan University found that the DNA of a crocodile was much closer to a chicken than to a snake. This is counter to the evolutionary 'fact' that species in a class (reptiles) are genetically closer than to species in a different class (birds). There are greater variations between species of frogs than between a bat and a blue whale. Another problem in the theory: the complexity of the animal should be mirrored by genetic complexity. But a garden snail has more chromosomes than a human. So does a goldfish.[216] The plain plant adder's tongue has 1440 chromosomes - over 7 times the second place and more than 10 times almost any other species on the planet. These facts refute some of the most basic evolutionary tenets. Pointing this out does not make someone a creationist – it makes them a scientist.

Physical structures make the problem worse. Homology is among the best evidence for evolution, but it has significant problems. Homology is the idea that the similarities between species must have underlying genetic correspondences stemming from common descent. Why are there similarities between a hand, a claw, and a paw? Oddly, common features are correlated to different genes in those animals. To say that genes are the source of transmission of common traits requires that the similar traits map to a common genome. But they frequently don't. Even worse, identical genes create distinct structures. [217]

Phenotype change can be rapid – blue-headed wrasse, for example, can change gender. If the male dies, the largest female becomes a male. Their gender is not genetically pre-determined. The MS fails to account for such rapid changes of form, origins of structural novelty, and the establishment of homologous character complexes called body plans.

And there is still no understanding of aging – all 20th Century theories are overturned. (Telomeres, or gene terminators, hold the most promise currently.) Researchers are starting over with complexity assumed rather than simplicity. Likewise, there is no plausible theory to explain sexual reproduction – the Modern Synthesis predicts asexual reproduction overwhelmingly – it's more efficient. Again, the theories were overly simplistic. Sex does not provide a single function in current theory – it provides many.

Neo-Darwinism is a 'random generator and filter theory.' In 1979, Gould and Lewontin challenged it with the notorious free-rider problem. They used a church analogy. Arches bear weight and spandrels decorate arches. Without knowing the mind of the architect, we assume the spandrels are extras, free riders on the arches' necessity. But it is unverifiable – it assumes a hypothetical world where, if churches could be built without arches, they would also lack spandrels. In the example, we could ask the architect, but we cannot ask natural selection. The critical point – when two traits are co-extensive, always occurring together, natural selection theory cannot prove which trait was selected for. It can only speculate.

For example, were polar bears selected for being white or matching their environment? The two different traits are co-extensive in the far north. At first blush the difference seems minor, but natural selection is a conceptual theory. If the concepts cannot be properly parsed, then the theory lacks the precision necessary to claim truth. "The moral is selection for problems need to appeal to counterfactuals [hypothetical worlds] if they are to distinguish between coextensive hypotheses."[218] But a hypothetical world, by definition, has not been experimentally confirmed.

A worse consequence – one of the two traits is selected for, but what does the selecting? All theorists rely on the metaphor of artificial selection, or breeding. Though they try to remove the 'mind' they fail. And natural selection has no mental process. Thus the analogy is false. Natural selection cannot make choices.

Challenges to evolutionary theory come from many angles, not just creationism. Fodor and Palmarini challenge natural selection – it is not law-driven theory, but merely interpretation of the history of species. As such, it's empty. Among the problems of adaptation theory are "its failure to distinguish utility [of a trait] from reasons of origin ... unwillingness to consider alternatives to adaptive stories ... reliance on plausibility alone for accepting speculative tales ... failure to consider such competing themes as random fixation of alleles, ... non-adaptive structures [arising with] selected features ... separability of adaptation and selection, multiple adaptive peaks, and current utility as epiphenomenon of non-adaptive structures."[219] We don't need to go into all these things – but it's critical to realize the endless possibilities of life to see that we don't yet get it.

In theory, phenotypic traits are connected to the environment by fitness to reproduce. But if natural selection theory cannot tell the difference between the free-rider and selected trait, then it cannot account for the phenotype. The problem breaks down as follows: natural selection either must be intentional – having a mental design process – or it requires natural laws to operate. These don't exist. We have stories about evolution, but nowhere are there inviolable laws – meta-operations superseding all other processes. No specific trait is better for fitness; it all depends on the environment.

But the environment is merely the entire planet. The local ecology is pointed to as the determining factor. Adaptationists gush about the 'exquisite fitness' of creatures to ecology. But ecologies are not separate from inhabitants; they are defined by them. Adaptation is not necessary to explain 'exquisite fitness' because it's not real. Any phenotype that still exists is by definition adapted to its environment. If the phenotype were absent, the ecology wouldn't exist. There would be no niche to adapt to. Fitness to ecology is not empirical – it is tautological. It 'predicts' that organisms will survive that have traits that help them survive. Thus fitness is not from natural selection, but from definition. Moreover, creatures modify ecology – humans certainly do. So do beavers and viruses. We sneeze when ill – spreading the virus.

Another confusion is the notion of selecting for traits. But phenotypes aren't 'bundles of traits. They're fusions of traits.'[220] Natural selection can't select traits – it can only select organisms. A change in a trait affects the phenotype in many ways, not just one as specified by theory. Explanations about inherited characteristics sound sensible in the context of historical narratives, but they don't rely on a framework of natural law.

Another strike is the 'problem of adaptation.' Evolutionary instances are called 'solutions' to older problems. The theory is thus non-falsifiable. Because it is assumed that every trait solves a problem, a trait emerging without random-generate and external-filter causes is conceptually impossible. If no problem is found, it is plugged in as non-adaptive rider on an adaptive trait, but such a situation cannot challenge the NS theory of population genetics.

Even one of the founders questions the theory of population genetics. Using evolutionary math, Haldane's dilemma shows that it takes 300 generations to fix a beneficial mutation in higher primates. It proves that the claimed rate of evolution is impossible under Modern Synthesis assumptions. Moreover, the rate of mutation is 999 negative to 1 positive. Another calculation shows 1.5 negative mutations per human which should result in error catastrophe – species degeneration, unless the species is young.[221] But then it lacks the time to evolve, hence the dilemma. The math stems from the idea that things are incremental and genetics is the driver. That idea is being challenged.

There are biological arguments against NS as well. The Darwinist idea is that a series of gradual, random mutations in an organism are selected for fitness. Unfortunately, there are a number of internal constraints on the phenotype. Each one restricts natural selection from performing its function. In other words, the traits are selected by genetic and epigenetic operations and internal biological processes before encountering the environment for selection. The more these restrictions apply, the fewer opportunities natural selection has to operate.

Non-selective adaptation occurs, too. In an example ridiculed for years, Conrad Waddington put flies in hot environments. Their eyes grew larger for no adaptive reason. It's been replicated many times.

Another bizarre non-adaptive trait – certain reptiles produce 100% females in high or low temperatures and 100% males in median temperatures. Any selective advantage is unclear, probably absent. "Selection without adaptation, genetic assimilation, genotypic and phenotypic plasticity, contingency, sudden explosions of new forms, transposable elements, epigenetic regulations, and interchangeability of reactions, internal and external factors"[222] are all non-adaptionist mechanisms for evolution. This number of mechanisms should require a serious assault on the reigning theory – it cannot account for them.

The saltation hypothesis comes from the Cambrian explosion – a huge increase in species in the fossil record. The MS attributes this rapid expansion of variety to older species having no hard tissue, therefore not appearing in the fossil record. New biologists believe this was a dodge and say the explosion was quite real. Implications are that evolution can jump – it's not restricted to incrementalism. 'Punctuated equilibrium' originates most new species in a geological 'moment.'

Two experimental findings militate against natural selection as the primary force of evolution – conservation of genes and gene complexes. Many genes have survived intact for millions of generations and exist across millions of species. Obviously, this comes from internal constraints on those genes – they never mutated to be 'selected for' even when performing different functions. Gene complexes work in concert to create a multitude of phenotypic traits. Simplistic change in a single gene almost never modifies a single trait – that is a neo-Darwinian myth. Few biologists subscribe to such a theory anymore, but it defines the popular belief.

The standard MS mechanism of micro-evolution does not create distinct phyla – groups of species with common traits. These must come about through gene-complexes. "Large effect mutations act on conserved core pathways of development. The connection between specific biological traits, specific evolutionary dynamics, and natural selection is complicated at best, impossible at worst."[223]

Many recent discoveries disagree with natural selection. Robustness means a trait does not correlate with ecological changes, thus meaning it is not tied to fitness. A master gene controls a number of different traits. If NS selects one of these traits, then a host of unselected traits come along. Those other traits will create a much greater load of phenotypic change than the selected trait. This directly opposes the random mutation of a gene creating a single change in the phenotype. It's simply not possible. Mutation, especially in a master gene, creates a number of phenotype changes. The problem is one of real complexity versus desired simplicity. Organisms are complex, coordinated units, not 'sacks of selectable traits.'

Evolution has many endogeneous (in the body) factors. As evidence of these piles up, the known internal constraints on the phenotype become greater, leaving less and less for natural selection to do – if an organism can never grow a third arm, natural selection cannot act on it. By accumulating many mechanisms for the fixation of phenotypes, any central theory of evolution falls apart. It cannot be a unified track with a causality so varied. The theory has simplified legitimately complex processes into a single idea – natural selection. It's like pointing to a radiator and calling it a car.

Evo-devo

Darwinism is not a testable scientific theory,
but a metaphysical research program.
—Karl Popper

Opponents question many MS assumptions: heredity solely by transmission through the germ line; solely from recombination and mutation; heritable variation has only small effects; unit of selection is the gene; phenotypic innovations are a result of cumulative gene mutations; targets of selection are individuals; evolution is a matter of descent with modification from a common ancestor. The emerging new field is called evolutionary developmental biology, or in stylized 21st Century lingo – evo-devo.

By focusing on the complexity, evo-devo destroys the project of biological reductionism. Simplistic computational models of population genetics cannot solve the complexity of genotype-phenotype creation. This was known by the creators of population genetics. Since this is the basis of the Modern Synthesis and since it cannot accommodate the findings of evo-devo, a revolution is occurring.

The 'epigenetic turn' which began in the 1990s has three components: the structuralist approach (generative plasticity); the Waddington approach (genes as followers in evolution); and the heredity-oriented approach (soft epigenetic inheritance).

The laws of form, in one example of the structuralist aspect, exist everywhere – spiral shells, sunflower patterns, and cauliflower buds draw a precise arc called the Fibonacci sequence. Natural selection cannot be the mechanism – such patterns are found in galaxies and other inanimate forms. In other words, it's a super-ordinate law of physics forcing the phenomenon, not a rule of fitness to survive.

Within the laws of form we find optimal solutions to phenotypes, but these shouldn't occur. Locomotion, the structure of leaves, wing movements, and neuron mapping have optimizations – the perfect solution. The lowly nematode has an optimal brain architecture – neurons are arranged for the shortest possible dendrites, hence best communication. Out of 40 million combinations, random mutation could never chance upon the optimal one. Natural selection predicts a good fit, but never the perfect one.

Prominent biologist Mary Jane West-Eberhard summarized the Waddington approach: "genes are more often followers than leaders in evolutionary change...phenotypic novelty is largely re-organizational rather than a product of innovative genes."[224] It's a shocking statement directly contradicting the MS. It's called *plasticity*, a huge topic – e.g. self-organization. The idea, from physical chemistry, is the ability of molecules to arrange themselves in complex forms. Most biologists do not understand it – it is not easy. Because of this, the phenomenon is marginalized, although it has a profound presence in phenotype formation. It extends to larger forms. Even Stuart Kauffman says that self-organization is the primary source of biological order.[225] This force is not recognized in the MS.

New biology perceives the failure of simplistic assumptions – life is too complex for tidy summations. One of the big mistakes in older theory is the common ancestor. It is assumed since so many organisms share DNA there must be a common ancestor. The mistake should have been realized decades ago, when Barbara McClintock demonstrated transposing genes. Unfortunately, she was mocked, but her recognition could have led to a much earlier knowledge of horizontal transfer – genes moving from one organism to another. Up to 45% of our genes were inserted by other organisms, then carried down through countless species. In symbiogenesis, two organisms merge to make a new one. This modifies the classical theory of competition and replaces it with cooperation. Evolution, Dr. John Dupré said, is "much more about mergers and collaboration than change within isolated lineages."[226] He challenges the tree of life model, calling it a web, rather.

Another new biology term, *evolvability*, means an organism can adapt towards the environment. Through evolutionary capacitance, silent mutations accumulate but are not expressed in the body. When the population encounters environmental pressures, the constraints come off and adaptations quickly occur. Evolution can thus be far more rapid than previously thought.

A related property missing from the Modern Synthesis is *emergence* – or the arising of traits not in the constituent elements. There is no wetness in hydrogen or oxygen, for example, yet combined properly they are water. All systems display emergence in innumerable ways. Part of emergence is downward-causation, or the ability of the system to affect its parts.

Emergence fairly shouts the ultimate failure of reductionism – properties of a system flatly do not exist in the components, therefore reductionist principles cannot predict them. An atom has no color, but a group of them do. In physics, even mass, space and time are considered emergent. Since the MS is definitively reductionist in ascribing overwhelming control to genes, it is mistaken. This recognition is on the horizon of biology, but is fiercely resisted. "An irreducible downward causal power cannot be due to micro-level potentialities," Mark Bedau explains. "Such powers would be quite unlike anything within our scientific ken. This will discomfort reasonable forms of materialism."[227]

The standard system is too basic in light of the intricacy of molecular biology and of cultural systems. Further, molecular biology heaps scorn on the simple one-to-one correspondence theory of characteristics. Genes interact with each other and other cellular systems to the point that a gene means nothing in isolation, but only by its place in the overall structure.

Genes switch on and off. How the system knows to do so is a mystery, though material causes are always assumed. Neil Shubin at University of Chicago in 2004, working on the Tiktaalik, a 375-million-year-old fossil from Canada, discovered that the "genetic machinery needed to make limbs [is] already present in fins."[228] The implications are enormous. Primate limbs are *previously encoded* in the genetic structure of an ancient fish – 300 million years before primates appeared. This is a potent challenge to the random idea of mutation. And it destroys the belief in strict genetic correspondence to traits.

Evolution alters developmental processes (genes and gene networks) to create new and novel structures from old gene networks. Phenotype is not fixed by genotype – we're not skin-bags for DNA. Physical change can appear first, forcing genetic change. In 1917, D'Arcy Thompson claimed that differential growth rates could produce widely divergent body parts – fins or feet – rather than different genes. It took 80 years for his ideas to be taken seriously.

The 'genetic-developmental toolkit' operates gene regulatory networks – and it has deep similarities in organisms of radically different architecture. The complexes involved in making animals as different as a fruit fly and a human being are fundamentally the same genes. The toolkit was already there in the ancestry. "The same genes are used over and over again, just in different ways and combinations. And we're using a ridiculously small number of genes."[229]

The real secret to variation lies in the gene regulatory network. Proteins turn genes on and off at different times and locations. They regulate the strength for different amounts of gene expression. The operation is extraordinarily complex and poorly understood, but at least now it is acknowledged. The developmental-genetic toolkit holds the 'master' genes. These few genes control torso segmentation, placement and growth of limbs and body plan. They are the same in different phyla. In other words, neo-Darwinism is wrong. Variation in form is not reflected in the genes. The genetic mutations intended to account for species *never occurred.*

Michael Skinner, epigenetic researcher at Washington State University, showed that exposure to pesticides in rats creates an extremely high prevalence of multiple diseases in off-spring who are never exposed to the pesticides. Such epigenetic changes often occur with no change in genome. Children conceived during the Dutch famine of 1944 were much shorter than average – and so were their children.

Jablonka and Lamb challenge the genetics-only stranglehold that has dominated evolution for fifty years. Among their assertions – other causes contribute to heredity, information acquired during a lifetime can be passed on, there are non-random factors, and changes in evolution happen from inner instruction as well as natural selection.

"Coding sequences are only a small part of DNA and DNA is just a small part of the cellular network determining which products are produced. It depends on what goes on in other cells and environmental conditions. It is so complicated that it is impossible to predict what a person will be like merely by looking at their DNA. Genetic astrology is a dream."[230]

One fact known by few non-biologists – RNA is capable of rearranging DNA. It can chop, splice, move genes around, and it does so frequently so that individual cells in a body have non-identical genetic information. The immune system has radically different DNA.

Geneticist James Shapiro disagrees strongly with the establishment, citing this evidence. The ability of the body to restructure its genome may not be restricted to somatic (body) cells, but could also occur in germ-line cells. It's an enormous proclamation. Evolution can be essentially guided. "Rather than being restricted to a slow process of random, blind genetic variation and gradual change, we are now free to think in realistic molecular ways about rapid genome restructuring guided by biological feedback networks."[231]

Plenty of experiments show that genetic variability is not completely random. Randomness as a sole source of genetic mutation is not well-evidenced – it is assumed. (Mathematicians can't even prove randomness is real.) Biologists who suggest otherwise are treated as heretics. An example of complexity: cellular processes 'proofread' DNA and correct mistakes. The error rate is 1 in 10 billion nucleotides. Without this system, it would be about 1 in 100. Directed mutation is the biological term.

Note that even a contrarian still offers fealty to materialism. They are very careful to point out that they are not positing God. Fine, but we do not know that immaterial causes are non-existent. It is a scientific approach to look, see, hypothesize, and experiment – but the fear of God blocks any such research possibility. Science has lost its courage.

Though all biological processes are explained in strictly chemical terms, we still find gaps in the record, openly acknowledged, and a linguistic formulation implying sentience. It seems the only way to explain the phenomena.

There are a few types of directed mutation. The most common form is increased rates of mutation due to environmental stressors. By the mainstream view, a lack of resources increases the error rate, leading to higher mutation. But this fails to account for local hypermutation. Specific parts of the genome mutate at thousands of times the main genome rate. Randomly created changeable mutation rates are nonsensical.

Hypermutation defies the mainstream logic that evolution only favors the individual and never the species – most mutations are negative, so a higher rate would punish the individual organism. Local hypermutation favors species survival, not individual survival, by creating high numbers of phenotypes, most of whom will die, but a few of which will be selected by the stressor conditions.

By central dogma, DNA is a one-way process – DNA to RNA to proteins – nothing swims upstream. DNA cannot be affected by chemical or biological processes. In more flexible theories, acquired characteristics can be transferred by non-DNA methods. It's a huge deviation from the old school. But in spite of strong evidence, it's sailing into the wind of dogma.

These systems are extraordinarily complex – all sides agree. The origin of the systems is a vexing question – one with various answers which only kick the can backwards. Where did the processes which led to these non-genetic processes come from? No one can ground the explanation in DNA. And that's a problem for the Modern Synthesis. It cannot explain the creation of any cellular-level directed process. It denies their existence as a matter of principle. This ongoing, fundamental problem assaults the baseline of materialism.

In fact, non-DNA inheritance is proven in any complex species. If the DNA is exactly the same in all cells, then why are there different organs? DNA alone should create exact copies of a single cell type. It's called cellular inheritance. It works through extra-genetic material. It lives in a wider field of study called epigenetics.

"Epigenetics," a prominent biologist explains, "is a modish buzzword now enjoying its 15 minutes of fame in the biological community."[232] The old guard stands firm here – new discoveries are scornfully dismissed. But it might be helpful to peek under the hood of this 'modish buzzword' to see if the criticism is accurate.

Epigenetics is one of the most complex fields in existence. To approach it, a 1960s paramecium study will help. Tracy Sonneborn, an American geneticist, surgically altered paramecium by inverting their cilia (the wiggling arms). The offspring inherited the surgical mutation, disproving the dogma of genes-only inheritance.[233]

Four types of epigenetic systems are currently known. Self-sustaining loops turn genes on or off and this continues in the cellular reproduction. In structural inheritance cellular structures are transmitted, as in the above example. Chromatin-marking systems attach molecules to DNA to make it behave in different ways. RNA interference manipulates genes. The last was noticed when genes were spliced and no effect happened. At the cellular level, RNA suppressed the genetic innovation – a downward causation denied by the MS.

Epigenetics goes back billions of years – existing in most bacteria and all single-celled eukaryotes. In spite of extraordinary complexity, it had little evolutionary time to arise. Some of the systems may have been around as long as life itself. One idea is proven wrong – that biological time scales are all that is required for such complexity to arise. These time scales are patently too short. As consequence, epigenetics struggles for recognition – it threatens the Modern Synthesis.[234] And the MS has powerful political allies who write best-selling popular science books.

Aside from genetic and epigenetic, Jablonka and Lamb have two more modes of evolution – behavioral/cultural, and symbolic/linguistic. Newborn ducks will follow a string pulled on a shoe, then bond to it like a mother. Baby rabbits fed by adoptive mothers that eat carrots are more likely to eat carrots than rabbits with non-carrot fed adoptive mothers. Behavioral inheritance systems are curious. It's absurd, Jablonka and Lamb point out, that animals wouldn't learn from other animals. These behaviors are not encoded in the genes.

The presumption that animal cultures are too simplistic to transmit hereditary information is unjustified. Endless experiments show socially learned behaviors in animals.

Behavioral theories have not come into vogue because they are not sexy enough to entice funding. If the direction is toward laboratory projects, then field research cannot gain validity and research withers. Because of the belief that all inheritance is genetic, cultural evolution is flatly denied. The genes-only theory has smothered evolutionary science for decades.

Symbolic/linguistic inheritance is for humans only, they contend. It is simply the ability to understand conceptual fields – language. All notions of a 'language gene' are unlikely – and without evidence. But the reverse is not false. Though no gene exists for language, a language of genes is undeniable. And it carries a big mystery – no one knows its origin.

The Secret Code

Fanatical atheists' intolerance is the same as religious fanatics, and it springs from the same source.
—Albert Einstein

Atheist astronomer Fred Hoyle, calculating the information content of life at $10^{40,000}$, gave similar odds against abiogenesis – life from non-life – in a finite universe. The co-founder of DNA believes life came from outer space – there are fossilized bacteria in meteors. Still, in order to have any kind of life as we know it, a planet needs to "be in a right kind of galaxy, be in the right place in the galaxy, have the right kind of star, be the right distance from the sun, have a proper mass, spin, and tilt, possess a magnetic field, the right atmosphere, and abundant water." Astrophysicist Hugh Ross calculates that "fewer than a trillionth of a trillionth of a percent of all stars will have this." Since the known universe has about a hundred billion trillion stars, this math leaves only a 1 in a thousand chance of any planet in the observable universe being capable even of supporting life, much less of its appearing.[235] Whether Ross is right or wrong, the origin of life is anything but simple. It's assumed to be reducible to material causes – but immaterial causes are not probed. In fact, they are ridiculed. Of course, like every other biology question, the origin of life pivots around the hinge of DNA.

DNA is a language of enormous complexity. It has four letters with limitless combinations. The unproven idea that this beautiful, sophisticated code arose purely by accident is not fully satisfactory. Random occurrence equals non-causality. It is not possible to prove a negative. The belief cannot be verified and is mathematically impossible. Therefore many scientists desire research into other possible causes. It is true that ID proponents have pushed this agenda as proof of God, which it in no way is. It is a very strong argument that something beyond the strictly material is occurring, but that could be many things. A promising doorway is quantum entanglement. We know that some connecting principle, inexplicable by current 'laws' of physics, operates in this domain. There is no logical reason to insist that it vanish at the molecular level, particularly in specialized sets where phenomenal complexity and order reign. Good luck to any scientist pursuing such research – they will probably not be significantly published no matter what they find. And research monies will be scarce.

There are many other troubles with any theory of life's origin. Materialist theories have the following unexplained problems. 1) Labs can duplicate early conditions and even massively cheat by injecting DNA and RNA into cells – still no speciation occurs. 2) There are 500 enzymes in every cell, needed by DNA to reproduce, but DNA constructs the enzymes. It's a chicken-and-egg problem. 3&4) Mitosis, or cell-division, is extraordinarily complex. Without cells, there is no means of protection for DNA – it would have been destroyed. There is no mechanism for teaching a cell to divide – and no idea how the first cell chose to do so. Without mitosis, there is no meaning to DNA replication – it has nowhere to go. How did DNA get in cells and teach them mitosis? 5) Random amino acids and sugars in solution will be both left and right-handed molecules, but in organisms all sugars are right- and proteins left-handed. 6) The formation of DNA, at millions of base pairs long, is formidable odds – ages of the universe. Antony Flew, atheist turned theist, describes a statistical thought experiment. If every atom in the universe were programmed to randomly put together letters into sonnet length at 1 million sonnets per second, it would take 10^{600} universes to generate one poem of Shakespeare by now. Monkeys actually typed 50 pages without a single word – not even the letter 'a' or 'I' separated by two spaces. A gene is exponentially more complex than a sonnet.

DNA's only provable function is the production of amino acids. These are simple enough – each one comes from three adjacent base pairs in DNA. The 21 amino acids join to make the vastly more complex proteins. But there are 64 combinations of three base pairs, leading to 'degeneracy.' Degeneracy means the third DNA position, for many of the amino acids, can be changed without changing the amino acid produced. It's a kind of molecular magic. It's highly resistant to point mutations – a fiercely robust and desirable feature. The process is a self-administering, standardized, nanotechnology code with this degenerate mutation protection in a particular place. No one has the faintest idea how it got there and why it works, but the 'accident' theory looks more and more like a dodge.

For example, there are $1.5X10^{84}$ genotype possibilities, trillions of times the number of electrons in the universe. Such is the power of combination. It rapidly exceeds the ability of random generation. The simplest viruses have more than 2,000 base pairs. This makes it quadrillions of times more complex than inorganic molecular systems. This leap in complexity is an unaccountable mystery of biology. Mostly it's dismissed with the weird non-explanation that it's just an old problem.

Stanley Miller and Harold Urey experimented in the 1950s with organic compounds in water. Running electric currents through it, they came up with amino acids. These are 10^{50} less complex than the simplest DNA – a long way short of life. What would cause a self-replicating molecule to arise without external impetus? DNA has no known intrinsic method of copying itself. Attempts to create replicating RNA have failed. Some idea suggests that naked RNA is the first life form, although there is no such life-form today.

Bartel and Szostak provided evidence for a mechanistic origin of life. They passed bits of randomized RNA sequences (300 molecules long) through a solution. After a few passes, catalyzation occurred. It's a mile short of the goal line, but it's a good extension of the earlier experiment. However, it still presupposes large pools of RNA floating in the prebiotic soup with reagents at hand – a pretty big leap. The processes themselves are manipulated in numerous ways that belie natural conditions. Left alone, most of them move away from life-formation. In can be argued that the experiments suggest Intelligent Design – after all, that's what these researchers are doing.

At any rate, there is only one form of DNA – made by four binding molecules. This strongly suggests a singular origin. Thus life probably only occurred on Earth once. Under any scenario, for life to originate is extraordinarily unlikely. There is no reason to rule out an alternative to the materialism hypothesis. It is possible that life originated in part from non-material causes. This does not require God.

Other theories exist, such as David Bohm's holographic universe or morphic resonance. Both theories rely on some pre-existent awareness. It is no less plausible than immensely complex molecules spontaneously organizing into self-replicating entities which evolved and gave rise to consciousness.

In all biology, we find a linguistic implication of sentience – "Something is recognized by an enzyme…the enzyme ignores sequences."[236] 'DNA is referred to as the language of life and things are said to be written in our genes.' Who does this writing? Who speaks this language? It's acceptable to use metaphor for ideas, but when the metaphor dominates the dialogue, one wonders why. Perhaps it points to a deeper reality. The metaphor is used because there are no concepts to explain what is 'really happening.' There is no understanding how the process could be strictly material. We get DNA with 'efficient memory systems.' We are talking about a different level of awareness – we cannot see it in the way we envision it. Yet it still behaves as if it is aware. "A protein that recognizes the problem is activated."[237] How does it recognize it? What activates it? Nothing can do this without awareness.

It's an oblique angle on Intelligent Design. The resistance to such research speaks poorly of biology. If an idea is incorrect, it should be shown wrong through experimentation, not censorship. Richard von Sternberg, former Smithsonian editor, published a peer-reviewed article arguing in favor of soft Intelligent Design based on the Pre-Cambrian explosion. The article was done under standard scientific procedure – peer review. Sternberg was castigated, subjected to inquisitorial processes on his beliefs, barred from his research materials, and removed from his job. A formal inquiry showed it was retaliation. The most absurd point – he didn't believe in ID. But being a good scientist, he thought it merited scientific discussion.

The human genome director, Francis Collins, believes in theistic evolution. Faith and science for him are completely compatible. Evolution does not provide evidence for God, but the moral law does. It's the sense of internal goodness and guidance we feel and the desire to help others. Even if we disagree over particulars, we feel some sense of right and wrong. This culminates in *agape*, the powerful upwelling of emotion in the face of overwhelming goodness. This is his evidence for God.[238] He's not the only prominent biologist–Christian.

When considering "the impossibility of conceiving this immense and wonderful universe, including man, as a result of blind chance or necessity," Darwin wrote, "I deserve to be called a theist."[239] He vacillated between logics and finally settled on agnostic, but Darwin claimed he hadn't been comprehended properly. Towards the end of his life, he said there could be other factors. "Mind has always existed as the matrix," Nobel Prize-winning physiologist George Wald said, "physical reality is constructed of mind-stuff."[240]

Life, in its endless complexity and beauty, cannot be forced to fit into any set of words and ideas. Inconsistencies will leap out immediately and everywhere. Darwinism as theory is neither true nor false. It is a heroic, insightful, vigorously researched and well thought out early attempt to explain the process of life's adaptation. It may still be the best map we have, but that does not make it true. It only makes it the best guide available *thus far* to navigating a difficult terrain. It needs more flexibility from its prophets. It needs to become more robust and able to handle the outlying data. The task is difficult, but that is the task. The best approach would be to drop the above assumptions and let some creativity surge through the discipline. Like most challenges in science, it is a political problem.

In its broadest formulation, only evolution is sensible. Life changes and is related to all other life. Biologists have not discovered the entire means of its adaptability. Genetic coding could turn out to be a lagging, rather than a leading, indicator. Other forces could be at work. An inability to conceive them does not mean they are not there.

Paradigms without Progress

The act of observation creates the entire universe.
—Jim al-Kalil, physicist[241]

Thomas Kuhn is one of the most important science philosophers of the 20th Century. He rejected the notion that science is a slowly building edifice – knowledge added to more knowledge – as we rise higher and higher. Science is a paradigm-driven operation. The paradigm occurs by solving a key intractable problem. Once established, practitioners fill in the universe around it. It gathers force and detail, solving more problems. But there are always anomalies. Though mostly ignored or shelved, when enough accumulate, the discipline has a crisis.

A new paradigm arises to challenge the old one. If the new wins, the process reinitiates. The field can split or add other fields. Logical induction and the like exert great force, but random social ideas appear, too. A new paradigm is not 'rational' nor is it 'progress.' Kuhn compares Aristotelian time-space as closer to relativity than Newtonian, for example. After the shift, normal, non-crisis science shoehorns the natural world into the new paradigm. This is then imprinted on students.

The randomness of ideas is not negative – it is the creativity of science. Without it, science flounders directionlessly in the data ocean. But it's not pointed at truth. The idea of science finding the truth is philosophically impossible. When we look back at discredited systems – Ptolemaic astronomy or caloric theory – are they unscientific because they were wrong? If they are scientific, then science is not synonymous with discovery of truth. Otherwise, it could not persist in error for so long. Any system now could be overturned at anytime. Therefore, such a theory is either non-scientific or science cannot move strictly at truth.

The notion that science 'completely understands the world' causes serious problems. The 'correct' view must be defended. Non-conforming research is culled and even suppressed, as Kuhn shows.

Once a paradigm emerges, certain data fall away. Former problems seem irrelevant – the question for biology 'what is the force of life?' is no longer sensible. At early stages, widely different interpretations of the same data are common. They fuse over time. A paradigm is born. Its survival is only loosely correlated to its robustness – it can merely solve a prominent problem (dark matter), be pushed by a prominent authority (HIV / AIDS) or ride a feeling of excitement (neuro-science).

New paradigms stand on shaky legs. They have solved a clear problem, but still must account for all other data and should break new ground to thrive. Such 'mop-up operations' become the life's work for most researchers. Data is forced into the paradigm. The focus narrows enormously – individual research studies the finest detail imaginable. Huge resources strive to establish theoretical parity with nature.

The larger aim of research is to experiment within the paradigm – to prove it. Science is at heart a puzzle-solving endeavor, hence the focus on utility over meaning. A predetermined result is sought. If an experiment fails, the researcher is always at fault – never the paradigm. Without desired results, experiments are discarded along with data. In this way, evidence is forced into the paradigm, rather than paradigm adjusted to evidence.*

The proper criterion for research becomes a 'solvable problem' – unsolvable ones are labeled not scientific. Not fitting in the paradigmatic phrasing, they become metaphysical, rejected as category errors. This is restrictive, but functional. Science needs the paradigm to focus. Nevertheless, much is excluded. The paradigm trumps all other forces.

Examples used to discredit often become the new theory. Robert Boyle is recognized for inventing the chemical element – but he was trying to prove they didn't exist. Curiously, wrong assumptions often lead to new ways of seeing. Lavoisier's 'principle of acidity' merged with caloric, or heat particles, to produce oxygen. Now, the notion is laughable, but it was necessary to break the old paradigm. The Leyden jar came from the now-dead fluid theory of electricity and was critical in the establishment of the modern theory.

New discoveries always encounter forcible resistance from the paradigm. An experiment illustrates this. People were given card decks with black hearts. They couldn't understand at first and 10% never understood what they were seeing. Paradigms restrict perception; it is their function. Anomalies accumulate, though. These are assimilated into or overturn the paradigm at which point they become the expected. Old paradigms hit a crisis – then they can be more easily overturned.

---

* The psychological definition of homosexuality is a fascinating example. Psychologically, all difference from the normative state were presented as pathology. There was no healthy deviation. Tellingly, the change came from without – a group of homosexuals stormed a psychology convention to force a rewrite.

Crisis stages are identifiable. Disagreements become widespread as theoretical constructs multiply. Simplicity vanishes; complexity rules. Contradiction overwhelms. Hypotheses appear and disappear at a ferocious pace.

In a crisis, the criteria for determining the hierarchy and properness of questions lie outside the discipline. The crisis resolves only when a new paradigm emerges to address the central problem. Without a replacement, the crisis continues. It can lead to the death of the discipline.

In academia, textbooks present cases as if they proved the theory. But that belief comes from mere authority – instructor and text. Lacking the critical skills of the discipline, students accept teachings on faith. In the process, they are inducted into the paradigm. The exercises are not proof – they are training for following the field. In learning the system, theory always precedes evidence. But paradigm does not equal truth. As has been repeatedly shown, a given set of data can be adapted to many contradictory interpretations.

A paradigmatic view is necessary for analytical perception. The question becomes: does objective data present itself and theory interpret or is data subjective, as well? Before Copernicus, no moving objects were discovered in the night sky. After, many were soon found.* After such changes as Lavoisier discovering oxygen, the scientists literally inhabit a different world – one with oxygen. Perception creates the worldview. Without a concept, a phenomenon cannot be perceived. Some South American natives were unable to see ships on the ocean or planes in the sky – they lacked a concept. Likewise, any experiment demands a tight data focus with a consequent enormous data exclusion. But reality does not dictate levels of importance in data. It is a subjective choice.

According to reigning epistemology, raw data emerges from experiments on nature. A framework upon that is called knowledge. Kuhn's paradigm-change epistemology disagrees. Old data lack the context. Old questions and problems no longer apply. Mental perception is restructured.

John Dalton revolutionized chemistry. Before him, chemistry combined elements in percentage amounts. Dalton combined in whole number ratios. He calculated atomic weights and wrote the law of constant proportion. Here's the interesting part: Dalton was not a chemist. He invented these approaches to solve a problem in his field – meteorology. It's a key lesson. Because

* The Chinese had found these centuries earlier – with a non-fixed theory of celestial objects.

he was not constrained by the paradigm, he solved a deep problem that chemists were unable to even perceive.

The scientific psyche virtually disposes of history. Science is seen as a smooth upward movement rather than a series of upheavals and junking of washed-out paradigms. When old theories are looked at, they're seen in a sad and archaic light – past scientists were a bunch of bewildered kooks. But they were excellent scientists and their theories were just as true then as our theories are now. Revolutions occur by alterations in the "formulations of questions and answers more than novel empirical discoveries."[242] Textbooks mask these changes in perception, presenting a linear view of science. It obscures a fundamental process. Because only the latest theory survives a crisis, science manages a mystique of progress.

No hard line shows an impending crisis. If any anomaly meant rejection of a theory, then all theories would fail. Anomaly-free theories do not exist – even mighty general relativity has flaws. New paradigms rewrite areas of investigation. Newton's theory of gravity discarded any statement of the underlying mechanism of gravity. Newton removed a question from physics.

Because two mutually exclusive paradigms cannot exist simultaneously in one field, the scientist must switch suddenly and completely. For this reason, many older, entrenched scientists never change. Paradigm shifts mostly come from young people – they are not as deeply imprinted with reigning ideology. As Max Planck said, "a new scientific truth does not triumph by convincing its opponents and making them see the light, but rather because its opponents eventually die, and a new generation grows up that is familiar with it."[243] This can leave a field in confusion for decades.

This stubbornness ironically makes a field advance. In normal times, researchers patiently chip away at a problem, confident in their paradigm's robustness. But in crisis, this manifests as stuckness. The process lends the discipline an illusion of its own sentience. Though the totality of science exhibits order, challenges old theory, takes new directions, and serves human utility, no single researcher engages in those activities. They are meta-activities arising from the whole.

Art was once cumulative – it had 'progress.' Skills were discovered and added to repertoire in an effort to move toward perfect realism. The word 'art' applied to scientific endeavors. Creativity was a scientific virtue. When no school could dominate as 'correct,' art moved from progress to expression – no longer 'science.' In science, competing paradigms cannot co-exist – one is retired in favor of another. This factor creates an illusion of progress. The end of an art school makes it fully explored – not wrong. The end of a scientific paradigm makes it invalid – not fit for theoretical study.

A new theory must extend beyond current data and observed phenomena – otherwise it has nowhere to go. Normal science then tests the extensions through experimentation. Numerous examples defy the idea that science is cumulative knowledge. Newton discarded mechanisms of gravity for sheer description – a regress. He had no explanation for what gravity was, only how it operated.

It's an open question if an old system is now wrong or different. Did Einstein overturn Newton? One could say Newton is a special case since relativity math reduces to classical mechanics. However, the fundamental posits do not. Space is no longer fixed, and is inseparable from time. The systems are mutually contradictory.

Often scientists are attacked with their own theories. Descartes put forth the idea of corpuscles to link mind and matter. His corpuscles are gone, but materialism is still fundamental. Descartes was a dualist, believing in mind and matter. His thriving empiricism was used to undercut his dualist philosophy. Ironically, half of Descartes' duality destroyed the other half. Likewise, Newton's theory was turned on his most precious belief – God. He believed his orderly universe proved God; now it's cited as disproof.

Consensus Deceptus

What used to be called propaganda now plays
a major role in shaping public opinion.
—Al Gore

Apparently, anthropogenic global warming (AGW) can cause mosquito-borne disease, tsunamis, resource shortages, and increases in terrorism.[244] The catastrophe looms large in society: "Agriculture will fall. A third of species face extinction. Millions will be at risk of floods. Heat waves, droughts, floods, and wildfires…" It's all four horsemen rolled into an invisible trace gas. It keeps getting worse – "billions of us will die and the few breeding pairs of people that survive will be in the Arctic," said environmentalist James Lovelock. But in 2010, he recanted – "everybody might be wrong."[245]

In a 2007 document released in the US Senate, 400 scientists spoke out on AGW.[246] All were skeptical of alarmist claims. The updated 2009 paper featured 650 and in 2010 it was over a thousand. 27 were authors for the IPCC – the leader in climate change promotion. Several were Nobelists. Hundreds were climatologists, physicists, and meteorologists. Here is a sample of their statements.

"Warming is not a big deal" – Dr. John Everett, IPCC lead author. "[It is] a blatant lie in the media that only a fringe of scientists don't buy into anthropogenic global warming" – Atmospheric scientist Stanley B. Goldenberg, NOAA. "There isn't a consensus among scientists" – Dr. Charles Wax, State Climatologists President, ret. "The quantity of CO_2 we produce is insignificant" – Dr. Philip Lloyd, IPCC lead author. "[Alarmism is] the worst scientific scandal in the history... When people come to know what the truth is, they will feel deceived by science and scientists" – Dr. Kiminori Itoh, environmental chemist. "I am a skeptic…Global warming has become a new religion" – Nobel Prize Winner for Physics, Ivar Giaever. "The scientific method has been abandoned in this field" – Atmospheric Physicist Dr. John Reid.

It's not new, either. This is from 1996 – "I have never witnessed a more disturbing corruption of the peer-review process than this IPCC report. 15 sections were changed or deleted to remove skeptical statements, e.g. 'None of the studies has clear evidence [to] attribute the observed changes to the specific cause of increases in greenhouse gases.' Whatever the intent, the effect is to deceive policy makers" – Frederick Seitz, former president of the National Academy of Science.[247]

"We have to offer up scary scenarios, make simplified, dramatic statements, and make little mention of any doubts we have," NOAA climatologist Steven Schneider said, looking for "the right balance between being effective and being honest."[248] A number of IPCC members have resigned in protest over conclusions. Lead author Richard Tol said the organization had been 'captured.'

As long as they worked for the IPCC, even skeptical scientists are still used as part of the 2500 consensus scientists, a blatant deception. Climatologist John Christy engineered the first survey of satellite temperatures. A lead author for the IPCC, Christy agrees that CO_2 has an effect on the climate, but disavows any catastrophe. "Our own research indicates that alarming changes in the key observations are not occurring."[249]

The International Panel on Climate Change *is* global warming. They write the poster document (the assessment), and a team of mostly non-scientists writes the real document: the summary for policy makers. The most important AGW document, the summary is put together by government and NGO reps, with a token handful of scientists. Tail wags dog – the assessment instructions are to match the summary's conclusions. Professional authors of IPCC papers are seldom climate scientists. They include medical doctors, entomologists, graduate students, and uncredentialed dilettantes. In fact, none of the 2007 lead authors on health effects of global warming had ever written a paper on climate change.[250]

An article about the WGII IPCC group found "of the 70 US contributors, there were 7 economists, 13 social scientists, 3 epidemiologists, 10 biologists/ecologists, 5 engineers, 2 modellers /statisticians, 1 full-time activist (and 1 part time), 5 were in public health and policy, and 4 were unknowns. 17 worked in Earth/atmospheric sciences."[251] By the IPCC's own statement, only 20% of its scientists have any climate credentials. The president, Dr. Pachauri, has a PhD in industrial engineering and economics.

A report written for the IPCC by two pro-AGW authors denies the touted agreement. "The consensus that human activities are having a significant influence on the climate is reached by only a few dozen experts."[252] Of 23 reviewers, only 5 agreed that man-made CO_2 was forcing climate change. For another claim of consensus, the National Academy of Science and American Meteorological Society issued pro-AGW statements. Members were not allowed to vote on these statements, however.[253] Consensus is not a silent act. Most scientists have never made any official statement about global warming – *that does not imply agreement*. But it is deceptively presumed to be so.

In a poll of meteorologists – "Most of the warming since 1950 is likely human induced" – only 25% agreed. 29% felt global warming was 'a scam.'[254] Even Patrick Moore, co-founder of Greenpeace, has become a skeptic and complains of politicization of AGW.

Climate change is not a scientific issue – it's a political one. Three state climatologists were threatened with job loss for AGW skepticism. The primary spokesman for the American Meteorological Society has only the unscientific credentials of former Al Gore staff. The prestigious National Academy of Science allowed backdoor nominations. Only candidates who endorsed Global Warming didn't have to be voted in. Once in, they joined all groups and vetoed decisions, even on non-climate topics, from scientists who disagreed with AGW. They also were elected to executive council and one of these people is now the President of the entire organization.[255] MIT's atmospheric physicist Richard Lindzen calls it a takeover. In May 2010, the 1,000-scientist letter above was answered by the pro-AGW contingent when 255 NAS members published an angry response.[256] Most of the signatories are biologists. A few are paleoclimatologists.

260 physicists petitioned their own American Physical Society for "an independent, objective study," which was denied in violation of the group's regulations.[257] University of California emeritus physics Professor Hal Lewis resigned from the group with a scathing letter claiming politics had trumped science.

Freeman Dyson was attacked for cautious skepticism and physicist Will Happer was fired from Princeton because of skepticism. Skeptics have been compared to Holocaust deniers. Climatologist Tim Ball has received death threats. A popular liberal blog called for executing climate skeptics.[258] Skeptics have been accused of taking about $10 million from big oil, but it's neither proved nor criminal. AGW research, by contrast, has been funded by $50 billion – a 5000-to-1 ratio. One environmental group received $12 million from BP. Big oil money supports AGW theory.

It's a financial boondoggle – Enron helped write the Kyoto protocols. The cap-n-trade market is estimated to be worth more than a trillion – Goldman Sachs runs the carbon exchange. Al Gore has a cap-n-trade software company. If the legislation passes, he'll be a multi-billionaire. Lord Monkton challenged him to debate the issue, but has received no response.

The US Climate Action Partnership writes legislation seeking lower greenhouse emissions. It includes a number of interesting corporations – DuPont, AIG, British Petroleum, Conoco, Alcoa, Chrysler, Ford, GM, Dow Chemical, and Shell. Chicago Climate Exchange, European Climate Exchange and others all have similar members, including coal companies. Oddly, this rogue's gallery of pollution is accused of funding the skeptics.

"I live a low-carbon life," one skeptic wrote. "I have a small, energy efficient house, I don't drive much, and I grow my own food. They should be mad at hypocrites like Al Gore and Sting, who talk about warming and have multiple mansions, private jets, and large entourages. If AGW is real, then their heroes are the worst offenders."[259]

Expert opinion should be taken into account. The unfortunate tendency is to take it solely into account and to buy into easy formulations like, 'the consensus of opinions concludes...' Unfortunately, the 1950s are over – blind faith in authority is no longer a smart option. Each citizen must be savvy to his own understanding. We have to dig deeper and not accept facile answers in the search for truth. Theories come in layers. We are presented with the seed: CO_2 traps heat and correlates with temperature. Without additional details, the premise makes sense – if CO_2 traps heat, then more of it must trap more heat until the effect runs out of control. We're not given both sides of the debate. We're merely told there is a consensus of scientists, but no proof is offered even for that. Expert opinion is hedged to make it appear unanimous. It's a rhetorical fallacy – the self-sealing argument – which admits of no means to debate it. Every point is falsely interpreted to support prevailing theory. Anyone outside the consensus, for example, is a lunatic, a self-serving right-wing capitalist, or in oil company pockets. Any evidence they present, even if validly established by mainstream research, is rejected. Carefully inspected, information turns out to be disinformation. In science, this pattern occurs as often as not. The old ideals no longer work.

Apocalypse Soon

In searching for a new enemy to unite us... the threat of global warming fit the bill. The real enemy, then, is humanity itself.
—The Club of Rome, 1991

If the 1920s War of the Worlds fiasco showed us anything, it was that the masses are easy to fool and the media is easy to manipulate. We think people then were naive, but maybe things haven't really changed so much. A substantial body of skeptics offers evidence that anthropogenic (man-made) global warming is deeply flawed science based on a grain of truth.

Here is the basic AGW theory. For the past century, planetary warming exceeds variable cycles of the past millennium, thus cannot be natural. The majority of warming since the 1950s is from greenhouse gas emissions. The limited CO_2 warming will be roughly tripled by positive feedback of methane, water vapor, and lost albedo from ice melt. This will increase temperatures as much as 10°C by 2100 – and possibly tilt us into climate catastrophe. Negative effects of warming dwarf positive effects and this has begun. We must act now because even a small risk warrants a massive effort.

CO_2 and temperature do have a correlation, and a strong one. More detailed geologic measurements upended the theory – but were ignored. In a non-controversial finding, *Science* magazine showed that the presumed causation of CO_2 to temperature is reversed in actuality. Temperature rises precede CO_2 rises. *The most basic assumption of AGW theory is wrong.* CO_2 rise comes after temperature change. (See figure 9, next page.) In spite of this, Al Gore used the graph to imply the opposite. "All that the lag shows is that CO_2 did not cause the first 800 years of warming, out of the 5000 year trend," RealClimate.org says. "The other 4200 years of warming *could* in fact have been caused by CO_2, *as far as we can tell* from this ice core data." Thus, they save the theory with a speculative fog. The IPCC report ignores this lag by claiming that nothing 'definitive' can be said. This is deceptive – temperature rise definitively preceded CO_2 increase in every study.

All parties agree – initial heating releases oceanic CO_2. AGW claims that the CO_2 then 'takes over' the initial cause and drives the warming. Skeptics argue that the original theory is falsified – CO_2 was the initial cause. Now that is disproved, so the bull's-eye is simply being repainted to salvage the theory.

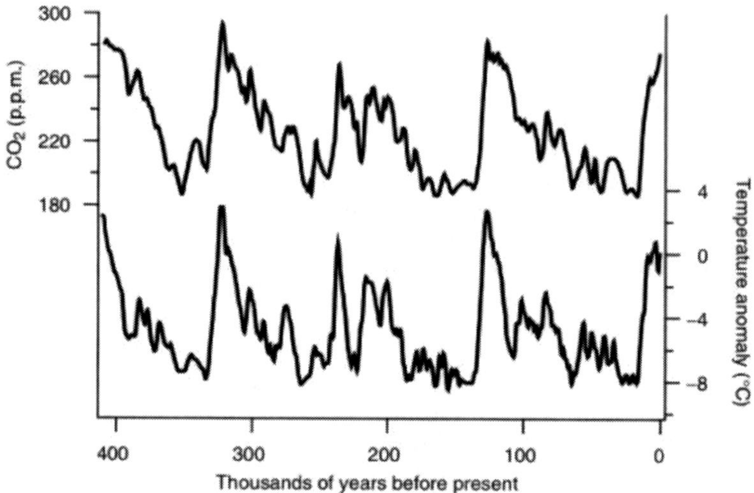

Figure 9.

Water vapor is the most abundant and potent greenhouse gas by far, accounting for 95% of the greenhouse effect. CO_2 is weak. CO_2 warming is asymptotic – it's capped. A doubling of the gas would increase temp by about 1.5°C. It's further weakened because it absorbs only a narrow band of radiative frequencies. Beyond a certain level, CO_2 will be absorbing all the radiation it can and will have no further temperature effect in spite of any increase. CO_2 alone cannot cause a runaway greenhouse effect. This is not contentious. AGW theory posits force multipliers – increases of water vapor and methane – from the limited CO_2 warming. This is based on computer models, and, as we shall see, is thoroughly speculative. The idea has no real-world evidence at all.

The climate is phenomenally complex. The greenhouse argument grossly simplifies it from an established truth – CO_2 absorbs heat and correlates to geological temperature changes – to a fantastical hypothesis – less than a thousandth of the atmosphere will heat up and overwhelm planetary systems. Even the IPCC doesn't say that, but they let the public believe it.

A popular comparison, publicly voiced by Bill Nye the Science Guy, is the Venus argument. Venus is hot because of a runaway greenhouse effect, so it could happen to us. The missing points – Venus gets 3 times the sun's energy, its atmosphere is 96% CO_2 vs .038%, it has no life, and the atmosphere is 93 times as dense. Any comparison is nonsense.

The backbone of AGW is twofold – known natural causes allegedly cannot account for all the warming seen. Not being able to think of another cause, AGW is presumed. Second, computer models have been adjusted until they match the history. Pre-programmed to assume CO_2 is the climate driver, this is exactly what they find.

In the 1970s there was a global cooling hysteria. The same consequences as warming were predicted – massive famine and desertification. The globe was cooling, but the catastrophe never happened. Most anthropogenic global warming skeptics take a similar position about the current alarmism – warming is happening, but it's not a runaway disaster. It's probably not even a bad thing. Warm weather correlates well with increased wealth and agriculture.

The moderate skeptic believes it is incremental. It will amount to about 1.5°C over a century and never spiral out of control. Of course, the phenomenon has been rebranded climate change. This is a ruse to mask the lack of real warming. The entire CO_2-bad theory rests on accelerating heat content of the Earth. If that acceleration cannot be found, then the problem is a will-o'-the-wisp. Giving it another ID is a marketing ploy. It still relies on warming – no other cause has ever been proposed.

But all the ice is melting! "Stay calm," said a Nobel Laureate in physics, "Earth will heal itself."[260] Glacial retreat has been happening since the 1850s. The retreat has actually slowed in the last 30 years. It makes little sense to blame another cause from 1850-1950, then claim that cause stopped and AGW took over to continue the same trend.

The idea of melting ice causing sea levels to rise is incorrect. Arctic sea ice is floating – even if it all melted it wouldn't raise the oceans any. In fact, it might lower them because ocean rises are due to temperature increases. Adding that much water at near freezing would drop temperatures. The IPCC says that oceans rise by heat expansion of the water – all Greenland ice-melt goes right to Antarctica. Any rises go back 150 years and have been in a consistent trend. Gore's prediction of 20 meters is not backed by IPCC, which claims 4-12 inches by 2100. While the smallish Antarctic peninsula is indeed melting and warming, the main continent is cooler than in the 1950s and adding about .5 cm of ice each year, thus lowering the ocean level.

A number of studies show that Arctic ice declines have been happening for hundreds of years. Glaciers in Alaska have done likewise. On the day the lowest reported ice in the Arctic was reported, the highest ice in the Antarctic was recorded. The media only reported one. Arctic temperatures were higher in the 1930s than now. In fact, there was a global warming scare then. And a cooling scare in the 1890s.

Storms aren't increasing either. Chris Landsea, IPCC hurricane researcher, resigned in 2005, blaming "an unsupported agenda that recent hurricane activity has been due to global warming." He said there was no increase. Atmospheric science professor William Gray believes anthropogenic climate change is so slight as to be meaningless. 1900-49 saw 101 hurricanes, he notes, while 1957-2006 saw only 83. The increase in storminess is a myth.[261]

Meteorology science shows that storms come from temperature differentials, and warming will lower those differences. Global warming should lessen storms. The trends show no increase in droughts, floods, hurricanes, or tornados, only an increase in reporting. In 2009, the total hurricane energy index hit an all-time recorded low.

In historical warmings, there were longer growing seasons, more rain, and increased arable land. The same will happen again. What we hear are increases in storms and rising sea levels, neither well established. Tornados have increased in frequency, it is claimed. Detection equipment has dramatically increased, however. A look at large, category 3-5 tornadoes , shows no increase at all, in fact it declines steadily from 1973. The government data used in *Inconvenient Truth* came with a warning on the site – "be careful with this data – the trend is a result of measurement changes."

Mann made

In theory, there's no difference between theory and practice.
In practice, there is.
—Yogi Berra

Most AGW proponents use surface temperature data. They ignore atmospheric and satellite data. However, greenhouse theory claims that the lower troposphere should experience the greatest temperature increase – that's where the CO_2 is. But the troposphere is warming at a much lower rate than the surface. Moreover, the Southern hemisphere experienced only one-third the warming of the Northern – flying in the face of the theory. It should be evenly distributed.

NOAA and GISS, the US temperature gathering stations, both adjust their measured temperatures upward, by about .3°C the last decade. This adjustment accounts for most of the 'warming' in the US. "The cumulative effect of all adjustments is approximately a one-half degree Fahrenheit warming," the NOAA website tells us. In other words, the temperature rise was not actually measured – it was 'adjusted' from the raw data.

The temperature data is not released, blocking replication studies. East Anglia's CRU destroyed most of its surface temperature data, claiming lack of storage space. Phil Jones of the climate-gate email scandals wrote that he would delete the raw data before sending it for a legal Freedom of Information request. This is the principal charge and it is a serious one – the data is public property and it is not a state secret. The requesters wanted to independently verify the claims of the IPCC. All they had to do was release the data. If they had committed no wrong, they could have defended against charges of fraud.

Other problems exist. Temperature collection stations have severe data distortion. They are supposed to be in grass and open-air situations. People have photographed these in hot parking lots, next to metal buildings, air conditioning exhausts, jet runways, and even an outdoor incinerator. The Tuscon station is in the middle of an asphalt parking lot – adjustment is less than 1°C.

CO_2 is still going up while temperatures have been going down for 10 years. (See figure 10.) Cooling is warming, it seems, making the theory pretty much non-falsifiable. It's reasonable to ask if such statements make sense.

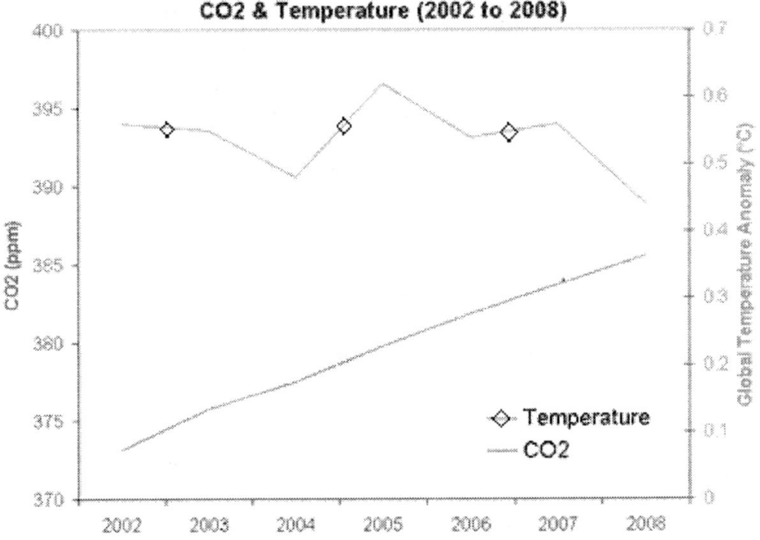

Figure 10: Rising CO2 (NOAA) vs. falling temperatures (GISS)

The current warming has been happening for 160 years. Warming occurred in the first half of the 20th Century, due to natural causes. When CO_2 began its big upward push in the 1940s, Earth cooled for 30 years. The AGW theory has no specific reason for the initial rise (or subsequent cooling), but assumes the mystery force stops and is replaced by AGW in the 1980s. As the graph shows, however, the prior temperature rises at roughly the same rate as the latter. (See figure 11.)

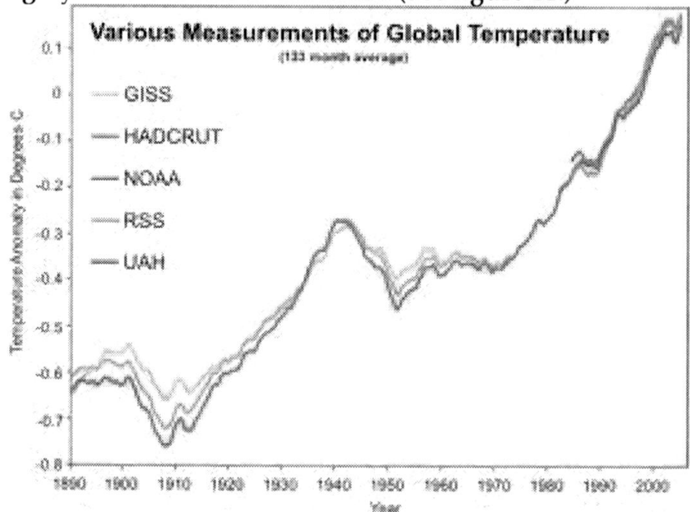

Figure 11.

Then there's the big one. The infamous hockey stick graph comes from Michael Mann. (See figure 12, next page.) It shocked the world and woke everyone up to climate catastrophe. It's now mired in controversy and openly acknowledged as fatally flawed. Skeptics call it fraud.

The sharp rise at the end comes from temperature data, while everything before comes from tree ring data. It's not credible science to graft together 2 data sources – tree ring proxy data with the surface temperature record.

Rings are used to determine past temperatures. The comparison set was from 1960 to 2000 – when temperature records were good enough to use. This was then extrapolated back 1000 years, assuming the growth would be linear with respect to age and to variations in temperature. But this bases the extrapolation on a tiny data set – not valid practice. Tree rings only grow for about half the year and during the daytime – they are useless for the rest. They say nothing about Earth's primary climate – oceans. Rings can be affected by rainfall, soil erosion, plant cover, wind, etc.

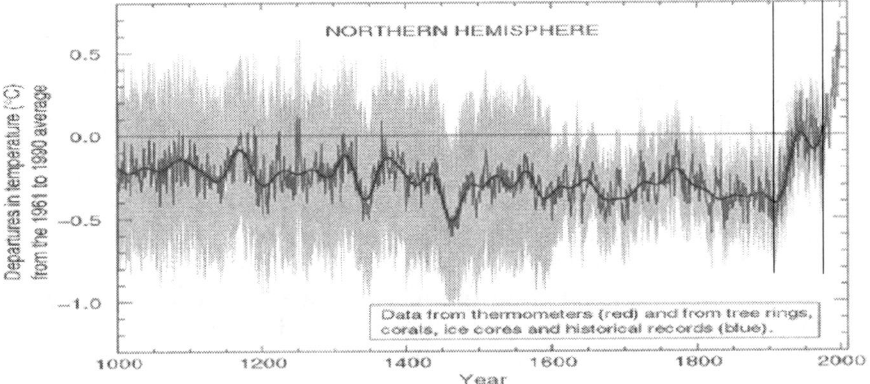

Figure 12. Mann's hockey stick. Left vertical line begins temperature data. Right vertical line ends proxy data.

It's probably why temperature records diverge from recent ring data. The 'divergence problem' is critical. The claim is that proxy data worked well until the time we could confirm it against solid temperature records – then it failed. Or from a different perspective – the only correlating data falsifies the assumption. So the assumptions somehow worked in the past when they can't be checked, then quit working when they could. It's absurd. Tree ring data is a Rorschach – any preconceived idea can be mapped onto it.

The IPCC said not to use tree ring data to determine past temperatures. The hockey stick graphers used such data, and preferentially weighted supporting data over contradicting data by 390 times. The IPCC used the hockey stick graph extensively (as did Al Gore) in spite of their noted disavowal of the methodology. The source data was withheld. A FOIA request took it from a file on the author's computer labeled CENSORED_DATA.

McIntyre and McKitrick obtained the software used to produce the hockey-stick graph. In a number of trial runs, random data always produced a hockey stick pattern. They had difficulty publishing because *Nature* magazine, meanwhile, instituted a policy of non-publication for papers questioning the AGW hypothesis. The magazine refused to make public the methods for the hockey stick article. When published, M&M caused a scandal – Congress investigated and three analysts confirmed their accusations.[262] Though vindicated scientifically, they are not welcome in the climate community.

Both sides hold Mann's analysis to be flawed, but his ideas still drive the science. It verges on the criminal because the hockey stick wiped out the known climatic record – the Middle Ages were warmer than now. The IPCC even said so in 1990. Unfortunately, this fact roundly discredits any catastrophic AGW theory – it had to go. Meantime, the well-established little ice age had to go, too. Otherwise, we would be coming out of its long cooling trend and reverting to the mean. And that's the real scandal with the Hockey Stick.

Tree rings, ice cores, and the historical record demonstrate a medieval warming period. Growing seasons were longer. The Viking burial ground in Hvalsey, Greenland is now under permafrost. The AGW proponents claim that the little ice age and medieval warming were isolated to Europe – they ignore historical data worldwide. (See figure 13.)

Other proxies contradict the claim. Carbon dating of sea sediment in the Bermuda Triangle shows temperatures 1.2°C

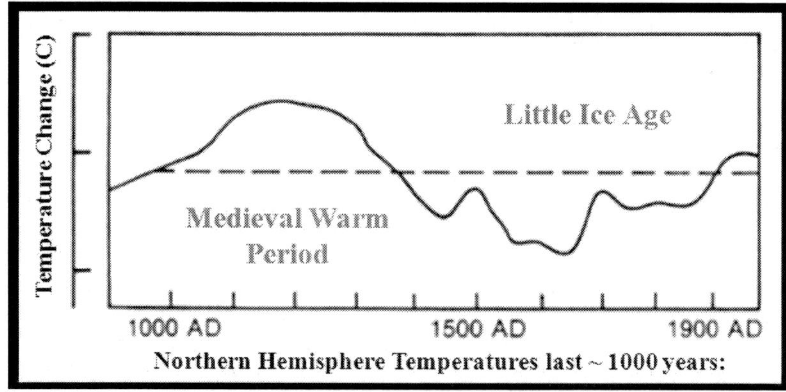

Figure 13: 1990 IPCC 1000-yr temperatures.

lower in the little ice age and 1.2°C higher in the medieval warming. (Temperatures were 2.4°C warmer 2,500 years ago.) De Menocal showed even greater variation off the West African coast. Peruvian glacial ice cores show the same. Kuo-Yen Wei found both periods in sediment dating and tree rings in China. The Japanese historical record (freezing/thawing of lakes) synchronizes with the two periods. The Australian record shows muted, but still present periods – the greater water content would have dampened the swings. Idaho, Argentina, South Africa – all show both periods through a variety of proxies.[263]

Mann was replaced by Keith Briffa. His proxy data (ice core, tree rings) showed a decline in the last 50 years. He threw the data out, with "the assumption that it is likely to be a response to some kind of recent anthropogenic forcing."[264] It's called cherry-picking the data. Here are his two results, reconstructed by the same team that exposed Mann. The rising line is adjusted from measured values. The dropping line uses proxy data. (See figure 14.)

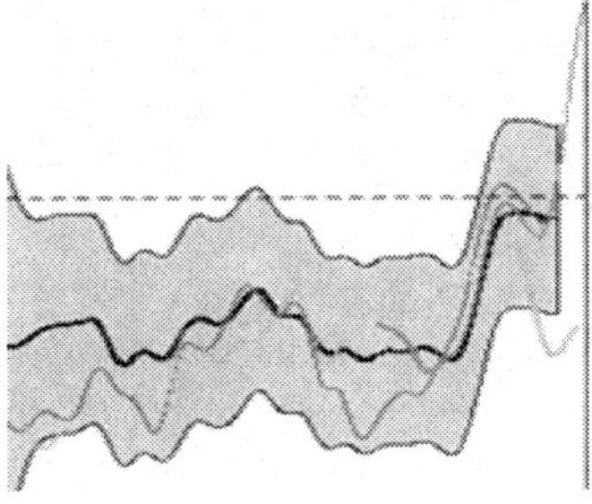

Figure 14.

The IPCC has jettisoned plenty of disagreeable evidence. Its Cambrian record shows CO_2 twenty times higher than today. Yet obviously there was no runaway effect. Earth reverted to the mean.

Models and predictions

All models are false.
—George E.P. Box, statistician

All climate fear is based on modeling. Computer models failed miserably to reconstruct historical data. Constants were inserted, then adjusted. Parameters modified, inputs tweaked, until the model, which assumed a priori that CO_2 alone causes warming, matched the record. But adjustable parameters dispute the validity of theories. Based on these results, computer modelers claim to accurately predict the future.

They cannot. In 1961, Edward Lorenz was doing mathematical modeling for weather. As is common, a groundbreaking theory occurred through a trivial accident. A bit lazy, he entered data to 3 instead of 6 decimal places, an insignificant change in values. He got wildly differing results. The classical idea could never predict this.

The implications are profound. All systems have this chaotic disorder built in. Slight changes in value create enormous, rapidly escalating behavioral differences. It violates the cherished idea that a deterministic universe is understandable by a sophisticated enough calculus. The complexity exponentially buries any system in short order. For weather, a doubling of processing power gives an extra two days of forecasting power. A redoubling adds another two hours. "Chaos is a reversal of the classical view that underlying laws are what count and local perturbations are trivial. In chaos, local perturbations can be overwhelming and you cannot tell when they about to overwhelm."[265] This butterfly effect shows that a tiny change in assumptions can lead to huge differences in outcome – it is the truth of all chaotic systems. Computer models can be made to do anything. Anything except give an accurate prediction.

The models don't find that CO_2 causes warming – they presume it. No alternatives are ever modeled. This is the first flaw. All models also assume a stable temperature based on the hockey stick idea. If either idea is wrong, then the models are wrong. The models drive all the predictions and all policy decisions. One skeptic compares it to a money-laundering scheme – legitimacy comes from passing it through the model.

Most models double the actual amount of human CO_2 – otherwise they would fail to find a problem. More dramatic predictions get attention. The media doesn't cover the 'slight change' outcome – it's boring.

The models are tweaked to fit the past, then presumed to work for the future. James Hansen's 1988 model perfectly fit the prior data and is wildly divergent since then. Year 2000 models are overshooting by around 100%. (See figure 15.)

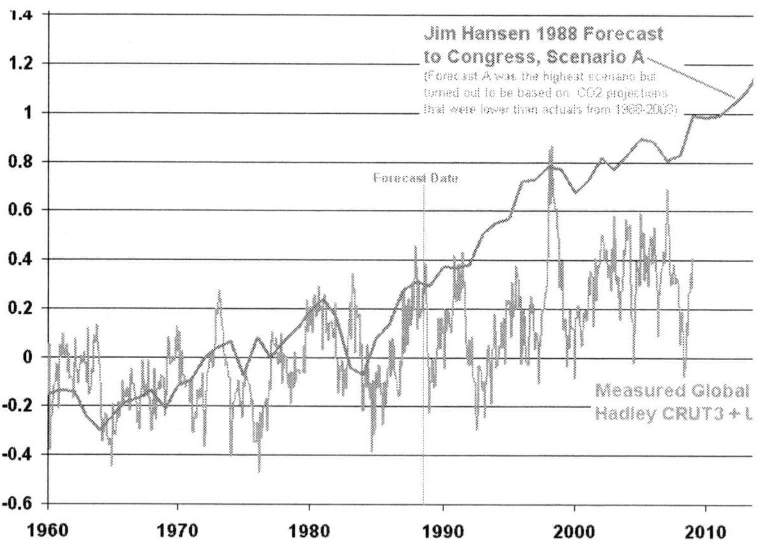

Figure 15.

This is corrected by aerosols, which theoretically reflect heat – though the phenomenon has no evidence. Each modeler plugs in different parameters to retrofit their curve to past data. Then the large divergences can be blamed on aerosols. Adjustable parameters are the saviors of bad theory.

All models and theory predict greater increases in troposphere temperatures than surface – that's where the CO_2 is, so it must warm first. No observations match this prediction. Satellite and atmospheric temperature records agree – the troposphere has not warmed as much as the surface. IPCC does not use atmospheric and satellite measurements – only surface. IPCC lead author Richard Lindzen says they're about as reliable as a "ouija board."[266]

The science of turbulence is among the most complicated. It has the shortest predictive window. It is also the science underlying weather and hence climate change. Hedrik Tennekes, Research Director at the Royal Netherlands Meterological Institute, claims it is ridiculous to make long-term claims on a science that does not predict anything beyond a few days. He rejects the "blind adherence to the harebrained idea that climate models can generate 'realistic' simulations of climate."[267]

Even formal predictions are made with no evidence. The 2007 IPCC report claimed Himalayan glaciers would be gone by 2035. This came from a non-profit leaflet and was shown to have no basis in science – the glaciers will last for hundreds of years in the worst case. The report, which won the Nobel Prize, also claimed the shrinkage was 135m per year. It is only 23. The UN climate science panel claimed weather phenomenon were linked to global warming – but a weak correlation forced a retraction.

The IPCC estimates that global warming would destroy 40% of the Amazon rainforest came from a World Wildlife Fund pamphlet. It had no scientific basis. In 2010, IPCC underestimated Antarctic sea ice by half. The claim that Africa would experience a 50% reduction on rainfall over the next ten years was based on a consumer advocacy statement. The IPCC believed that 55% of the Netherlands was below sea level. The Dutch authorities clarified this error, noting that only 26% was below sea level.[268]

The models have an even worse common flaw – positive feedback is assumed. CO_2 has risen from .028% to .038% or 1.36 times. Temperatures have gone up .6°C since 1900. Because CO_2-heat is a suppressive cycle, a rise to .056% (double the start) would work to a rise of another .6°C. This sensitivity of 1.2°C for a doubling of CO_2 is a median AGW estimate. Such a result would bring no problems to the planet. It would even help grow more food. The max increase would be about 1.5°C. (See figure 16.)

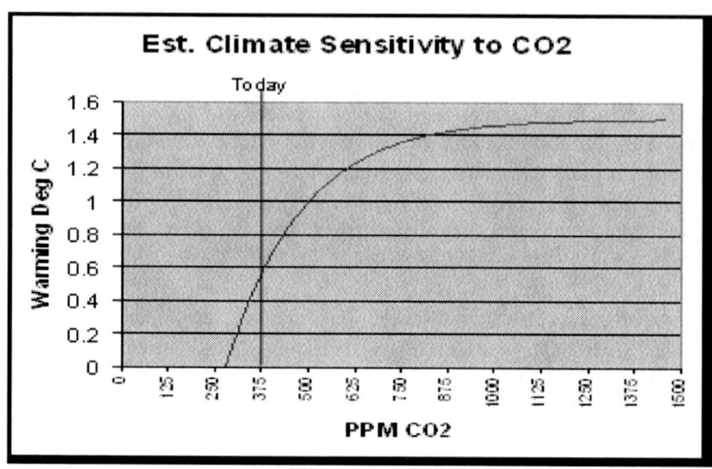

Figure 16.

Like 99% of natural systems, climate is negative feedback. Input forces are constrained by the system – nothing spirals out of control. The system dampens inputs. AGW, by contrast, is hypothesized to be positive feedback – against any evidence, normative theory, and collected climate data. The IPCC claims that climate sensitivity of 1 by CO_2 jumps to 3 when combined with other factors – leading to runaway warming in the models. The climate has been stable, within a range of temperatures and much higher CO_2, for a billion years. If a process has such undeniable stability, it is not scientific to posit a sudden overwhelming reversal of that trend for no valid reason.

To keep it scary, we need a positive feedback system. Lost ice reflectivity, humidity, and methane make models spiral out of control. Besides the lack of current evidence – higher temps, humidity, and much higher CO_2 in the past have never caused this spiral. We are not changing a law of nature.

Water vapor is used as a powerful feedback mechanism, a force multiplier to get awful predictions. However, the IPCC admits that it doesn't know whether water vapor is net rise (humid air) or decline (more clouds reflecting), though it's probably a balance considering long-term stability.

Aging models overestimate the water vapor and methane now being measured. Methane increase is tapering off and water vapor is actually declining. Since this is a critical aspect of the out-of-control feedback process, models should be revised, or better, scrapped.

The pernicious mistake is the nature of CO_2. It's simply not a pollutant. CO_2 is the lifeblood of the plant kingdom. It's a trace gas – less than one molecule per 2,000. All gases are greenhouse gasses. Oxygen, water vapor, nitrogen – if it has mass, it absorbs heat. CO_2 is being framed. We don't even produce that much. Animals, bacteria, and land produce 430 gigatons/yr, and oceans 332. We make 29 – about 4%.

The major miss is the sun. Ignoring the sun in global warming is ridiculous – it is the source of all energy in any form on the entire planet – hence the only real climate driver. Yet ignoring it is exactly the contention of AGW – the sun has no variable effect. When the sun is considered, the Maunder minimum – a time of no sunspot activity – correlates strongly with the little ice age. Sunspots are colder spots, which sounds counterintuitive. Why would colder spots make it hotter? Sunspots indicate increased solar activity, so while the spots are cooler than the rest of the sun, the overall output is greater – and that's the key measure. Solar activity, by official data, is much stronger in the last half of the century. (See figure 17.)

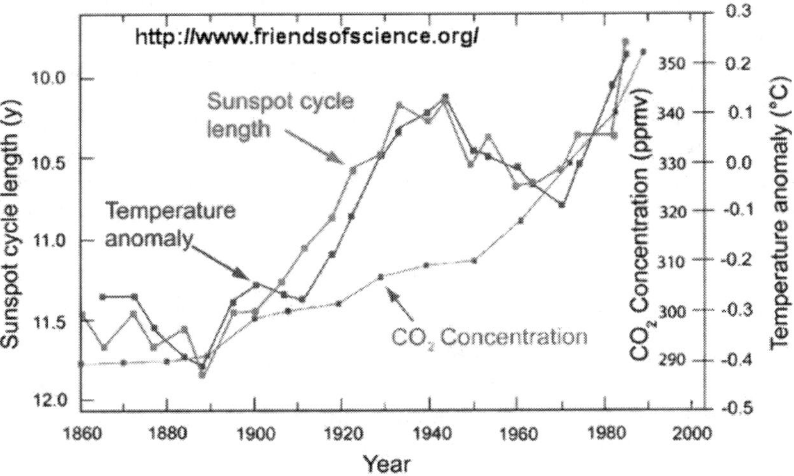

Figure 17. (Courtesy www.friendsofscience.org)

Second, we are emerging from the little ice age. Probably the coldest period ever experienced in human history, this ended in the mid-19th Century. We're reverting to the mean as the negative feedback system corrects itself. Third, the oceans have a

20-year heating/cooling cycle as various flows relocate heat to top or bottom. All these phenomena are well established. There are many explanations that graph out better than AGW. All have some effect

Conclusion

The law of unintended consequences happens when a simple system tries to regulate a complex system.
—Andrew Gelman

The idea that skeptics all believe in a conspiracy is untrue. Some may, but disputes are about the science. Most supporters of AGW simply believe the theory and if they do a bit of data massage, well, science is about choices. The stakes are too high to be overly scrupulous. Of course, there will always be profiteers who manipulate any situation for personal gain. If this constitutes conspiracy, then so be it – only the most naïve would deny such an obvious truth.

There are endless statements that claim absolute agreement by all scientists. This is a lie and such uniform agreement on anything as variable and poorly understood as the Earth's climate would be impossible. Such claims should be treated with extreme skepticism. Most scientists do agree that some warming has occurred and that a fraction might be due to CO_2 increases. Anything else is up for grabs.

CO_2 helps warming as a greenhouse gas, but we cannot attribute all or even most of the warming to it. We cannot by any means estimate the impact of man-made CO_2. Counter-measures will be useless – "the scientific community is pretty agreed those things [carbon offsets] will have virtually no impact," Richard Lindzen, IPCC lead author said.[269] What they will do is maintain the developed-world control of fossil fuels and consign Africa and other undeveloped locations to the Dark Ages of death by fouled water, malaria, exploitation, and famine.

The cap-and-trade scheme was authored, in part, by British Petroleum. General Electric has lobbied for it extensively. Electric rates, according to President Obama, will 'skyrocket' under the plan. Enron designed the first cap-n-trade scheme. Oil, electric, and finance will benefit from the projected $2-trillion industry.

The IPCC predicts up to 10% of hunger/malaria/flooding mortalities by 2085 could be from climate change, given a worst case. Any protocols, even if fully implemented, would reduce climate change by 10% tops. Therefore, mitigation would alleviate 1% of global deaths at the most generous estimate. At 2-6 million total, they estimate 20 to 60,000 preventable deaths. If the money for the protocols (which will do little by any estimation) were put into other humanitarian efforts, half or more of the 2-6 million lives could be saved – 50 times the human benefit. Hunger/malaria/bad water provably kill 36 times the worst estimates for climate change. Infrastructure/disease prevention/clean water programs could easily save 1-3 million lives instead.

"Over 4.5 Billion people could die from Global Warming-related causes by 2012," a 2007 Canadian article reported.[270] "It's completely immoral," a UN envoy declared, "even, to question, on the basis of what we know, the reports that are out."[271] There are proposals to take away or deny professional certification in meteorology for climate skepticism. A commercial even featured the brutal murder of schoolchildren for skepticism. This sort of McCarthyism will freeze valid science – based on disagreement. When skeptics are suppressed, it is no longer science.

AGW is a cash cow for climate research, having increased moneys from $50 million to billions per year. If the AGW alarm shuts off, so do the funds. All researchers have a financial stake in continued public fear.

The precautionary principle is invoked – better safe than sorry. But the policies are killing Third World people. Without electricity, they get cancer from dung-smoke, food poisoning without refrigeration, cholera and dysentery from lack of water. Solar and wind are said to be the answer – but that is too expensive for average Westerners. It's impossible for almost any African. Former environmentalist Patrick Moore of Greenpeace says that this type of environmentalism is intensely anti-human. Africa should be allowed to use its own oil and coal for its people.

The notion that we need to do something just in case is terribly flawed. Policy changes like cap-n-trade merely punish the less affluent without changing CO_2 concentrations at all. They provide open doors for special interests, lobbyist abuses, and financial graft. Other projects worsen AGW, if anything. The ethanol trade caused Brazil to cut down huge swathes of CO_2 sinks called rain forests to grow corn for ethanol which created more CO_2 to grow than it saved by using it. The biofuel scam that arose directly out of the climate scare has taken one third of US agricultural land out of food production in just two years. These lunatic plans caused food prices to soar and people to starve. Global governance-style policies will not deal with the problem, even if it is one. AGW has taken up the entirety of the environmental movement for decades, leaving far more serious problems like mercury pollution, depleted uranium weapons, islands of plastic, and BP oil disasters ignored. The environmental movement has fallen for the War of the Worlds.

Peer Review

A well-informed, 'jargonized' laity could not be distinguished from an expert discussing a scientific topic – Collins *et al.*, 2006[272]

Peer review has two types – funding review and publication review. The functions are diametrically opposed – one examines the potential payoff of future research and the other examines interpretations of completed research. Notably, publication review does not examine the research per se, only what the author says about it. Though it therefore cannot detect fraud, it is the only system for detecting fraud. As Elizabeth Knowle said, "there is remarkably uncritical faith in the peer review system." She speaks of how the system attempts a hidden function it was never intended for. "Formal peer review has taken on the supposed objectivity of research the peer review process was meant to judge." In other words, peer review has become a means to proclaim the validity of the science itself. It pushes certain claims to the forefront so that peer review has become the gold standard rather than research.[273]

Funding review, by many accounts, is unreliable, has inherent biases and lacks efficacy in choosing good projects. It is expensive in scientists' time. According to cell biologist Robert Pollack, "the system of grant review has virtually collapsed."[274] People have lost dedication because it is demoralizing. The bar has been set so high that projects with equivalent merit must be chosen between. The politics of reputation, institution, gender, race, and friendships makes the decisions.

Reviewers tend to pick projects sure to be successful. Such projects are based on science that has 'proven itself.' This eliminates the possibility of radical breakthroughs. Considering the enormously competitive market, long-term, expensive, cutting-edge science is almost never funded. The only exceptions are studies put forth by scientists of tremendous renown. But even here, as Peter Duesberg shows, to go against profitable dogma is to lose all funding – even for unrelated projects. Defunding is thus simultaneously punishment and warning to others.

Another concern is 'leakage,' a polite term for intellectual property theft. Reviewers see the vanguard of ideas. They can, and have, denied funding, then applied with an equivalent idea. Based on common reviewer relationships, their grant will more likely pass.

Also, the system reinforces the problem of non-replication. People that want to confirm previous research do not receive funding as policy. Science, as driven by expensive funding sources like NIH, is definitively incapable of self-correction.

Editorial review is wholly different. As defined by one analyst, it is "the evaluation of research findings for competence, significance, and originality by qualified experts."[275] The aim of peer review is to publish papers of higher quality and to improve the quality of all submitted papers. The criteria: it should be important, useful, relevant, methodologically sound, ethically sound, complete, and accurate.

Tom Jefferson presented a large-scale analysis to the 2001 conference on peer review. He found little research into the efficacy of the system. "Editorial peer review, although widely used, is largely untested and its effects are uncertain."[276] In spite of this, peer review is an unquestioned metric in most fields. Peer review may continue for unstated reasons. Journals now require it to guard their reputations or create suitability for funding. According to this paper, the aims of the system have not been honestly codified.[277]

Most research claims are provably false. Smaller studies, smaller effects, more relationships, lower selectivity of relationships, flexible design/ definition/ analysis/ outcomes, financial pressures, single-source research, and exciting new fields, are high predictors of false positives. Smaller effects are now the norm in epidemiology, leading to a firestorm of false positive results. Flexibility allows for the transformation of negative to positive results by changing the target. Data mining software is often specifically designed to produce statistically significant results. Epidemiological studies fared among the worst for false results – see autism and mercury.

Editorial review presents several sets of issues. Source data is seldom included with papers. Consequently, referees are 'blind.' They lack the tools needed for confident analysis, but their analysis is the ultimate validation of the paper. The problem, Horace Judson writes, is "hidden but not trivial."[278] It creates faith without merit.

Peer review faith is based on a fallacy – that the system will publish all truth and block all falsity. The system is not even aimed at that goal. Peer review aims to publish the 'best' papers. While a perception of truth-value is necessary for acceptance, it is neither sufficient nor proved. Most correct papers are rejected. Many people will only consider a paper that has passed peer-reviewed as true. The error leads to a misconception that rejected papers are false.

Massive studies by pharmaceutical companies form a special, though common, case. Analysts rely on data gathered by hundreds, even thousands, of field researchers. The study is usually a trivial part of their job. The data collection is haphazard and often fraudulent – a common complaint of analysts. The studies cannot be replicated. Supervisory controls are virtually absent. Research controls have no precision and mostly don't occur. The studies are enormously costly. There is almost no central hierarchy. More often than not, studies are based on mere data-gathering exercises that are not focused on any research question. This reverses the meaningful system of hypothesis leading to study design and implementation. Scientifically, it is valid to make a supported hypothesis from uncoordinated data, but not, as the industry does, to draw definitive conclusion rather than following up with controlled studies.[279]

If a researcher makes novel claims, these are *far* more likely to be rejected. But herein lies a pernicious problem. What if the 'peers' are out of their element? If the publishing researcher has found a new area of study, then there is no basis for peer review. There are no peers to review. No one has studied the discipline. Of course, if the researcher makes a compelling argument with supportive data, then it should pass review. Unfortunately, much of this depends on rhetorical rather than research skills.

According to Harvard's William Starbuck, "Empirical evidence indicates that editorial decisions [in peer review] incorporate bias and randomness." One group submitted 12 previously published papers – titles changed – to the same journals. 3 were spotted, 1 accepted, and 8 rejected for bad methodology. They also found a median 36% error rate in citations. "There is no evidence that peer review is effective."[280]

Would Darwin have survived peer review? Probably not. Casedevall and Fang argue, quite convincingly, that Galileo was tried by his learned peers. The inquisitors questioned why stellar parallax (the movement of stars as the Earth travels from one side to another of the sun) was not detected. It is a highly pertinent scientific question. Galileo recanted when they showed him the implements of torture. The current method is admittedly more civilized, but the principle still exists – conform or be rejected. Alderson, et al. claim 'the practice of peer review is based on faith in its effects, rather than on facts.'[281]

Peer review cannot detect the truth of a paper, only the merit of publication. Hwang-woo Suk is a Korean biotechnology researcher. He published papers in *Science* and peer-reviewed journals on stem cell research. His data was found to be fraudulent, but it passed review. Dr. Shön, mentioned earlier, published hundreds of papers regarded as major advances in solid state physics. They had serious and obvious misconduct, yet passed internal and external peer review for Bell Labs and highly credible journals. It's nice to believe the system works in that he was exposed, but it does prove that fraud happens. Peer review was not the method of exposure, either. No one knows how many don't get caught.

The system requires 'objectivity,' but that is strongly subject to pre-existing variations in ideology, conflicts of interest, and desire to circumvent contentious findings.[282] *Nature* rejected two unconventional theories that later won Nobel prizes. Companies have blocked publication of articles reflecting negatively on their products. People will vote with their pocketbook, if they have funding, employment, stock interest or other remuneration from a company.[283] Reviewers are less critical of friends and acquaintances than of strangers. They are hostile to people they dislike. A reviewer encountering an idea that competes with his research is likely to dismiss the paper.

Criticism of the process includes incapacity to find distortion or scientific misconduct, partiality for particular writers, and failure to perceive significant errors.[284] According to one paper, peer review is "slow, expensive, ineffective, something of a lottery, prone to bias and abuse, and hopeless at spotting errors and fraud."[285] A 1998 study intentionally included 8 major flaws. Reviewers discerned only 2 on average.[286] One analysis demonstrated that randomness played a significant role in peer review,[287] and another showed "agreement between reviewers in clinical neuroscience was little greater than would be expected by chance alone."[288] Lutz Bornman's meta-analysis showed a coefficient of .2-.4 for peer reviewer's agreement. Below .5 is low, indicating "judgments in peer review are not very reliable."[289] Another group found that journal staffers made similar review decisions as experts – there was no reason to favor expert peer review over informed laity.[290] Interestingly, a double-blind study showed whopping reverse sexism. Men accepted female or male papers at the same rate, but women accepted female authors at 62% and males at only 10%.[291]

Groupthink drives the system. To obtain NSF grant money, scientists need peer-reviewed papers. The more reviews required for publication, the more likely one is to go along with prevailing modes of thought. But cutting-edge science, by definition, does not go along with the status quo. In a field with a wide variety of opinions, the peer review process often works to shut down unpopular opinions. Only the conservative center remains standing.

According to David Horrobin, "quality control appears overwhelmingly important and the encouragement of innovation receives little attention. That is a recipe for failure." Innovations in patient care between 1930 to 1960 were dramatic, but have suffered enormous declines since. Though successful, Lithium would have never passed funding review, thus never made it as a treatment. This is almost certainly happening today with some of the best ideas. Horrobin details a number of cases where researchers were shut out by the peer review process. Only through their own exertion and faith were they capable of making great advances in medicine. Several even won Nobel prizes.[292] "There is a powerful tension," science philosopher Michael Polanyi said, "in the history of science between originality, creativity and profundity and accuracy and reliability. Success requires the balanced contribution of both."[293]

Within the system, when an editor sends an article for review, if it receives 30% negative responses, most journals will reject it. But those negative responses may be from reviewers who hold to an outmoded view and cannot free themselves. There is no guarantee that they have valid scientific insights. One study showed that an educated layperson with the right words couldn't be discerned from an expert in physics.[294]

Once a thought style is established, it is extremely difficult to break. Those who separate from the pack do so at their peril. They are vilified as fools. Without generous doses of confidence, exertion and genius, they will drown whether their research is valid or not. The money goes to continually reinforcing entrenched opinion. In essence, the funding becomes detrimental to progress. This is not to say that changes don't happen, but they are so difficult and require such an overwhelming body of evidence (hard to get without funding), good connections, and a forceful and dynamic personality, that they are far more rare than should be. The process cements opinion. It does not open new ideas.

People have difficulty admitting they are mistaken, especially if they have spent years in entrenched views. They will fight evidence. It is an emotional argument against evidence, not a logical one. But it is human nature, and to insist that science is somehow immune is foolish.

Mature fields give rise to 'research cartels' viciously guarding their territory, squashing minority views, and blocking publication of unconventional ideas.[295] In response, articles go conservative.

NASA is a case in point.[296] The peer review system was composed of in-house people. The reviewers worked under a small team of leading scientists. Few employees will be completely objective and honest in disagreeing with a boss when their job depends on it. And this is not an exception – it is the norm. Many universities and corporations have internal review systems. The process is very tightly controlled from the top, rendering the idea behind it meaningless. And worse than meaningless, detrimental by the pretense of non-existent open-mindedness. According to Thomas Gold, NASA could have been much greater. It is little more than a superb space photography group with a decent ability to gather evidence through probes. All its other programs are sub-standard and have stalled.

Another example of peer review groupthink (thought styles) is the theory of oil production. The prevailing theory is that oil is biological in origin. However, a probe found oceans of methane on Titan – proof that hydrocarbons have come from abiotic sources. The principal theorists will not admit this incontrovertible data – the peer review system shuts out all such speculations because they don't conform to existing theory. Literal oceans of critical evidence are discarded. The insidious nature of this process is that once a theory gains a solid foothold and the theory is established, funding often goes to bring contradictory facts in line with theory. An enormous theoretical structure rises from an inexistent or contradicted foundation.

Peer review is also biased against negative studies, or studies that show a treatment does not work. Among other ills, this problem results in a lack of critical inquiry into pharmaceuticals that are being pushed for profit with no valid benefit.

A serious and oft-overlooked question is whether the methodology can be co-opted for illegitimate gain. And of course the answer is always yes. This is a major flaw for the communality of science. The methods are now used as often as not to arrive at a pre-determined, profitable conclusion. Until it acknowledges this obvious corruption, science does not deserve our unquestioning trust. Journal editors choose what to publish. If funded by a certain industry or company – and most are – will they criticize it?

Scientists have a great deal of conviction in the process, but there seems little reason for that conviction. Journals must take a researcher's data on faith – it is too expensive to comb through raw data. Therefore, scientific misconduct is invisible to peer review. Tests have shown that judges catch fewer than 25% of intentionally planted, serious methodological flaws. Therefore it is almost useless to detect incompetence. Peer review is little superior to random selection.

Implicate Order

To see a world in a grain of sand and a heaven in a wild flower
Hold infinity in the palm of your hand and eternity in an hour
William Blake

Though it may be underfunded in science, courage is not a trivial quality. In 1951, David Bohm refused to testify against Oppenheimer in the McCarthy hearings. He was fired from Princeton and barred from teaching in the United States. One of the giants in his field, he is now revered for disputing most of the last century of physics. He explains his contention with a simple, but unusual, experiment. A drop of ink placed in a slowly turned viscous fluid disappears into it. When the turning is reversed, the drop reforms. This is one example of a hidden dimension to the universe. The dispersed form of the ink appears to have lost its 'order,' but it must be there in a hidden way. Else how could the drop reappear?

Bohm's theory has an implicate (enfolded) and explicate (unfolded) order. The explicate is the manifest reality we readily perceive. These physical perceptions are taken as the sole reality by materialists. But there is more, Bohm claims, and quantum physics proves it. "An electron is not one thing, but a totality or ensemble enfolded throughout the whole of space."[297] A constant movement flows between the implicate and explicate orders. Movement and flow are far more meaningful descriptions than singularity of physical objects. This interchange between the orders explains how an electron can emit a photon. The electron enfolds into the implicate and the photon unfolds to the explicate. An electron does not constitute a fundamental particle. It is a facet of the ongoing movement of the hologram. Particles are vastly complex entities engaged in consciousness – they 'use information.'

Alain Aspect (1982) proved non-locality in physics. The results of non-locality are the Copenhagen interpretation and various many-worlds theories. Both insist, if subtly, on the primacy of material reality. Copenhagen claims that wave-particles exist in a super-position. A particle exists in two mutually exclusive states simultaneously, and probabilistically. The idea works well mathematically, but it eludes the conceptual mind. Many-worlds theory claims that a quantum choice splits the universe into separate realities. Neither idea is testable or falsifiable – hence not scientific, per se. Neither is Bohm's, but his idea is considered too unusual to merit solid consideration.

A careful analysis shows that multiple universes created by quantum events is not any more normal than an enfolded order – the latter is just not 'Western.' The splitting universe comes from reductionism. Bohm's theory is rejected because science cannot cope with holism – it simply lacks any such idea. Bohm's theory is not so much odd as written in a foreign language that Western science cannot yet understand. Physics is finally showing signs of moving toward such an approach. Flow, connection, and hidden realities are returning as more or less mainstream ideas.

Einstein brought space and time together. Bohm extends this logic – *all* things are united in a single continuum. There is no separateness. All things that appear so are merely extensions of implicate into explicate. The two orders are not really separate – that is an illusion. They slide into each other. The denial of the continuum, the tendency to fragment reality, causes all our difficulties. It creates the struggle. There is no difference between living and non-living. Life is "enfolded throughout the totality of the universe."[298]

At the same time he extends the holism of relativity, he overturns its ultimate explanatory power. Space and time, for example, are no longer dominant realities. Moreover, "in relativity, movement is continuous, causally determinate, and well-defined while in quantum mechanics it is discontinuous, not causally determined, and not well-defined."[299] The theories apply to the explicate order, but not the implicate. The root-level disagreements show that they only describe aspects of reality, but not the totality. They are limited. They lack totality because they lack wholeness. These contradictions between fundamental theories demand a new type of theory, dropping some of the 'basic commitments.' In the primary phenomenon of quantum entanglement, Bohm's holism removes causality, replacing it with implicate order. Everything is connection, a hologram. Everything contains everything else. In a hologram, each part of the image has the entirety.

Implicate order argues against a number of axioms in physics: All theory is limited. The theory of everything is an impossibility. The Cartesian coordinate system is not really a deep-seated order. No fundamental difference lies between reality and thought, or observed and observer. Phenomena cannot be reduced to fundamental particles, laws, or unchanging existence. There can be no discrete space-time events or discrete quantum states. Human knowledge should not be focused so primarily on mathematical constructions and statistical descriptions of particulate matter. In short, nothing is completely separable from the holistic reality, "the undivided wholeness in flowing movement. Flow is prior to the things seen to form and dissolve in this flow."[300]

Brian Josephson, who won the 1973 Nobel Prize for physics, supports the implicate order theory. He believes it will allow for a cosmic mind to one day be part of physics' overall approach. The mind explains and analogizes the underlying reality of QM and directly manifests implicate order principles. Thinking has a quantum style – one state jumps to the next instead of Newtonian linear movement. It has a non-local connection. Fundamental particles are enfoldments of the underlying order – they move too fast to be discrete quantities. Information is diffused throughout the universe, like the brain. Any part contains the whole.

Karl Lashley, in 1946, performed experiments to cut out memories in rat's brains. No matter what part he removed, they still retained the ability to navigate a maze, though they were clumsier. Memory is not localized at any point in the brain. Karl Pribram, a successor of Lashley, inspired Bohm. His holonomic brain model showed that memory is holographic. "As with consciousness," Bohm said, "each moment has an explicate order. In addition, it enfolds all others in its own way. The relationship of each moment to all others is implied by its total content: the way it holds all others enfolded within it."[301]

Everything is connected. There are 100 billion neurons and a trillion connections. More neural pathways are possible than electrons are in the universe. We have a tendency to break things down to particles as explanation, but connectivity is the real key. Connection is a deeper reality than what is connected. Nothing has meaning in isolation – in fact, it cannot even exist so. "No one is bounded at the skin."[302]

Physicists, Bohm claims, have an "unshakeable faith in fundamental particles."[303] The mechanistic universe leads to meaninglessness, but quantum theory does not require a clockwork construction. Energy is infinite. Ignoring this reality, physicists concentrate on material objects. The cosmos is not self-existent, but is a minor manifestation of a far greater reality. This reality cannot be probed by rational analysis.

Meaning could be inherent and, for David Bohm, that is likely. The LaPlacean, reductionist view has led to a breakdown of thought. Modern thought styles, inasmuch as thoughts create reality, are hyper-complex and reductionist. This leads to most of our cultural problems – especially nihilism. Bohm wanted to unite a holistic physics with the communal consciousness. This would overturn the dividedness and pain of modern society – seeing ourselves as integral movement of the whole, as non-separate.

The implicate order has been compared to Buddhist thought – the parallels are many. Bohm even worked with Krishnamurti. Such a system places mind at a high level of influence. It even becomes the creator of reality. This is more than idle theorizing – any number of mind-over-matter phenomena have been well-documented, even published in scientific journals.

Emotionally disturbed and retarded people, for example, have only 25% the cancer rate. They almost never get leukemia.[304] 'Jack Wright,' a cancer patient, was given Krebiozen a few days before his doctor expected him to die. The tumors 'melted like snowballs on a hot stove.' He left the hospital cancer-free. Months later, the patient heard Krebiozen was useless. The giant tumors returned in days. The doctor told him that only one batch of Krebiozen was bad. He administered water injections and told the patient it was the drug. Again, the tumors vanished. When he found the drug was completely useless, the tumors returned and he died.[305]

Mind may very well exist independently of the brain. In a normal person, brainwaves never change. But with a multiple personality, each one has a different brainwave. One personality can be allergic, but when another comes online, rashes and swelling will mysteriously vanish. A drunk will become sober. Left-handedness can switch to right-handedness. Even scars and eye color have been documented to change.[306]

Jack Schwarz, in the 1970s, demonstrated bizarre abilities, all very well documented. He could push enormous needles through his flesh without bleeding. When withdrawn, they left no wounds. He could alter his brainwaves and was unaffected by toxic injections. These abilities were verified by many medical practitioners.[307] "All your body is in your mind," he said, "but not all your mind is in your body."

Mirin Dajo put a fencing foil through his body repeatedly. The

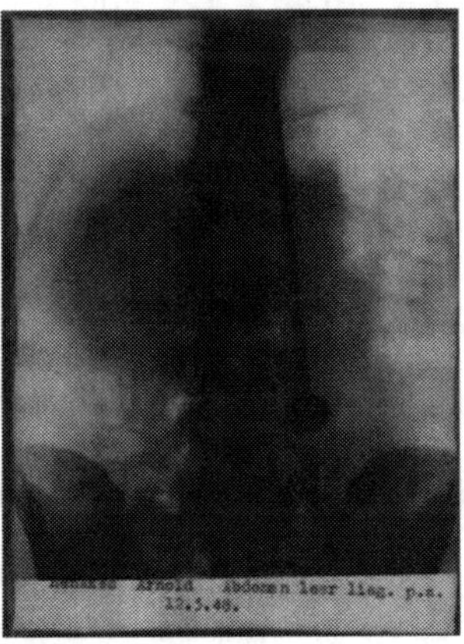

Figure 18: X-ray of pin swallowed by Mirin Dajo, 1948.

Zurich Cantonal hospital verified it with multiple doctors and X-rays showing the foil penetrating vital organs. (See figure 18, previous page.) The wounds closed when it was removed.[308] In 1962, the military hospital of Verona Italy verified that Vittorio Michelli actually regenerated bone tissue after significant degradation.[309]

Mohotty was a boy who offered penance to his deity in exchange for saving his father's life. According to *National Geographic*, he learned to push skewers through his arms and bury giant hooks in his back to pull a large weight. The hooks were removed without blood and the wounds closed.[310] Such phenomena are not limited to individuals. In India, a different person in a village was chosen each year and swung through the air by hooks in their backs. When removed, *Scientific American* reported, the hooks left no wounds.[311]

One of the most fascinating cults in history was called the Convulsionnaires de Saint-Médard. The Abbe de Francois of Paris died in 1727 after a lifetime of opposition to his own Catholic Church. Mourners came in sheets. Thousands report of the crowd's amazing powers – many die-hard skeptics confirm the stories. People went into convulsions. To deal with the pain, they asked to be beaten as hard as possible with stones and hammers, some even laying their weight on sharp points first. They showed no sign of injury. It being an anti-authoritarian movement, the Church and civil authorities sent teams of investigators to disprove the 'miracles.' Every one of them validated the reports. Many skeptics disparaged the movement's fanaticism and religiosity – but even the fiercest critics agreed the occurrences could neither be dismissed nor explained by rational analysis. The phenomenon lasted for a decade and, according to skeptic poster child David Hume, "many of these miracles were immediately proved upon the spot before judges of unquestioned integrity, attested by witnesses of credit and distinction in a learned age and on the most eminent theater in the world." But similar to a modern skeptic, Hume denies what he has just affirmed, "What have we to oppose to such a cloud of witnesses, but the absolute impossibility or miraculous nature of the events…? And this surely, in the eyes of all reasonable people, will alone be regarded as a sufficient refutation."[312]

Robert Jahn was a professor of aerospace engineering at Princeton and a professed skeptical materialist. In 1979, he oversaw a student project in psychokinesis and rejected his materialist viewpoint. He has since created a number of tightly controlled studies showing telekinesis – "small but replicable and statistically significant correlations between operator intent and output characteristics" of mechanical/electrical systems.[313] Jahn and Dunne (his partner) believe that the influence comes from the intersection of matter and energy's wave properties.

Stigmatist Therese Neumann quit eating and drinking for a two-week period – verified by a doctor and four nurses keeping a 24-hour watch. It is, of course, medically impossible to not drink for two weeks and live. Supposedly, she didn't eat or drink for decades, though this is impossible to verify.

One easily validated immaterial skill comes from archeology. Norman Emerson, vice-president of the Canadian Archeological Association, works with George McMullen, a truck driver. McMullen found several sites, and once traced out an Iroquois long-house. It was found in the exact place he marked, according to Emerson.[314] "I have received knowledge of archeological artifacts ... from a psychic informant, who relates this information without any evidence of conscious reasoning."[315] Stephen Schwarz, *National Geographic* editor and MIT staff, also believes in intuitive archeology. "The time and space framework so crucial to the Grand Material world-view is by no means as absolute as most scientists believe."[316]

Dr. Ian Stevenson investigated reincarnation for decades, going to India. Many children related stories of past lives which checked out in detail. From the *Journal of the American Medical Association*, he "painstakingly and unemotionally collected a detailed series of cases in which the evidence for reincarnation is difficult to understand on any other grounds ... He has placed on record a large amount of data that cannot be ignored."[317] Yet amazingly, it is.

Michael Sabom, a cardiologist, was a determined skeptic. Tired of hearing about 'OBE* fantasies,' he constructed a study to debunk it. The study made him a believer. He divided his patients between those who, during his surgeries, had experienced OBE's and those who had not. He asked all to describe their surgery. Of the 25 without OBE's, 22 were completely wrong, and 3 correct but vague. Of the 32 OBE patients, 26 were correct but vague, 6 were correct and detailed. One gave such a detailed, extensive, and accurate account that Sabom felt forced to change his position in the fashion of a true scientist. He is now an OBE believer and has written widely about it.

Valerie Hunt, a kinesiologist, monitored frequencies of the human body. Normal organ cycles are 250 cycles per second (cps). Hunt, who was not a spiritualist, recalibrated the machine

* Out of Body Experience.

for experimental purposes. She found that the highest cycles were in the 'chakras.' People who are more material have below 400cps, those with moderate psychic feelings have 400-800cps, and those who experience trance have 800-900, and mystics have up to 200,000cps.

Sri Aurobindo was an Indian savant who stated many of these ideas in a profound way. He posits a 'higher vibrational reality' and as we descend through it, a 'progressive law of fragmentation' overcomes us. This lower vibration of consciousness keeps us in a divided belief system, blocking our ability to encounter the blissful, joyous and compassionate emotions normal in higher realms.[318] "[T]he snare of the mind and the senses, ... the snare of the thinker, the snare of the theologian ... the meshes of the Word and the bondage of the Idea ... are within us waiting to wall in the spirit with forms ... we must always go beyond, always renounce the lesser for the greater, the finite for the Infinite ... to proceed from illumination to illumination, from experience to experience ... [We must not] attach ourselves even to the truths we hold most securely, for they are but forms and expressions of the Ineffable who refuses to limit itself to any form or expression."[319] Half a century later, David Bohm echoed him: the implicate reality "could equally well be called Idealism, Spirit, Consciousness ... The separation of [matter and spirit] is an abstraction. The ground is always one."[320]

But human experience is a narrow gorge. Everyone knows of amazing animal stories of this connectedness – e.g. dogs finding their way home from anywhere. Not all dogs can, but some have done a lot more. In 1582, Fidelis found his master 300 miles from home at the court of Versailles. Prince made his way across the English Channel during WWI to reunite with his master on a French battlefield. Tony went from Aurora 200 miles to East Lansing when his family moved. Sultan found his master's grave, despite never having been there, and stayed day after day.

After 150 years of serious research, biology and evolution cannot find any mechanism for animal navigation. Despite the failure, all alternative theories are ridiculed or ignored. In 1931, Max was left in unfamiliar territory. The dog sat and looked around for a time, then focused attention diligently homeward for 30 minutes, then set out in the correct direction. The process is not automatic, but seems to require 'attunement.' Max didn't appear to use any of the normal senses.

Homing pigeons' skill is an enduring mystery. All theories – sun, stars, magnetic field, and generational teaching – have been disproved. When confused with artificial light beforehand, the birds first go in the wrong direction, then correct course. But if it's cloudy, they immediately go correctly. The sun can actually disorient them. The magnetic field theory is nonsensical – it can only account for the direction of the magnetic poles, not East-West. The poles also migrate constantly and birds with magnets attached easily find their way home. Generational teaching is disproved – cuckoos are raised by other birds, yet they still migrate to ancestral cuckoo homes. Butterflies return to ancestral homes 4 generations later – all the originals having died long before. Yet the community remembers. Tribal peoples have this sense of direction. Most Aborigines and Kalahari unfailingly point homeward immediately, no matter where they are.[321] Materialism has failed to explain this deeper reality.

There are many abilities beyond the material realm. Dogs warn of epileptic seizure by herding and pushing people to sit. These pets never make a mistake – they cannot be faked out, and can do it from another room. In a bizarre result, Renee Peoch imprinted caged chicks on a robot as mother. While control robots moved randomly through their room, imprinted robots stayed near the cage.

Abundant historical evidence speaks of animals' ability to detect earthquakes hours and days ahead of time. The Chinese don't labor under the bias that 'earthquakes cannot be predicted.' Their system combines modern seismic gear with animal prediction. Hundreds of thousands of people are trained to call in with animal anomalies. In 1995, they successfully predicted the Yunnan earthquake. In 1997, they predicted one a week beforehand. Hai-Cheng was flooded with reports of cattle and horses panicking, geese flying into trees, rats acting drunk, and pigs biting each other. A few days later, a 7.3 Richter quake flattened the evacuated town.[322] Their record is 7 out of 8 correct.

Even examples of great beauty must be ignored in order to coherently maintain the materialist thought-style. Male loons each sing a different song. When a male dies, a new male comes and takes over the song without ever meeting his predecessor.

There is no shortage of scientists who are not materialists, but they keep a low profile. A 1979 poll revealed that 55% of professors in the natural sciences believe in ESP, for example.[323] Brian Weiss, a Yale psychologist, wrote *Many Lives, Many Masters*, detailing his change from skeptic to believer in reincarnation. He received a tidal wave of letters from psychiatrists who also had come to believe, based on patient stories, but were afraid to publicly say so. This is the ugly secret of science – many believe in an immaterial reality, but cannot admit it for fear of censure.

Some of the greatest physicists of the past Century were anti-materialists. They believed in a spiritual reality supercessory to the physical. Sir James Jeans, a foremost physicist of the 20th Century, claims the universe is not material – it is pure thought. "Matter must be of the same nature as mind – thought, not extension. We are but thoughts in the great mind." The nature of the atom proved to him that "things are not what they seem. We are not yet in contact with reality."[324] The theory of quanta even negated causality. The creator of the exclusion principle, Linus Pauling, agrees. Pauling allows "an invisible reality transcending the causality of classical physics."[325]

Max Planck, father of modern quantum theory, believed any serious person knew that the religious element was necessary for 'balance and harmony.' Faith is 'indispensable' in science and 'the pure rationalist has no place' there. Science is incapable of solving a mystery it is part of. Reason cannot even confirm the reality of the external world – that is a metaphysical belief.

The most eloquent writer, Sir Arthur Eddington, performed the eclipse experiments which gave relativity its first empirical test. Eddington sported a potent humor to discuss his beliefs. Reality is spiritual, he claims, not material. A new moral materialism not only doubts the spiritual, but 'despises' it. Notwithstanding, the world is "mind-stuff. Solidity is an illusion, a fancy projected by the mind. We have chased it from liquid to solid to atom – and there we have lost it. Science has shown that things are very different from what they seem. But it is a one-sided view of truth which finds in these representations [our perceptions] nothing but deception, which takes the conscious spirit to be inessential."[326] A universal mind is a plausible idea given modern physics.

"Multiplicity is only apparent," Schroedinger said. "In truth there is only one mind. Mind is indestructible since it is always now."[327] Louis de Broglie, 1929 Nobelist for the matter-wave thesis, believed in "profound realities which conceal themselves behind natural appearances."[328]

Werner Heisenberg, who won the 1932 Nobel Prize and created the uncertainty principle, had "no problem with the idea of metaphysics – questions of fundamental concepts. Why ever should we not be able to ask such questions in physics? We should not talk the deeps in which the truth dwells out of existence. That would be a very superficial view."[329]

It's hard to find any great mind of 20th-Century physics who does not believe in a deeper reality, be it spiritual, mental, or mathematical. But such realities are difficult to speak of, especially in the teeth of skepticism, or at least its club-footed modern namesake. Subtle truths are invisible to such gross perceptions. According to Ken Wilber, the physicist looks at nothing but abstract equations, not reality itself. It's a confusion.

To reverse it, Wilber points out the critical difference between immanence and transcendence. If we look at the universe as the chain of being – a series of nested realities – then matter is at the base, transcended by life, then mind, soul, spirit, subtle dualism, and essence. (There are many different ways to map the chain of being.) Each level transcends the previous – physics can study matter, but not life. Biology cannot study mind, nor psychology soul, nor theology spirit. Meditation cannot quite crack duality, and only direct perception knows the essence. But as each of these higher levels transcends the lower, they are still immanent within. (See figure 19.) Otherwise, mind could not formulate any ideas of biology or physics. With clarity of discussion, much confusion can be avoided. Are we talking about immanence or transcendence?

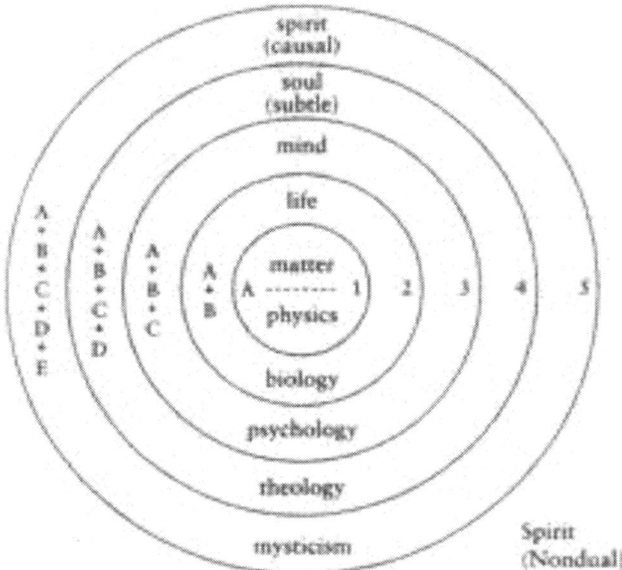

Figure 19: Ken Wilber's chain of being.

A direct appeal to experience applies to all domains, but the method differs between domains. In physics, it is extension in space-time, thus measurement is primary. In biology, it is cellular structures/genetics. Psychology values quality and intention. Theology seeks God, meditation – focus, mysticism – connection, and direct perception seeks naked reality unshorn of ideation.

Internal structure is another aspect of all domains. Physics has only four forces. Biology adds hunger, thirst, shelter, motive power, and procreation. Mind adds jealousy, hope, envy, pride guilt, remorse, justice, art, and morality. Theology has divine beings, the spiritual domain adds universal love, grace, compassion, skillful means, and intuition, and the essence domain includes wisdom, clarity, non-thought, non-duality, and stark awareness of reality. It is absurd to abnegate higher truths simply because lower methods cannot perceive them.[330]

By confusing the domains and methods, physics appears fundamental, thus more genuine. Religion appears stratified, or more nonsensical. But seen properly, each domain has its own methods for sorting the salient ideas which speak within it. All realms of experience have valid knowledge tests that can be applied. They differ in objectifying criteria, however. Try proving 'life' through physics – but to theology it's bluntly obvious. Any level can be faked. Just as there is pseudo-science, there is also pseudo-religion and mysticism. The real battle is not between science and religion, it is between genuine and deceptive.

Shunyata

I dislike the use of the word reality.
—Sir Arthur Eddington

This part ends where it began – epistemology. Buddhist theory of knowledge has elements of Western epistemology. Empiricism is valid, but not all-consuming; rationality is a tool, but not a master. The senses can fool us; logic has limits. If we navigate these waters skillfully, then our senses can tell us what we need to know and logic cuts away false ideas. It's important to realize these two functions. Direct perception knows, but the mind is easily confused by rational deduction. Logic is not used to know or understand – it is used to eliminate false understanding. "Fidelity to rationality," Prigogine wrote, "isolates man in a silent world."[331]

Rationality must be defeated by rationality – it is the only language it understands. Not seeing intuition, it cannot believe it exists. While the languages of intuition, emotion and spirituality have difficulty understanding the language of rationality, they can acknowledge it. Rationality can only acknowledge itself – it is blind. To discuss reality with a diehard rationalist, one must employ rational arguments – these types are too dim to see other lights – or perhaps too Brights* in their own minds. Those who speak only one of these languages becomes its victim. To speak two makes one a partner. To speak more makes one a master.

From the Buddhist point of view, all rational understanding is definitively flawed – rational mind cannot perceive absolute truth. Logic is used to destroy itself. It functions as a guardian against the untruths of logical certainty, not as a discoverer of truth per se. This is one of the big mistakes of current science – faith in logic as reality – but it doesn't add up. Let's look briefly at logic first.

Logic has many forms; it is multivalent in the extreme. There are formal, inductive, deductive, syllogistic, sentential, predicate, modal, mathematical, informal, philosophical, and computer logics. All of these are bivalent – they have only yes or no answers. But as Hegel said, "neither in heaven nor in earth, neither in the world of mind nor of nature, is there anywhere such an abstract 'either–or' as the understanding maintains."[332] The creation of such systems as fuzzy logic have helped Western

---

* Brights is the name R. Dawkins recommended for new atheists to call themselves.

thought modes to deal with this problem, but they are ill-developed and not mainstream in usage.

Logic is not a study in truth-value – it is a study in coherent connectivity and non-contradiction. Logic rests on nothing in the tangible world. But, science claims that logic is a formula for truth. Logic's relation to truth must be either – 'logic creates truth' or 'logic discovers truth.' If truth is taken to be a real-world property (and it must be to have any meaning), then it is impossible for logic to create it. It is also impossible for a conceptual abstraction (logic) to discover an actual physical property. *There is no demonstrable connection* and without connection, logic fails. The most fundamental aspect of logic is the connectivity between propositions, evidence, and conclusions. Without connectivity, it is illogic.

Aristotle's law of the excluded middle is among the most restrictive thought rules imposed on our world. No one is aware of it, being so deeply embedded that it seems intuitively obvious. By this law, for every proposition P, either P or not-P is true, but not both. In formal logic systems this is accurate, but it has leaked out into the everyday approach. We believe any statement is true or false. This fails to account for temporal, relative, conditional, contextual and ambiguous truths. Wood will burn – not if it's soaked, underwater, without oxygen, or petrified – conditional. It was a cloudy day – but if only the morning was cloudy, the statement is neither true nor false. 'This meat is overcooked,' for example, depends on the individual. Any opinion is neither true nor false. Yet the pervasiveness of this law leads us to take our opinions as truths rather than preferences. We fail by an inability to distinguish opinion from reality.

Implied comparatives also fail, e.g. Jane is tall. Compared to whom? Jane is neither tall nor not tall, but only so in comparison to another. Contradictory statements, both of which can be true, are another flaw. Mount Everest does not move and Mount Everest moves 20 miles every second. The first is true from our perspective on the ground; the second from space. Or future truths – Bob is going to the beach next week. It's not yet true or false since he may not make it. The law of the excluded middle is wrong. Formal logic is inapplicable to actual experience.

Classical and other logical systems contain a principle of explosion – anything follows from a contradiction. If a system shows that A and not-A are both true, then any statement can be proven. For example, we accept Earth is large or Earth is not large. Earth is large (compared to me) and Earth is not large (compared to the universe). Both statements are true. Then we state: either Earth is large or fish are mammals. Since Earth is not large, it follows that fish are mammals. The law of the excluded middle assumes absolutes within a relative frame, leading to logical absurdity.

To assume that reality is inherently logical is to assume that it cannot contradict itself, but it does. The principle of identity is the most fundamental in logic – yet it fails. The principle states that A=A, dividing the universe into object and other outside the object. It demands singularity and absolute separation. If we examine an object – a car, say – then it has the identity of being a car. If we take the engine – is it a part of the car or not? Clearly it is, so it shares identity with the car. Therefore, as car, it shares identity with all other parts. As engine, it does not. The principle thus fails – the engine is both self to the chassis' other and a common self with the chassis as car. One may say this is nitpicking, but why? There is nothing to the car except its parts – no other materialist analysis of its identity makes sense. Set theory gets around this problem in formal systems, but it demonstrates the flaw of conceiving of the world as a formal logical system – it does not work. Reality is not inherently logical.

It has serious consequences. Our modern theory of free trade comes from the game theory of John Nash. The theory claims that in all instances people will pursue their self-interest. The theory never worked in testing – people cooperated much more than models predicted. Nevertheless, it was scientifically instituted, via the Rand institute, throughout public service systems. Governments radically privatized government functions on the presumption that true democracy would emerge from the market. Results are debatable, but one point is well-agreed – those who pursued radical self-interested wealth have bankrupted the citizens who worked in cooperation. The democratic theory of markets destroyed the economy by turning it from production to finance. It came from a scientific, mathematical model – a formal logic system. Now we are paying the consequences.

An alternative system is called atheorism. Though tongue in cheek, it captures the essence – aspects of the real world are beyond theoretical understanding. Theory cannot capture reality. Another permutation might be irrational theorizing – the world may not be rational at heart – so only irrational theories will describe it. Or it's indescribable – as in Buddhist doctrine.

The science of Buddhism begins with epistemology and ends with empiricism. The fundamental aim is to elevate the individual's understanding of and place within this reality. It differs from the Western comprehend–and-conquer approach. It is observer participancy in a dual form – not only does observing mind affect the observation, but the observation changes the mind, as well.

The Buddha's most important problem was suffering. The way to end it was by knowing the truth. Psychology and science are not separable. The best way to track this down is through the first Buddhist teaching – the Four Noble Truths: suffering, its cause, its cessation, and the means to that. To exist is to suffer. That does not mean that all of existence is joyless – he did not say that. But even within great joy is the suffering of knowing it will end. Buddha said that no form of existence can escape suffering. It has many forms. Everything born must grow old and die. We lose things we like, we can't get things we want, and we have problems we don't want. These are inescapable, but we still struggle against the reality, making the pain worse. A very subtle form of suffering exists as well – conditioned existence. We are not in touch with reality and this creates an almost imperceptible, but constant unease. We can never fully relax.

The origin of suffering begins with this subtle, out–of-tune situation – ignorance of reality. It is the first of the Twelve Nidānas – the links of interconnectedness. All phenomena are connected to all other phenomena in ways beyond comprehension. Failing to realize this creates a false sense of separateness – an ignorance of what is. From another angle, the connection is more important than what is connected. The human brain, for example, is the most complex object under scrutiny today. That complexity comes from interconnectivity – the linkages far outnumber the individual neurons.

These twelve nidānas comprising an individual's journey through time can be analyzed. The person is a spatio-temporal construct – an entity inhabiting space and moving through time, if you will. The nidānas are the temporal map.

The five skandhas (or aggregates) are the spatial constituents of the self.* Form, or the idea of body, supports the others. Feeling is the meeting of internal with external – it includes a blunt emotional sense of like, dislike or neutrality. Perception is the conscious glimmering of that and allows for a bit more strategy in approaching reality – envy and pride arise. Formation, the fourth skandha, creates all the more developed forms of thought and emotion we can experience – loathing, hatred, love, logic, opinion, etc. Consciousness, the fifth, is the perceiving aspect of the self. This set of things moves through

---

* This is my own explanation.

time, riding the rails of the interdependent links of existence – the nidānas, also called karma.

The nidānas begin with *ignorance* (first nidāna) of fundamental reality – not knowing the true nature of what is and of the self. The self begins in confusion and wants to solidify some image, to grasp at understanding. This desire to exist and deepen the tenuous sense of existence links one chain to the next, turning the seed of basic ignorance into mental and physical strategies – the formations of the skandhas. The two modes – skandhas and nidānas – are fully interpenetrating. They are different ways of explaining the same basic thing. The *formations* (second nidāna) form (hence the name) the karmic net, entrapping the entity. The *consciousness* arises from this – the entity considers itself as a separate thing – a delusion.

The nidānas are posited on the idea of rebirth – we continually cycle through the layers of existence. The first three – ignorance, formations, consciousness – describe the important considerations of the past life. They tell us how we got here. The next seven lay out the critical details of the present life – how we perpetuate the cycle by inattention. The fourth, *identity* gives rise to the *sense consciousnesses* (fifth) which *contact* (sixth) the world through the sense organs. *Feeling* (seventh) causes *craving* (eighth), leading outward to *grasping* (ninth) – this can include aversion. Integrating the desire as part of the ego causes a subtle alteration in the identity – *Becoming* (tenth) a different entity. This self, a projection into the next life, is constantly changing.

The third (future) lifetime is summed up as *birth* (eleventh) and *aging and death* (twelfth). The Buddha taught this to scare people – the cycle is self-perpetuating and without an active, intent approach, it will never end. Suffering will go on forever. As a brief aside, this is a counterargument to an atheist argument against reincarnation – that it is a desire for immortality. The Buddha said, basically, immortality sucks – get out while you can.

With a focused approach, we can escape – the third noble truth. Cessation of suffering occurs through realization of reality. The fourth noble truth is the eight-fold path to that realization – right view, intention, speech, action, livelihood, effort, mindfulness, and concentration. In other words, the entire propulsive force of karma can be unwound by cutting through ignorance about reality. The whole scheme falls apart and one is free. Buddhist science, for this book, is the understanding of that reality. It is also called the View. Study of the View leads to conceptual understanding, but this is insufficient. Realization brings it into the mind-stream so that one perceives the world that way directly.

As a side note, there is a simpler way to halt the nidāna chain. The practitioner can meditate on the arising of craving (eighth), letting it go before it turns into grasping, thus cutting the karmic propulsion and liberating the mind from rebirth. This is nirvana, but it falls short of enlightenment.

To move into the empirical orientation, a basic axiom needs to be established: all things are impermanent. This is fundamental to Buddhism, and is the Buddha's initial departure from other schools. Without this understanding, study begins on the wrong foot by assuming some permanence.

The term Buddhist science has no immediately clear referent. There are thousands of lists – the 8-fold path, 3 marks, 9 yanas, 10 virtuous and non-virtuous actions, 4 foundations, 5 precepts, 6 paramitas and 10 bhumis to name a few. These are divided among the three 'baskets': the Vinaya rules of monasticism, the Sutra discourses on meditation, and the Abhidharma teachings on mind and matter. After relegating the first basket to ethics, we might consider dumping the second in religion. This would be premature. Meditation is critical to Buddhist science – it is how to do it. Meditation frames the mind in a more open way, receptive to information and sensitive to the ego's desire to distort it to save the theory. Meditation is the scientific method of Buddhism. In sharp contrast to Western science, a theory cannot be separated from those who believe in it. Without a mind to interpret, theory is only black marks on a white background. Meditation is the means of minimizing bias so that reality can emerge.

So a reasonable definition of Buddhist science would be investigation of the nature of reality. This leads to what is called the View – one's understanding of reality. The Buddhist view consists of five graduated schools.*

The first is the Shravaka. Their goal is to liberate the individual from suffering. It takes a narrow field of reference – the self. All creatures behave as if there were a self – something to protect. Though many atheists have come to the logical conclusion that no self exists, there is still an experiential and emotional sense of one. The instinctive idea is that it is 'lasting, separate and independent.' Any logical scrutiny reveals the personality is a changeable stream of occurrences suffused with many factors. It is a varying relation between internal and external with nothing substantive or constant found. The

* Taught by Khenpo Tsultrim Gyamtso, Rinpoche, this is not the only approach.

instinctive feeling can be analyzed meditatively. The actuality of the self is impossible to grasp, understand or explain.

Relaxing in this paradoxical irritation – the conflict between feeling the self is there and the inability to find it – is the key to Shravaka meditation. The way to arrive at not-self is to search for the self within one's being. Not-self is easy to establish logically, but realization is far deeper and requires meditative scrutiny. Logically, one contemplates where and what the self is – the body or a thing inside, a physical substance, a brain-module, and so forth. One searches the immaterial stream – the emotions, concepts, and consciousness. This last is the prime suspect, but consciousness is merely the stream of instants of perception, constantly changing. Its only stable trait is an ability to perceive. But since it takes a different object moment to moment, it is thus different moment to moment. The emotional content changes as well.

Further, the criteria of 'ability to perceive' does not differentiate one self from another. So the Buddhist belief is that our suffering comes from clinging to this changeable set of characteristics and traits and falsely imputing a lasting, independent and singular self onto it. If we can overcome that, not just logically, but experientially, one finds cessation of suffering, or nirvana. That is far short of Buddhahood, however.

In sum, the Shravaka concludes that reality is composed of tiny, discrete instants of consciousness and tiny particles of matter – atoms. Self is an illusion. Shravaka is Buddha's reductionism.

The second stage is Cittamatra, or mind only. "All realms of existence are mind," the Buddha said. This is not solipsism – there are other minds that interact. Nor is it idealism, though that is the closest Western doctrine. Cittamatra points out that mind cannot experience anything outside itself. All objects of mind are formulations of the mind. Characteristics of color, solidity and shape are mental imputations. For example most objects, according to science, are empty space. Mind therefore is both perceiver and perceived. Mind and its objects are the same substance. "All phenomena occur as inner perceiving aspect or outer perceived aspect,"[333] so everything is mind. Anything beyond mind cannot be proved by definition – only mind can encounter a phenomenon. Everything mind experiences has to be formulated by itself.

Two methods can help in contemplating this difficult doctrine – first is the back door of the Western approach. Matter and energy are not different – they are a gradient. It's received wisdom that every particle has a wave nature and every wave a particle nature, but that those aspects are not reality. The reality is beyond our ability to explain. All we need do is place mind in that energy spectrum. In neuroscience, mind is the electromagnetic energy of the brain – Delta, Beta, Alpha, and recently discovered Gamma waves. Since electromagnetic energy can exist in a medium, like a computer, or without a medium, like light traveling through space, there is no reason to presuppose that mind cannot exist without the brain – its basic signature, electromagnetic radiation, provably exists with no medium.

If mind is conceived as a subtle form of energy, which is a thoroughly logical, well-evidenced idea, then it fits comfortably within the mass-energy spectrum. If it is a part of the spectrum, then it is all of it. Not that conscious mind occupies the entire spectrum, but that the entire spectrum has subtle qualities of perception. *Consciousness has to come from somewhere because it exists.* It is no more valid to claim that matter has magically become conscious than to claim that a subtle level of awareness pervades phenomena and attains consciousness at a certain level of organization. Either claim is metaphysical. In other words, the electromagnetic spectrum is integral to all forms of mass-energy. It is also the defining characteristic of mind. Therefore, mind and substance are the same nature.

The second explanation is the dream example. Can you prove you are not dreaming right now? We know we're fooled by dreams, but we claim the continuity of existence as proof that waking experience is not a dream. But when we die, how do we know that this will not seem like a long dream? Further, the continuity proof would turn the waking experience of a schizophrenic into a de facto dream.

An argument against mind-only is our consensual reality. But the consensus is only an approximation. Each of us experiences the world in our own way and cannot tell the experience of another. And the further we move from our group, the less consensus there is. Is God real or not? What food is healthy? What activities are fun? There is no agreement on such questions. And once we leave humanity, there is no question of consensus – a dog or mosquito has a thoroughly different reality. Why? Because of its perception – mind creates the world.

According to this doctrine, mind is real. Self-aware, self-knowing, self-illuminating. Cittamatra divides the world into three conceptual aspects – imaginary, dependent, and absolute natures. The imaginary is external objects. The dependent is the seeming aspects of mind and its object – the dualistic world. The absolute is mind beyond division or concept.

As each instant of perception arises, it depends on its other aspect for existence – i.e. the perceived aspect needs the perceiving aspect to have any meaning. The next school criticizes the Cittamatra for this fault, saying that mind can have no substantive reality – it is a dependent entity. The school is called Madhyamika, the Middle Way, and divides into Rangtong – empty of self – and Shentong – empty of other. Rangtong has two branches. Svatantrika demonstrates the emptiness of relative phenomena and establishes emptiness as absolute nature. Prasangika is more rigorous in terms of establishing emptiness of phenomena but strictly avoids any statement about absolute reality. Rangtong focuses on logical refutations of normal notions of reality. Rational approaches always undercut themselves and a rationalist worldview fundamentally conflicts with experience. There are a few common arguments to establish emptiness of fundamental phenomena – the one and the many and the tiny vajra.

The one and the many points out that any singular phenomenon is made of parts, thus it is also multiple. A car is the sum of engine, tires, wheels, body and so forth. But nothing can be both one thing and many things – it is a direct contradiction. Therefore the normal idea of singularity in objects does not withstand scrutiny.

Likewise, an analysis of time shows it to be unreal. Ponder a near future instant. It is not yet here, and is not yet determined. (At least not provably so). With no one to experience it, it cannot be real – no precise characteristics exist. The present is what we think of as real – here, now, tangible. Our future instant moves closer to the present, then enters it, then recedes into the past, never to be seen again. The past is irretrievable – it does not exist. But it makes no sense to say that an unreal future instant moves into the present, becomes temporarily real, then recedes into the unreality of the past. At what point could it become real, then lose its reality? This analysis takes away the substantive reality of the present moment and thus of time itself.

The next analyses dispute all notions of causality, including acausality. The logic is somewhat aggravating to contemplate. The normal response is to reject it without full understanding. The key is that they do not prove any idea about causality. It is solely a disproof of any causality concept, which is extremely disagreeable to quotidian mind. It takes a serious effort to understand the logic. It doesn't happen immediately because it is foreign.

Causality works temporally – a cause gives rise to a later effect. On a gross level this works and that's why we believe it so strongly. But on a precise level, it has contradictions. First problem – a cause must precede an effect in time, but to do so, the cause must end before the effect begins. However, this would make cause and effect unconnected in time. Contrariwise, if the cause connects in time with the effect, then they are simultaneously existent, violating the principle that cause must precede effect. It's important to realize that disputing causality does not mandate acausality – that is an assumption of the law of the excluded middle. It does not apply here. This is the Middle Way.

The argument called the 'tiny vajra' disputes the four ways of arising – the cause and effect are the same, they are different, they are both, or they are neither. If they are the same, then cause has no meaning – it is no different from effect, so there is no means to distinguish them. But an acorn and an oak are different. If they are different, then how can a cause give rise to an effect on a predictable basis? Remember, by the law of the excluded middle, a cause is either the same or not the same. If it is not the same, it is different.

If cause/effect are both the same and different, then the flaws of the first two positions merely add together. And if the cause is neither the same nor different, then what can it be but nonexistent, implying acausality? But acausality cannot be correct, because inputs have reliable outputs – planted grain produces wheat and water flows downhill. Neither causality nor acausality can be precisely established. As Karl Popper said, "causality is a metaphysical assumption."[334]

Without a precisely established causality, things are said to be illusory – such that interconnectedness is the fundamental reality. Phenomena can be described in grosser terms, but they always elude sufficiently precise analysis. At some level of close examination, they are beyond conceptual formulation.

The difference between the Svatanttrika and Prasangika is the establishment of the absolute nature. Svatantrikas claim the absolute is emptiness. Prasangikas say that to establish emptiness by reasoning creates a subtle conceptual approach. However, the logic itself dictates that conceptual mind cannot correctly ascertain the ultimate. Since rationality can always find a contradiction in any rational argument and since contradictions invalidate rational arguments, rationality cannot perceive the ultimate. Conceptual mind is a rational formulation based on symbolic logic – words map to phenomena. Therefore, nothing can be said about the absolute nature. Since every argument is self-defeating, it is better to remain silent.

The position is quite uncompromising. Meditatively, it amounts to the cessation of all concept, allowing the absolute nature to come forth. Mind can rest in the absolute nature. Where Svantatrika assaults non-Buddhist views, Prasangika assaults subtle concepts in lesser Buddhist views. The end goal of all schools is the same – direct perception of reality beyond the interference of logical, conceptual mind. That is why meditation is not considered a form of thinking. The main point of Prasangika philosophy is to reveal contradictions inherent in any logical position. This gives the conceptual mind no place to be, no means of solidifying conceptual reality. Svatantrika overcomes the belief in Kant's 'noumena,' the thing in itself – self-nature. Prasangika overcomes the idea that things definitively have no self-nature, which is still a conceptual formulation. The school also overcomes the divide between absolute and relative, or essence and appearance. Any such division is a conceptual imputation.

Physicist L.Q. English compares Prasangika madhyamika to condensed particle physics, finding three types of emptiness. First, objects arise in dependence – they cannot have independent existence. Otherwise, they would be unable to interact. All phenomena arise from other phenomena, but cannot be reduced to their causes. Second, all phenomena arise in dependence on a conceptual label. Third, all phenomena are made of parts, but the parts do not contain the object.

Water is not the sum of its parts. A few molecules are not water, but without them no water exists. So water is not found in its parts, in a group of parts, or beyond its parts; no water identity can be found. Water has no essence and does not inherently exist.

Likewise, molecular crystal lattices (ice, salt) have unproven virtual particles such as phonons, excitons and polarons. These show no demonstrable reality, but are mathematically imputed. They cannot exist at the microscopic level without the overarching crystal lattice. However, they are needed for macroscopic explanation. They neither exist nor not exist. In semiconductors, a 'hole,' or absent electron, must be treated as real as an actual electron. It is dependent arising – emptiness. Inferred particles fulfill their functions, but by appearing in dependence on other particles, they cannot be found in isolation – only mathematical signatures are left. Condensed matter physics proves that no one theory can explain all phenomena – laws vary with complexity and scale. New characteristics appear and others vanish.[335]

Shentong, the final school, means empty of other. Considered by many teachers to be the highest view, it applies especially well to meditation. Rangtong is the best view for contemplation, for cutting false views. Shentong reveals the true view. Being inherently conceptual, logic cannot perceive any reality beyond concept. It is like trying to feed somebody the word 'hamburger.' The Shentong critiques Rangtong in a simple manner. If everything is, in fact, empty and without essence, there would be no basis to give rise to the world. The Shentong master claims that reality has its own nature, that it is not empty of self. It is empty of other – no conceptual idea can capture it. This reality has many names – Buddha nature, clear light essence, and wisdom mind. It cannot be perceived by consciousness. It cannot be a divided object, and dividedness – perceiver and perceived – is the definition of consciousness. From this point of view, Rangtong meditators have such a powerful skill at negating even the subtlest illusion that when the wisdom mind arises, they negate that as well, blocking true realization. So the ultimate reality appears as emptiness, or even non-existence, to conceptual mind. Logic can never find the ultimate reality. Logic is extremely skilled at cutting away false realities – that is its function. The genuine reality is perceived by direct meditative perception. The task is formidable and requires expert guidance from a highly skilled meditator who can perceive it. Illusory manifestations can be very seductive and convincing. They lead the practitioner astray.

The grosser afflictions of anger, pride, lust, rationalism, materialism, atheism, Buddhism and so forth, obscure the wisdom mind. Thus from a Western scientific perspective, such a thing cannot and does not exist. Because the approach is experiential and inwardly focused rather than experimental/theoretical and outwardly focused, Western methods cannot discover it any more than Eastern methods can determine the speed of light in a vacuum.

Buddhism has an epistemology and philosophy of investigation at the core of its process. Study of theory, then contemplation to shape the mind's understanding lead to meditation which perceives beyond the contemplation. In taking conceptual attainment as the highest goal, Western science excludes itself from proper dialogue with the higher schools of Buddhism. It simply negates this meditative understanding. The practitioner will be curious about Western arguments, but ultimately unswayed by the fundamental assumptions about reality.

Many scientists affirm this type of belief. It is simply a lie to claim that science believes only in material reality. Certain scientists clearly do believe so. Being loud and vocal, they bear an outsized influence. They attack scientists who do not subscribe to the materialist paradigm. They use humiliation, ridicule, ostracization, and other forms of academic terrorism. But that does not make them right.

Conclusion

From the valleys, one cannot see what it is like at the summit.
—Longchen Rabjam

In 2001, an English girl named Laura Buxton released a balloon with her name and address. It descended in the tree of another ten-year-old girl, 140 miles away. Her name was also Laura Buxton. When the two girls met, they both wore a pink jumper and shorts. They had the same hair and eye color and were the same height. They both had a three-year-old black lab, a grey rabbit, and had brought their pet guinea pig, brown with a beige-orange patch on their 'bums.'

This true-life set-up for a surrealist joke received wide attention. Skeptics pulled out their pellet guns of logic to bring this balloon down in a puff of air. There is some point. For example, the evidence focuses only on what they had in common instead of favorite colors or foods (both different). Or siblings, parents, etc. Obviously, millions of differences exist. That still doesn't invalidate how unusual the incident is. Surely there are wildly unlikely coincidences. This may be one of those cases. *Or it may not be.*

James Randi discounted the story for a different reason – it's an anecdote. An anecdote is a short account of a particular incident or event of an interesting or amusing nature, often biographical. Every experiment performed is an anecdote. Anecdotal evidence needs to be considered precisely because it operates where traditional science fails – outside the laboratory. Empirical investigation demands statistical corroboration – it must be repeatable. But this explicitly assumes that all reality is replicable, an unverifiable hypothesis.

Anecdotes are perfectly acceptable as evidence if they meet two conditions. The events must be verifiable – video cameras have already changed the scientific field. Second, the conclusions must be a logical consequent of the evidence. With these criteria fulfilled, an anecdote is valid for study. Otherwise, the collapse of the three buildings on 9/11 would be invalid for study. It was no more than a sum of different pieces of anecdotal eyewitness testimony, not repeatable by experiment.

Shopenhauer stated the problem with biased debunkers pretending objectivity, "everyone takes the limits of his own vision for the limits of the world." The first explanation becomes 'it cannot be different than what I already believe.' Therefore, instead of investigating the hypothesis that an unknown force influenced the balloon, the pre-determined conclusion that it can only be a coincidence is certified with the seal of undeniability. Where is the proof?

Anecdotal evidence is inadmissible scientifically is because it is unverifiable, not because it is a story. If it can be verified, it is valid for study. And the case of the two Lauras has been verified. The world's most prominent skeptic can't understand this simple principle. "Too much skepticism," Carl Sagan said, "and you're closed to the advance of science."[336] Skepticism has fallen from the fine discipline it once was. A modern Gestapo, it now aims only to attack, not to understand.

These days, skepticism has degraded to psuedo-skepticism, a bias toward negation rather than an open skeptical position. The true skeptic has the liberty of not stating a position and thereby avoiding the burden of proof. Modern skeptics claim they have no burden of proof, but they do state a position. They state that something is *not possible*. A negation is also a claim, requiring proof. These negative claims frequently amount to strange alternate hypotheses which are unbacked. For instance, "a UFO is actually a giant plasma, or someone in a psychic experiment was cued by a high pitch others which normal ears would fail to notice...the result is that many critics feel that it is only necessary to present a case for their counterclaims based upon plausibility rather than empirical evidence."[337] This tactic is so common on skeptic blogs as to be universal. They seem not to even realize they are doing it. It is a form of acculturation, a thought-style, now invisible to the group. It is so rigorously ingrained that it cannot be successfully revealed to the members. They will ignore it.

The character of scientific dialogue has changed radically in the past 10 years. It has become angry, even venomous. A simple disagreement on any science blog is typically met with hostility and insults. Any idea of science as neutral or free of emotion vanishes with such interactions. Science is the people who do it and the discussions they have. In that case, it is now a blood sport.

The most profound skeptic actually wants to believe in something, but will rigorously test it for proof. These modern skeptics simply deny without any investigation. It isn't science; it's arrogance. A genuine skeptic would side with a person proposing an unpopular concept and try to prove it, just as much as he would try to disprove it. Skepticism has lost its dignity and its joy.

It's a long-standing habit. In the 1800s, a town reported rocks falling from the sky. The scientific community dismissed it as mass hallucination. The debate was fierce – museums destroyed valuable specimens because scientists said they couldn't exist. Later, an investigation discovered meteorites.[338] The problem was an adherence to a pre-ordained theory – rocks do not fall from the sky, therefore, the people are delusional. But as Robert Oppenheimer said, "there is no place for dogma in science."[339]

Most debunkers take apart strawman arguments. Disagreeing prima facie, they don't bother to deeply understand oppositional positions. Valid skepticism is uncomfortable – stepping into indeterminacy, not grasping onto facile scientific answers. The world is unpinnable, fluid and everchanging. Uncertainty is both philosophical and experiential. Genuine skepticism demands courage, not of convictions but of convictionlessness. It demands the certainty that there is no certainty, the knowledge that nothing is knowable, and the vision of nothing to see.

Skepticism has a long history of both Eastern and Western styles. The Eastern is essentially Buddhist/Hindu. The Western style can be divided into philosophical and, more recently, empirical skepticism.

It seems to have begun when Pyrho felt he could no longer rely on dogmatic beliefs to order reality. His followers sought mental quiescence and proposed that scientific beliefs were unnecessary for it. They wanted to void all beliefs, but bumped against the unavoidable truth of appearances. The world and its contents appear, in other words, without proof. (The Buddha called this Maya, the play of illusion.) Sextus Empericus fleshed out this basis into a workable mode of investigation. Skepticism, he argued, can be summed as skepticism toward the perceiving consciousness, the perceived object, and the connection. For example, different states of mind produce different perceptions of reality – happy, fearful, querulous, or what have you. Objects have different proportions from different vantages – in front of or behind a door. They have different properties under different conditions – ice and steam. How do we know which of these contradictory appearances constitutes reality? According to proper philosophical skepticism, we can't.

In recent years, scientific skepticism has emerged. Also called empirical skepticism, it doubts less and demands more. Here, claims require an empirical basis. It's a sensible position. The proper method is to subject varying claims to a rigorous investigation by experiment. It is an axiom that unusual claims not be rejected out of hand, but that they require extraordinary evidence. This seems fair enough, but the typical modern skeptic does not evaluate the evidence. He rejects it automatically.

These skeptics invalidate the true skeptical position by categorically denying a host of phenomena. They tend to class these together as 'supernatural': spirits, psychic powers, dowsing, intelligent design, UFOs, and conspiracy theories. But they give mainstream ideas a free ride. Expert opinion and peer review are the only truths, not individual analysis.

Seat yourself in the heart of the science, then attack it. Nothing else is Western science. No one does this anymore. Science, by this ideal, is over, possibly forever. Human failings, desire of success, and pressure for money have stolen that integrity away. In a capitalist system, only a deluded man would believe that science is not for sale. Its own noblest goal, science is merely a commodity in the all-powerful market. Those who espouse its sacred purity as a current reality are guileless or liars. No one outside of science gives a damn about it – the center did not hold.

The proponents of reigning scientific theory cut off all debate. They seem not interested, even hostile. The point of this book is to bring out contrarian theories, to give the debate reality. Any theory not properly challenged is almost certainly wrong. Points of failure are not exposed; flaws are buried. The basic notions may be valid, but such a theory will have mistakes not subjected to the process of discovery.

The book counters the idea not only that science is objective, but also that some group called 'scientists' possess a mysterious power whereby consensus becomes truth, and that this group's conclusions escape the mundane considerations of the rest of us: money, politics, ego and career ambition.

One of the main confusions in science and logical theory is that truth is inherently valuable. It is a moral foundation. This idea is assumed, unexamined, and unproved. Of course a positive illusion may be better than a nihilistic truth, but a philosophical contradiction lives in this materialist framework. Truth, as value judgment, is an abstract concept. In a strictly materialist world, there can be no value judgments. To claim that murder is wrong, for example, is to appeal to an immaterial reality – ethics. Truth is widely touted as a principal value of science – but that is mere propaganda. It is the individual or the group's truth that holds forth while other truths are routinely suppressed.

Science needs an atheism pertaining to itself. As a great yogi said, "the proclamation of truth is fearless."[340] The need is practical, not philosophical. There may be areas of reality beyond the scope of rational analysis – e.g. the quantum plane or human behavior. Under the current approach, rationality and testable hypotheses allegedly move inescapably to truth, and nothing more is needed.

Sir Arthur Eddington, one of the greatest physicists of all time, offers a contrast – mind is the first arbiter of anything and precedes logic. "The ultimate data must be given to us by a non-reasoning process, a self-knowledge of what is in our consciousness. To make a start, we must be aware of something. But that is not sufficient, we must be convinced of the significance of that awareness. Without the ability to make judgments of significance, we cannot even reach a physical world."[341]

Put bluntly, the materialist doctrine is absurd, so much that we may question its sanity. Time and space are root-level realities, affecting all other material entities. They are not corporeal substance – neither time nor space has physical reality. Space is even defined as non-materiality, and time essentially so. To call oneself a materialist is to diagnose oneself with psychosis.

Before science, man had no means to destroy the planet. Now because of science, we may have no means of preventing it. In spite of this, recent attempts to pull morality into science have happened. "All moral issues in a liberal society are intrinsically unresolvable," Bryan Appleyard says. "All such issues will be progressively decided on scientific versions of the world and values. In other words, they will cease to be moral issues, they will become problems to be solved."[342] Science and religion are not even having the same discussion. The problem-solving ethic turns into the handmaiden of convenience.

Science can, and has, created an endless stream of gadgets to distract people from the existential angst or joy that is their natural lot. This is called 'progress.' No one knows why. People are measurably less happy and more stressed. They are obese and have the attention span of a flea. Is life better? Science has taken away certainties about the world and the internal self and now we have only a perpetual indeterminacy – an endless fragmentation. 'Efficiency is the end of culture,' Manley Palmer Hall said.[343] Comfort is meaningless – we obsess over process and cannot even appreciate our ease. Perpetual distraction is our real economy. Science has disposed of questions of meaning.

'This elevation of Narcissistic self-cultivation to virtuousness closes a circle,' Appleyard writes. 'The self is denied its place in the world and its source of values. It resorts to a pagan act devoted to its own cultivation and worship. This, in justification, is said to be a virtue. The circle is closed. A morality is deduced from the facts of materiality. What the enlightenment philosophers could not honestly do, we have chosen to do dishonestly."[344]

The material bias of science separated ethics from knowledge, or value from truth. Science's efficiency gives it an outsized voice of authority in the world. Thus its underlying premise that everything is material and there is no inherent meaning becomes the truth of the world. Naturally, some people resist – humans cannot live without meaning. In the absence of higher spiritual, religious, or philosophical truths, a meaning built on the deification of self arises. The consumer society becomes the prevalent value. Buy things to be happy. Cut fat, visit the psychologist and take a great vacation. Those are our celebrated values. Krishnamurti said, "it is no measure of health to be well-adjusted to a profoundly sick society."

Nietszche predicted this – his last man, small of mind, blinkered in spirit. Spiritual values cannot exist, morality is a degraded paean to indulgence, and humans are genetic robot vehicles. Mass production and the cultural degradation of a disposable society leave us saturated in trivial distractions. Where has religion gone?

Part II

Faith

Religion keeps the poor from murdering the rich.

—Napoleon

Syncretion

Covenant of Genocide

Only a true follower can properly misunderstand a great leader.
—Karma Namgyal

"What is hateful to you, to your fellow do not do," Hillel said. "That's the entirety of the Torah; everything else is commentary." Perhaps, but one wonders if Hillel read the book. His idea is difficult to reconcile with flooding the world, murdering all first-born, committing genocide, and enslaving the surviving virgins. It would be nice to believe this teacher, but when he closes with 'now go and study,' one puzzles if the student will find this Golden Rule in the space of blood that is the first five books of the Bible.

A very different, but more commonly accepted basis of Judaism is Maimonides' 13 principles of faith. 1) God is the creator and guide of everything. 2) He is a unique unity, 3) free from all material properties, 4) the first and the last, and 5) the only valid object of prayer. 6) All the words of the prophets are true. 7) Moses is the chief of prophets. 8) He received the entire Torah. 9) There will be no other Torah. 10) God knows all deeds and thoughts, 11) rewards the faithful, and punishes transgressors. 12) The Jewish Messiah will eventually arise and lead Israel to dominate the Earth. 13) The dead will be revived. Better than Hillel, Maimonides still leaves a few serious gaps and plenty of questions.

Asked to list the five major world religions, most people say Christianity, Islam, Hinduism, Buddhism, and Judaism. The first four are the top four by numbers, but Judaism is an odd 12th. Where Christianity has almost 2 billion, Islam 1.5 billion, Hindu a billion and Buddhism 600 million, Israel boasts a meager 14 million extended citizens. For every Jew, there are over 100 Christians. Measure for measure, it is the most politically potent religion on the planet. In part because it is the only tribal religion that hit the major leagues.

Judaism is cohesive, but not coherent. It is tribal, but its parts disagree. This, of course, is the source of its profundity. Without this conflict, Judaism would be trivial.

It is wedded helplessly to Christianity. The bulk of the Christian Bible is the Judaic Tanakh – the Hebrew Bible. It's a fantastic book. While it is foolish to regard it as literal truth, it is not so to mine it for truth or insight. The atheist who dismisses the Bible dismisses his opponent's central argument. The Hebrew Testament makes a lot more sense by knowing the summary. It's still a mash-up, but it has a historical, theological movement subject to dissection.

God creates the world with Adam and Eve, then floods it – saving Noah, makes a covenant with Abraham to create a great nation, and renames the grandson Jacob as Israel. Jacob has twelve sons – the twelve tribes of Israel. Moses leads the Israelites out of Egypt, into the desert where they get the formal covenant – follow the Law and expel/destroy the Canaanites. Joshua accomplishes this genocide. The tribes split into warring fiefdoms. Around 1000 bce, the warrior David appears from the peasantry to become king. His son Solomon receives a singular covenant – no matter his actions, God will favor him. After this apogee of culture, Israel divides into Judah and Israel. The Assyrians conquer Israel, scatter the Ten Tribes, and destroy Jerusalem and the Temple. Babylon conquers Judah. Cyrus of Persia, the only non-Israelite called Messiah, sends the Israelites back to rebuild.

The time of the latter prophets occurs during the conquest/exile/return – God no longer acts, and speaks only through them. A tradition of love and wisdom emerges with Second Isaiah, Psalms, and Proverbs. In the most potent theological book in the Bible, Job challenges God. Afterwards, God hides. He is either not mentioned, or becomes Daniel's cosmically removed Ancient of Days. He is now both an absence and a powerful, distant, silent figure, sitting on a throne, staring into the future. The covenant degrades and falls into confusion. The chosen people await the end times, more or less bereft of God. The Tanakh ends by reliving the past – I and II Chronicles recaps the time of David until the fall of Jerusalem. It gives the book a peculiar recurrence – rolling again and again through the Judaic history.[345]

With this map in place, a deeper analysis can help to comprehend Judaism. Not fully, of course – it's an ancient and deep religion, not well understood even by its most serious practitioners. But the point of this book is to move atheism out of a smug, self-righteous, condescending shell. The atheist worthy of the label humanist longs to communicate. Aware that any ideology, including his own, has shortcomings, he wants to understand first, then critique. In this, new atheism has utterly failed.

Many approaches to looking at Judaism are possible: contemporary relations in the Middle East and the world, Palestine, the Diaspora, the emergence of Israel since 1948, the oppressor/oppressed cycle of history, the monotheistic fulcrum that pivots half the religious world, the tribal religion, the various covenants, the separation from others as the Chosen People, and the inexplicable aspects of the religion.

All of these can be analyzed through the Tanakh. The books are the same as the Old Testament, but the order is different. The prophets are in the middle, giving the book a theistic flow from "action to speech to silence."[346] The approach here analyzes the Tanakh as both Judaic history and cultural insight, using the shifting notion of God as proxy for the changing face of Israel. Using a literary entity as metaphor for a nation, if it tracks a lengthy period, leads to a schizophrenic history.

God opens from on high, creating the world and man. He immediately becomes more mundane as he switches from El – the god on high, to Yahweh – the boots-on-the-ground god. The first covenant, pre-Israel, is to 'be fruitful and multiply.' Man is given dominion over the Earth. When he kicks Adam and Eve out, he is worried they would eat from the Tree of Life and 'become like us.' For unclear reasons, he destroys the world through flood. The second covenant comes to Noah – God will not again destroy the world. After this, Abraham gets the first tribal covenant* – "I will make of you a great nation."[347] Abraham gets a reproductive advantage and, in a recurrent theme, must travel to a promised land. Abraham challenges God before the destruction of Sodom and Gomorah. God seems fine with the challenge and even compromises. He also has a rather weird morality – Lot, who has children with his own daughters – is saved, even though the towns are destroyed for sexual depredations.

God adds a new aspect to his character, one which plagues religion to this day – the personal deity. He performs the trivial task of helping a servant find a bride for Isaac. The move conflates the transcendent with the mundane. It's a pivotal moment in religion – a powerful creator attends to individual affairs. A personal god can be commanded and is always there – leading to the bizarre modern contract where an all-powerful creator of the universe guides the smallest human details and knows every thought. At this early point, however, he cannot yet read minds.

* Islam lays claim to the Abrahamic covenant, as well, through the illegitimate son Ishmael.

Isaac begets Esau then Jacob. Jacob steals Abraham's proxy blessing from God by pretending to be Esau – the nation is founded on deception. Jacob is renamed Israel and gives birth to the twelve tribes, his sons. The oldest, Judah, fathers the Judeans – who will become the Jews proper. By modern standards, Judah is not a good man. The youngest, Joseph, is sold into slavery by his brothers because Jacob loves him the most. When they come to Egypt, the saintly Joseph is overjoyed to see them and instantly forgives all.

God is not yet aware of the consequences of his actions. He makes decisions on the spot in response to events. There is still no sense of prophecy.* He is not yet omniscient. Up to this point, we have a history of betrayal, deceit, destruction, and ugly tests. Soon, it becomes anally obsessed. God regularly hands out hemorrhoids and bowel disease. People eat dung, and get it spread on their faces.

Along comes Moses, God's only friend. Moses speaks directly to God, interpreting for others. This is the first 'revelation.' At this point, Yahweh-El subsumes his adversary Baal. He is now part warrior-god. It is the ongoing theme of the rest of the Bible – victory/defeat with Moses as mythic hero. After leading the Israelites from Egypt, Moses gives them the Law – 613 commandments. It is not a happy time.

God springs a peculiar trap on his people. There is no previously codified law, or even any idea of such a thing. When Moses descends with the tablets, he finds the golden calf and becomes enraged. The punishment is extreme – tens of thousands of people are slaughtered. It's arbitrary – the people are convicted of violating a law they did not know existed. He also tricks them into sacrificing their own children.[348]

Aside from the Law, the 'no other gods' commandment formalizes the singularity of God. The Israelites move from a national god in a world with other gods to The God who no longer allows other gods to exist. In the process, he subsumes the competition. It is a 2,000-year process toward monotheism.

The first five books comprise the Torah, or teachings. After Exodus, they wander in the desert, with God, the people and Moses all complaining about each other. God actually lives with them in a tent – cloudy by day and fiery by night – because Moses convinces him not to leave. During the forty years, the tribes fight and massacre each other again and again. God and his people come to an understanding – the covenant. The Mosaic covenant is the rock-meets-bone agreement with God. The

* The Abrahamic covenant reads more sensibly as promise to action than as prophecy.

fulfillment is the Holy Land. This great Jewish prison extends to the present day – they must expel or destroy all the Canaanites so that their religion does not infect the Israelites. By divine command, they must commit genocide on an innocent people. "If there is a town that worships other gods, you shall put that town to the sword," even its livestock.[349] The Canaanites did nothing wrong – they were just in the way. The devout Jew thus has the most insidious mandate – kill or be killed. If they fail to remove the Canaanites, then God will turn on them and they will be destroyed by the Canaanites. *This is the heart of the covenant, still in effect.*

The modern feeling of most Jews may be different, but in the Bible they were born to fight. Deuteronomy best expresses this fierce nationalism with God on the side of a specific people. This tribal brutality finds extreme expression when the Benjamites want to sodomize a man from another tribe. He offers his concubine, then goes to bed. When he finds that they raped her to death, he is enraged at the insult to his honor. He cuts her body into 11 pieces and sends these to the other tribes. They wipe out the Benjamites save a few soldiers and vow their daughters will not marry them. This threatens the covenant, they suddenly realize – one of the 12 tribes will fail without women. Fortunately, the town of Jabesh did not participate in the Benjamite destruction. So they annihilate it, except for the virgins, whom they offer to the Benjamite soldiers to freely rape for progeny. This vicious act saves the covenant.

Joshua, the first king, enacts a genocidal pogrom. They fail to expel all the Canaanites, violating the covenant. The tribes fracture, and fall into conflict. Uniting the tribes, King David emerges in God's favor over the previous sovereign, Saul. Saul made a mistake. He was supposed to massacre the Amaleks to fulfill a 600-year-old vendetta for God. Saul spares a small contingent out of mercy and from an old connection. God wanted them all dead, so Saul gets knocked off by David. Outwardly, Saul was punished for not being vengeful enough. But there's another angle. During that period, nation events required a God-explanation. He who failed had lost God's favor, so Saul's defeat needed an explanation.

The emergent reason says a great deal about the Israelite ethic. This religio-culture never lets go of a tribal vendetta. Military victory is the seal of God's blessing. Genocide is a divine command. Revenge is righteousness. Individual guilt is a meaningless concept – if a man sins against God/Israel, his whole people becomes a lightning rod. As a corollary, multi-generational punishments may have been the pre-heaven/hell deterrent. Back then, religious people just died, so God/priests had to threaten their progeny to keep them in line.

The great king David fought for the Philistines and slaughtered thousands of Israelites. A willingness to slaughter the chosen people seems like a big plus for God's favor – Moses killed a lot of Jews. David was arguably a traitor to his own people, but he was loyal to God. He never succumbed to Baal worship. This great hero of Israel devolves into five terrible traits – cowardice, adultery, blasphemy, treachery, and gluttony. Though still a beloved Jewish figure, David had one of his loyal men sent to death in battle so that he could take the man's wife into his vast harem. God sends a servant to accuse David. His punishment – "the sword shall never depart from your house."[350] He was not allowed to build the Temple because of his warlike past, so his son Solomon built it with slave labor. God says, "my eyes and heart will always be there."[351] Considering the Temple was destroyed later, God's statement seems a bit premature.

In David's time, God promises to protect his people "so that they shall dwell secure and tremble no more. Evil men shall not oppress them anymore as in the past. I will give you safety from all your enemies."[352] David is unique – his lineage is unconditionally protected by God. His heirs will be treated as the children of God. In light of this unconditional covenant to David's progeny, any idea of a New Covenant with Christianity names God a liar. The Jews are the Chosen People. Of course, the New Covenant is a reasonable claim – the ensuing history makes God a liar – not long after, Israel is enslaved.

God now moves from action to speech. In I Kings 18, Yahweh performs his final miracle before a 'multitude.' He moves away from man and into Heaven. Soon after, the prophets speak for him, beginning with Elijah and Elisha. Biblical prophecy means a conduit from God to the people – only the latter prophets predicted the future. Also with them came the first inkling of righteousness. They fought against political and rabbinical corruption and they first spoke out for the poor. All the prophets were loyal to the covenant – they preached against Baal worship and the like, predicting the wrath of God. Sure enough, Samaria fell to the Assyrians in 722, Jerusalem to Babylon in 587, marking the decay of a 1,000-year covenant.

Isaiah, the most famous of the later, is generally regarded to be two prophets. The first, a ragged mishmash of ideas and the breeding ground for subsequent prophecy, was written around

750 bce. It introduces the Messiah – a warlike, perfect man who will lead Israel in world conquest.

The Israelites firmly tie the thread of the covenant back to Moses and Deuteronomy. If "you return to the Lord your God, heed his command with all your heart and soul, God will restore your fortunes. He will bring you together to the land that your fathers possessed and you shall possess it."[353] In the prophets, an odd extension of the covenant happens. At this point, possessing the Holy Land is small beer. They are promised conquest of the entire world through various means. Isaiah 19 parcels it out with Assyria and Egypt. In other parts, it is apocalyptic. Elsewhere in I Isaiah, it is peaceful – Israel emerges as lord of Earth with other peoples being their servants.

Second Isaiah was written during the Babylonian exile. The exile and return is a critical period which resonates strongly to this day. Many Jews were taken captive into Babylon. Jerusalem was sacked and the First Temple destroyed. Tens of thousands fled to Egypt, initiating the Diaspora. The alphabet changed from Israelite to Hebrew. The prophets rose to prominence and the Torah became the central text. The entire Bible became canonical. When Cyrus took Babylon, he sent the Jews home to rebuild the Second Temple. The period is the punishment for apostasy and redemption by God.

Second Isaiah (40–66) presents a far more unified vision. The time of tribulation is over. The Israelites will return from Babylon to Jerusalem. All of humanity is included. War is virtually absent. It does not accuse Israel of spiritual failings. Israel appears peacefully ascendant. All other nations will pay tribute. God is clearly and definitively established as the sole God in existence. The covenant of Mosaic Law is now diminished against one of divine inscrutability. Up until II Kings, God was knowable. In the now standard image, God is remote, mysterious, incomprehensible. He is edging towards omniscience. This inscrutable all-knowingness enters God into a new relationship with humanity. Rather than the bulging trivia of Mosaic Law, there is now a Lord working in mysterious ways. He also gains the power to read thoughts. Israel, he knows, has doubts, whereas before someone like Moses had to explain it to him.[354]

The close of the age of prophets brings a change – God goes into hiding. He no longer speaks directly, and his messages are no longer interpreted. They become riddles rather than allegories. Zachariah 13 ends the age – "I will remove from the land the prophets and if anyone again appears as a prophet, 'they shall not live, for they speak lies in the name of the Lord.'"

Israel finally rejects prophecy and it does not appear again in the Bible per se. (Daniel is interpretable as visions). Prophecy seems to have died because it is discredited – the prophecies failed. Some say the fall of Jerusalem fulfills prophecy, but predicting a foreign power to attack Israel is not too impressive – war was inevitable. It would be a lot more amazing if there had been no war.

In Psalms, a divided God leans towards the peaceful side. Divine wrath still gets a few nods – "A blessing on anyone who dashes your babies against a rock."[355] The idea of worship, absent in the Torah, becomes prominent. Omniscience is now total and personal: "You discern my thoughts from afar. There is not a word, but that you, O Lord, know it well."[356] The morality of Psalms moves from the large-scale morality of Israeli victory to one of familial happiness as reward for keeping the covenant. The idea of righteousness for its own sake is in the future – an idea Job will put forth and strike down. Before then, we get a glimpse of the Lord's gentler side in Proverbs.

Beginning with Second Isaiah and into Proverbs, God offers comfort to his chosen people, introducing a 'loving' God. The idea has not appeared before at all. Since God stands as a mirror for Israel, this absence of love until now is critical. It is only and ever a flickering, except for a few individuals – Solomon and Joseph. Despite oceans of wrath and a harsh loyalty, he has shown no happiness, love, or enjoyment. These emotions are unknown, one might conclude, in Israeli culture. At this time, there seems to be some desire for them – a deep cultural shift.

This change in character begs the question – how and why did monotheism arise? Hosea is considered a more accurate historical portrait because it was a contemporary history – most other books were written up to a thousand years after their events. Hosea violently opposed any foreign alliance, believing it would weaken Israel. Out of this arises monolatry – the worship of a single god, but belief in other gods. Soon after Hosea, the Assyrians dominated Israel.

Hosea's opposition is integral to Israel's mindset. Earlier, King Josiah went on a religious extirpation. He destroyed other temples, smashed ritual implements, banned other divination, outlawed household gods, and "slaughtered on the altars the high priests."[357] This purge refocused Yawhew's fragmented identity. The tendency of economic subjugation, divine claim of the king, and the shadow of foreign military hostility pushed Yahweh (god of war and foreign affairs) into the top slot.

"I am the first and the last. Besides me there is no God," Isaiah says,[358] but this monotheism is new. El stood for Elohim, a plural designation for a group of gods. "Do not serve other gods and bow down to them."[359] Yahweh acknowledges competitors – he is not monotheistic yet. In Exodus, he is 'a jealous god.' Without other gods, what is there to be jealous of? "Now I know that you are greater than all other gods."[360] There are other gods. Biblical polytheism is well-accepted by scholars. In Psalm 82:1, "God takes his place in the divine council and holds judgment among the gods," then sentences them to death. In Psalm 86, he addresses his fellow council members – "You are gods." Most polytheistic references were probably culled as part of an editorial agenda.

In Habakkuk, he commands Deibert, a god of pestilence. This has been re-translated through syncretism – absorption of other gods. It's an ancient political tool to unite cultures. In 2350 bce, Sargon of Akkade conquered Mesopotamia. In doing so, he fused his Goddess Ishtar with the Sumerian Inanna, saying they were different names for the same entity.[361] Similarly, Yahweh breaks the heads of the dragons in the waters, crushes the Leviathan, battles the gods of the sea and controls storms – acts of Baal.

"I am Yahweh. I appeared to Abraham, Isaac, and Jacob as El-Shaddai, but by my name Yahweh, I did not make myself known."[362] Shaddai translates as almighty, so he's saying he was formerly called El, the almighty. Julius Welhausen claims the union of two tribes – the Exodus-author fuses the gods into one.[363] The archeological record is not definitive, but the massive exodus probably never happened. Most likely, a small band left Egypt. The main body of Israelites probably broke from the Canaanite peoples, co-opting this wandering tribe. They took the lead god, El, and molded him into their Yahweh. The Bible supports this interpretation. The '-el' in Israel is associated with El – a common practice in those days. Israel (translated as who fights alongside God) probably comes from the union of three Egyptian gods. Isis was a mother god who loved the downtrodden (they were slaves in Egypt), Ra was the sun god, and El was the creator god. When the tribe left/escaped Egypt, they took the gods with them.

Biblical scholars agree that the polytheistic tendencies of earlier Israel withered during the Babylonian exile and return. Israel was conquered, Josiah killed, and the people scattered. But this was not a failure of their god – it was a weird victory. Yahweh proved his might by using foreigners to punish his people. His control of foreign empires but inability to control his chosen people is overlooked. The logic must have inculcated a sense of the highest irony among Judaic thinkers – an all-powerful God born of catastrophic defeat. The desire to make sense of defeat, clinging to cultural identity, and the charisma of Yahwistic prophets probably pushed monolatry into monotheism – it seems not to have existed before anywhere on Earth. The apocalyptic culture gave them a clinging thread. The more debased their situation, the more grandiose the revenge fantasies.[364]

Though clearly male, God is here and throughout asexual. He subsumes competing deities' personalities, but not their lust. God, and by implication Israel, is a creative and destructive force, a distant monarch, and a household companion, a legislator, a being without a childhood or parents. But he is also El, who had a wife – Ashterah. Why did she disappear? Scholar Patrick Miller believes the king did it. As the son of Yahweh, he pushed his 'father's' worship to consolidate political control. He privileged the prophets who stayed on message – ancient propaganda.[365]

God has a female aspect. Only Proverbs hints of her. Lady Wisdom speaks, from herself, but for God. God's femininity appears nowhere else in the Tanakh. Proverbs also introduces a work ethic – elsewhere Israel is mostly told to subjugate other people and live off their labor.[366]

But the dark side has not vanished. God is increasingly obscure, deceitful, and malevolent. "I gave them laws that were not good and observances by which they could never live. I polluted them with their own offerings, making them sacrifice their first born which was to punish them so that they could learn that I am Yahweh."[367] God brags that he tricked Israelites into burning their own children alive. This conflict – power versus morality – has been slowly building. It took almost 2,000 years for the next book of incredible courage and power – Yahweh is put on trial.

Indicting God

The warrior with a broken heart can never be corrupted.
—Chokyi Gyatso

The Hebrew testament has a peculiar ethic. The Israelite covenant with God holds a supercessory position to all other structures – moral, financial, familial. The covenant is a powerful lacuna in the book of Job – it is not there. Job is not clearly an

Israelite,* but God calls him the most righteous man. This functions as a hidden question. Why are Israelites more important than others? Does the blood oath of the covenant overpower God's Psalmic commitment to righteousness?

Job raises the ultimate profound theological question. Part of that profundity is that he asks it directly of God – or so it would appear. Theodicy – why is there evil with a just God – has brought low many a true believer and it is never better expressed than in its first formulation – the book of Job.

There have been many exegeses of Job – Aquinas, Gregory the Great, Calvin, even Kafka allegedly interpreted the book. Most begin with the idea of vindicating divine justice and finding meaning in suffering despite inscrutability. The interpretation fails – the author intended nothing of the sort.

The wider El-Yahweh morality suggests, rather typically, that the good are rewarded and the wicked are punished – except when God breaks that rule. His reasons are inscrutable. The Job author asks what those reasons might be. The text refines righteousness, taking away the reward-for-goodness model, replaced with a more absolute version of righteousness. In the face of no reward, even terrible suffering, can love of God remain? But God does not introduce this morality – the 'adversary' does. A superior philosopher to God, he suggests that virtue practiced for reward is not genuine virtue. God allows him to test Job on that basis.

One might suspect the writer of a sly agnosticism – why did the Creator of the Universe not think of this himself? The Job author is a masterful theologian. He essentially asks the question of Euthyphro's dilemma. If morality is right because of God's authority, then it is arbitrary – subject to God's whims. If it is right in itself, then God has no power over it and cannot be omnipotent. But Job goes further, stepping straight past this question and, it can be read, dealing God a silencing blow.

In Hebrew, *satan* is a verb – to obstruct. 'The satan' – adversary – appears only three times in the Hebrew Bible: to wager over Job, to incite David to make a census in Chronicles, and to accuse the genocidal king Joshua in Zachariah. (Eve's snake is never said to be him.) The satan is a minor character, little more than a pebble in the shoe. He certainly doesn't stand out as evil. Job's satan seems to be part of a divine council with the mandate of philosophically challenging God.

The adversary claims that Job will curse God if afflicted. He takes away family and possessions. Job passes the test. The

* This is an ongoing Rabbinical debate – not clear in the Bible.

adversary claims if his body is struck, then he will curse the Lord. God agrees to the challenge. Job gets boils and falls into misery – one of the most wretched characters in literature.

More subtle agnosticism – God does not win; the devil simply vanishes. Job, scholars agree, was written by two different authors. The later added the frame story – the wager and the restoration of Job to his former status. It is a very different story without that addition, spookier and far more threatening – it yields no comfort.

The Hebraic text does not submit to the tidy conclusions of Job cursing God or cleaving to belief in God's virtue. Job does neither, but walks straight into the ambiguity. Taking this middle way, he questions God directly without fear. Beforehand, his friends counsel that God is punishing him for an act of wrongdoing. He does not agree. He neither accuses God, nor validates God's justice. He wants answers. Ultimately, Job has his confrontation and speaks to the whirlwind in the desert.

The symbolism is clear. A whirlwind is chaotic and powerful, and cannot be a metaphor of rectitude. Any such interpretation is an after-the-fact salvage job. The whirlwind never specifically identifies itself as God. After Job speaks at length about justice, the voice rages at him about the authority of power. "Shall one who should be disciplined complain against Shaddai? He who arraigns God must respond."[368] This is a loaded verse – God is on trial. He has been arraigned and accepts that. Second, he is deceitful – Job is not 'one who should be disciplined.' He is the most righteous man in the Bible, by God's own witness. His only possible crime is daring to question God, but of this he is never accused.

The voice says that one who is guilty should not complain, but never says Job is that man. It is intimidation without truth. God prevaricates. He bluffs. Job offers two responses. First, he says, 'you are mighty, I am powerless. I've said what I came to say and won't repeat it.' Up to this point, Job has questioned God vigorously about justice. God responds with the answer of power. He ignores the question of justice. Then he demands an answer from Job, who refuses to answer.

A third point of the agnostic case – Job never uses honorifics to address the Voice. Everywhere in Israelite society and the Hebrew Bible, God is addressed honorifically. But Job ceases to do this when he encounters the whirlwind. He addresses the voice as an equal.

The Orthodox interpretation is that he recants: "I know thou canst do all things and no purpose of thine can be thwarted. 'Who is this that hides counsel without knowledge?' you ask. I have uttered what I did not understand, things too wonderful for me which I did not know. 'Hear and I speak. I will question you and you declare to me,' you said. I had heard of thee by the hearing of the ear, but now my eye sees thee, therefore I despise myself and repent in dust and ashes."[369]

The inner quotes are Job's repetition of God. This brief, stunning speech ends with a clearly repentant phrase – but the translation is deceptive. The suddenness of his reversal jars the reader and makes no sense. Up to now, he has been resolute in demanding an accounting from God about His justice. Not getting it, Job has no reason to reverse his position. He has held a steadfast integrity and courage in the face of all adversity. "Though he slay me, yet will I trust in him: but I will maintain mine own ways before him. He also shall be my salvation: for an hypocrite shall not come before him... make me to know my transgression and my sin."[370]

Were he to reverse his position, we would expect some more substantive comment on it. The text was subversively translated to support the 'God is just' theology – but the writer intended something very different. All Job wants is God's verdict. Is Job innocent or guilty? Otherwise, his suffering is ambivalent and ultimately without meaning. God will not comply. But Job's uncompromising demand, his righteousness, puts him above God morally. The trial he demands for himself turns into a trial of God. God may be found guilty of arbitrary injustice.

Job readily acknowledges the superior power of the Lord, but does not switch from his demands to self-despising in a mere two lines without explanation. Utterly consistent and precisely logical, he has not received any answer to his simple question – *what are my sins?* Job, of course, knows nothing of any wager with the Devil. He knows only his own failing faith in God's justice. His reversal makes sense only through exegesis – an imposed ideology of later interpretation. Job's recanting is an artifact of translation.

After defying God by silence, in his second response Job does not recant – he restates. *On this difference hinges the entirety of the Hebrew Bible.* Can a fully virtuous man convict God? Jack Miles, a biblical Hebraic scholar, offers a more consistent translation of Job's final statement, "You know nothing can stop you. You ask, 'who is this ignorant muddler?' Well, I said more than I knew, wonders quite beyond me."

Job realizes that his demand to know his sins uncovered a deep truth about God – 'I said more than I knew.' Job continues:

'You listen and I'll talk. I'll question you and you'll tell me,' you say.
Word of you had reached my ears.
But now that my eyes have seen you,
I shudder with sorrow for mortal clay.[371]

Miles, whose book took the Pulitzer, capably defends his translation in detail. Most importantly, the word myself (I despise myself) never appears in the original. Job never recants. Job, in fact, defeats God on ethical grounds. He emerges as a superior moral entity. By force of integrity, his trial is swept off the table and God's is put on. The idea of a just God is invalidated. For Job, God is the greatest curse humanity could ever have.

The book of Job holds the final words of God. Taking out the frame story (where God praises Job for his righteousness), then God ends as a voice of chaos whose sole ethic is power. The most stunning fact of this presentation – in the remaining ten books, God says nothing. Job reduces God to silence. Not only is the Job-author agnostic – he denies a just God. The last words of God in the Old Testament may have been written by an atheist.

Divine Void

Why do you sleep, O Lord?
—Psalm 44

In the last third of the Tanakh, God is gone. He does not act; he does not speak. He is silent as deep space. This is mirrored by his journey from early ignorance with Adam and Abraham to all-knowingness as Daniel's Ancient of Days. Omniscience is silent.

Ecclesiastes makes an interesting denouement for Job. A book of poetic philosophy, it looks into the ways of the universe by implying that God is inert. 'Time and chance happeneth to all men.' Israel has finally moved past the strict covenant and Law as absolutes. Indirect questioning of God, as opposed to the earlier direct questioning, is the new philosophy. Looking at the apparent absence of God, Israel determines its own independent attitude.

Esther gives that absence narrative form – God is not even mentioned. An Israelite, Esther becomes queen of Persia. She turns the tables on a minister oppressing her people by intervening with her husband the king. The Jews are granted 24 hours of impunity to wreak pre-emptive vengeance.

From Kings until Esther, the unified Israelite narrative has been absent. The stories form a hit-or-miss hodge-podge of people and prophets. Here, Israel emerges as unity, almost a character in the story. But she has no God.

Notable in Esther, the Israelites are now the Jews, but the Judeans were only one of the twelve tribes. It cannot be determined whether the eleven tribes disappeared or changed their collective identity. Israel has returned with a serious national personality, but with the largest gap in the Bible. Esther mirrors Exodus – it is an intervention to prevent genocide against the Jews. God's absence is not incidental – Israel has abandoned the idea. She is on her own as a people. No one even calls on God in this time of incredible peril. The Jews have lost Yahweh.

The coherent, but incohesive Israelites become the cohesive, but incoherent Judeans. The critical point helps explain the modern Israel/Judaic reality. The tribes were incohesive by inter-tribal warfare, but they cohered in sensibility through the covenant. After the apostasy and the loss of Israel to foreign powers, the covenant is not clearly in effect. The relation with God is neither true nor false. Its powerful force is no longer a presence, but the historical echo sweeps through the people. From twelve tribes, a single unity of Judea emerged, but the understanding of their place, their historical coherence, has dissolved into Job's whirlwind. Their meaning as a people is no longer well established, but their tribal unity is stronger than ever.

Daniel sets a new tone. Taking a cue from I Isaiah, he has apocalyptic visions. An apocalypse is a revelation of God, seeing him. It is characterized by destruction and warfare with a divine intervention. It happens at the end of time. Daniel reintroduces God, but he is now impossibly remote. The Ancient of Days, he sits, white-bearded, on a throne and silently awaits a distant future. This will be a time of terrible trial and powerful retribution carried in bloody metaphor. At the end, of course, Israel will emerge triumphant.

Ezra and Nehemiah close the chronology of the Bible by introducing a current theme in Judaism. A large Diaspora has powerful emotional, financial, political, and spiritual ties to Israel. Nearing the end of the Hebrew Bible, the Mosaic covenant is slyly re-upped. "When God delivers other nations to you and you defeat them, you must doom them to destruction, grant them no terms and give them no quarter. You shall not intermarry with them. Otherwise the Lord's anger will blaze forth against you and he will promptly wipe you out."[372]

Ezra and Nehemiah reintroduce Mosaic Law, the Torah, and the covenant. They claim the power to accept the covenant on God's behalf. God is no longer needed. Nehemiah becomes harsh and brutal as the story of Israel closes. He tortures people who have intermarried. Thus the final prohibition in the Tanakh chronology is against marrying outside of Judaism.

"We will not neglect the house of our God."[373] Though written in the 4th or 5th Century bce, this near final biblical injunction reads to modern Jews (and Christians) as a command to rebuild the Temple, destroyed in 70 ce. But the Islamic Dome of the Rock is now there, finished in 689. This is the central bone of contention between Christianity/Judaism and Islam. This building site may yet be the spark setting off the next world war. The Temple demand is fiercely reinforced as the Tanakh closes.

Chronicles forms an unusual coda – it appears as past but commands the future. The book recapitulates the apogee of Israel from David to the fall of Jerusalem. The closing words of the Tanakh are the same as the opening words of Ezra. The king of Persia says that God has given him charge of all the nations of the Earth and wants him to build "Him a house in Jerusalem. Any of you of all his people, may his God be with him. Let him go up."[374]

The final words of the Tanakh are to return to Jerusalem and rebuild the house of God, like a drumbeat on top of Nehemiah. There seems to be a calculated idea in the placement – Ezra/Nehemiah comes after this chronologically. In the Christian Old Testament, Chronicles comes before Ezra. The idea of a recurrent Israel cycle suggests itself – a rise and fall within the covenant parameters. But the specific ending is this demand to re-instate Israel, which happened then and again in 1948. The Third Temple, however, must be built in blood. All three monotheistic religions share this vision – the apocalypse is imminent.

Savior

Gospels

Sell all you have and give it to the poor.
—Jesus Christ, Gospel of Luke

Christians don't follow Jesus. Jesus taught to never save money, toil for bread, give away all possessions to anyone who asks, sell everything for the poor, and not marry if they wanted heaven. A beggar who died in agony at 33, he promised to bring division but not peace. He split up mother from daughter and told people to hate their family. He told Christians to pray only in closets – no school prayer or Evangelism.[375] He proscribed wealth repeatedly – an obvious recipe for spiritual fulfillment. True followers would see the beatitudes as goals rather than categories. They would strive to fulfill the letter of the law, fast secretly, and study Judaism because Jesus was a Jew. There is a reason that Christians fail to do these things. They don't really believe the Bible. And with good reason – it's filled with internal contradictions, it's been edited to shreds for political reasons, and uncountable versions of it exist.

In Judaism, Messiah is not the Son of God, but is God's anointed – a mortal man. This is clear in the Old Testament. Jesus' lineage is forced back to David – the Messianic prophecy requires he be 'a son of David.' It's flawed reasoning – Joseph was not his real father, God was.

One of the great Christian questions is how a Jewish sect became so rapidly and rabidly anti-Jewish. Mainly, the Jews denied Messiah-ship. The Messiah was supposed to make Israel ruler of the planet. Being tortured to death was not part of the deal.

'Forgive them father, for they know not what they do,' was taken out of many early Bibles. It referred to the Jews, not the Romans. But in that case, the New Christian Covenant would be compromised, so the line was cut. Many Bibles exist with many differences. These are best viewed as political agenda and opportunism.

The first printed Greek New Testament was published in 1517 by Desiderius Erasmus. Using inferior texts, he rushed the translation and publishing to beat out a competitor. The other text was vastly better researched and prepared, but the Erasmus speed earned his Bible the standard of authority for 200 years.* Being so soon after the printing press, this Bible spread widely and became the basis for the King James version. The source texts of Erasmus were mostly made in the 11th Century, hence useless for authoritative reconstruction. In other words, the King James Bible is thoroughly flawed.

In the 1700s John Mill put together a deeply cross-referenced Bible from the old Greek codices including 30,000 textual variations. Modern scholars estimate 300,000 variations exist. The old scribes had a tendency to harmonize the texts, bringing the Gospels in line with each other. For example, Matthew was changed so that Joseph was not Mary's husband but her fiancée. In the original text, she was not a virgin, either. These revelations in the 1700s created a religious tussle. The Protestant Reformation created the *sola scriptura* doctrine: the Bible was the inerrant word of God and all that was needed. The Catholics claimed a Christian requirement for apostolic lineage, which they held, of course.

In earlier versions, Pilate gives Jesus to the Jews, who crucified him. "His blood be upon us and our children."[376] From the Codex Bezay (a very early Bible), he says to "a man working on the Sabbath, 'if you know what you are doing, you are blessed, but if not, you are cursed and transgress the law.'"[377] The unusual interpretation is that someone could violate the Judaic Law if they understood something and receive blessings, but not if they didn't understand.

All these changes came from politics. Some early Christians believed in 2 Gods, 12 gods, even 365 gods.[378] Some felt Jesus was human, some divine, some both. Some felt the Resurrection was a means of salvation, some an example for repentance, and some even felt that he had never been crucified at all. This last is interesting – it is what Mohammed believed and remains Islamic doctrine. No one knows where he got the idea from. The school that won the day, Orthodox Catholics, espoused the Trinity – Father, Son, and Holy Ghost. The Son is fully human and fully divine.

There were other schools. The adoptionists believe that Jesus was born a man, then adopted by the spirit at baptism. The Docetics (Greek: *dokeo*) stressed the divinity without humanity. Timothy 3:16 was changed from *'who'* to *'God* – was made manifest in the flesh,' by a scribe to counter the Docetic view. "This cup is the new covenant of my blood which is shed for

---

* Not until 1551 did anyone organize the Bible by Chapter and Verse.

you,"[379] was arguably a later change in Luke – it stole the covenant for the Christians.[380]

The common way to read the Bible is devotionally. Passages are memorized, earmarked, and mined for wisdom. Critical analysis differs – the text is taken apart for internal consistency. Christian seminaries, to their credit, analyze the Bible in this way. Though pastors know of the many inconsistencies revealed, they don't preach about them. This is mostly about job security – the faithful won't tolerate a skeptical minister.

Biblical contradictions abound. At the last supper Peter asks Jesus, "Lord where are you going?" and Thomas says, "Lord, we do not know where you are going." A few minutes later, Jesus says, "none of you asks me 'where are you going?'"[381] Mathew's Judas returns his ill-gotten silver, then hangs himself. In Acts, Judas buys a field with the silver and falls "headlong [and] burst open in the middle so that his bowels gushed out."

Jesus cleanses the temple. In Mark, it's a week before his death and leads to arrest and crucifixion. John has him do it at the beginning of his ministry. In Mark, Jesus eats Passover (which begins Thursday after dark), is immediately arrested, and crucified the next morning, Friday, at nine. In John, he is captured on Thursday morning (before Passover), condemned at midday, and crucified that afternoon.

The pedestrian point is that the Bible cannot literally be true – Jesus cannot have been crucified both Thursday afternoon and Friday morning. Why the difference? Best speculation – John wrote symbolically. Jesus, the Lamb of God, died when the lambs are slaughtered for Passover.[382]

The first three Gospels are called synoptic (for synopsis) because they have verbatim chunks of text and many of the same stories. Mark was written first, probably around 70 ce. Most scholars, Christian and otherwise, believe Mark is the main source for Matthew and Luke. Matthew and Luke were written not long after Mark. 75% of Mark's short Gospel appears word for word in both of the other two. 97% appears in one or the other. The later two are much longer. They share an additional 25% not included in Mark. This material is called 'Q' for Quelle – the Source.

There are deep character and thematic contradictions. The synoptics have simple statements made by Jesus at his trial. Mark only has two words – *su legeis* – 'you say so,' in response to Pilate's question, 'are you the king of the Jews?' John has long passages, including a discussion of heaven, Pilate's ultimate powerlessness over him, and his mission to speak the truth. With the greatest temporal distance, John exercised the most revisionism, turning the story into a fiction of divinity. Mark reinforces the chosen people theme of the Old Testament. John's Christ tells the Jews their father is the devil.[383]

Jesus' birth is garbled. Matthew and Luke give different genealogies, and both are paternal. But if Mary was a virgin, Joseph was not the father. Jesus had no paternal lineage except God. Matthew has Joseph's immediate paternity as Jacob, Matthan, Eleazar, Eliud to David. Luke's immediate paternity is Heli, Matthat, Levi, Melchi back to David. Mathew's genealogy is 14 generations times three for 42 total. Abraham to David (14) to the fall of Judah (14) to Jesus (14). He skips names in the source material (Mark) and in the actual text there are only 13 from Judah to Jesus. Luke, by contrast gives 57 names back to Abraham.

In Matthew, Joseph and Mary flee to Egypt because Herod intends to kill all the children. There are no extra-biblical historical records of this mass slaughter by Herod. Luke has an Empire-wide census calling Joseph to return to Bethlehem, but the excellent records of Caesar Augustus mention no census. The census makes no practical sense. Joseph returned to Bethlehem, where his ancestor David had lived 1,000 years before. This census would have thrown the entire Roman Empire into chaos. It would have been impossible for each person to trace ancestry a millennia in the past. There would be no way to feed the mass migration since most people would be gone for the census. Half the towns would have ceased to exist over the preceding millennia. Joseph went to Bethlehem to fulfill an Old Testament prophecy.[384]

Matthew and Luke diverge completely on the birth. Matthew has wise men, the slaughter of the infants, and the family fleeing to Egypt. Luke doesn't mention these things, but does mention the shepherds, the census, the birth in the manger, John the Baptist, travel to Bethlehem, and the circumcision. Luke has the birth of Jesus when Quirinius governed Syria, beginning ten years after the death of Herod, when Matthew has the birth. Matthew never mentions the journey and implicitly contradicts it. The wise men visit Jesus in a house – no inn or manger. Mathew's holy parents are from Bethlehem, Luke's from Nazareth. Mathew's escape to Egypt, Luke's return to Nazareth.

Here Christians reverse the logic of sense – they claim that the birth fulfills the prophecy in Micah – 'a savior will come from Bethlehem.' The two irreconcilable versions suggest that the writers forced the narrative into the prophecy.

The Virgin birth is confused. Mark skips the birth and goes straight to adult Jesus. Matthew hashes through the Old

Testament prophecies, achingly fulfilling them. It's based on a faulty translation from Isaiah, very important in the Jesus pre-Matthew. "A virgin shall conceive and bear a son and then call him Emmanuel."[385] The original Hebrew word *alma* usually means young woman – *betulah* means virgin. Matthew made Mary a virgin to fulfill a flawed translation. It was probably not even a prophecy, but merely a statement of fact about something happening in Isaiah's time. Christian preachers make contortions to get around this – it is a central tenet of Christianity. And it is demonstrably false.

The Resurrection takes the prize. John has Mary go by herself. Matthew has two Marys. Luke has two Marys, Joanna and other women. Mark's stone is already moved; Mathew's witnesses watch an angel move it. In the tomb, the women find an angel (Matthew), a young man (Mark), two men (Luke), and nothing (John). Mathew's women inform the 11 disciples; Mark's tell no one; Luke's tell an unnamed disciple and Simon Peter. Mathew's Jesus appears immediately to the disciples; Luke's disciples disbelieve the women; John's go to the tomb to see. Mathew's disciples go to Galilee and Luke's remain in Jerusalem for the Ascension.

The spookiest part is the original end of Mark. The source texts have 666 verses. 12 were added in the following centuries. "Trembling and bewildered, the women went out and fled from the tomb. They said nothing to anyone, because they were afraid."[386] And that's the original ending – no wonder someone rewrote it. Matthew ends with an exhortation for the Apostles to begin ministries. Luke continues till Jesus flies up into heaven. John ends with a healthy assortment of miracles and Jesus still on Earth. Acts begins with Jesus rising up after 40 days.

The Gospel of John differs radically from the first three. The forty days of temptation doesn't occur in John – such tests are for the human Jesus of the synoptics, not the divine of John. Jesus meets John the Baptist and immediately begins the ministry. The only event John shares is the Passion of the Christ. In the synoptics, after the Virgin birth, he performs exorcisms and transfigurations, teaches in parables, and has the Last Supper. None of this makes the fourth Gospel. He is not baptized, does not go into the wilderness, does not teach the kingdom of God, and there are no parables. John's Jesus alone washes the disciples' feet, but does not institute the Lord's Supper. He has no trial before the council. John proclaims that Jesus is the word of God made flesh, an idea completely absent from the synoptics. John's Jesus performs seven miracles – to prove his status. He unabashedly glorifies himself – 'I am the resurrection and the life.' None of these self-aggrandizing statements occurs in the synoptics. He has long speeches, few aphorisms and is weirdly detached from witnesses.

Here is the heart of the differing symbolic interpretations. In John, Jesus pre-existed his birth as 'The Word made flesh.' The synoptics do not have a pre-existent, (eternal to the past) Jesus. The debate is extremely significant in Christian theology* – it underscores the doctrine of the Trinity, and is a major disagreement with Islam. John's Word made flesh has no birth story. John has no genealogy, no Joseph, no Mary. This Jesus is not a prophet born of man – he is a divine presence only revealing a tiny part of his being.

All four originally anonymous Gospels were titled by Church Fathers in the 2nd and 3rd century. By wide scholarly consensus, the Gospels were not written by Matthew, Mark, Luke, or John. None of the authors claims eyewitness status. All four alleged authors were Galilean peasants who spoke Aramaic but almost definitely could not read. Acts 4:13 says that John is 'unlettered.' The Gospel authors were highly educated. The original New Testament, and especially John, is in sophisticated Greek. It's wildly improbable that any of the disciples could have learned spoken Greek beyond a pidgin form, and certainly not written Greek.

Numerous other gospels never made it into the Bible. Thomas, Peter, and Philip all have ascribed gospels. Irenaeus, a 3rd-century Church Father, tackled the authoritative gospel problem. With no substantiating evidence, he determined who the authors were. The Gospel of John clearly states the author was not an eyewitness. He refers to his source, "the disciple who testifies to these things and who wrote them down. We know that his testimony is true."[387] As does Luke 1:1-2, the accounts "were handed down to us by those who from the first were eyewitnesses and servants of the word."

It's not contentious, even among Christian scholars, that most Bible books are misattributed. Only 7 Pauline letters and Revelations (John of Patmos) are considered valid, though some hold to the authorship of the Gospel of John.

There are three reasons for doubt – most texts were anonymous, then later attributed to Apostles by Church Fathers for credibility reasons. Second, non-anonymous books were attributed to a famous namesake – the Book of James, a common name, became James the brother of Jesus – without evidence.

* Isaac Newton kept his Arian, non-Trinitarian beliefs secret for fear of losing his job at Cambridge.

Third, outright forgery is well-established through hundreds of records. Again, a Pauline letter carries tremendous authority over Church doctrine. There was an all-out war over theology between differing branches of Christianity.

In looking at the Gospels, they seem the sole source of information about Jesus. During his time, he was but one of many backwater prophets. Nothing is said of him in Greek or Roman histories until 130 CE. In the Judaic record, he is only mentioned by one historian.

The scholarly application to determine what the historical Jesus might have said has several criteria: it must be close to the time he would have said it, it must be verified across sources, and not be pushing a particular viewpoint. The last is to counter the proven tendency to edit the Gospels for theological agendas.

The Gospel of Mark is arguably the most important for historical testament – it is the oldest, hence closest to Jesus' time. Matthew and Luke are mostly important for their unique material. John, the last Gospel, is far more mystical in its approach. Points where all the Gospels coincide, some scholars say, show the likeliest true material. John changed the original message of Jesus, probably because the prophecy, by that time – 90 CE, had been disproved. The kingdom of God had not come to Earth in the lifetime of any witnesses.

The historical Jesus seems to have been a 'near-term apocalyptic preacher,' a common type in that day. The apocalypse, in brief, is the coming of God to Earth to establish his kingdom. In Jewish mythology, it puts Israel above all others. Jesus believed it was a time of evil and demons. A Son of Man was to come in judgment on mankind. Though presumed to be Jesus, he may not be referring to himself. "The Son of Man will send his angels."[388] "Be prepared because you do not know the hour when the Son of Man is coming."[389] Yet Jesus is already there. It takes an interpretive leap to turn Jesus into the Son of Man – the Messiah. In other Son of Man passages, he does refer to himself, but some of these verses were added in later centuries – the earliest texts do not have them.

"When the Son of Man is seated…you who have followed me will also sit on 12 thrones judging the 12 tribes."[390] But Judas is one of the twelve. He speaks of the kingdom of God on Earth, not in heaven. This type of quote is considered a real one. It does not conform to later beliefs – Judas as betrayer, the kingdom in Heaven, not Earth. Jesus' original preaching on the coming kingdom was revised when it did not happen in the allotted time.

The Bible cannot, of course, be literally true – internal inconsistencies make that impossible. But the more interesting story, for the atheist, is what the Bible really means. And to figure that out, we need to look at the individual author's intent.

According to apostate Bible scholar Bart Ehrman, Jesus was crucified for two reasons - Jewish elders and Roman desire to keep the peace. Jesus came to Jerusalem during Passover because the crowds were there. The religiosity was high. Many people were open to apocalypse. He visited the Temple, knocked about a few tables. It was a symbolic gesture – the destruction of the Temple indicates the Kingdom of God is near. The elders didn't like it. They watched him. As his ministry grew rapidly over the week, they took action. By calling him 'King of the Jews,' he became guilty of rebellion against the Emperor. The Temple priests called on the authorities to kill him. They did so in an almost negligent manner.

Each book has its own messages. Mark's Jesus is totally isolated by circumstances. Everyone mocks him – Jews, soldiers, and even other prisoners. At the end he cries out, "My God, my God, why hast thou forsaken me?" In Mark, the centurion says, "Truly this was a son of God." In Luke, he says, "Truly this man was innocent." The distinction is critical. If a son of God could not understand his suffering, then how could anyone? It is the ancient Jewish lesson – suffering is not ours to comprehend.* For both, Jesus speaks to the Gentiles. The Centurion was neither disciple nor Jew.

Luke's Jesus is more concerned about others – "Father, forgive them, they know not what they do." One criminal begs for and receives redemption. Luke's Jesus offers himself as a ritual sacrifice, rather than the awful tribulation in Mark. For Mark, suffering is incomprehensible, but God is invisibly at work in the act. For Luke, one can understand suffering in the midst of it – indeed it becomes trivial compared to the reward.

The tearing of the curtain is hugely symbolic. For Mark, the tearing ends the rabbinical intercessory power. Jesus provides a link directly to God with his death. Luke's curtain rips while Jesus is still alive. Jesus is not forsaken here – God was present in the act. Jesus' death has redemptive power. By one Luke reading, the tearing condemns the entire Jewish system of worship. Quoting Psalms 31, Jesus 'commends his spirit' into God's hands. This Jesus is not alone, but next to God the entire time.

---

* A son of god is not as exalted as one would think – it means a pure follower. The Son of Man is the real thing.

The thrust of Ehrman's critique is that these different stories have been merged into a single narrative. The different interpretations are not only lost, but emerge as schizophrenia. What mind confidently states, 'You will be with me in Paradise today,' then howls out 'Father, why have you forsaken me?' Certainly the agonies of crucifixion would create many bizarre experiences in a normal mind, but this was not a normal mind. As part of God, his words are supposed to have a deep and abiding meaning. If we interpret them as temporary madness, then Jesus' last words are not particularly profound. And they're contradictory.

Mark's Jesus tells followers they must follow the Law better than the Pharisees to enter heaven.[391] Paul made the Jewish Law an obstacle. The basis of Christianity is the latter. Paul's writings led to the rising persecution of Jews – against Jesus' desire. After Constantine and the officialization of Catholicism, persecution of Jews became systemic. In a massive historical irony, a Jew teaching what he saw as the truth of the Jewish God, was hailed as a savior of the horrifically anti-Semitic Catholic religion.

Scholars agree on a number of points. Jesus preached to the Jews. He considered himself fully Jewish. He was not trying to create Christianity, nor trying to break with Judaism. He preached as an apocalyptic Jew. If so, then the Christian point of view makes no sense. Jesus did not espouse it. Jesus never broke with Judaism. He criticized certain members, to be sure. But the Judaic tradition had no central human hierarchy. Many groups had different views. Christianity did not arise from Jesus. It came from Paul.

With 7 verified and 6 disputed books, Saul of Tarsus (the Apostle Paul) weighs in as the real heavyweight in Christian theology. Before his Jesus vision, Paul oppressed Christians. Afterwards, he became an itinerant preacher. A skillful diplomat, showman, and CEO, Paul founded the early churches that morphed into Catholicism. Using 1st-century communications, he guided the wide network through its challenging early decades.

Paul's accounts of his life are in sharp disagreement with Acts. (Acts recounts the activities of the Apostles after Jesus.) According to Acts, Paul preached to Jews and Gentiles alike. In Paul's own words, he only preached to Gentiles. Acts has his views come from consultation with other Apostles. Paul claims he met only two Apostles and acquired his views directly from Jesus in a vision.

The distinctions are vital. If Paul had a different view of religious conduct than Luke – who wrote Acts – and a different view of Jesus, then which interpretation of Christianity should we take? And here we have a central critique of the tradition. If one wants to understand the Bible, then it is critical to compare and contrast the different authors. Problematically, most Christians simply gloss over the contradictions of the Bible. It's more comfortable. But with the numerous contradictions, viewing it as unerring seems delusional.

A longstanding biblical debate centers on the relation between the Book of Matthew and Paul's letter to Galatians. Paul ardently believed in salvation through Jesus. Those who tried to keep the Halakha (Jewish Law) were in danger of forsaking salvation. Mathew's Jesus, by contrast, said, "Not one stroke of the letter will pass from law until all is accomplished." The Law refers to the 613 ancient Jewish commandments from Moses and the Talmud.* Paul forbids Gentiles from keeping the Jewish Law and Matthew requires it. The two views cannot be reconciled under a literal biblical interpretation. Paul clearly won the debate – no Christian observes the Halakha.

Matthew has Jesus speak of charitable acts – food to the hungry, clothing to the naked – as a necessity of salvation. The lack of those results in damnation. Compassionate acts and observance of Halakha can lead to salvation without Jesus. Paul allows salvation only through belief in the death and Resurrection of Jesus. The two salvations are completely different.

The demonstration of counterfeit letters by Paul is fascinating. In 2nd Thessalonians, Paul talks about an antichrist taking the Temple throne, proclaiming himself God, and leading people astray – clear warnings of the Apocalypse. It directly contradicts 1st Thessalonians 5, where Jesus will "come like a thief in the night... destruction will come upon [people] suddenly." Here there is no warning.

Colossians and Ephesians are forgeries. The theology of the undisputed letters disagrees sharply – the Baptism is a death uniting one in death with Christ, but the individual's resurrection will not occur until the future when Christ comes.[392] In the forged books, a person's resurrection has already occurred at the moment of Baptism. In most letters, Paul opposed this vigorously. It was very important doctrine in his undisputed letters. By large agreement, the others are pseudepigraphic, not Paul's letters.

There is more evidence of falsification. He addresses disputed letters to church leaders. But in Paul's day, there were no such

---

* There are four laws against eating grapes.

leaders – churches were chaotically democratic. The letters give instructions to gird the Church for long-term stability. But Paul was adamantly apocalyptic – Christ's eminent coming would solve all those problems. Most of the canonical and non-canonical gospelists felt Jesus' arrival to be eminent.

These criticisms come from Christian scholars and most Christian scholars hold these opinions. Thus, Christianity has a serious problem. Many seminarians do not agree that the Bible is the literal word of God, but their flock does. Divinity schools and Bible study textbooks include these critiques, yet few Christians know about them. They are also ignorant of the lost gospels.

The original New Testament featured the Gospel of Barnabas, a fearsomely anti-Semitic rant. Barnabas reinterprets the Old Testament as a Christian book not fit for Jews – they have broken the covenant with God.

There are hundreds of other culled Gospels. An ancient New Testament, on papyrus, includes Jude, 1st and 2nd Peter, Melito, and the Nativity of Mary. The fourth-century Codex Sinaiticus, puts in the Shepherd of Hermas and Barnabas. The Codex Alexandrinus from the 5th Century places 1st and 2nd Clement in the New Testament. The Muratorian canon, around 200 ce, is a list of the 22 New Testament books plus the Wisdom of Solomon and the Apocalypse of Peter. In light of this historic revision, differing canons, and inclusion of forgeries, it's hardly possible that the Bible is the unerring word of God. Even the idea is bizarre – it was never stated to be so during the formation of the canon. It was only alleged to be the word of various Apostles.

Serapion formulated an early canon. He chose books only if written by an Apostle. Concerned about forgeries, he had criteria for apostolic origin. The principal one was Orthodox view. The argument, of course, is circular. It assumes orthodoxy to be valid, then supports the view by assigning Orthodox texts to Apostles. Athanasius, in 367 ce, created the list of the current canon, which was never made official. In sum, the problems with the canon are: it took many centuries for the canon to emerge, there is plenty of obvious forgery, and certain parties omitted all dissenting views and added in verses supporting the orthodoxy.

Orthodox Christianity faces an intractable problem conceiving of Christ. It is a monotheistic religion, yet most of its beliefs draw from John and Paul's divine Jesus. But then, of course, one has two gods – father and son. Arianism claimed God created the Son who then created the universe. The Son is subordinate to the Father. Athanasius authored the victorious view – the Trinity.

Based on the Johannine Comma (John 5:7-8), it is not in the oldest Greek Bibles. This most important theological verse in the entire New Testament delineates the Trinity doctrine. "There are three that bear witness in Heaven: the Father, the Word, and the Spirit and these three are one. There are three that bear witness on Earth: the Spirit, the Water, and the Blood, and the three are one."

The Holy Spirit became a third aspect of divinity. The fourth-century Nicene creed fortified the Holy Spirit as an equal part of God, as the ever-existent spirit breathing power from the Father through the Son to create the universe. The spirit guides and arouses the prophets. At one level it's schizophrenic – three cannot be one. At another level, it's a sophisticated theology. God can manifest variously but extends from a singular essence.

Orthodoxy means right view. The struggle between heresy and orthodoxy is a perennial and age-old problem for religion. It opens a heart critique of all religious traditions. Many cling to the mask of tradition, holding onto views outmoded by the modern inroads of science. They grudgingly change only to stay relevant. The early Christian Church held many doctrines. Only the conversion of Constantine in the fourth century made the Roman Catholic Church the orthodox one. It was not that much more powerful, but it existed at the heart of the Empire. The historian Eusebius, soon after, rewrote the history to make the Roman Catholic view appear to have been dominant all along. Other groups were painted as powerless fringe groups.

This led to the brutal hegemony of the Catholic Church over Europe and later South America. But political implications aside, it destroyed any semblance of spirituality. The whitewashed version of Luther had this spiritual aspect.* He tried to remain loyal to the Pope, but in the end accused him, too.

Religion needs heretics to break it free of tired doctrine. Stamping out all disagreement destroys spirituality. Such a dead religion may still thrive socially and politically. 'It is right because the leader says it is so,' is anti-spiritual. 'Our way is right, other ways are wrong.' 'You can buy your way into heaven.' These are purely religious, in the most profane sense. The *spiritual* struggle occurs within; the religious without. Religion is political. That is not bad, per se, but it speaks to baser desires. Political altruism requires enormous wisdom and strength. Few succeed. Despair, marginalization, compromise for ideology, noble victory in religious politics – it is a narrow gate. Centuries of Catholicism have utilized the canon, doctrine, and

* The real Luther was also a Jew-hating zealot – see his book *On the Jews and their Lies*.

priesthood to extend authority. It is not a spiritual end; it is a political one. Even the most devout Catholic comprehends this.

One of the most pernicious problems of Catholicism comes from this: priest as intercessor. Ignatius of Antioch, to the Ephesians, said "regard the Bishop as the Lord himself." The Pope is the direct line to God. But if there is no God, or God is silent, then what is the Pope? The Pope's primary mission historically is not interpreting the will of God; it is holding the Church together. The primary tools are the desire for heaven and the fear of hell.

The earliest Christians did not believe in heaven, hell, or the soul. They were apocalyptic, an answer to the problem of theodicy – why do people suffer under an omni-benevolent, omnipotent God? According to the ancient form, suffering is temporary. God allowed evil to overcome the world for some reason – test of faith probably. At some point, he will come to Earth, raise the dead, and pronounce judgment. All wrongs will be righted.

There is neither heaven nor hell in this view. Paul seriously believed it. Christ would come to usher in this age and lead as a king. He preached that the end times were about to happen any day. The Resurrection signified the pending resurrection of everyone. If someone died in the meantime, they would be with Christ in a temporary heaven, then be reborn on Earth. If righteous, they would be transformed into immortal bodies here.

Thus eternal life for Jesus, Paul, and early Orthodox Christians was a physical life here on Earth in this body, resurrected by God. Not in heaven, not in hell. When the apocalypse failed, the message was reinterpreted. Heaven and hell were created.

The Astonishment

Just be normal, that's already strange enough.
—Dutch saying

The Jesus Project, started in the mid-1980s, sought the actual Jesus within the historical record. After peeling the layers back, many researchers came to a shocking conclusion: Jesus never existed. In high atheist countries like Sweden, it's long been the standard view. Most modern scholars accept that the historiography to establish Jesus is insufficient. "The gospel authors were Jews writing in the Midrashic tradition and intended their stories to be read as interpretive narratives, not historical accounts."[393]

Pontius Pilate existed, but the excellent Roman records show no evidence of any execution of a Jesus. No historians of the day mention Jesus. The first appearance (aside from the NT) is almost a hundred years later. The Gospels themselves were written decades after Jesus' time. They are written in the third person – no Gospel author indicates they were ever in the presence. There are no eyewitness accounts of the physical Jesus. In fact, The Bible offers no physical description of Jesus anywhere. Jesus often spoke while alone – how did the authors know what he said when alone? They also report on his thoughts – how could they have known them? These are tools of fiction, not history.

All Greek and Roman writers who mention Jesus were born after the Crucifixion. None provide sources. They appear to reference contemporary stories – the same kind of evidence as Athena or Hercules. Most believed in these figures, too. All the miracles of Jesus were rehashed from the Old Testament and all his sayings were common in the day.

Matthew 2 describes the mass slaughter of infants, but no historian recorded it. King Herod even died in 4 bce. In Luke 23, Pilate sends Jesus to speak to Herod, 37 years after the man's death. Pliny the Elder and Seneca wrote history at the time – neither said anything about Jesus. Philo Judeas, born in 20 bce, lived until 50 ce. He scrupulously recorded all Judaic history in and around Jerusalem, but never mentioned Jesus.

Outside of the Bible, there is no evidence for Nazareth. It is not in any of the epistles (which predate the Gospels), in the Old Testament, or in the writings of any contemporary historian. There is no surviving physical evidence. Modern Christians claim it was tiny, but the Bible calls it a city, using 'village' and 'town' for smaller places. Paul never mentions Nazareth. Archeological efforts found only tombs where it should be – but the Jews never put tombs in towns.

The apocryphal Gospel of Philip gives a different slant. Ancient Hebrew had no vowels, which allows for easy misinterpretation. *Nazara* means truth. In Philip, Jesus is called the Nazarene, one who speaks truth.[394] The Nazarenes were an ancient Jewish/Christian sect with no connection to a place. Mathew's obsession with fulfillment of prophecy caused the confusion: "He came and dwelt in a city called Nazareth, *that it might be fulfilled* that spoken by the prophets. He shall be called a Nazarene."[395] Writing in Greek, Matthew misses the boat. Judges says, "for the child shall be a Nazarite,"[396] a man with long hair.

The Bible speaks of the wide renown of Jesus – Herod and all the great priests knew of him. "Great multitudes of people from

Galilee and Jerusalem, Judea and beyond Jordan" followed Jesus.[397] "An innumerable multitude trod upon one another."[398] According to the Gospels, everybody knew about him, but not a single record keeper or historian alive in his time wrote about him. And it's not for a lack of records – there are plenty. The eclipse and the rending of the Temple veil (at the Crucifixion) went unreported.

It's a long-standing puzzle in Christian scholarship. In fact, it is a set of puzzles with a potential common answer. The easiest expression of the problem is in Paul's letters. Strangely, Paul never refers to Jesus as a living man. There is no reference to his ministry or life. We'll get to the evidence for the surprising statements, but Paul, who wrote before the Gospels, only speaks of the Crucifixion and Resurrection of Christ. There is no place, time or disciples. Paul's Jesus was not of Earth.

Outside of the Gospels and a few cursory references in Acts, the New Testament makes no mention of a human Jesus. This may be why Acts, written in the 2nd Century, allied Paul with the Jerusalem Apostles. Paul never made this connection in his own writings, but Acts was written during a time of inter-church battles.

Five of the six major Christian apologists of the day make no mention of a physical Jesus. (Justin Martyr is the exception.) It's a bizarre omission since the man Jesus is the fount and foundation of the Catholic Church. How could the readers of these earliest Christian writers have understood the doctrine with no mention of Jesus and his redemptive qualities? Modern apologists weakly explain that these ancients were hiding Christ. But this sits ill with the martyr tradition – proudly proclaiming Christ even to the point of being tortured to death for belief. Besides, these authors wrote before the systematic persecution and had little to fear.

Justin shows this early lack of knowledge about a historical Christ. "But Christ, if he has indeed been born and exists, is unknown. And you, having accepted a groundless report, invent a Christ for yourselves."[399] Even more interesting is Felix's Octavius. Speaking of the future Resurrection, he asks, "what single individual has returned from the dead that we might believe it for an example?" This Christian apologist *never mentions Jesus* as such an example. Later, he says, "men who have died cannot become gods, because a god cannot die, nor can men who have been born (become gods)."[400]

This knowledge has been around for a long time. The problem is how it fits into the modern Jesus mythology. The long-standing idea of him has been overturned in the past few hundred years, a change with increased force in the past few decades. It is now considered that there was an itinerant preacher named Jesus, a wise man who was crucified. The ideas and miracles were, willy-nilly, attached to him by religious force. But it still fails to explain the absence of the man himself in these early documents.

A number of theorists have turned the idea on its head. Euhemerism means a mythical figure came from a real person. This would be reverse euhemerism – a fictional figure bridging into the historical record. The divine Christ spoken of by Paul accumulated a historical Jesus, one who never existed. The concept is off-putting and requires a suspension of the normal thought-style. The historical Jesus has so much cultural force that it is automatically assumed, even by most atheists. But the evidence can be analyzed from the opposite perspective – Jesus never existed.

The evidence is extensive. According to this theory, instead of a single expanded story, many threads consolidated. These included Hellenistic influences, Platonic monotheism cross-pollinating with Judaic monotheism, an apocalyptic tendency, a wisdom tradition without revelation (the Cynics), a particular Midrashic tradition which invented tales based on the Tanakh, and the ubiquitous savior cults. The Diaspora was in full swing – spreading Judaism and absorbing Greco-Roman influences. It was an uninhibited exchange, people becoming and ceasing to be Jews. All of these elements existed at the time and all appear in Christianity.

Dividing Christianity into its two traditions – Galilean and Jerusalem – gives a better handle on the material. The Galilean spoke of the pending kingdom of heaven, the return of the Son of Man, the judgment of the world and the general apocalypse. Anti-establishment, an ancient rural tradition, it preached a new society and a radically changed ethic, sometimes even casting off the Law of Moses – a prevalent theme in Paul.

The Jerusalem tradition united pagan and Jewish themes. Based on itinerant preaching, it spread much more widely – also a Pauline feature. (He united these trends, in fact.) This tradition spoke of Yeshua (Jesus) the Christ (Messiah or anointed one), a supernatural savior. This is the revelatory tradition – the divine God (or Son of God) speaks to the prophet, but appears only in visionary form. In certain instances, the Son of God underwent a mythic-realm death and Resurrection. The death was an act of sacrifice and in some cases supplanted the animal-sacrificial tradition of Judaism. This realm was considered real, but in a higher dimension. The Son of God linked humans with the deity.

This syncretic answer brought salvific mystery cults into the Jewish tradition.

The Hell above us

Imagine there's no heaven.
—John Lennon

The record of Paul sheds the most light. "This is what we all proclaim, that Christ was raised from the dead."[401] Paul discusses the Crucifixion and Resurrection again and again. Despite this, the latter 22 books of the NT do not mention Jesus being the Son of Man, the Messiah, or from Nazareth. The few Nazareth exceptions reference historical events after Paul's death – thus from false Pauline letters or later insertions.

For Paul, the supernatural Christ was a very real being. In a verified letter, he puts words to Jesus in the Lord's Supper. This is often taken to mean the Last Supper – but this is not indicated in Paul. He claims the idea of the Lord's Supper came from revelation.[402] A common question for all Christian scholars remains unanswered. Why did Paul put forward this super-powerful, cosmic, divine Christ who bound the world together, an alpha-and-omega Son of God, but completely ignore all details of his earthly life? In Paul's theology and ethics, *he never quotes Jesus*. "If you are observing the sovereign law 'love your neighbor as yourself' that is good."[403] He says many of the savior's ideas, but when he quotes, it is from the Tanakh. Bible expert Helmut Koester said of Paul, "surprisingly, there is no appeal to the authority of Jesus."[404] Earlier Christians noticed the discrepancy.

"God has shaped us for life immortal," Paul writes, "and as a guarantee of this, he has sent the spirit."[405] Why not Christ sent as guarantor? The omission makes a hash of current Christianity. "For I deliver to you what I received, that Christ died for our sins *according to the Scriptures*, that he was buried and raised on the third day, again *according to the Scriptures*."[406] Paul wrote before the Gospels – he draws on the ancient Tanakh tradition to speak of the Crucifixion, not on any recent historical record or personal knowledge.

Paul writes about the Jewish guilt for ignoring his message of Christ. He never speaks of their guilt for ignoring Jesus himself or for any part in the Crucifixion.

He speaks of apocalyptic visions, 'the Lord himself will descend,' but Jesus is not involved. He does not use Jesus' own apocalyptic statements.[407] Apocalypticism, also called two-age dualism, was a national fervor. Centered on the poor, it would set right the scales of justice. Good people would get good things and the wicked punishment. Jesus' appearance would be the hinge between these ages – the Christian interpretation. Over the decades to follow, when the apocalypse never occurred, there should have arisen an 'apologetic industry.' But that didn't happen for centuries. Paul even ignores the Son of Man idea. At the time, Jesus was not part of the Pauline apocalypse – that was added later.

He locates the time of apocalypse in his own day, not in the time of Jesus. "God says, 'Behold, now is the acceptable time, the day of salvation.'"[408] Paul's quote is lifted from Isaiah to enforce Paul's message – not Jesus'.

Paul never puts Jesus in any historical setting. He is not crucified on Calvary, nor by Romans. He never mentions an empty tomb or its discovery. He has no time delay between Resurrection and Ascension, no notion that Christ ever walked the Earth, and no statements by Jesus at all.

None of the epistle writers place these events on Earth. There is no desire of any to see Bethlehem, visit the Mount of Olives, or the site of the Last Supper. Jesus is never placed in Jerusalem. He is not resurrected and does not appear on Earth afterwards in these texts. This is an enormous hole – the Resurrection is the most important belief in modern Christianity. The central belief *is not even mentioned* in most of the NT books. It makes no sense.

Paul mentions the appearance of Christ to people. If the reader removes the shadow of the Gospel, these are properly interpreted as visions. "Jesus appeared to Cephas, then to the twelve, then to all the apostles, and lastly to me (Paul)."[409] The Apostles and Paul both saw Jesus in the same mode – a vision. Paul is very clear about his encounters being such. He appears to 500 people at once. Paul himself sees Jesus in his famous conversion on the road to Damascus, but this is decades after the Resurrection/Ascension. And it appears only in Acts, which is bizarre. Paul himself never describes this critical appearance of Jesus. At any rate, it had to be a vision to be congruent with the Gospels timeline.

In Galatians, Paul talks about his two-week trip to Jerusalem to make the acquaintance of the Apostles Peter and James. He does not ask them any questions about the life of Jesus. He does not visit Calvary, the tomb of Jesus, or any sacred site. They were either unimportant to Paul, or they did not exist for him. He explicitly denies an earthly Jesus – "If he had been on Earth, Jesus would not even have been a priest."[410]

Even the Didache, a first-century Christian tradition, has but a brief mention of Jesus and he has no corporeal entity. Scholars have strained the meaning of 'The Lord' to mean Jesus, but it is unlikely. The Didache has no apostolic tradition and no Crucifixion/Resurrection.

Church forefathers Ignatius, Clement, Polycarp and Barnabus wrote in the first half of the 2nd Century. None show any knowledge of the Gospels. This was as much as sixty years after Mark. They have no knowledge of the narrative of Jesus' life on Earth. They believed that Jesus did exist as a human, but never mention the key events. Jesus was divine, they claimed, then became a human.

It was a common understanding that supernatural realms existed, ascending over Earth for seven levels. "Scripture was not the prophecy of the Christ event," Earl Doherty explained, "but its embodiment."[411] In other words, Scripture was the human means to look into these divine realms. These were not prophecies of an earthly future; they were descriptions of a higher order. In Paul's day, reality was much richer, replete with gods, angels and seven levels of the heavens. At one point, Paul speaks of a man "caught up to the third heaven."[412] The reigning belief held God's heaven at the top down to Satan, just above Earth, causing havoc for us. "None of the rulers of this age have understood wisdom, for if they had, they would not have crucified the Lord of Glory."[413] These supernatural "rulers and authorities in the heavens,"[414] not knowing wisdom, turned their back on God. They actually crucified Jesus in this supernatural realm. "Cosmic powers, authorities and potentates of the dark world, the superhuman forces of evil in the heavens," Paul writes.[415] Men did not crucify Paul's Jesus.

For Paul, the Son descended to the lowest of these supernatural levels, where he committed an act of sacrificial atonement. He was crucified by these forces, who didn't recognize him as the Son of God. Then he ascended back to heaven. Christ's sacrifice occurs "in the real sanctuary, the tent pitched by the Lord and not by man…a greater and more perfect one, *not part of the created world.*"[416] He died for our sins, and that is the entire story of Christ according to Paul. There is simply nothing more. But Paul is interpreted by the Gospels, despite never seeing them. He should be interpreted in the light of Hebrew Scripture, which he refers to again and again.

The non-canonical Ascension of Isaiah lays it out. Isaiah rises to the top layer, gets a glimpse of God and the chosen one, and hears that the chosen one will descend to the lower world (not Earth), be killed and raised back to the heavens. In the process, he will save the righteous from Sheol, the Hebrew underworld. "The Lord will descend into the world in the last days. He is to become Christ after he has descended and become like you in form and they will think he is flesh and a man. The *gods* of that world [not our world] will lay their hands upon him and hang him upon a tree, not knowing who he is. Thus his descent, as you shall see, will be concealed from the heavens."[417]

This does not refer to Jesus' of Nazareth or any birth. The god of that world is Satan, by the contemporary mythology. Though Paul draws deeply on Judaic tradition, he also incorporates many Hellenistic notions. The mode of salvation, the characteristics of redemptive divinity and the ritual are derived from Hellenism. The sects included baptism (conferring eternal life and rebirth) and the Lord's Supper – a common shared repast, and a blood-drinking ceremony (Eucharist). Dionysus was murdered and resurrected. Orphism offered notions of good and evil – one of the few mystery cults which did. It introduced sin to the Greeks. Tarturus – the Greek hell – had no Judaic parallel. In a new century of cultural mélange, Paul was a consummate man of his day.

False Prophet

Error is powerful.
—The Gospel of Truth

Toward 100 BCE, even Orthodox Jews began to seriously consider the return of a great prophet. The three ideas were fused and the Messiah/Christ took on the traits of Rabbi, monarch and prophet. Elijah and Elisha cut the Jesus template – 40 days in the wilderness, multiplication of food, and ascension to heaven for Elijah. Elisha resurrected the only son of an old woman on the hill of Moreh. Jesus raised from the dead the only son of an old woman on the hill of Moreh. Elisha cured a leper and restored the sight of an army. The hugely popular book of Enoch contributed the visit to hell, eternal life, the heavenly throne, and judgments of humanity. "You are the Son of Man who was born to righteousness."

Some theorists place Jesus in the Midrash tradition of biblical and legal interpretation. One style of Midrash takes Hebrew Scripture and creates a morality tale – the protagonist endures suffering and demonstrates/fails at morality and so forth. These are meant as teachings, not as factual accounts. But the Jesus story migrated.

Other cultural forces contributed. In Platonic thought, God lay at an infinite remove. He/it created the universe and left. Unfortunately, this left us with no connection. Enter the Logos – the word. It is evident in the opening verses of John – "in the beginning was the word." The Logos manifested from God to connect to the world. It's a quick hop from the Logos to Paul's Christ. The Judaic tradition has a similar theme in the female character of Wisdom. "By the gate, wisdom calls aloud. The Lord created me in the beginnings. I was at the Lord's side."[418]

Though speculative, Wisdom may have morphed from a female to the mythic Son of God. Modern scholars are cognizant of a similar Pauline tendency. By modern interpretation, Paul put his mythical Jesus onto the actual itinerant priest Jesus. But where did the man's life go? It appears that later Christians are reading into the text, seeking the man Jesus by extrapolation from the faint traces Paul left. But the resounding lack of reference to a physical Jesus is stunning.

Even the Gospels don't leave much meat on the Jesus bone. One source document for Matthew and Luke, the hypothetical document 'Q,' is the set of common Jesus sayings between the two. Q has no context – the setting and time for each saying are completely different between Matthew and Luke, but the words are nearly identical. Some interesting facts about the source material emerge. Q never speaks of Jerusalem. The Gospel of Thomas has some of these aphorisms – 'blessed are the poor, for they enter the kingdom of heaven' – and some of the characteristics. The only link to Jesus is that each aphorism is preceded by the words 'Jesus said.' It has no narrative, context, Crucifixion, nor any other events. With Q and Thomas, we find two distinct lineages. Both ignore the Crucifixion and Resurrection.

Q has two layers – the earlier wisdom tradition and the later apocalyptic tradition. Going back to Q, it is impossible to make final judgments, but it appears that Jesus was not originally in there. The reason for believing in two layers is the radical opposition in message. The wisdom sayings are tolerant, peaceful, and loving. The apocalyptic sayings are anything but – they are almost hateful. Best guess is that an apocalyptic Jewish assembly integrated the first Q layer into their apocalyptic tradition.

"[I]mportant to the first-century Jew ... were the key issues of Temple, land, and Torah – race, economy, and justice. When Israel's god acted, Jews would be restored to their ancestral religion, with the rest of the world looking on in awe, and/or making pilgrimage to Zion, and/or being ground to powder under Jewish feet."[419] The set of aphorisms in early Q does not correspond to this victory ideology and is not well grounded in the Judaic tradition. The other tradition should come from that same place and time. A number of scholars since the 1980s point to the Cynic tradition.

Cynics were itinerant preachers, with a message that society was too structured, top-heavy, and hypocritical and that only by attunement to nature would people escape suffering. "Consider the beasts yonder and the birds," Dio of Prusa said, "how much freer they live than man."[420]

Q preachers had the same motif. The preachers had to sever family links, sell possessions and take to the road. Judaic values were tribalism, wealth for being righteous, and living in the Holy Land as per the covenant. When a man wanted to bury his father before following Jesus, he said, "Leave the dead to bury their dead," a strange ethical position, but perhaps a Cynic one.

Interestingly, the apocalyptic layer of Q does not specifically incorporate Jesus either. Each saying always happens in different settings between Matthew and Luke – there was no context in the source material. We might forgive Jesus his absence from the early Q – it was grafted on from Hellenism. But since he was rooted in the apocalyptic tradition, it makes no sense why he is not in the original apocalyptic source material – unless he didn't say it. The alleged founder is absent from the beginning.

Scholars have found two or three anecdotes tacked onto Q – they appear in Matthew and Luke, but not in Mark. So it looks like Mark pulled pieces, especially prophecy, out of the Tanakh and placed them in a narrative. The stories are fiction, meant to instruct like *Pilgrim's Progress* or Dante's *Inferno*. The evidence suggests creation of the Midrash by Mark. Matthew and Luke then took the Q document, retrofitted with a 'Jesus said' frame, and independently folded it into Mark.

John was written from Mark, but with a completely different message and theology. In John, Jesus no longer interacts. He talks like a psychotic – "I am the way, the truth and the life…I am the door to the sheepfold."

The emergent picture is not one of a historical Jesus giving rise to various stories of his life, but of a number of itinerant apocalyptic and salvific traditions unified into a single religion – Christianity. This then coalesced on the Midrash of Mark, transforming it gradually from morality play to received truth. The strongest indication is the tone difference between the Q material and the rest of the Synoptic Gospels. He is at times a parable preacher – gentleness, concern, love of fellow man. The image is of slow transcendence, seeds growing into trees. He even implies it is already here if we only perceived correctly. "The kingdom of heaven is in your heart."

The apocalyptic tradition is full of 'rumors of distant wars,' locusts, earthquakes, and zombies. It will be soon, sudden and intense. "There will be two in a bed. One will die."[421] It is not a moral situation – it's just random violence. A person believing both of these futures simultaneously is schizophrenic. Jesus contradicts his own ideology. "The law should not be changed one jot…I come to fulfill the law," versus "the Sabbath was made for the sake of man and not man for the Sabbath."[422] He even heals someone on the Sabbath.[423]

Virtually every action in Jesus' life has a corresponding reference somewhere. A solid source of material, especially for Mark, is the Tanakh. "Then the eyes of the blind shall be opened and the ears of the deaf unstopped. Then shall a lame man leap like a hart, and the tongue of the dumb sing," versus "the blind recover their sight, the lame walk, the lepers are clean, the deaf hear, the dead are raised."[424]

According to fundamentalist Christianity, Jesus fulfills the prophecies, but this is wrong. Most of the things taken from the Tanakh were not prophecies; they were just events. Elijah uses 20 loaves of barley and some corn to feed a multitude.[425] Mark uses the same event twice – loaves and fishes. Jesus didn't fulfill prophecy, he recycled miracles. The theology is a New Covenant with God, a Christian covenant superseding the old. Jesus needs to have the same signs as those prophets. Thus they are borrowed from the Old Testament.

An interesting quality of Matthew and Luke – they are parallel until the Resurrection, where Mark ends. Each then invents their own post-Resurrection sequence. Mark's Passion is a literary creation, not an oral account of history.[426]

The Passion narrative itself is a leitmotif of older scriptures – the suffering and vindication of the innocent righteous one. The innocent man is the object of a conspiracy and bogus accusations. He remains loyal to God and suffers, then is sentenced to die. God either intervenes before death or raises him after. His innocence is vindicated as he ascends to heaven. The narrative is in Genesis 39-41 (the story of Joseph), Esther 3, Tobit 1, Suzannah, Daniel 3 and 6, III Macabees 3, II Macabees 7, and Solomon 2-5. It dates back at least to the story of Ahiquar in 500 bce.[427]

Specific Midrashic elements pulled from the Scriptures – Zechariah 9, the king rides in on "a colt, the foal of an ass." Zecheriah 11 has 30 shekels of silver. Exodus 24 – "the blood of the covenant the Lord made with you" compares to Mark 14:24 "this is the blood of the covenant poured out for many." The Apostles flee at Jesus' capture. In Zechariah 13:7, "Strike the shepherd and the sheep will be scattered." In Psalm 2, "the rulers conspire together against the Lord and his anointed," just as Pilate colluded with the Pharisees.

Isaiah 50 says, "I offered my back to the lash, I did not hide my face from spitting and insult." In Mark 15, Jesus is whipped and spit upon. Micah 5:1 – "With a rod they strike upon the cheek the ruler of Israel." Mark 15:19 – "Soldiers beat him about the head with a reed." Psalm 22:16 – "they have pierced my hands and feet." Psalm 22:18 – "they divided my garments among them and cast lots." Both occur in Mark's Crucifixion. Psalm 22 opens with "my God, my God, why has thou forsaken me," which Mark's Jesus says verbatim. Psalm 69:21 – "and for my thirst they gave me vinegar." Jesus gets a sponge of vinegar on the cross. Amos 8:9 – "I will make the sun go down at noon and darken broad daylight." Mark 15:33 – "At midday, darkness fell over the whole land." Mark 15:39 "Truly this man was the Son of God." Solomon 5:4 "Fools that we were, he is one of the sons of God." Hosea 6:1-2, "After two days, he will revive us, on the third, he will restore us." "For three days and nights, Jonah remained in the fish's belly."

This taking from the Scriptures is even present in the negative. In crucifixions, it was normal to break the legs, but it did not happen to Jesus. John specifically denies it. "You must not break a bone of the Passover lamb," from Exodus 12:46. Psalm 34:20 – "he guards every bone of his body. Not one is broken."[428]

Mystery Cult

Truth is not static.
—Ebrahim Moosa

The Jesus story had many mythical sources. Mithra helped the souls enter heavens after death. Born on Dec. 25 with shepherds attending, he could raise the dead and would pronounce judgment at the end of the age. These similarities were claimed, by later Church fathers, to be the retroactive work of Satan. In fact, Christianity can be seen as the sole survivor of the Greek mystery cults. However, Christianity was not kept a mystery, which probably accounts for its survival – it was widely available.

Such pre-cursors are too numerous to mention. In a contemporaneous story, Chaereas finds the "stone moved away...one sent in...the dead girl was not there...the shroud stripped off." Later, he is scheduled for crucifixion.[429]

The story has recurred for millennia. Amen-Ra was the great god of Egypt and arguably the source of the word 'Amen.' Jesus is referred to as the good shepherd, ruling with a rod of iron. Pharaoh was the good shepherd, carrying a rod of iron in representations. Pharaoh was an emanation of Amen-Ra, the son of God. He is also called Horus – his adversary is Set. One of the Pharaohs, about 800 years bce, nullified the pantheon of gods. He only allowed one god – Amen-Ra – and he claimed to be the emanation.

Jesus is thought to be cut from this Horus cloth. Both were born of virgins informed by angels, in a low place with shepherds attending, the only son of an only god, with a foster father descended from royalty, and heralded by a star. Horus was born in the place of bread. Bethlehem was called the house of bread. Herut-Herod tried to murder Horus-Jesus, the families fled, each child had a coming of age at 12, then disappeared. Both reappeared and were baptized at 30 in a river. Anup/John the Baptizers were both beheaded. Horus was KRST, the anointed, called shepherd, lamb, lion, the sword, son of man, the Word, and the fisher – like Jesus. Both were tempted on a mountain by Set/Satan and resisted. Jesus was 'the living bread,' Horus the 'possessor of bread.' Both came to fulfill the Law. Both had 7 loaves to feed the multitude. Both came by the water, blood and spirit. Both were called the 'morning star' and gave the same to their followers. They performed the same miracles – raising the dead, walking on water, restoring sight, stilling waters, and exorcising demons. Both had a conversation with their father on the mount at sunset. Both transfigured on a mountain, gave a Sermon on the Mount, and were crucified with two thieves. Three days later, they were resurrected with women as witnesses. Each was prophesied to reign for 1000 years.

The Hindu Krishna has a similar story – Crucifixion, Resurrection, second coming with stars falling from the firmament and sky darkening. Thousands of years before Jesus, men were claimed to be the Son of God with a mother named Mary or equivalent. They scolded their elders at 12. The ruler tried to kill them at birth. They began ministries at 30, died on the cross at 33. Sixteen such prophets predate Jesus – Krishna, Ioa of Nepo, Hesus of the Celtic druids, and Quexalcote of Mexico among them.

Alkmene had a mythical union with Zeus and gave birth to Hercules. Hera (Herod) wanted to kill him. Hercules wandered, doing miracles. Josephus, in antiquities, speaks of Hercules and

Jesus as equals. Perseus, Mithra, Osiris, Hermes and Prometheus all died violently – Prometheus was even crucified. All were rescued from mass infanticide by monarchs. All were born just after the winter solstice (Dec. 25th) of virgin mothers. Their fathers were all gods, all fasted for forty days, and all were resurrected. Mithra was buried in a tomb of rock and had a eucharist.

Other interesting interpretations exist. "There you will meet a man with a pitcher – follow him into the house."[430] Some critics believe that this means the Age of Aquarius – the legend of Christ is zodiacal. While this is often taken too far, certain references are probable. The endless fishes symbolize the current age – Pisces. According to this theory, the Crucifixion/Resurrection is the winter solstice. The sun goes into a three-day low on Dec. 22nd, then is born again on the 25th – the death and Resurrection. Of course, that's celebrated in Spring, but it would explain the Resurrection. The zodiac has a cross and a circle for the sun. The cross divides the sky into the four seasons. The disciples are the twelve houses. The symbol appears on many churches – cross with circle and sometimes twelve spheres.

The Old Testament Joshua ben-Nun is also translated Joshua of the fish. Jesus (Joshua or Yeshua) means savior. Nineteen Jesuses appear in the Jewish histories of Josephus. Four were high priests, nine were contemporaries of the Gospel times. The question, in the end, is not really whether a Jesus existed – many did. The question is how much of the biblical story is grounded in human history. And the answer seems to be precious little.

Gnosis

Be an arrow of awareness.
—Ekajati chant

Like science, like anything, Christianity is abused for political and material gain. But that is not its own crime – it is the fault of manipulative sorts. As religion, however, it long ago committed the worst sin: self-mutilation. 2,000 years ago, Christianity destroyed its most profound ideas.

Their re-emergence was spectacular. In 1945, Muhammed Ali al-Sammân found an earthen crock in a field. It held ancient Gnostic texts. His mother burnt part of them to start a fire. Soon afterwards, he and his brother murdered a man as an act of revenge for their father's mother. They hid the texts from the police who were hunting them. Then the priest holding them offered them for sale on the black market. Eventually, the Egyptian authorities recovered the texts and placed them at the museum of Cairo. Professor Gilles Quispel travelled to Egypt to study them. The first thing he read was, "These are the secret words which the living Jesus spoke."[431]

The Gnostic gospels present a completely different picture of Jesus – shamefully ignored by Christians. The spiritual aspect is formidable. "If you bring forth what is within you, what you bring forth will save you. If you do not bring forth what is within you, what you do not bring forth will destroy you."[432] Gnosis accuses Orthodox Christianity of degrading God.

Early Christian groups practiced very different systems. The Ebionites retained their Jewish heritage and followed Christian teachings. Jesus was the Messiah, sent from a Jewish God to the Jewish people. To follow him, one had to become Jewish. Paul taught the opposite. The Marcionites followed and surpassed Paul. Jewish Law and Jesus' salvation were different. They radically concluded that Yahweh was the enemy of Jesus' God. According to Marcion, the Old Testament god created the world almost maliciously. When people disobeyed him, they suffered eternal damnation. Yahweh was evil; the Christian God was good. He sent Jesus to die and redeem people so that they could escape the old god.

Gnosticism has many flavors, but most are related to Marcionism. Here, the transcendent is genuine reality. Physical reality, a cosmic accident, entraps the divine nature. We must understand our true identity to escape. Christ was a divine being not entrapped. He showed the means of liberation. Some schools posit two entities – the man Jesus and the divine Christ. The latter entered at the baptism and taught until death, prompting the cross-borne cry – 'why hast thou forsaken me?' The public teachings are irrelevant to salvation. Jesus gave secret teachings.

Orthodox Christianity became the official doctrine during the fourth-century reign of Constantine, a political phenomenon. By orthodoxy, Jesus is both God and man. Sent by God, he shed his blood to atone for sins and open the door to salvation through faith. "I am the truth and the life," the Bible Jesus said. "No one comes to the father but through me."[433] The Catholic Church used this statement to mandate people's participation in the Church. As interpreter, only the Church opens the door to God. It appeals to the many. Even the lazy have only to confess. The simple-minded have but to turn to the pastor. One's decisions and consequences are not one's own. Guiding principles come clearly to the follower and society is unified under a central code. Though atheists insist otherwise, the system has benefits.

The negative aspects are obvious, too. Rigid hierarchy allows tyranny – an evil Pope makes an evil Church. Corruption pervades. Individualism is stifled – the Bible was originally kept in Latin to prevent peasants reading it. Any personal, creative connection with a higher power must be filtered through Church dogma. Without Holy See validation, the consequences are severe, even today. Among the most grievous is the closure of the spiritual. Spirituality is an inner experience. It cannot be codified – especially by harsh application.

History has many faces. The Catholic Church's unobstructed appearance as a unified form in the early days is one. It is wrong. Catholicism was weak, one of many traditions. Gnostic Christianity was the opposite of orthodoxy – hence a war between the two. Any Gnostic could have revelation. Women held the same authority as men. Democratic to the point of anarchy, the role of pastor changed weekly by drawing lots. In fact, the Gnostics were part of the Church. They attended any meetings they wished, but claimed no need to submit to the codes. They were not bound to monogamy, for example.

Battle lines were drawn – the one creator God who invests the orthodoxy with power against the nameless divinity beyond God, accessible to all. Irenaeus, an astute political theologian, took the battle to the grounds of doctrine. All Christians, he proclaimed, must believe in the single true God, the creator. Clement, the first Bishop of Rome, declared that people who spoke against reigning church leaders violated the authority given by God to rule. Such people should be put to death.[434] Other fathers said the bishops should be treated as if they were God. These speakers are so blunt that they must have believed it. The Old Testament gives plenty of support for a rigid authority.

Gnosis, or knowing, is an ancient Greek word. It has two meanings – the rational and the intuitive. The second knows essence, character and fate. But it has roots in rational knowing. Philo of Alexandria believed the rational mind was the extension of God's wisdom. Elevating this mind and suppressing the base desires of the flesh was the road to godhood. He also wrote about the Logos as God's way of connecting with Earth and even creating the world through it. It unified natural and moral law – acting in accord with nature.

Gnosis claims that the god we perceive is merely an image – a demiurge which created the world and became confused. Gnostic language is a bit cagey; different texts have different beliefs. In a common approach, men who look to the primal Godhead mistakenly see a manifest sentient creator. Thus the Bishops' claim to power is based upon error. The Gnostics, representing spirituality, did not want this battle. The Church, representing religion, did.

Valentinus, one of the most important Gnostic leaders, was also politically clever. He merely agreed that anyone who wished to submit to the creator god and the mundane Catholic Church should do so. After all, it was a proper gateway to true understanding. Many Gnostics were even priests who held their initiations secret. Irenaeus accused them of being agents of Satan, so the Gnostics posed a dual level. The outer church was elementary Gnosis, and the inner, secret church gave the real teachings. Though Irenaeus was uninitiated and didn't understand the inner teachings, the inner church accepted him as a true follower of Gnosticism. His counterstrike, *Against All Heresies*, introduced the doctrine of repentance. It was the seed for witch burnings, the Inquisition, and centuries of torture that plague the Church's image.

Probably the most important take-away is that many early Christians disbelieved the current doctrine. The Church was not formed from a solid belief in God. Jesus was not the sole salvation. These beliefs emerged, by force of violence, over time.

Gnosticism is not easily summed up – there were too many strains of it. Some were vitriolic against Jews, some apocalyptic, some even hateful. But the records found in Nag Hammadi show shocking doctrinal differences from orthodoxy. Most notably, the Old Testament God is not the New Testament God: "'I am God and no other exists except me.' But when he said these things he sinned against all the immortal ones. Faith was angry. 'You err, Samael (blind god). An enlightened immortal humanity exists before you.'"[435]

The Valentian sect spoke of "a sole Lord and God."[436] However, Gnosticism generally referred to the Godhood not as a sentient being, but as "an invisible, incomprehensible primal principle."[437] It has a strong non-conceptual strain. "To call God by any particular name is deceptive, for it diverts our thoughts from what is accurate to what is inaccurate. The one who hears the word 'God' does not perceive what is accurate. So also with the Father, the Son, the Holy Spirit, the Resurrection and all the rest. People perceive what is inaccurate."[438]

The fundamental problem is political. The Church claimed one God, one Son, and one appointed Apostle – Peter. From him extends the Papal lineage. Without it, no one can approach. The Gnostics emphasize a direct approach to an ineffable Godhead, neither masculine nor feminine, without hierarchy. To go through Bishops was to adulterate the genuine reality with conceptual poisons. The battle is age-old – the individual versus the group, the spiritual versus the religious. "For whoever has not known himself has known nothing," Gnostic Jesus said, "and whoever has known himself achieves knowledge of all things."[439] Who needs a priest?

The world is an apparition, according to the treatise on Resurrection. Ordinary life is the death of the spiritual. "Those who say they will die first and rise are in error. They need to receive the resurrection while they live."[440] Here the fleshly resurrection is mocked – it is an inner, metaphorical act. Even the biblical Jesus hints of deeper teachings – "To you has been given the secret of the kingdom, but to those outside everything is in Parables – they may indeed see, but not perceive, hear but not understand."[441]

The Gnostics run with the idea. "Bishops and deacons, [claiming] authority from God, are waterless canals who do not understand mystery yet boast the mystery of truth belongs to them alone."[442] They reject Orthodox authority by attacking the source. The Papal lineage extends from Peter. In the Book of Mary, her spiritual wisdom surpasses Peter's. We have a number of counter-orthodoxies in this one notion – women are equal or superior to men; a hidden, higher lineage holds this wisdom; and the orthodoxy is confused. A single formula expresses it – feminine principle. It begins with creation.

Some Gnostic schools call the origin story a birth metaphor. Adam and Eve is conception, Eden the placenta, the river out the umbilical cord. Exodus is birth, the Red Sea menstrual blood.[443] The virgin birth represents the innate purity of the 'Ground of Being,' untainted by its creation, no matter how degraded that becomes. It is ever youthful and fresh in experience. For Valentinus, the cosmic womb gave birth to divine manifestations with masculine and feminine compliments. Similarly, "the Mind of the Universe, which manages all things, is a male … a female … produces all things."[444]

Gnosticism was very appealing to strong, independently minded women. *Sophia* and *Hochma* are feminine terms for personified wisdom – an approach harshly suppressed by the Church. The Orthodox position is non-scriptural. The Gospel Jesus preaches openly to women and has Mary Magdalene with him always. Women found the open tomb. In the early Pauline church, women took positions of authority as preachers and prophets. Though on the whole masculinist, Paul acknowledges a female apostle as his own superior.[445] He disallowed for cultural and political equality, but did observe that women were 'equals in Christ.'

It's easy to say that patriarchal fathers took control, but perhaps more reasons exist for the excision. Feminine principle is unpredictable, even dangerous. "I am the first and the last, I am the whore and the Holy One, the wife and the virgin, I am the silence that is incomprehensible."[446] Such forces cannot be tamed by doctrine, nor by men. In Valentinus, Wisdom conceives without a male counterpart. This violation of the laws of nature leads to a malformed creature – not in accord with the basis of reality. The being, and the earth he creates, are characterized by anguish and fear. His name is Yahweh.

Spirituality, in all Christian traditions, means approaching God. But for the Church, if a spiritual experience disagrees with doctrine, it is 'wrong.' Certain ideas of God block the individual seeker. For both camps, again and again the creator God speaks of jealousy and no other gods. Orthodoxy makes this a right of God, but Gnostics condemn him for this neurosis. "'It is I who am the god of all.' But Wisdom cried out, 'you are wrong, Saklas.'"[447]

Justinus, another Gnostic teacher, speaks of a creator god experiencing fear, then overcoming that to his own amazement. The god then accepts what the feminine Wisdom had taught. It resonates with the biblical Jesus hiding secret teachings for the elect.[448] "God created humanity;" the Gopel of Philip says, "but human beings created God. That is the way of this world – human beings make gods and worship their creation. It would be appropriate for the gods to worship human beings."[449]

The debate has interesting echoes of scientific debates over knowledge. By Gnostic doctrine, any conceptual form of the truth is inferior – only a means of approach. The orthodoxy believes truth can be stated directly, clearly and definitively in words. It is not an approximation, but is the truth itself. Moreover, their statement is the sole truth – outside the Church, there is no salvation.[450]

For the Gnostics, there is no salvation without self-knowledge. "Wisdom calls you, yet you desire foolishness. A foolish man goes the way of every desire, like a loose horse. Before everything else, know yourself."[451] Self-seeing is seeing God.

The lack of Gnosis is described as "terror, instability, confusion, doubt and division… ensnared by many illusions."[452] People are "fleeing without strength… involved in striking blows, receiving blows, falling from high places, as if people were murdering them. When people awake from these disturbances, they see nothing for they are nothing. Such is the way of those who have cast ignorance aside as sleep, leaving such things behind like a dream in the night. This is the way everyone has acted: as though asleep at the time of ignorance, and this is the way he has come to knowledge: as if he had awakened."[453]

Paradox and contradiction are a Gnostic reality. "I am knowledge and ignorance. I am shameless, I am ashamed. I am strength and fear. I am foolish and wise. I am godless and one whose god is great."[454] The idea is non-duality – world is not other than self, and vice versa. "In everyone divine power lies dormant. Seeking itself, mother of itself, father of itself, unity, being a source of the entire circle of existence."[455] The principle is called self-secret – one cannot understand until one is ready. "I am thought that abides in the light, she who exists before the all. I am the real voice. I cry out in everyone and they know that a seed dwells within.[456] When you make the two one and the outside like inside and above like below, when you make male and female one and the same, then you will enter the kingdom."[457]

This tradition is uncompromisingly self-reflective. It assaults the great problem of orthodoxy – defiled emotion and belief. "How do you know that someone is ignorant? You are ignorant when you hate them and are jealous of them."[458]

According to Valentinus, our reality is a corruption of wisdom. He offers a deified parable. "Thus the earth arose from her confusion, water from her terror, air from ... her grief, while fire ... was inherent in all these elements ... as ignorance lay concealed in these three sufferings."[459] The Gospel of Truth states it without symbolic overlay – "Ignorance brought about anguish and terror, and the anguish grew solid like a fog, so that all are unable to see."[460]

The Nag Hammadi library references many meditative techniques for Gnosis – mantra, stillness, the nine levels, the triple power, primary revelation, and transcendence of concept.[461] The techniques are not clearly explained. The instructions were either lost or they existed solely in oral transmission – a common means of maintaining spiritual secrecy. Like Othello, Christianity "threw away a pearl richer than all its tribe."

The Gnostic adept becomes a "disciple of his own mind."[462] The best texts emphasize a recurrent theme – the need for personal insight. Always there is the rejection of dogmatic knowledge in favor of experiential knowledge. "If one does not understand how the fire came to be, he will burn in it. Not knowing the water, he does not know anything. Not understanding how the wind came to be, he will run with it. Not understanding how the body came to be, he will perish with it.

Whoever does not understand how he came does not understand how he will go."[463]

This internal aspect is the key to the entire project. The individual spirituality begins with the mind. "The mind is the guide, but reason is the teacher ... Live according to your mind ... Acquire strength of mind ... Enlighten the mind ... Light the lamp within you,"[464] "... the kingdom is inside you. When you know yourselves, you will realize you are the son of the living father. If you will not know yourself, then you dwell in poverty. You are that poverty."[465] In the Gospels, when Jesus said some would witness the kingdom of God in that lifetime, [466] he meant they would attain Gnosis.

unChristian

There will be no mercy for those who have not shown it.
—James 2:13

A Tufts University study examined 5 active pastors who were closet atheists.[467] Several spoke of a 'moral faith imperative' they could no longer fulfill. One preacher, 'West,' entered the seminary without belief. He is happy in his role, instilling democratic and liberal values in his congregation and aims to 'make his job obsolete.' West thinks atheist clergy are quite numerous because experts speak to the uneducated – they know the truth. He wants to serve – helping people 'damaged by Christianity.' 'Darryl' feels he is a believer by his own standards, but would fail a strict test of belief. He knows many other liberal pastors in the same position and wants the movement to attain transparency in the Church. 'Adam' read the book *unChristian*, by Dave Kinnaman. Though not the book's intent, it moved him from his beliefs.

Jack is a Southern Baptist who spent 15 years ministering. To confirm his faith, he carefully read the Bible. An atheist came out the other end. He expressed the most cogent critiques in a colloquial style: If God is perfect, why did he create people who needed someone to die for their sins? If he's so wise and wonderful, why did he need worshippers? No one could survive three days in the belly of a whale. The numerous contradictions, the paradox of sacrificial love, and the cryptic language of God nullified it for Jack.

These are the good guys, but the list of hypocritical preachers caught in illicit scandals is large. Jimmy Swaggart was brought low by hookers, Ted Haggard by a male prostitute, and Jim Baker blew $158 million in donations on the high life. David

Berg created 'flirty-fishing,' using sexual techniques to get converts – it ended badly. Robert Tilton made $80 million a year until a TV exposé knocked him down. Pat Robertson was a friend and investor of Mobutu Sese Seko and Charles Taylor – murderous dictators who control diamond mines. Of course, it's not just the famous – in 2006, 4,392 American clerics were named as sexual abusers of children – and that was just the tip of that iceberg.

Most followers are not so heinous – they're more or less good people. Kinnaman, however, found a serious image problem. His study is brave – an unflinching look at the backwards beliefs of the faith. Christians, it seems, need to change their approach to magnetize young people. The unflinching candor is admirable – far superior to the smugness characteristic of most atheists.

His group found six major topics: Christians are perceived as anti-homosexual, over-zealous, judgmental, hypocritical, too political, and sheltered. Some of this, they concede, is true. And what they found about the average Christian is useful for anyone who wants to communicate.

Though Christians are more likely to donate money, they live the same lifestyle as anyone. Born-agains are as likely to use porn, argue, gamble, fight, abuse others, drink, steal, do drugs, lie, enact revenge or malign. As the Book of James points out, without inner examination of one's performance, faith is meaningless. 60% believe that cohabitation and gambling are morally acceptable, but only 7% believe that saying 'fuck' on TV is.

Proselytizing is a big negative for Christianity, and it's a major perception gap. Large evangelical efforts create up to ten times the negative press. It's not useful – most people come to the faith through a person they trust. Most non-believers don't think proselytizers care about them, but typical believers feel sincere when proselytizing. Non-believers often have better Bible knowledge than their Christian peers, which gives them particular disdain for Christians who "ignorantly follow Christ."

Christianity is known for anti-homosexuality. A close relative once informed me that 'AIDS is God's punishment for fags.' He probably never noticed the rift – all respect vanished in an instant. One infamous preacher has his congregation demonstrate with signs – 'God Hates Fags.' A sizable percentage feels that 9/11 and Katrina were punishments for the sin. This sort of frothing vitriol embarrasses Christianity and is not terribly representative. 60% of older Christians find homosexuality a problem, but only a third of younger ones do. Older Christians think that gays are politically organizing to destroy the Church. Considering one of three homosexuals is a Christian, the belief speaks to the sad ignorance of such people. The Bible does not single out homosexuality as worse than any other sin, however. In fact, it does not make the Ten Commandments, so it is less sinful than, for example, coveting a neighbor's wife.

Jamie Tworkowski shows the good side. His congregation works with 'cutters,' teens who cut themselves – caring for them and finding them a home. "Is this what Christ knows when we surrender our broken hearts, when we trade death for life," he said. "We are only asked to love, to offer hope for the many hopeless. We won't solve all mysteries and our hearts will certainly break in the search, but it is the best way. We were made to be lovers, bold in broken places, pouring ourselves out again and again." [468] If the faith produces this kind of person, then it has good to offer. Martin Luther King proved it. Religion does not poison everything.

Non-Christian youth find that Christianity lacks genuine spiritual vitality and a quality of mystery. It relies on law, dogma, and specified behaviors. As a corollary, the authors find Christians to be judgmental. It stems from the sin of pride – the 'acceptable' sin. It is subtly encouraged, it seems. The cure would be respect for others. A Buddhist teacher dubbed the problem 'spiritual materialism,' and pointed out that it applies to all groups. One's view is seen as utterly correct. Christ is here to save the follower. He lives in a right relation with God. One understands the universe and has a special place in it. Spiritual materialism is an enormous obstacle – a person with pride cannot be taught. How does someone reach a person who knows they are right?

UnChristian still has several serious problems. The book cannot question certain ideas – Jesus lived a sinless life, God is the all-knowing creator, still ruling, salvation is a gift and cannot be earned, Satan is real, a Christian must share their faith, the Bible is accurate in all the principles it teaches, unchanging moral truth exists and is defined by the Bible. [469]

The book is primarily prescriptive. While it looks to a humbler spirituality, it fails to question the basic premises – Jesus as savior. The honesty and self-evaluation are laudable, but the tired message is not.

In a related problem, they don't ask people if their feelings about Christianity are based on disbelief of fundamental views. Only concerned about modern perceptions, they never ask others if the whole Christian project makes sense. Does God have a place in modern life? Does the idea of someone dying for sins make any sense? Do they believe that modern Christianity represents the actual teachings of Jesus?

As much as this group has questions about itself – its motivations and image – it must go further to attain real spirituality. Spirituality questions itself and the more deeply it does, the more it is genuinely spiritual. Where science offers evidence without truth, religion proclaims truth without evidence. The assumption is that a biblical worldview makes the Christian. However, many educated Christians believe in God and Jesus as teacher, but find the Bible to be a fallible and human document. Though a good step for the faith, it needs a lot more. In the end, an untested faith is worth little. And testing does not mean unflinching belief contra persecution; it means critically examining one's beliefs. That is the spiritual approach.

Impressively, the spiritual aspect is clear and worthwhile. It's defined as biblical worldview, being Christlike, following Christ, and loving others in word and deed. They mean it. But being Christlike cannot be the beginning and end – no matter how spiritual he was, there must be other examples. And here Christianity founders on its own rocks – spirituality is open by definition. Infinite paths to it exist. Commitment to message, desire to communicate, and the wish for humility are spirituality, but any insistence on the one and only true way is its antithesis.

Dominionism

It is Dominion we are after. World conquest.
—George Grant, Coral Ridge Ministry

Two-thirds of young outsiders and half of young born-agains perceive the political involvement of Christians to be a problem facing America.[470] Most young people, faithful or not, feel that Christian politics is too focused on the faith aspects. Christians are pushing a particular agenda, forcing out other approaches. Many use politics to line their pockets. Leaders are seen as demonizing certain groups for political gain. Jesus, critics claim, would never use politics in such a manner. Unfortunately, these critics haven't the vaguest idea of the true scope of Christian politics. Or the ultimate aims.

With Psalm 45 as source material, Jonathan Edwards gave eloquent voice to the dominion of Jesus in 1839. Satan's rule was slated to end, and God's to begin. "Christ, whose dominion will never end, has a supreme appointed dominion over heaven and earth by delegation of God."[471]

Strange seeds grow strange fruit. Abraham Kuyper created Dominionism as a specific theology in the early 20th Century. His 'Dutch neo-Calvinism' was a means of influencing people in a Christian manner, offering 'common grace' to anyone. Only the Christian worldview made sense, Christ underpins and rules over all aspects of life, and each person feels antithesis – desire for God and desire to escape God. Kuyper's philosophy was a well-structured attempt to reconcile an orderly and immanent God with modernity's rapid change. Sphere sovereignty, a central idea, gave each area of culture autonomy, although all existed to serve God. The state could not determine the arts, education, or civil justice, for example. This anti-totalitarian ethic, Kuyper's most enlightened idea, was later scrubbed from Dominionism.

In the '40s, Christians responded to the encroachment of scientific power with *The Fundamentals*. The book laid out the undoubtable Christian topics – Virgin Birth, Jesus' death for our sins, his Resurrection, the Second Coming, the infallibility of the Bible, and Dominionism. Against this backdrop, Kuyper's student Francis Schaeffer upped the ante and distorted his teacher's idea. Schaeffer warned against secular humanism and the erosion of the Judeo-Christian underpinning of society. He felt that legalization of abortion indicated a cheap approach to life and a society bent on destroying itself.

The theology kicked into overdrive in the 1970s with R.J. Rushdoony's Reconstructionism. This uncompromising system believes that Christians alone should administer the government with the Bible and Ten Commandments as the solitary basis. Though not a prominent overt doctrine, it is a powerful covert one. It's too harsh to be generally accepted – the death penalty is applied for most every 'sin' – such as homosexuality, blasphemy and not being a Christian. It's affecting the planet. Anti-homosexuality laws are being passed, with the help of The Family (discussed below), in selected African nations. Punishment is death. Such is the Christian shame – it is divided by a strong outcry against these draconian laws and a strong support for them. Which side really speaks for God? Christian leaders cannot openly endorse Reconstructionism, but many, such as Falwell and Robertson, have endorsed the books and admit to reading them.

Dominionism, from *dominate*, is a twisted re-interpretation of Genesis 1:28: "For man rules over every living creature." The re-interpretation claims that only when all churches on the planet are Christian will Jesus return. Other religions are inferior and heretical. It legitimates any means necessary for political takeover. "Dominionists preach that Jesus has called them to build the Kingdom of God in the here and now," Chris Hedges explains. "America becomes an agent of God. All political opponents are agents of Satan."[472] Dominionism obsesses on political power and, in its own terms, "will use guerilla tactics to undermine the dominant regime."[473] There is wide concern among observant liberal Christians and secularists that Dominionism has come to control the right wing and even infect the left wing.

There are two flavors – soft and hard. Soft Dominionism holds that the US was not founded in the Enlightenment tradition as widely believed, but in Christian principles. Accordingly, it should return to those. Critics counter theologically with John 18:36: "My kingdom is not of this world." They also counter politically with several arguments. A treaty is the high law of the land. The Treaty of Tripoli, ratified in 1797 by George Washington, reads, "the government of the United States is not founded on the Christian religion."

The Constitution does not mention God as governing principle. The Declaration of Independence is thus invoked by Dominionists as the superior document, though it mentions only 'Nature's God' and 'man's Creator,' but not the Christian God.

Hard Dominionism seeks a theocracy, asserting the need to control society for its own good. The roots are threefold: Satan usurped dominion from Adam. God created the Church to get dominion back. Jesus won't be here until the Church controls all "governmental and social institutions."[474] The Declaration of Independence specifically negates hard Dominionism on almost every account – all men are created equal (no elect), governments are instituted among men, deriving their powers from the consent of the governed (not from God, nor without consent), it is the right of the people to alter or abolish the government (not a theocratic principle). But this crowd isn't overly concerned with such niceties.

The control happens by creating the 'Kingdom of God' here and now. It is not metaphorical; it is definite and embodied. World conquest is the policy. Military methods are promoted, even glorified against 'enemies of the Kingdom.' People can be forced to become Christians, or killed. The job of Jesus is reassigned to elect believers who "incarnate Christ to establish the Kingdom."[475] These 'Manifest Sons of God' would become the same as Jesus and receive gifts of God – teleportation and knowledge of all languages even.

Dominionism has great propaganda. It is not openly presented. Most evangelicals are unaware of the term or its meaning – they are deliberately deluded by their own leaders. The movement is intelligent – savvy leaders are picked for gradual transformation of belief. The Promise Keeper Men's movement, for example, was integral, infiltrating the theology into the large and moneyed Protestant circle.

The movement has gone global, according to Christian Sarah Leslie, with "sophisticated psycho-social methodologies, statistical research, socio-economic development tools, marketing research, strategic planning, assessments, data banks and monitoring, and technical assistance. They are also aggressively forming alliances with national and international governments, corporations, individuals, private agencies, philanthropic groups and other entities."[476] The Coalition on Revival has faded, but its agenda of seventeen spheres, mandatory for all Christians, has oozed into governmental and NGO documents all across the planet. The entire approach unifies government, business, and Church for the 'Global Kingdom.'

Dominionism has three thrusts – Spiritual Warfare, the Patriotic American movement, and Mission as Transformation. C. Peter Wagner describes Spiritual Warfare: "Once we have the apostles in place, we will then bring the intercessors and the prophets into the inner circle, and we will end up with the spiritual core we need to move ahead for retaking the dominion that is rightfully ours."[477]

The Patriotic American movement conflates the United States with Kingdom – disavowal of Christianity is equated with lack of patriotism and ultimately treason. Ann Coulter pushes the agenda. It stems from James Dobson's Focus on the Family and Grimstead's Coalition on Revival. "All humans on earth," Grimstead wrote, "whether Jew or Gentile, believer or unbeliever, private person or public official, are obligated to bow their knees to this King Jesus, confess Him as Lord of the universe with their tongues, and submit to His lordship over every aspect of their lives in thought, word and deed. Personal neutrality before King Jesus is sin and treason."[478]

Transformation embeds the codes of Dominionism into social organizations and overt theology, deliberately and gradually changing their character to the desired end. Traditional one-on-one missionary activities are slickly phased out, replaced by corporate nation-building approaches. Campus Crusade for Christ is a key study in all three tactics – they have taken over the Air Force Academy. As pastor Rick Joyner believes "God is a military God."[479]

Lieutenant General Boykin has been involved in numerous high-level military campaigns since 1971. He ran an intensive two-day seminar called the Faith Force Multiplier. Catherine Eureka, a journalist, wrote an exposé. High-level military personnel indoctrinate the evangelical, fundamentalist Christian churches with this military ideology called the force multiplier. Worse, according to Michael Baigent, is "The introduction into the military of the extreme religious zealotry of fundamentalist Christianity...the progressive ideological indoctrination of the armed forces in support of one narrow view of religion."[480]

The harrowing story of Mike Weinstein frames the problem. As an Air Force Academy freshman, Weinstein began receiving notes with swastikas – 'You can run, Jew, but you can't hide.' Later, he was beaten and hospitalized. His psychologist accused him of faking the harassment, even though his roommates had seen the notes being slid under the door. Given the choice of leaving with a confession or going through a lie detector test, he punched the officer and ran. A lawyer met him, then threatened to go public with his story. Weinstein was restored to full status and the harassment ceased.* But a generation later, his son went through the same harassment.

The policy of Christian oppression at the Air Force Academy is systemic. A PowerPoint presentation by Lt-General Harry Raduege had the "eye of God watching over them in divine surveillance.'[481] "This goes far beyond the academy," Colonel Richard Klass, a Rhodes scholar, said. "It's hard not to find the correlation between the abuses and the Bush administration's ongoing attempts to breach the wall of separation between Church and state."[482]

For Weinstein, the metaphor of soldiers of Christ easily translates to real bullets and real deaths. This connection is obvious when it appears as a takeover of the most lethal military in history. "Are we at risk of equipping an army of our own fanatics, single-mindedly ushering in the Kingdom of God by converting or killing every last unbeliever? The Gospel must be preached to all the world, according to evangelists. Every knee will bow and every tongue confess. *That is a mission of conquest.*"[483]

The broader Dominionist movement has hundreds, if not thousands of offshoots. Some are enormous, like the evangelical churches. Some are secretive and very powerful, like the Family.

---

* He made the Dean's list 7 times in a row and graduated with top honors.

Some are training grounds. Patrick Henry College near Washington D.C. teaches strict biblical belief as a mandate for political power. The students, all home-schooled, are rigorously groomed in debate and work in the House, Senate, and judiciary bodies. Other projects include paramilitary camps for evangelical children. Dr. Hope Taylor charges the Church "to execute the will of the King concerning the war in Iraq and the war on terrorism."[484]

The Fellowship, or The Family, is perhaps the most powerful Christian political organization on the planet. Every President since Eisenhower has attended at least one National Prayer Breakfast – their sole public event, once a year. Members include senators, congressmen, judges, diplomats, ambassadors, CEOs, and connections to almost every world leader. Quite a few brutal dictators have ties. Leader Doug Coe is portrayed as unflappable, extremely charismatic, and worshipful of dictators like Hitler and Pol Pot. The association has a flat, open hierarchy, a loose structure, and exerts enormous power in extreme secrecy – all for Jesus, apparently. The theology is slippery – mostly it finds that might makes right. The elect are powerful to do God's work, so anything they do is forgiven. Pacts of brotherhood and invoking Jesus seems to be the key.

But Dominionism can have a more detailed, if blunt, theology. Yuri Cari explains, with quotes from Pat Robertson's *Secret Kingdom*, "the believers who are destined to rule are called the 'elect,' and are separated from those believers who do not and will not accept the predestined superiority of the chosen ruling class. A Christian who raises his voice against the 'elect' could be labeled a 'false prophet or a dreamer of dreams,' and therefore, according to the Deuteronomic law 'shall be put to death.'" In other words, Christians aren't meant to rule – only special Christians. Others are part of the 'flock.'

The rulers are pre-ordained by Calvinist doctrine. Calvinism and Evangelicism rub against each other. Evangelicals believe in free will to choose Christ, Calvinists believe in a predestined elect who can commit no wrong and will arrive in heaven no matter their actions. Any wealth, of course, is just a mark of God's favor. Evangelicals, however, don't study theology. Many of them worship with 'gifts of the spirit' – glossolalia, healing, and possession by Christ. This puts the fewer, but more doctrinaire, Calvinists in the driver's seat. So long as this conflict is not clearly stated, the Evangelicals will go along with the Calvinist program – Dominionism.

One organization sports a bevy of the elect. The incredibly secretive Center for National Policy hides its website from searches. There is no content in any case. The IRS forced it to go public with its 'publication' to maintain its non-profit status, but it is virtually impossible to obtain a copy. In 1999, George Bush addressed the Council. The text of the speech remains secret. ABC news called it the most powerful conservative group you've never heard of. Alberto Gonzales and Clarence Thomas have spoken there. Senate majority leader Bill Frist and Dick Cheney have attended meetings. In 2002, they had a meeting with Karl Rove and President Bush. All agreed that Saddam Hussein needed to go immediately.[485] A year later, after the war began, Cheney and Rumsfeld addressed the CNP.[486] It has a corporate agenda.

Kingdom building via corporation has become virulent – especially in resource-rich nations. Getting 'God to the marketplace' is the technique of corporate Dominionism – an integral CNP tactic.

Membership includes Richard Devos, one of the co-founders of Amway and the brother-in-law of Blackwater founder Erik Prince. Also on the CNP are Jerry Falwell, Pat Robertson, Tim LaHaye, and Clayland Boyden Gray. Gray's father founded the Bowman-Gray medical school which surgically sterilized numerous children for low IQ scores.[487] Ted Haggard and Holland Coors are members. Almost all members subscribe to Dominionism.

Leslie warns about the construction of an "antichrist zeitgeist that is frightening, appalling and massive."[488] From Romans 13: "it is not for nothing that they [government] hold the power of the sword, for they are God's agents of punishment, for retribution on the offender. That is why you are obliged to submit." War seems to be always on the horizon, and glorious. "The angelic activity surrounding the Church," one publication exults, "will carry a militant characteristic as Michael and the warring angels of Heaven are released."[489]

These leaders can do anything they want under the Calvinistic doctrine – certain souls are predestined to enter heaven. They are ushering in God's Kingdom, so all means are acceptable. Even slavery is justified – it's good for the enslaved! "Heathen slaves ... were actually favored by [slavery], since it placed them in contact with believers."[490] It's uncertain why that's good, since they're going to hell in any event.

The consequences are destroying Africa – Uganda emphasizes the problem. Tens of thousands of orphaned children sleep together in abandoned buildings and hospital basements. Often, they have to mop beforehand so their cardboard boxes are dry. They're sardine-packed, sleeping in a heap. In the morning, they rise early and a stream of little humanity runs barefoot several miles to school – their only hope for a better life. These are the lucky ones. The unlucky are soldiers – abducted and forced to kill. The child soldiers hunt the school-goers as recruits or victims. Child-soldiers attempting to escape are beaten to death by former comrades. They are indoctrinated into brutality by watching people's throats cut with machetes or shot in the head. They must do so themselves or die. Joseph Kony leads one such group: the Lord's Resistance Army. They are Dominionists.

Children too weak to walk are chopped up with knives and left to die. "Even when I'm not asleep I have bad dreams," one escaped child said. "I saw people's arms and legs being cut off," another said. "I was afraid and asked for mercy. They beat me until nightfall." In three months, over 3000 were abducted. 'We only eat once a day," a non-abducted orphan said. "It is better if you kill us. Maybe I will see my brother in heaven." Every night when the children arrive safely to the shelter, they sing group praises to God for their safety. The soldiers, by contrast, are taught that the Holy Spirit will make them invulnerable to bullets and that God will make the stones they throw explode. [491] They are ushering in Christ's Kingdom.

It even goes to the left, Leslie says. Beneath numerous Christian poverty programs is an agenda to 'disciple the world.' Hunger and AIDS are manipulated for political traction – who can argue with compassionate activity? The consortium of state-Church-business steam-rolls in on a tide of goodwill. Poverty within the Church is stated as the worst problem – a genius strategy. As Third World Christians get the booty first, their numbers will swell for a stake in prosperity. At least it's a bloodless coup, but the mission behind the message is not hard to fathom.

Rick Warren, 'America's Pastor,' has synthesized the three movements of Spiritual Warfare, Transformation, and Patriotic American with the three spheres of Church, state and business more than any man alive. He gave the 2009 inaugural address for Barrack Obama. Friends with Bono and the Aspen Institute, he seeks a 'billion-man army' for his P.E.A.C.E. agenda. He may get there yet.

"The darkest place in hell," Dante said, "is reserved for those who remain silent in times of moral crisis." The quote is a rallying cry for Dominionist critics – most of them Christians. The best critics of a tradition come from within. Dominionism, Sarah Leslie claims, can only be an 'aberration' of Christianity. The Bible itself, such critics note, explicitly revokes Dominionism: "Man has no superiority over beast since both amount to nothing."[492] Dorothee Sölle coined the phrase Christofascism out of concern for the loss of Christian goodness. These critical Christians want to preserve the compassion and dignity of their tradition. They fear it will be destroyed by demagoguery. Reverend Dan Vojir believes the warning signs of impending Christofascism are all around – nationalism, corporatocracy, militarism, scapegoating, phony enemies, national security state, criminalization of everything, and rising imprisonment.* "When fascism comes to America," Sinclair Lewis said, "it will be wrapped in the flag, carrying a cross."

There is cause for hope – most Christians would never support the agenda if they saw it clearly. They are being deluded. If the aware Christians can wake up their fellows, then the tide can be stopped. From an atheist point of view, it is the same as seeing the corruption of science. If we unblinkingly submit to any ideological abstraction, be it 'science' or 'religion,' then we allow corrupt men to own it, and us as well. As Thomas Jefferson warned, "the price of liberty is eternal vigilance."

* The US has the highest per capita prisoner population of any country ever.

Submission

Before you judge, you must understand.
—Sanggye Chodrak

Islamic theology has a host of factors, but the Koran is probably the best beginning point. Mohammed claimed it was a Middle Way, beyond extremes. The Koran is the word of God. It means the Recital and is meant to be spoken. Archangel Gabriel, it is said, gave the Koran to Mohammed. It is 'that which brings together all wisdom.'

Critical dissection of the Koran is more challenging than the Bible. The Koran was written by one man in 50 years, not a hundred men over millennia. It is not internally contradictory, especially not its narratives. The Koran has little narrative substance in any event – all stories clearly lie in the service of religious themes. It is more an extended poem with endless riffs on God's greatness framing a religious philosophy. The philosophy is not particularly well-developed, but apparently the Arabic poetry is exquisite.

The Bible is self-contradictory – it cannot possibly be true. Christian clerics are the first to see this in intensive studies. They have an intellectual bind – ignore contradictions and convince themselves it's true, lie to parishioners, teach it as a human text, or quit preaching. The Koran does not fail in that way. Accepting the basic premise – God gave the Koran to Mohammed – makes it work. The Koran never proves itself false as the Bible does. This gives Islam a strength that Christianity and Judaism can never have. Islam does not require tortured logics to explain glaring inconsistencies. It does not suffer the cognitive dissonance of ignoring fault lines in its most sacred text.

The Torah is also a holy book, a furqan, 'that which separates truth from error and provides criteria for distinguishing wisdom.' Moses is mentioned more than any other figure in the Koran.

Jesus is a great prophet named 154 times and Mary is the only woman mentioned. She gives birth alone in the desert. Joseph and the Manger are absent. Christian theology, however, is wrong – "Say not Trinity: desist: it would be better for you: there is one God."[493] Original sin is not part of Islam. Adam's departure is seen as a stepping into God's creation and not a fall from grace. God intended Adam for the Earth, so it was no mistake.

The Koran insists that Mohammed was not creating a new religion. He was creating an Arab seat for the same God. "There shall be no coercion in matters of faith," the Koran says. Any other religions or ideals of God are valid for their peoples. "Our God and your God are one and the same."

The Koran accepts neither Jesus nor Mohammed as divine. Islam doesn't believe in the Crucifixion or Resurrection of Jesus, but does believe in his Ascension to heaven. Muslims believe he will return, in the Resurrection of the body, and in life everlasting.

Islam is not anti-Judaic or anti-Christian – Mohammed and the Koran both validated the Abrahamic tradition. In fact, all other traditions are validated because so many prophets are acclaimed.[494] It might therefore seem contradictory for some Muslims to claim Jews follow a false path. The path laid out by Moses and Jesus is not wrong, but people have lost it. They no longer follow the path of their prophets. The faith became corrupted – that is the criticism. But if people can remember the original faith, it is still valid. Prophecy thus does not mean seeing the future, per se. A prophet is a messenger of God's qualities, or of his instructions.

From the Koran come the all-important five pillars. 1) Profess the faith of no other god but God, and in Mohammed as his messenger, 2) face Mecca and pray three or five times a day, 3) give alms, 4) fast during Ramadan, and 5) pilgrimage to Mecca. There is, incidentally, no monasticism in Islam.

Related to these, Ed Hotaling says, Islam has four core beliefs. There is no god but God. God is the all-powerful creator of the universe and every being. Upon death, each human will face a judgment day. Those who have not embraced Islam will be in hell and believers will enter heaven. Looked at so bluntly, such views are extreme. The pressure to avoid hell, based on a single lifetime, is unlimited. But like most Islamic critics, Hotaling sees only the mundane – and misinterprets that.

An important critique of Islam is the inability to question the basic assumptions. Every Islamic thinker, no matter how insightful, has utter faith that a solitary God created the universe who spoke to Mohammed as his prophet. There will always be the various rank-and-file who accept the tenets, but this gap in even the most critical thinkers is a failure.

Theology is not so top-down in Islam – it is best left to the individual, and best not thought about too much. God can't really be understood, so just know the basics – there is only one. Maintenance of a just society is a far more useful discussion.

The word 'Islam' means submission – to God's will. While there are the two pillars of acknowledging and praying, the particulars of this God are not overly specified. Social justice is His first virtue – the *ummah*, or community, the primary goal. The original doctrines of Godhood were taken largely from Judaism and were more or less apocalyptic. To discuss such things in Islam is mildly negative. Godhood is ineffable – what would be the point of discussing it?

Yet ulama, learned ones, have still built a sophisticated theological construction. The vision of God stems from *tanzih* and *tashbih* which unify into *tawhid*. *Tanzih* is God's uniqueness, difference, and distance from his creatures. *Tashbih* is his similarity and immanence within them. Those who unify the two experience the *tawhid*, the oneness and interdependence of all things. Those who can bear the majesty of *tanzih* can experience the mercy and gentleness of the *tashbih*. Those who cannot will be blinded. This is the meaning of hell – separation from God because of one's inability to face the stunning truth.

God's aspects are not equally balanced. Mercy is granted to all creatures, but wrath is selectively dispensed. In the fullness of time, mercy will triumph. Wrath and hell-fire are not punishments for naughtiness; they remind the soul to return to God. In such a universe, the further one moves from God, the worse it feels.

"Everything is perishing, except his face."[495] Ulama say that hell is not permanent. Because its force is based on disintegration it will one day vanish. Then the soul will be able to return to God. Another sign of mercy's strength – good works are repaid many-fold while evil is repaid in kind. God uses good works to draw creatures closer. "Whoever brings a beautiful deed will have ten the like," one hadith says, "and whoever brings an ugly deed, its recompense will be its like or I will forgive him. Whoever draws near to me by a hands-breadth, I will draw near to him by an arms-length. Whoever draws near by an arms-length, I will draw near by a fathom. Whoever comes to me walking, I will come to him running. Whoever encounters me with sins, I will encounter him with forgiveness."

Light is a name of God. It is an essential reality, both the knower and object of knowledge. Light's reality eliminates the unreal darkness of ignorance.[496] They are not in balance – light is more powerful.

There are two poles of Islamic understanding – rational and intuitive. These translate to Western modes. From the perspective of oneness, rationality dissects the world. It moves toward separateness. The situation becomes 'yes or no,' mutual exclusion. This is associated with *tanzih*, the remoteness of God. The emphasis is difference rather than sameness. Rationality has no other language than establishing difference. The constant separation of things creates a world of multiplicity. This is an aspect of our relative existence, but the more it is emphasized, the more the mind moves away from the binding oneness that gives the universe its cohesive character.

For Muslim thinkers, this is a multi-generational historical process. The kalām, or dogmatic theologians, focus too much on God's transcendence, his different qualities. The ideas of his unity are excluded. The insistence of focusing on a God distinct from the creation ultimately separates God from the universe, from us. God is no longer necessary within the cosmos. The end result is atheism.

From the intuitive Islamic perspective, the modern thought style – a sort of secular kalām – leads to fragmentation of mind and society. Smaller differences become important. People feel divided over trivial points and the number of views explodes. This is a fairly obvious occurrence in the West, where science fields are splitting into almost infinite sub-fields, but it happens in Islam when rational thinkers predominate. Though poorly understood by the West, fundamentalists gravitate toward rationalist conceptions of God rather than the *tasbih* aspects.

"God is very remote, majestic, awe-inspiring and distant. He is the Lord of all." The remoteness is in contrast to the nearness – goodness, mercy, and beauty. These are aligned with revelation, or direct experience of God. Revelation is an unveiling. But God's light is the veil – it is too bright for the untrained soul. The unveiling reveals the similarity of characteristics – God is immanent within his creation. Humanness, properly understood, expresses divinity without being God himself. "Wherever you turn, there is the face of God."[497]

Kalām, or reason, would say that God has no face, he is not visible, and in order for him to be God, he must be separated. The unveiled approach is to see and feel God, or the sacred in every moment.

Both *tanzih* and *tasbih* are necessary. God must be approached rationally, as separateness, and intuitively, as immanent closeness. A lack of one creates distortion. Excessive focus on *tanzih* pushes God out of creation. *Ta-til* divests God of his function, like deism, where God did his job and left. Humanity then supplants God and erects a pantheon of abstract deities – science, democracy, progress, and equality, for example.

Overemphasis of *tasbih* creates an inversion. With God immanent and everywhere, there is no transcendent counterweight. The sacred is in everything. At some point, different grades of sacredness arise because the human mind cannot perceive the divinity in all. Then one focuses more on one's own divinity. Continuing along that path leads to lunacy.

Tashbih alone can also create the New Age styles of free-floating spirituality. Everything's sacred, everything goes because the sense of structure and order are anathema. All that's left is a sloppy love-in – the early Sufi problem. The kalām thinks of the *tasbih* approach as 'the error of the common people.' The idea is clear – most Muslims think God is a god of love. Immanence and presence fill the world with divinity and sacredness. The God of kalām is to be feared.

Unfortunately, the kalām approach is the front face of Islam. The imposing Lord and King style of God is presented to the West in its most severe form. What sells in our media is extremism. Some would say there is even a media bias and attempt to paint an extremist caricature of Islam as the mainstream. It is a natural consequence – as the logical, conceptual strain, kalām is the apologist of Islam. It becomes the spokesperson.

In contrast are the philosophical schools. Mostly, they saw Islam and Hellenism as a union. An individual could attain understanding of the divine will through strenuous effort and subjection to Sharia. The philosophers saw ethics as a central idea in preparation for the return to God. Their ethics are drawn more from Greek tradition than the Koran.

Islam divides into three dimensions. *Islam* – submission – tells people how to approach God. *Iman* – faith – explains the underlying rationale. It includes discussion of visible and invisible beings, the tradition of prophecy, the eschatology of end-times, the *tawhid*, or unity of God, and the measuring out, or the incomprehensible unfolding of reality. Iman suggests faith in the absolute reality. There must be some absolute reality, something permanent, iman says – we're calling it God.[498] *Ihsan*, doing what is beautiful, is the third dimension. It "brings motivation and psychological qualities into harmony with one's activity and understanding."[499]

Sufism explains ihsan nicely. However, it works better as 'being the beautiful' than doing. According to Murata and Chittick, the common translation of Sufism as mysticism is wrong. Sufism brings out and elevates the noble qualities which are expressions of the Godhood while excising the ignoble ones which express the unreal. Sufism objects to the excess of *tanzih*.

God is too remote. People engage in rationality without wisdom. They lose their nearness to God.

From this angle, Sufism fully manifests God's qualities. God is unknowable, but his attributes can be understood. The two classes – majesty and beauty – have eight categories: power, wrath, authority and justice are majesty, and grace, generosity, compassion and mercy are beauty. Many names, which can be mantrically repeated, fall into these categories. The 'Sincere,' for example, helps the Sufi gain sincerity and realization. The 'Guide' helps with scattered mind. The 'Guardian' protects against desire for possessions.

Sufi methods are similar to Eastern technique, but came about independently. In the graded path of retreat, asceticism gets one used to hunger so that food does not fill the place God can. Fear gets one used to death and judgment. Longing for paradise turns the mind from the mundane. Love of God fills the mystic with love so that others are magnetized by his spiritual light. Managed breathing, mantras, and visualizations of seven centers are used. The wise fool, drunk on closeness to God, compares to Tibetan crazy wisdom. The master is essential – the source of blessings.[500]

"Sufism is entirely adab," one maxim says. *Adab* means 'to invite, to offer a banquet.' It is a fundamental ethos – Islam in action. The idea of hospitality to travelers is not a nice Islamic thing to do – it is an obligation to God.* Adab is even broader than Sunna, the Prophet's behavior. It includes his inner qualities as well – a learned understanding of Islam, a strong conversance with arts, and beautiful handwriting. Each profession and station in the society has its own adab. Telling someone they have none is a terrible insult. Adab expresses 'beauty, refinement and subtlety.' It manifests *tawhid*, the unity of God. It is "cause and fruit of one's inner self. Knowing, doing, and being are inescapably one."0[501] Adab cannot be programmed. It arises from inner goodness, an innate expression of longing to express Islam.

Ihsan is thus a total approach to life that harmonizes one with the real. In so doing, it alters the being deeply. This transformative depth brings the person closer to God. Paradise is not a physical place; it is realization. It is transformation of human nature into the profound nature expressing God. In doing so, the mind moves from unreality of mundane life to the immanent reality of God.

* In one horrifying story, US troops blew up an old woman who was bringing them food.

Mohammed, like Jesus, was a near-times apocalyptic prophet. "When Gog and Magog are unloosed, they slide down out of every slope and the true promise draws near... We shall bring forth a beast out of the Earth to say that people had no faith in our signs."[502] He once held his finger and thumb closely and said, "I and the last hour are like this."[503] In Islam, the soul, spirit, and body are distinct aspects of the self. The spirit is the highest and closest to God, the body is the lowest. Upon death at a predetermined hour, two angels deliver judgment. Correct answers return a person to the grave in comfort, wrong answers in horror. Everyone waits there until the day of Resurrection.

"The hour is coming," the Koran says, "God shall raise up whosoever is in the graves."[504] The angel Seraphiel will blow on his trumpet and the laws of nature will unravel. "The Earth shall be changed to other than the Earth... You shall see the mountains passing by like clouds... When the sun is enfolded, stars are taken away, the seas are set boiling, souls are paired with their deeds and the buried infant is asked for which sin she was slain. When the scrolls are unrolled, when heaven is peeled back, when hell is set blazing, then the soul will know what it has made present."[505]

God becomes manifest. The former signs will vanish and he will appear nakedly. Those who have lived well and become accustomed to the light of God will see it and enjoy the mercy. Those who have not will be overwhelmed by the majesty and wrath and become fearful and blinded. Coming out of graves is an ascension, like revelation. The single day for God could be 50,000 years. The theme of light is ubiquitous. All obscurations are burnt away and people see bare reality.

Angels write people's deeds on scrolls. They have to pass over the Serat, a hair-like path over the fires of hell. Some go easily, but the majority fall. With Abraham first, the prophets intercede on behalf of their peoples. Those in hell will beg mercy and be given it.[506] One hadith says that God will eventually bring all beings from hell into his grace.* Trials are so that humans can know themselves and accept their fate.

On a less materialist interpretation, God is the source and embodiment of all good qualities. Any qualities in life are borrowed from God. He is the ultimate reality and moving away from Him one goes to the unreality of nothingness. The inability to face God is the inability to face truth. But truth in the light of God destroys one as a self-created, self-directed being. One has to submit totally to this more divine will. Mystically stated, the

---

* Christianity has a parallel – hell is temporary, but spoken of as permanent in order to frighten people onto the path of righteousness.

person has to give up the idea of one's self and of separateness from the whole. Hell is the idea that one is isolated from reality. The apocalypse is a settling of the natural state – those distant from God will be distant, those close will be close. No specific judgment need occur. It is also called the mystery of the measuring out – the unity of predestined qualities and humans' ability to choose their path.

Most of the Koran takes a more literal approach, but there is a tradition where the Koran has 7 layers of meaning, the highest known only to God. The final judgment, the subtext to everything, is the Return to God. People will be questioned about motives rather than actions.

A hadith says the end will not come as long as someone on Earth says 'Allah, Allah.' The hour of the end will be held off as long as a single Muslim (anyone true to God) lives in ihsan – beautiful works.

"God will never chastise them while they ask forgiveness."[507] A single pious person in a city can gain a stay of execution for all. In light of more elevated notions of God, when people turn their backs on the real, when transcendence becomes too remote, when the good and beautiful have no serious place, when ethical standards have degraded to selfishness, then of course society will fragment.

The Hadith of Gabriel ends with the Prophet telling Gabriel about the marks of the end. "The servant girl will give birth to the mistress. You will see the barefoot, the naked, the destitute, and the shepherds vying with each other in building." The social construct will crumble. The servant girl reverses the normal order. The barefoot, etc. refer to the spiritually impoverished. The building is the creation of ideologies and political structures. Thus the most spiritually degraded and debased people will be in charge of the political and social order. They will set norms and standards for others. They will enforce the rules everyone must follow. Mohammed said that each generation would be successively more evil – turning away from God. Social relations will become completely unglued, mired in deception, confusion and corruption. Religious sentiment will collapse and the fabric of civilization will shred. It will become increasingly difficult to live in accord with goodness, due to 'fabrications of human cleverness' from degraded instincts.[508]

Prophet

Peace be upon him.
—Islamic blessing on the Prophet

Mohammed's stated virtues, according to Yusuf Ali, are faith, hope, trust in God, devotion in service, love of truth, patience, constancy, humility, self-denial, attention to God's message, and charity.[509] Early on, he was forced to leave Mecca by the ruling powers when he taught that greed and accumulation were negative. Those who engaged in such modes would be called to judgment for not helping the poor. He formed a new bond in Medina, a serious breach. In pre-Islamic Arabia, to break with the blood tribe was blasphemy.

Of course, it created the new possibility of ideological tribal union. This gave Islam quite the leg up – tribes could grow by melding rather than just birth. The ability to overcome tribal disunity and grow exponentially in years was the primary factor in the survival and strength of Islam.

Mohammed, who grew up a destitute orphan, revived the tribal ideal of protecting the weak and the poor. The original ummah in Medina included Jews and Christians – they took vows of allegiance to the ummah and swore not to attack and to defend one another. Also, Arabs believed Allah was the same as the Abrahamic God. Mohammed didn't bring in a new god. He just made it into the only one.

Despite polygamy being normal, he only had one wife for most of his life. Much is made of his multiple wives later, but it's not difficult to argue that these marriages were political and not prurient. They united tribes into Islam. He was also known for listening to women – a rare trait. He rigorously performed household chores and mended his own clothing. The other male leaders found this embarrassing, but could not stop him. He fervently supported women's rights. The Koran gave women clear inheritance, the right to divorce, and required men to financially support them. It does not require veiling or segregation. Polygamy was still common, but women outnumbered men because of constant warfare. An unprotected woman was in danger, so by marrying, the man served as protector. Men were to treat all wives equally. The women of the original Medina community were full partners in the public sphere. This original situation has disappeared – Islam is far more patriarchal.

Mohammed had a serious desire to unite with the local Judaic community, but was rebuffed. The situation was difficult for him. In reading Genesis, he was overjoyed to find Ishmael. By legend, Ishmael had settled in Mecca and built the Kaaba with his father Abraham. The Prophet was shocked and dismayed to discover that Christians and Jews were of different religions.

This inability to unite with Judaism caused him to change the direction of prayer. Initially, Muslims prayed to Jerusalem, not Mecca. Ironically, Mecca had declared war on him for breaking blood ties and he was not welcome there. By some interpretations, this change did not refer to Mohammed's place of birth, but to Abraham, who preceded the split of the monotheistic religions. By respecting the religion more than God himself, one was committing idolatry.

In 624, Mohammed raided a wealthy Meccan caravan. Raids were a normal means of support with limited resources, but it was bad form to kill someone. Vendetta would be declared. Raiding one's own tribe was a grand mistake – and he was from Mecca.

He was quite a competent general. His military discipline and superior tactics defeated a far larger force, but this brought the general anger of the Meccan powers on him. Much of his later years were spent in warfare as consequence. After a clever victory over larger forces, though, his Islamic God came to be seen as more powerful.

In what is regarded as his most brutal act, all the males of a conquered Jewish tribe were put to death and all the women and children sold into slavery. In general, he advocated and practiced mercy, so this demands real scrutiny. Possibly, he was just showing the true Islam, the true Mohammed – a violent, unforgiving, brutal man and religion. However, it was normal practice in the day. To not do so would show weakness – they would regroup and unite with other of his enemies, then attack again. It is still a disappointment to read of this massacre. It injects a blood fury into the ethic of Islam straight from the hand of the Prophet. But there is one critical detail – the Jews captured in the battle asked that their fate be decided by a Jewish chieftain. It was the chieftain who killed 700 men and sold the women and children into slavery.[510]

This battle is in the Koran and used to justify hatred of Judaism. That misreads the Koran. Mohammed maintained a respect for the larger Judaic religion and prophets all his life – he was only at war with the Medinan tribe. And they declared war on him first, fearing his growing influence. Islamic anti-Semitism is actually a recent occurrence, stemming from the Israel-Palestine situation.

The Koran states clearly that war is a disaster in human society and must be ended swiftly. The times of Mohammed were marked by perpetual warfare. So if he was proclaiming peace, he was in a terrible bind. He had to make war. The lens of history makes right and wrong easy to declare, but impossible to really know. Some consequences live through history, but no one can see what these will be. Perhaps he had no other options. Perhaps it was needful to quickly kill hundreds instead of letting the conflict drag on for years, killing tens of thousands. Or perhaps it was his worst mistake, haunting us today.

At any rate, he turned the war into a *jihad* of peace. His choice was courageous in the extreme and speaks well of him. Mohammed made a *hajj* to Mecca. No violence is allowed on hajj – with 1,000 Muslims, he made a pilgrimage unarmed into his greatest enemies' seat. His primary enemies, the Quraish, tried to attack the pilgrims before they reached the Meccan sanctuary, but the hajj evaded them. Determined to use peaceful means, Mohammed forced the treaty against the desires of both his opponents and his own people, who were eager for battle. An act of genuine spirituality, it was innovative, bold, against the baser wishes, and pointed at peace. The Bedouins were impressed and converted en masse.

The treaty lasted for 6 years, until the Meccans broke it by attacking. At this point, he was too strong. He marched on Mecca with an enormous army (10,000 men), and took the city without a single death. He ended the pagan significance of the Kaaba, restructuring it toward Allah.

The Kaaba is the central 'shrine' of Islam in Mecca – a black cubic rock 'from the sky.' It pre-existed Mohammed by a long time. Though the meaning of the ritual had been lost, he incorporated it into Islam and repackaged it. After several circumambulations, the hajj pilgrims kiss the black stone in the Kaaba. Other aspects include all-night vigils on the plains, a mass movement, throwing pebbles at a rock, shaving heads, and a final-day animal sacrifice. Despite a popular notion that any heathen entering Mecca would be killed, there is an absolute proscription against violence in Mecca at all times. Though spiritual, it began as a practical method of conducting trade – Mecca was always a safe zone. There are no weapons, hunting, or even swearing. Curiously, before Mohammed the Kaaba was worshipped by both Christians and polytheists side by side.

This conquest was the culmination. All the tribes were united in singular Islam. They were forbidden to fight each other. Mohammed brought peace to Arabia after millennia of tribal division.

In this interpretation, Islam is neither a religion of peace nor of war. It favors peace, but uses war to attain those ends. The religion also demands a just society caring for its most unfortunate members and disdaining ostentatious wealth. Islam, in contrast to Christianity, has no theological concept of heresy. It also has no intermediary, such as a priest. Every Muslim approaches God directly. Imams and the like teach men how to live with each other, but they are not a conduit to God.

According to its Prophet, Islam is in permanent crisis. The split between Sunnis and Shias is proof. Mohammed wanted a united Islam, a single tribe. He respected other disciplines and never mandated world conquest. Jews and Christians were people of the book – they had their own valid tradition. He only wanted the ummah to be whole. For a brief time, it was.

History

There is no true Islam.
—Pervez ali Hoodbhoy

Islam is inherently entrenched in its history as *Dar al-Islam* – the House of Islam. Though the tradition declined during the 20th Century, Muslims treasure their history and find many religious lessons therein. When God worked with them, it was because they worked for the ummah, community. When they lost God's favor, it was tied to the fate of Islam. When empires fell, it was from not tending to the strength of the ummah. But a central lesson is from the life of the Prophet.

After taking Mecca in 630, he required no one to convert to Islam. Much of Islamic warfare is just so – it is not specifically religious in character. Though various rulers and Caliphs invoked jihad, it was usually political. Jihads are not universally supported by Muslims. The most telling are *fitnah* – tribulations. These are civil wars, when Islamic governments are corrupted and the egalitarian spirit of the people asserts itself.

The great success of the religion is easy to link to early military successes. Within 9 years of the Prophet's death, the Arabs had occupied Egypt, Syria, and Palestine and defeated the Persian Empire. Islamic conquerors were greeted as liberators because the Byzantine Empire had decayed and overtaxed the population.

The infamous Sunni-Shia split came from a succession contest of blood versus faith – the first fitnah began in 656. The Shiati-Ali wanted the bloodline of the Prophet, his cousin Ali, to lead Islam. The Sunnis believe the leader should be chosen by Sunna

– the customs and practices of Mohammed. The most righteous man should be elected to lead. Ali was a good Muslim, but a weak leader. When he was deposed and assassinated, a permanent schism split Islam.

A century after his death, the empire stretched from the Himalayas to the Pyrenees. The rapid expansion and incredible success created a sense that Islam was ordained by God, lending divine strength. The expansion was not a product of Islam – Arab tribes had been raiders for centuries. But because of their newfound unity, they were successful in conquering and holding. The expansion was not a means of spreading religion, as many believe. They were just expansionist wars. They were religious in the sense that God was on their side, but they were not jihad – the word actually has no military meaning. The early internal wars, by the Caliphs, were religious. They tried to keep the ummah together against the tendency to fracture upon the death of the founder.

The Caliphs, as first heirs, were religious and military leaders. They conquered the largest empire in history within a hundred years. The first three were murdered. The pre-Sunnis then expanded the empire. They massacred Shiite rebellions led by blood-heirs, furthering the division.

Around 700, Hassan al-Basri lived in accord with the Prophet's teachings. He instilled a piety, disdain for wealth, and equality that remains common to Islamic thought. He created meditation on the Koran, combining it with surrender as a means of overcoming ego by striving in the way of God. He preached free will and questioned the Caliphate's dissolution, but still supported their rule. This began the tradition of critical examination of rulership. Islam is not dictatorial, despite all statements to the contrary, nor has it ever been. Islamic rulers have certainly imposed dictatorships, but this violates the spirit of Islam. Most dictators have been extremely secular – even repressive of Islam.

A concurrent doctrine said only God can judge the contents of men's hearts. The Mutazalites had a plain theology – God was single and simple and the ummah was a manifestation of him. The early glimmerings of *fiqh* – jurisprudence – arose against the questionable practices of the rulers. The desire was to make rulers who were the best Muslims – following in detail God's will.

Around 725 ce, the Shia i-Ali movement elevated Mohammed's progeny Ali to divine status, contradicting the tenets of Islam – no man is divine. In the first glimmerings of mystical and apocalyptic traditions, the early leaders who had died in battle were 'discovered' to be in occultation (hidden from the world), but would someday return and reveal the kingdom of heaven in the Last Days.

The Umayyed family came to power. Though strong rulers with expansionist tendencies, many were dissolute Muslims. 90 years later, their power fell to Abu al-Abbas al-Saffah, a new kind of Caliph. He murdered the Umayyeds. At this point, Islam entered a more strict monarchy. This sat badly with many Muslims to whom Islam is deeply egalitarian. The hadith tradition – sayings of the Prophet – as well as Shariah and *fiqh* law traditions began soon after.

The Koran has a simple legislative approach, so they needed something much more involved to run an empire. The A-hadith tradition was born, collecting stories and sayings of the Prophet to glean lessons from his life on governance. A second tradition took the Sunna, the customs, and built a legal system from that.

The law grew out of the need for a better legal system. It has four roots – the Koran, the Sunna, qiyās (analogy), and ijmā' (communal consensus). The last is the misunderstood democratic strain of Islam – the community has authority to change its law, and has done so frequently. Law is developed by the ulama, or learned men, but the community is not obliged to accept it. Further, they can sponsor their own law by consensus. God would not allow the ummah to make a mistake.

The Sharia is the basis of the law, based itself on the life of Mohammed. By living as much like the perfect man as possible, one comes closer to God. The great devotion for the Sharia has brought an image of Mohammed into their stream of consciousness. The Sharia worked against aristocracy and haughty culture. It kept the Caliphate's powers in check. It is a democratic ideal including protection for the weak. It forbids any interference in personal choices.

In the ninth Century, the twelfth Imam, Abu al-Qasim Muhammed, disappeared into hiding. His legend is extremely important, most notably in Iran. Partially because of this, the four mystical traditions appeared. These gradually leaked out into the general Islamic view, giving the religion a deeper sense of itself. Spirituality became more inwardly available.

Soon the esoteric schools bloomed. Many people wanted a more spiritual, less mechanical, approach. In most religions, mysticism has a somewhat uneasy relationship with the Orthodox. It favors a free interpretation and self-reliance for the individual's spiritual path. It also believes in a far higher level of attainment. Esoteric schools typically hide their beliefs to avoid persecution. From these schools' point of view, it was not heresy

– it was a delimiting of theology. Mystics felt that deeper meanings lay in the Koran.

The Faylasufs get the nod for Hellenism. In one version of history, the Hellenes created an abundance of knowledge and Islam later guarded these treasures, especially the Faylasufs. They regarded rationality as the highest sacrament, the alpha and omega, with God the ultimate rational ordering of the universe. They had a more Hinduistic approach to history – it was evanescent, less important than the elevation of rationality. Only by purifying the mind of non-rationality could God be attained. The more mundane Koranic arguments, such as hell, were an emotional prod for the illogical masses. Because of their Hellenism, they co-opted Platonic doctrine. The philosopher-monarch could morally fabricate a theology to push the masses to proper religion.[511] Mohammed thus created Islam as a political tool. The inherent contradiction exists here as in science – to believe in a fundamentally rational world is not a rational argument. It is a bootstrap statement of faith. The universe cannot be proved inherently rational.

Sevener Shias, or Ismalis, believe the 6th Imam was the last valid one. They meditate on the Koran for hidden meanings. Mathematics and science are sacramental gates to transcendence, but rationality is only a part of it. Communication with the divine must also happen through symbols. They believe in six prophets – Adam, Abraham, Noah, Moses, Jesus, and Mohammed, and that each had countered the downward cycle of history from Satan's rebellion. The Kingdom of Heaven on Earth is to be initiated by the Mahdi – the 7th prophet. Ismali Shiism recognizes other systems as proper expressions – no human system can contain God. Importantly, they do not believe the gate of revelation was closed by Mohammed. The 7th Imam will turn the wheel of Islam further, ushering in a higher age of truth. Ismalis push for an age of social justice.

Twelver Shiism later rose to predominance in Iran in the 16th Century. It is an apocalyptic version. The twelfth Imam will return with Jesus at his right hand to usher in a just society. As a mystical tradition, it is not necessarily a literal doctrine. It can imply immanence. This might be expressed as calling on the wisdom of a divine figure. The 'ilm, knowledge of how to behave on Earth, disappeared for the Shia at the wrongful death of Ali. Only by calling on such wisdom can the Shia perceive the deeper reality of right action. From this point of view, the practitioner manifests the just society on the spot by calling forth the hidden transcendence. Justice is in the world, but not of it.

The fourth school is Sufism, from *safwa* – purification of inner heart. In the words of one master, it means "you own nothing and are owned by nothing."[512] Branching out of Sunni philosophy, Sufism was a reaction to the trend of all religions to turn into a mere set of behavior rules. The practitioner looked inside himself for God and found revelation in all things. The tenth Century saw persecution of the Sufis and elevation of this doctrine from drunken ecstasy to spiritual profundity.

At the same time, the centralized power of the Caliphate dissolved, but Caliphs remained as symbolic religious figures. The dissolution came from the size – the empire was then larger than Rome at its peak. It fractured into smaller empires and dynasties.

In the 10th Century, formal Sunni Islam combined from several strains – jurists, hadith followers, and the old-school Mutazalites. The theology pointed out that God may not have human attributes – throne, physical form – but that he must have some attributes or else he was merely an abstraction. Asharam emerged. It had a hint of mysticism and almost a New Age ideal. God was available to everyone, everywhere in all things, a suffusing principle hidden in mundane principles. God was accessible to the focused religious mind.

Around 1105, the most important thinker in Islamic history published *The Revival of the Religious Sciences*. Al-Ghazali, after a nervous breakdown, said he knew too much about God without knowing God. After ten years of Sufi practice, he wrote his masterpiece. Theology and rationality, he said, were unable to offer access to Allah. Prayer and ritual were essential elements. He gave an important depth of meaning to Islamic ritual. It helped the ordinary Muslim to engage with greater force and spiritual directness. It connected all activities to God. He spoke of the three types of practitioners – the simple who pursues religion without objection, the intellectual who creates a logical framework, and the mystic who simply engages directly with the divine. The authority of the imams went against the democratic essence of the Koran and created an unnecessary barrier between the individual and God. After al-Gazzali, Sufism entered the mainstream. Islam became a way of life, rather than an externally religious empire.

Eventually, the tacit retirement of the Caliphate changed the character of the Dar al-Islam. It became more Muslim, but less politically unitary. A second phase of expansion began. Shia had regained the upper hand until the 11th Century when Sunni returned with a vengeance. The Ismalis, the most political of the esoteric schools, rebelled by creating the Hashashim, known for taking hashish to get the courage for suicide attacks. They didn't actually take hashish – it was a libel of opponents. From the Ismali point of view, they worked for the ordinary Muslim, but their terrorist tactics were rejected as un-Islamic. Their marginalized fitnah threw power to their Sunni enemies.

The Sharia gave a long-standing code of behavior, Sufism gave a mystic approach to deepen the inner life, and al-Gazzali tied the two together. Islam broke free of its tight political dimensions. Like any religion, it would be used for political gain, but the end of the Caliphate allowed the religion of Islam to rise above the House of Islam as the meta-structure of all the lands.

Up to this point, Islam and Christianity occupied separate spheres, but the 12th Century began the Crusades and the reconquest of Jerusalem by Saladin. The 13th Century brought the Mongols who decimated the easterly parts of the empire. Many Mongols converted to Islam. Jalal al-Din Rumi, the great mystic poet, wrote at this time. In the 14th Century, Tamerlane's brief empire also flashed across the page of history.

The brutal conqueror, who loved Islam, retook much of the territory from the Mongols. Critics of Islam often use Tamerlane and other violent types to prove a contrived point about the violence of Islam. But in 1,300 years, every type of Muslim has lived, as have every type of Christian, Jew, Hindu, Buddhist and atheist. Anyone can cherry-pick individuals and apply them to the character of an entire people or religion. But the comparison is false. One important truth – a people, a religion, a culture, holds a large set of beliefs, rules and doctrines. No consistent whole or monolithic picture works for even a small group – it is impossible for 13 centuries of billions. The intent to paint a caricature of the barbaric, violent Muslim mythologizes a division the world does not need.

Around 1500 new Islamic empires arose. The Caliphs had not been under the law, but the new rulers were, at least in theory. Most did promote an Islamic view. In the Iranian former empire, Shiism dominated. Ottomans took the Sharia, and Sufism fell to the Moguls.

The Ottoman Empire's rise slowly pushed out the Byzantine. In the 15th Century, Constantiple fell and was renamed Istanbul. Widespread persecution of Sunnis was countered with Ottoman persecution of Shias. The Ottoman Empire reached an apogee under Suleiman the Magnificent.

At the same time India, under Akbar, hit a zenith. Akbar, an ecumenical reformer, created a period of Hindu-Muslim cooperation and mutual governance. In looking for a détente template, we could do no better than Akbar. He created a Hindu-Islamic Unitarian faith. Overt doctrines of sectarian tolerance and dialogue were the norm. He nullified the jizyah, a tax on non-Muslims, became a vegetarian in support of his Hindu subjects, and quit hunting. He erected Hindu temples and created a place of all faiths to gather. He founded a Sufi strain, based on universal love, with the idea that any proper religion could lead to God. Akbar was an enlightened monarch and came closer to the Islamic utopian ideal than anyone. The citizenry sought such a magnanimous spirit, some felt, that conflict almost ceased.[513]

In the 1700s, his bright legacy was destroyed by the last of the Moguls, who attempted to convert everyone to Islam but only created a permanent hostility. The damage of those policies still plague India and Pakistan.

Thinkers began to feel the decline of the Dar al-Islam. By 1800, the Ottoman Empire was failing and Islamic rule of India was over. (The British took it for resources.) A feeling of failure took hold as the West took power. Thinkers became hard-edged and darkly practical. They focused on the need to maintain political and military power.

Wahabbism, now generally and mistakenly thought of as Islam proper, appeared soon after. Various attempts were made to secularize and modernize the nation of Islam – some democratic, some brutally repressive. Western colonialism of Islam began in earnest. Attempts to prop up the failed Ottoman Empire to resist European hegemony made minor headway. Secularization ascended forcefully.

When religious defensive doctrine met modernity, it found a problem. Islam is not opposed to modernity, but the conditions therein differ from Western conditions. Primarily modernity has been applied under Western duress. They are not allowed to integrate it themselves – it is forced. It is not an exciting, chaotic arising – the spirit of invention is not part of their modernity. It is pre-delivered package. Western powers treated Islamic leaders as unenlightened and barbaric – racial inferiors. Britain felt it would 'civilize' the natives of India. Many of these ideas still thrive in the West – even among liberals, though few admit it. Notably the colonizing powers never share the full benefits – only those aspects which extract the resources and minimize disease.

After India, Algeria fell in 1830, then Tunisia, Egypt, Sudan, followed in 1912 by Libya and Morocco. The Ottoman territory was parceled between England and France in 1915. Attaturk fended off the colonization, but being a serious secularist, he mandated Western lifestyles. Even the end of an occupation left resources in control of Western powers.

In 1906, Iran created a popular constitutional government, but when oil became a critical resource the British colonized it, ending democracy. The Arab nations warred against the Ottomans. A number of rulers, notably in Turkey and Egypt, promoted fierce secularism – including concentration camps and executions. The most secular governments were the most brutal.

In Iran, the Reza Shahs ruled. Ruthlessly anti-Islamic, they tortured religious leaders to death and assassinated hundreds. Mohammed Mossedegh was democratically elected. After nationalizing the oil industry, he was deposed in a 1953 CIA-British coup. The Shah returned to power. The CIA and KGB helped the last Shah, who was an atheist, to set up his Savak – secret police. Increasing marginalization of Islam and brutality by the Shah set the conditions for an Islamic revolution. The Middle East does not trust secularism for a very legitimate reason – it has been used to oppress them for decades.

The Muslim Brotherhood was started by Hasn al-Banna. The movement embraced modernity and technology, but wanted a spiritual meaning to be embedded within. Al-Banna felt religion cannot be separated from life – it must suffuse and have a political dimension. He sponsored academic institutions, vocational ones, clinics, hospitals, factories, increased wages, medical insurance, and instructions to bring legislative power to the workers. In one of the most depressing occurrences in Islamic history, a secret splinter group of the Brotherhood engaged in acts of terrorism. The main movement was hugely popular, but the sect discredited the movement as a whole, ending it. The Brotherhood was revived a decade later with a more militant face. Most Muslims want modernity, only united with religious principles. The myth of rejecting it is simply untrue.

In 1932, Saudi Arabia was created. In 1947, the British left India and the country erupted in strife between Muslim and Hindu. Pakistan was carved from the Indian sub-continent to solve the Hindu-Muslim conflict. It failed. In 1947, the state of Israel was sliced from Palestine. 750,000 Palestinians fled during the wars and were not permitted home by Israel.

The humiliation of the Arab world and the series of military and political defeats gave rise to the fundamentalist movement. The thrust was to re-establish the ummah in accord with the Koran and God's will. The ummah is meant to attain dignity and independence.[514]

The 1900s saw the re-emergence of *itjihad* – independent legal reasoning. Thinkers felt the need to reconcile Islam and Sharia with modernity. Islam had experienced a multi-century fall from grace after a millennium of ascendancy. The mighty House of Islam became a servant's quarters to the West. In Islamic view, an ummah living in accordance with God is successful. The catastrophic political fall of Islam signaled a failure to live in the way of Allah. The larger collective thought community of Islam sought a return to the will of God.

Islam today

Whole cultures now doubt their own humanity.
—Sakyong Mipham Rinpoche

Only 15% of Muslims are Middle Eastern. If we want peace and friendship, then learning about our 'other' and finding something to respect is hands-down the best approach. It eases tension. Making a Muslim friend changes false perceptions. The best factor to improve relations would be for Westerners to find out more about Islam, soften their opinions, and understand similarities. Both, for example, admire technology and liberty in the West. Both fear moral decay as the most negative Western trait.

The majority of Muslims are from Africa and Asia. 85% are Sunni and 15% Shia. The latter are mainly in Bahrain, Iraq and Iran. 57 countries boast Muslim populations. Women form college student majorities in the UAE and Iran, but in other Muslim countries cannot even read. Women have headed the governments of Turkey, Pakistan, Indonesia, and Bangladesh, but not the United States. In a few countries, they cannot vote or even leave the house. Some countries apply Islamic law, while others apply secular law.

Islamic faith is central to 90% of Muslims. They value the traditions and guidance from it, though often only notionally. This contrasts with a bare majority in the US and dwindling minority in Europe. The Judeo-Christian roots, de-emphasized or ignored in the West, are fundamental to Islamic thought. If Western leaders sought rapprochement, they would trumpet this connection.

Most information on Islam comes from the TV. The account is spurious. It may serve another agenda or be prescribed. It takes a narrow truth and pretends it's universal. A 1,400-year-old religion cannot be taken in a sound bite. If we listen to pro-Islamists, we get proselytizing and contorted apologia, the same as Christianity. The accounts of apostates offer an inside view of a former believer, but there may be an ax to grind. Even an inside view is culturally narrow. There is no such thing as Islam, Christianity, or Buddhism. What we know is only our idea. Any central reality is indiscernible, probably non-existent.

This book looks at a more progressive face of Islam. This is not because it represents the 'true' Islam, but because most presentations use caricatures of militant Islam as the template. The overwhelming number of sound bites, and sound bites are all we get, come from conservative Imams. Progressive Muslims are unheard and believed oxymoronic. This is no attempt to ignore the fundamentalists, pretend them away, or apologize for their existence. But the admittedly simple research for this book suggests that violent extremism is antithetical to Islam.

A combination of overt and subtle forces manipulate the Islamic idea for control. That which works against justice or glorifies violence is not what Mohammed intended. He taught human unity and equality for all, including women. Other religions were to be embraced as friends, not viewed as enemies. And while the Koran certainly speaks of violence, it speaks more fervently for peace. The great majority of Muslims believe these things. They are critical of hide-bound, oppressive rulership in patriarchal Islam – Saudi Arabia, for example.

The Progressive Muslim Network defined progressive Islam in 1998 as "a commitment to transform society from an unjust one where people are mere objects of exploitation by governments, socio-economic institutions and unequal relationships to a just one where they are the … shapers of their own destiny in the full awareness that all of humankind is in a state of returning to God."[515] They oppose corporatism, globalization, ecological pillaging, animal cruelty, racism, sexism, homophobia, and authoritarianism within Islam and without. Islam is a path to peace, for the individual and the greater civilization, progressive Omid Safi believes. Peace is more than the absence of war; it is the active engagement for the rights of the downtrodden.

"Different circumstances require different methods, but not different moralities," a US policy document states. "But which morality should that be?" Safi asks. "The President and advisors get to determine what morality is. It is precisely such a hegemonic discourse that progressive Muslims challenge, the same as we reject Muslim literalist exclusivists."

Billy Graham's son Frank called Islam "a very evil and wicked religion." Pat Robertson called the Prophet "an absolutely wild-eyed fanatic, a robber and a brigand, a killer… to think Islam is a peaceful religion is fraudulent." Jerry Falwell referred to Mohammed as a terrorist. Fritz Bolkestin, an EU commissioner, thought that 83 million Muslim Turks would create the Islamification of Europe. "If he [Bernard Lewis] is right, the liberation of Vienna from Turkish Armies in 1683 will have been in vain." Jean-Marie le Pen talked about the "Muslim's domineering nature." The Kristiansand Progress Party said *Mein Kampf* and the Koran were one and the same. They lobbied for banning Islam in Norway. Arsonists targeted mosques and Muslims' business property.

The Islamification of Europe is a paranoid fantasy. At present, only 4% of the EU is Muslim. Adding Turkey would raise it to 17%, but would not create much intermingling. EU Islam is hugely diverse – coming from Asia, Africa, Turkey and the Middle East. Around half barely practice. The majority of the French rioters in 2005 did not go to mosque.

Anti-Americanism is believed an innate part of the Muslim mind. This is incorrect. When asked if they admired anything about the West, more than 95% said 'Yes.' Anger at the West stems from perceived condemnation and contempt for Muslims in general. They dislike military and political manipulation in their borders and overt/covert US backing of unsavory Islamic regimes. They fear the loss of their native cultures.

There is wide admiration for democratic principles and scientific basis of society. They are more upset at being denied these advantages. Despite the common perception by the West in the cartoon controversy, most Muslims support free speech. An overwhelming majority want it in their constitution. The outrage was from a lack of respect, attacks on identity, and mortification. A common complaint is that Mohammed actually represents all Muslims, but bin Laden only a handful. The Danish newspaper that published the cartoon, by the way, rejected similar cartoons of Jesus for fear of offending readers. To Muslims, this looks like a double standard.

Ignoring underlying causes is miscegenation. The catalyst event – the cartoon – is focused on to avoid deeper analysis. During the civil rights movement, the government backed away from quoting extremist nationalist voices and moved toward integrative voices like MLK. The effect was astounding. The same strategy would now be worthwhile. Instead of quoting extremists, we should focus on the thousands of voices speaking for moderate Islam.

Muslims want better economic conditions, employment opportunities, standards of living, law and order, elimination of wars, and promoting democratic ideals... enhanced national status, independence, and end of outside interference. Priorities are better education, end of illiteracy, gender equality, social justice, and religious freedom.[516] Battling for jihad is absent from life desires.

Islam is the second largest and fastest growing religion. After 9/11 and 7/7, few in the West take seriously the idea that it is a religion of peace. So why is it growing? Most Muslims do not agree with terrorism. Those who leave have lost faith in God. Most Muslims retain a life-long faith and eschew violence.

Muslims do not single-mindedly despise the West. Three-quarters of Muslims (and most Europeans) associate the word 'ruthless' with the US, but not with European nations. A high percentage of Americans wrongly feels that Muslims are not interested in furthering beneficial relations. One of the strongest wishes of Muslims is "better relations with the West."[517]

The misperception goes both ways – most Muslims think Americans don't care, but 89% want better Islamic-US relations. One in four Americans thinks growing tensions are due to US actions, but most believe it is faulty perceptions about US actions. Muslims are far more likely to cite a need for change on both sides. They want assistance to make Islamic nations more economically viable, a cessation to interference in their affairs, and a more balanced approach to Israel-Palestine. The majority of Muslims think it is their responsibility to prevent extremism and terrorism.

By contrast, 57% of Americans admired nothing about Muslim society. 82% of Americans would not want a Muslim for a neighbor. Ignorance has a price – those who claim more knowledge of Muslim countries find more value in those countries. Those who know at least one Muslim have a far more positive outlook.[518]

Fundamentalism

Let there be no compulsion in religion.
—Koran 2:256

For a thousand years, Islam felt itself in God's favor. For the past 250, the opposite seems true. Modern trends reflect this – all Islam now desires to return to God. Fair enough, but the big worry is fundamentalism. It is a typical Western media response to pin the label only on Islam. There are as many, if not more, Christian fundamentalists than Islamic. The tendency did not appear in Islam until the 1960s. It's ironic that fundamentalism is an essentially modern creation. It exists to protest modernity's threat to religion and begins as a schism within the community. It is not directed externally. Islamic fundamentalism is not violent and it is different from extremism. By enacting religious fundamentals – the five pillars, the hajj, and good adab – Islam can return to God's favor. By jihad, striving in the way of God, Muslim society can again find that light. If God is not capable of bestowing such a state, then they are trapped within their ideology. Or if he can, perhaps they are paying penance for a millennium of conquest. Perhaps it is a teaching on pride.

Islam is neither religion nor culture, but a civilization. As such, it is porous and mutable, not fixed and isolate. A handful of extremists and a near majority of the West have mistakenly portrayed it as an obdurate block of stone. But Islam can interpenetrate with all cultures based on shared values – e.g. desire for social justice. In fact, it already has – that's how it spread around the world.

Al-Raziq was an Egyptian reformer around 1900. He pushed for a divorce between religious and political. Shouted down at the time, his ideas are being revisited. This is the trend we need to know about in Islam. These are the people we need to encourage.[519]

Most Muslims like modernity. Any university science/engineering department holds a disproportionate number of Muslims. They crave knowledge and progress. It is incumbent on the West to embolden those strains within Islam instead of the political regressives. These voices hesitate to apply modern rationality to fundamentalist logic for fear of attack. But as the Tanzih/*tasbih* discussion shows, a bottom-up theology, a dialogue rather than a mandate, elevates itself. Rationality can strip away false projections to find the core transcending the rational. It forces theology beyond flimsy, contradictory, dogmatic, evasive or impenetrable expressions. Rationality can clean up weak ontology if it knows its proper function. It is not meant to prove truth, but to eliminate falsity. Truth reveals itself.

Islamic fundamentalism is not the source of all problems in the Middle East – both Nasr and Hussein were secularists.[520] Fundamentalism is partly a social movement. An enormous concern rests on the loss of Islamic identity under Western culture. It organizes along ideological, ethnic, religious, class, and national lines to achieve political ends against a perceived elite hegemony. The aim is social justice. To reinterpret this as an inevitable clash of civilizations is not only wrong, but perilous. When adopted by media and politicians, it becomes a self-fulfilling prophecy. The general situation between Islam and the

West is trade, tolerance and peaceful co-operation. We see it otherwise because acts of terrorism and war get all the press. These are recast as the Clash of Civilizations struggle rather than what they are – political maneuvering, hegemonic politics, resource grabs and resistance to those. From this, we get ridiculous statements from the UN head. Islamic fundamentalism is "at least as dangerous as communism" had been to the West.[521] People should be suspicious of all such good/bad formulations, anything that divides humanity along ideological lines. Hidden political purposes are generally not difficult to find. Common people want to get along – only politicians want war.

Islam is not about religious control. Any religious duties can be performed by any person. There are no priests or intercessors to God. Learning and teaching are egalitarian. Any person can speak in the mosque and anyone who is interested can listen. There is a deep tradition of learning as means of approaching God.

The mosque is not some severe place of religious orthodoxy, it is the community center – open for all public activities. No discussions are improper in the mosque, except ones improper to Islam in general. Islam does not recognize a difference between "sacred and profane, the religious and the political, sexuality and worship. The whole of life is potentially holy and [must] be brought into the ambit of the divine."[522]

As a comparison, David Loy analyzed capitalism as fundamentalism, the first global religion, "binding all corners, whose religion we overlook because we insist on seeing the secular."[523] Fundamentalism insists on a sole truth possessed by the believers, a desire to polarize us and them, a willingness to kill in Crusade, and the merging of ideology with one's nature leading to 'righteousness.' Capitalism has become the sole answer – omnipotent, omniscient, and omnipresent. Capital is a jealous God banishing Communism, shopping malls are temples, the golden arches compare to the crucifix. Rituals and beliefs include shop-till-you-drop fanaticism, the fervency of the American dream, the heaven of success, and the relentless desire to convert all others. The us-versus-them mentality falsely identifies terrorism as Islam proper, providing a clean enemy to destroy.

But to simply oppose extremist Islam is not enough, Farid Esack claims. The progressive Muslim must skillfully oppose the fundamentalism of capitalism. One must "destabilize the current world order, not to be conflated with political violence. An alternative vision of the world is possible. Islam is a religion of peace, but not exclusively that."[524] He is concerned, however, about the 'delusions of grandeur' in Islamic belief in governing the world.

One modernist critique is the brutality of Islamic punishments. Until 1974, it was legal for a man to kill his wife and the lover if he caught her in 'the act of infidelity' – in the United States. Brutal 'justice' is hardly isolated to Islam. Even the Muslim Brotherhood protested Wahhabist severity. Stoning was anachronistic, without place in the modern world. They pointed to far more serious Koranic transgressions, such as obscene disparities of wealth. Most Muslims would be appalled at Goldman Sachs CEO Lloyd Blankfein's claim to be 'doing God's work.' One can discourse on the horrors of female genital mutilation and forget the common Western horror of circumcision. Ignored are the overwhelming majority of Muslims who protest the practice on a simple grounds – it is contrary to Islam. It's easy to be outraged by honor killings and the hypocrisy of the Saudi Royals, but to overlook the tens of thousands of girls raped to death in the Western sex slave trade.[525] Both societies have plenty of flaws, but just because a society allows a practice does not mean the people approve.

Fundamentalism has an inner aspect that is worthwhile – the desire to submit totally to one's belief, to live with perfect discipline. To the untrained eye, it seems like loss of freedom, pleasure, and even good sense. But a strict inner discipline opens the door of purity and drops away grasping for meaningless detrita of the world. It turns the mind to transcendence.

Outer fundamentalism often forcefully emphasizes Sharia. The Sharia is the province of conservatives and that's a problem, because progressives are hesitant to engage. It becomes an external imposition rather than an internally understood doctrine to bring one to God. So they focus solely on submission, waving away iman and ihsan. But all three are equally important. *Tanzih* is emphasized to the exclusion of *tasbih*. Fundamentalism is enforced by those with political agendas. They do not represent the normative members. That wrathful capacity justifies two threads. In the extremist version, violent attacks are validated. The liberal version uses rational apologetics. Much of modern Islam has lost its intellectual history, except this hyper-emphasized political manifestation.[526]

The strength of Islamic fundamentalism comes from Saudi Arabia, specifically Wahabbism. The Saudis have deep pockets – Wahhabism has infiltrated other countries slowly by the backing of enormous madrasses. It is a restrictive, external fundamentalist doctrine. In another country, it would be isolated and unimportant, but Saudi Arabia holds Mecca and Medina, the two holiest sites of Islam. The nation carries enormous authority as the center. Millions of pilgrims make the hajj every year, and feel the strong religious side of Wahhabism. Strict discipline offers profound states of mind when taken voluntarily. Pilgrimage multiplies the effect. Few Westerners have undertaken retreat or pilgrimage, but those who have understand the power. It is meaningful and beautiful. The mind often feels inspired, focused, and thunderously peaceful. The experiences are indescribable and unattainable in ordinary life. Fundamentalism, properly constructed and applied, can bear amazing fruit, but when it is dictated rather than voluntary, when it is perpetual rather than selective, it becomes political – a tool of repression. It turns into a burden for the unwilling, and does more harm than good.

Wahhabism relies solely on ancient texts, rejects critical historical perspectives, considers the broad history of Islam as an un-Islamic aberration, and disallows varying schools of thought. It is hostile to rationality, creativity, arts, poetry, and music. The approach is rigid and rejects all outside input. It runs counter to the Islamic "love of entire humanity. Values like human dignity, love and compassion cannot be quantified and therefore cannot be integrated into legal determinations."[527]

Abd al-Wahhab wrote the doctrine in the 1770s, and it was a minor fringe sect until the House of Saud applied it politically in the 20th Century. The a-historicity helped validate their rule and the severity helped them keep tight rein. Even with their backing, it nearly disappeared twice. But each resurgence brought increasing authoritarian violence. The rest of Islam was opposed, but the Saudis had money and controlled the holy sites. This confusion gives rise to the Western misconception that Wahabbism equals Islam – and that is what the doctrine falsely claims. Most Muslims are not Wahhabists and have dubbed it with the derogatory name.[528]

The result is predictable. The doctrine has gained a controversial status as Islamic 'orthodoxy.' Such Muslim countries have the frustrated hostility of a victim and feel cut off from both modernity and cultural Islam. They are lost, unable to discuss other doctrine and deepen their understanding. But any doctrine that holds itself as the sole truth while demeaning all others is inescapably wrong. Different people have different paths – the failure to recognize that adds up to a spiritual zero. It is politics in priestly robes.

Westerners object that Islamic politics is incompatible with democracy, but it's not true. Separation of Church and state is not a necessary condition for democracy. Great Britain and Italy have state religions. Atheism is the state religion of China and the former Soviet Union. Though an argument can be made that democracy is against God's law, the reverse argument can be made. Monarchy takes away each man's right to stand before God. Most modern Islamic democracies have simply been a sham – the British, for example, rigged the Iranian elections. Democracy is inherent in the religion. Sharia has ijmā' or consensus. Two Rashidan, the first four or 'rightly guided' Caliphs, were elected.[529] The democratic ideals of social justice and equitable wealth are cornerstone values.

Ahmad Moussalli argues that Islam is democracy. The ummah, as the highest manifestation of the divine, holds its own governance as divine will. Doctrines of consultation, consensus, arbitration, voluntary allegiance, freedom, and human rights are divine prescriptions, tracing their origin to the Koran. No subset or minority group can legitimately claim divine providence over the ummah. In other words, Islam is inherently democratic by a root argument. Authoritarian governments are anti-Islamic and a government ignoring these fundamental principles delegitimizes itself.[530] The majority of Islamic intellectuals push for democracy.

In the context of democracy comes the question of law. Most Muslims want the Sharia as law, but not the sole source. They want Western rights, bringing together modern liberty with adherence to Islam. There is no felt conflict with Sharia.

Western misunderstanding of Sharia law is ubiquitous – it is a large, complicated body. The literal translation is 'the path to water,' but means the path to God. The Sharia is more repressive in many instances, but coming from a millennium of debate, it has a plethora of faces and interpretations. Parts are more enlightened than others, like any country's law, but the theoretical basis is social justice. The original intent was to counter the power of the Caliphate. Being 'divinely inspired,' the Sharia is technically not subject to change.

Sharia has five categories – the required, the recommended, the indifferent, the reprehensible, and the forbidden. Idolatry, or associating anything with God, is the only unforgivable sin. Though in favor of Sharia law, most Muslims are opposed to clerics holding government positions or designing a constitution.[531] They reject theocracy.

In Iran, known as conservative, fewer than 1 in 6 want Sharia as the only source of law. Though the Sharia has been used to diminish rights and oppress women, most feel this to be un-Islamic. Sharia is God's law and the *fiqh* is Islamic law. The

Sharia is fixed, but the *fiqh* is malleable. Public intent holds power over it. The Sisters in Islam, for example, pushed for a monogamy-in-marriage contract and got it.[532]

In the Islamic juridical tradition, there is a broad consensus that the punishment for apostasy is death. But according to Omar Farouk, these jurists do not separate the argument from treason. As in the Koranic "no compulsion in religion," there is no Koranic injunction against apostasy. In the hadith, a Bedouin wanted to cancel his religious vow. Mohammed refused three times, but did not punish the man. All punished examples include treason.[533]

Islamic philosophical traditions have a wealth of protections for community and individual rights, legitimate respect for political, social, and religious differences, and a view of the people as politically sovereign. Though the Caliphate was often oppressive, the history of political thought abounds with liberal doctrine: *al'musawat* is equality, *al'haryya* is freedom, and *al'adl* is justice. These date back to Mohammed, who ruled politically, but not religiously. They deepened during the medieval peak of Islam. A century and a half ago, this style of liberal Islam was on the rise, but was squashed by imperialism and resource struggles. Unfortunately, the mass of peaceful acts goes unnoticed. History is written in blood.

Women

If Islamic feminism strikes people as an oxymoron, we unapologetically suggest that their definition of Islam needs rethinking, not our linkage of Islam and feminism.
—Omid Safi

Up to a 90% majority in Islamic countries feels women should have the same rights as men. Even Iran gives this high numbers. However, the Western-style critique of Islamic gender inequality is non-existent among Muslim women.

The Islamic treatment of women is not understood by the West. In most countries, especially the Middle East, as many women get post-graduate degrees as men. Only in poor countries, such as Yemen, is there a gender disparity in education. But this applies in Western nations, too. More interesting is the Muslim woman's desire for equality and rejection of Western values. Both genders overwhelmingly believe in equal rights for women, but only 20% of women want to adopt Western values.[534] They see the gross sexual objectification of Western women as a form of subjugation. They find it degrading and reject it. Few Muslim women feel oppressed by their religion, though some feel repression by the political situation.

They are far more concerned with the same issues of male Muslims – US political/cultural domination, the vilification of Islam, and identification of mainstream Islam with extremism. Those seeking higher office feel their religion is an important aspect. Well-educated reformers arguing against female genital mutilation and the heinous Pakistani rape laws[*] claim they are against the spirit of Islam and the Sharia. They are finding success, too – the rape law was cancelled on Sharia grounds.

Some women do not want the same rights as men – they often have better rights! A woman is never responsible for financial support of her family, but any inheritance she gets is hers alone. The man is required to support his family. Women cannot be obligated to work, but men can. Amr Khaled, the most popular Islamic preacher, elevates women above men.

In most countries, men who support women's rights are more religious. With honor killings, the perpetrators are almost always lapsed Muslims. These acts are tribal, not religious – that is why they are localized. General Islam rejects honor killings overwhelmingly. Some women are outraged even in Saudi Arabia at the false idea that women are oppressed by Islam – they object in the strongest terms. They are also angry that their oppression is seen as coming from male counterparts, but the suffering endured from Western political actions is ignored. Also noted is the lack of concern for women (and men) in Palestine. They object to the use of 'liberating women' as justification for colonial wars.[535]

Feminism has been homogenized, Sadiyaa Shikh claims, under the symbol of white Western middle-class females. Islamic feminists find their approach in Islam itself, premised on the Koranic call to justice and the idea of total human equality. The *hijab* (veil) is an example – it is always assumed to be patriarchal suppression. In Taliban and Wahhabist places, this may be true, but in most places, it is not. Many Egyptian women adopted the hijab to protest British colonial rule. Professional Muslim women wear it symbolically, bringing work and religious life together. Iranian women wore the veil in 1979 to protest the secular totalitarianism of the Shah and his Western backing. Some feel it is mandated by God and a requirement of modesty. Others say the veil diminishes the 'sexual prioritization' men apply to them.

---

[*] A raped woman is guilty of fornication, but a man must have 4 witnesses to be guilty.

They further stand against the commodification of beauty that dominates the West and refuse to be measured by that yardstick.

The decontextualization of the hijab ignores its cultural legitimacy. To Westerners it looks bizarre and oppressive, to Muslims it does not. The veil is not a one-size-fits-all symbol. Different symbols carry different meanings – some are empowering. While we should rightfully question and probably object to the veil's enforcement, it is hypocritical to force women to not wear a veil.[536]

When the Prophet was asked who to respect most and in what order, a hadith says, "First, your mother, second, your mother, third, your mother. Fourth, your father." Islam is not anti-women – brutal and illegitimate governments are.

Extremism

Each man's sins are his own.
—William Shakespeare

Westerners and even many Muslims know little about Islam. The public wants a quick and easy answer, but the issues demand an information-dense analysis. Wide dissemination of disinformation leads to demagoguery on both sides.

The causality of non-Muslim terrorism is explored in strong academic detail, Hanaan Ashrawi claims, by looking at a broad range of political, economic, ideological, and religious factors. In the case of Islamic terrorism, it is instantly and always assumed religious. Worse, the label terrorism is bandied about with remarkable indifference to what it labels. Sufis were depicted as wild-eyed killers in the 1950s, as fundamentalists are now. Neither is true. It is critical to distinguish between the religious approach of the fundamentalist and the political approach of the extremist.*

Political dissent is legitimate and necessary to democracy. People defending against an invading military should not be called terrorists, yet they are. If someone speaks up for these people, they are 'supporting terrorism.' They become un-American. It is a de facto destruction of freedom of speech – made worse by its hiddenness. Lives have been threatened, careers lost, reputations destroyed because people spoke out against what they saw as oppression.

The divide widens. A market branding Muslims as religious fanatics or Westerners as rapacious imperialists is booming. The

* The earlier section on Wahhabist fundamentalism as politics refers to governments – this section refers more to individuals.

cycle of negative feedback draws us into a warlike world. Paranoia, vilification and hatred have become media commodities.[537]

After the Soviet Union collapsed, Islam did not fanatically leap into the void, knife in its teeth – despite endless predictions. A number of factors, political and otherwise, joined together. Islam exists in a socio-political matrix intricately connected to international politics, Christianity, Judaism, oil, wealth disparity, technological proliferation, the internet, devastating US military superiority, and media demagoguery. In busy lives, the need for quick answers – 'Muslims are fanatics' – is understandable, but facile. Terrorism is not so simple. While certainly true that the religious aspect of Islam can be twisted to justify extreme acts or program insane behaviors, that does not make the ideology of Islam the root cause. It is an obligation of intelligent, thinking people to critically analyze causes and to understand them.

Western spokespersons must become more educated to cultural nuance – else they malign from ignorance. The continuing myth of monolithic Islam increases the polarization of West and Islam, propelling us to war. As compassionate humans, we must battle simple vilification of an entire civilization.

Most Muslims see peace as the creation of a just world. To make that world, it is necessary to oppose corporate imperialism. "The rush to label Islam a religion of peace has forced it to accommodate the thing it most detests – a world of social injustice." The highest caliber of spiritual people will agitate against injustice in pursuit of a better world – this does not mean violence. As Farid Esack said, "Peace based on oppression can never be the goal."[538]

Muslim opposition to the US, Naeem Jeenah claims, is a response to "occupation of Palestine, murder of a million Iraqi children, carpet bombing of Columbia, assassination of Lumumba, terrorist dictatorships supported by the US government: Hussein, Noriega, Mobutu, Sese, Seko, the Shah, Suharto, Apartheid Africa and Israel. The World Trade Center killings were despicable, but every day 3500 children starve to death because of a global system that comforts the rich and causes misery for the poor."[539] Support for Osama bin Laden and the Taliban is misguided, Jeenah says. Support should be for the suffering Afghan people. Bush and Osama bin Laden are both extremists – both should be rejected. Focusing on good versus evil reduces everything to battle and cuts away awareness of suffering – the terrible confusion of the American people and the abject misery of the third world.

The majority of Muslims dislike extremism and close-mindedness and believes these are serious problems in Islam. Most feel extremism is a threat to their own country, and find causes to be poverty, unemployment, poor education, and US policies. High majorities want the US out of Islamic lands. Surprisingly, the majority of both radicals and moderates do not want theocracy.[540]

A 90% Muslim majority condemns 9/11 on religious grounds – it was un-Islamic. The single digit minority supporting 9/11 do so on political grounds. Deliberate attacks on civilians is the definition of terrorism. 54% of Americans say attacks on civilians are sometimes justified. 20% of Muslims think so.

The idea of hatred for the West does not ride the data well. The radical minority is significantly more likely to desire improved relations with the West than the moderate majority. Most radicals dislike Britain and the US (84%), but not Germany and France (24%). 78% of Muslims would be angry at a relative joining al-Qaeda. Only 2% would be proud.[541]

Racial profiling, surveillance/closure of mosques, and military interventions cause Muslims to feel the West is 'waging a war against Islam.' Most are suspicious of the stated US goals of Mideast democratization. Objections cited include the decades-long support of autocratic regimes, the invasion of Iraq even though no hijackers were from there, and the full backing of the eight repressive Mideast states forming the coalition against Iran.

They think the US intends to weaken and divide Islamic nations. Asked about fears for their country, they overwhelmingly cite US manipulation, occupation, and national security. Mohammed Sidque Khan, a 7/7 bomber said, "until you stop the bombing, gassing, imprisonment and torture of my people, we will not stop this fight." It is a political statement, not a religious one. The majority do not want war or terrorism.

The US is engaged in Iraq, Afghanistan, Yemen, Libya and Pakistan. Osama bin Laden is not found – hardly any terrorists are. Two twentieth-century empires died on the battlefields of Afghanistan. Ours might be the third. It's reasonable to ask if a geo-political reason exists for these trillion-dollar wars – and of course, the three-letter answer is oil. Questioning the government is not a right in a democracy – it is an obligation. A million Iraqis have died in our name. Virtually none were combatants. Many were children. Weddings are bombed in Pakistan, hoping for terrorists to be there. It is a strange peace. It is incumbent to let the government know that the citizens wish this ocean of blood stopped. We do not want a legacy of creating hell on Earth. We want peace. In that spirit of détente, let us look at this enemy called terrorism.

The overwhelming majority of terrorist attacks on US soil were performed by Christians. Nightclubs have been blown-up, abortion staff murdered, and Oklahoma City federal buildings bombed. Aside from being a lesser danger, the frothy, wild-eyed Muslim who despises modernity enough to sacrifice his life is a myth. Most extremists groups seek people with a very calm state of mind – it benefits the duties. Oddly, in the 1970s Bin Laden was a playboy in Beirut, "a drinker and a womanizer which often got him into bar brawls."[542]

Sayyid Qutb, the 'father of Islamic extremism' founded the Muslim Brotherhood. He began with a liberalizing ideal – Islam and Christianity could inform each other. Education should be academic and not just religious. In 1925, he was a secularist, but the torture he endured and executions he witnessed in prison made him turn toward religion.

Harsh suppression of fundamentalist groups will not lead to détente but will worsen the situation. Imprisonment and torture, such as Guantanamo and Abu Ghraib, create intense hostility among Muslims. Their lives are shown to be less valuable. Before the invasion, Iraq boasted 0 suicide bombers. Now there are hundreds.

Most extremists* are well-educated, middle or working class, but not poor, and not usually fundamentalist. Some are heavy drinkers and use porn. They are educated in the West. Few went to madrasas. About 7% of the general population feels terrorist attacks on military are justified, but only 2% feel attacks on civilians are. Of those who condone violence, not a single one quotes the Koran as justification. When moderates cite their reasons against, all cite quote the Koran, mostly the verse "taking one life is as sinful as killing the whole world."[543]

Though religious rhetoric comes from extremist groups, it does not necessarily indicate the rationale for violence. Religion and life are not separate – such statements happen in every conversation. Most extremist groups cite political reasons. The PLO was staunchly secular. Hamas began to protest Israeli occupation, but have drifted into religious rhetoric and justification. In Lebanon, the Hezbollah attacks against a Marine base included 8 Muslims, 3 Christians, and 27 Communists.

Most authoritarian governments were installed by colonial powers and are backed by those powers today. Muslims who

---

* Defined here as someone validating terrorism or military action, but not necessarily committing it himself.

had supported secular democracies are turning toward Sharia-based candidates in disillusionment. Islamic parties were doing well in the more secular Arab countries, but the authoritarian governments have begun labeling their opponents as extremists and terrorists. During Egyptian elections, the opposing candidate was jailed.

"Diagnosing terrorism as a symptom and Islam as the problem, though popular in some circles, is flawed and has serious risks," John Esposito wrote. "It confirms radical beliefs and fears, alienates the moderate majority, and reinforces the belief that the war on terror is really a war against Islam."[544] Misperceptions are rising. The percentage of Americans who blame Islam for increasing terrorism against civilians went from 14 to 33%.

The sentiment is worsened by the Islamic belief that the US represents freedom. Thus the Abu Ghraib and Guantanamo actions appear as hypocrisy. As one polled Iraqi said, "we would expect this from our own government, but not from you."

Jihad

There comes a time when silence is betrayal.
—Martin Luther King

Jihad can be used as a verb – to strive in the way of God. Of the 41 such Koranic uses, only ten are in a war context. Only four verses mention *jihad* as a noun. This nominal case is the more important – it defines jihad as a concept. Of the four occurrences, three are pacifistic. Arabic scholar Michael Bonner argues that the military-jihadic doctrine does not come from the Koran. Since only 25% of the word's usage is in military framework, it cannot be principally a military concept.[545] In the Koran, it's just an important word.

The doctrine of jihad did not exist until decades after Mohammed's death. Since the Koranic justification for military jihad is weak, the hadith form the basis. But the hadith are problematic. Notwithstanding the possible editing of the Koran before its compilation, the hadith are provably so. No scholar denies it. The hadith is a floating record of the Prophet's sayings, so anyone wishing for political cover could 'find' one. In other words, Mohammed probably never created the idea of military jihad. He waged war for political reasons and certainly used religion as a force multiplier, but jihad only and ever meant to strive in the way of God. Since Islam is pervasive, jihad would apply in battle, as well. But so do the inescapable needs for food, water, and sleep. That does not make them military doctrines.

The final verse in the Al-Hajj sura invokes a vigorous jihad – it is definitively peaceful. The hajj is the pilgrimage where violence is forbidden, even in self-defense. The Koran instructs to perform jihad by giving alms and praying.[546]

Most Koranic passages do not suggest vengeance – that is left to God. "Turn now from them and say 'Peace,'" and "To you be your religion, to me my religion."[547] Mohammed tried to create an interfaith community – religion was not the basis of his conflicts. Sometimes he fought with the local Jewry, sometimes he allied. That back and forth is clear in the Koran. This interfaith desire, interpreted here as political, can be seen in Abraham's 'creation' of the Kaaba – a Mohameddan invention – no one knows who built the Kaaba. Afterwards, all three faiths could worship there – side by side.

A main problem with Islam is taking the political document, the Koran, as the inerrant word of God. Mohammed wrote the Koran in response to current political situations. It may have been good policy then, but it cannot apply for all time, especially when it has internal philosophical contradictions. These vanish if one sees them as responses to temporal situations rather than the perpetual command of God.

The war suras are cherry-picked to make them doctrines of all-out war. "Make ready against them strong squadrons whereby you can strike terror into the enemy of God and your enemy." But the next verse is somehow forgotten when hating the Koran, "and if they lean to peace, lean thou also to it."[548] Both extremists and Western critics only quote the first part, implying that Islam is in a perpetual state of frenzied rage.

Aside from drawing on hadith, jihad formulators weighted the Koran toward the later verses. But the Koran is political, and these were written during wartime. It's flunky logic. Why would the word of God be more meaningful later than earlier? The original jihad doctrine spoke of a House of Peace inside Islam and a House of War outside where the conversion would be ongoing. Soon enough, there was a House of Treaty. Not long after was the greater and lesser jihad. "The greater jihad is the struggle against the self," a hadith says.

Jihad is quite an important doctrine. The idea that the main thrust is forceful conversion to Islam is insupportable. "If they leave you alone and do not fight you and offer you peace, then Allah allows you no way against them."[549] The Koran explicitly forbids mandatory religion. "We know best what disbelievers say, you are not there to force them."[550]

At the end of the 7th Century, for example, Islamic chieftains forbid conversion to Islam. After a time of coercion, in 929 the injunction to war against unbelievers was modified – they didn't need to convert, but only to pay tribute. Politics controlled religion – they wanted money, not more Muslims.

Certain Koranic passages can be taken out of context, but when read in context, they refer to specific wars. There are endless preconditions and qualifiers placed on war activities. Not all parts of the Koran are prescriptive – some are just historical descriptions. The critique applies to all holy books. When a religion takes its texts to always say, 'Thou shalt,' instead of 'this is what happened,' trouble will follow.

Even the lesser jihad is officially stated as being only for defense. Rulers will abuse any policy they can, of course, but a close examination of terrorist statements indicates they believe they are defending against an aggressive power. When bin Laden wants the military out of Saudi Arabia, he does not want to kill infidels per se; he wants them gone from the holy land of Mecca. Any jihadic act that kills innocent women and children is expressly forbidden by Koranic injunction. The Koran overflows with the idea of protecting the innocent.

The infamous sword verse from the Koran, sura 9:5, is usually quoted as "kill the infidels wherever you find them." It's used to justify the belief that Islam is inherently aggressive toward all non-Islamic people. But the verse is mistranslated to create a false idea. A better translation: "when the sacred months are passed, kill those who join other gods with God wherever you shall find them. Seize them, besiege them, and lay wait for them with every kind of ambush." The verse refers to polytheists – joining other gods with God. Christians and Jews are exempt. They are *not infidels* as the Koran clearly states many times. They are people of the book. They worship the same God by Islamic belief. Presumably atheists are exempt, as well. They have no gods to join with God. It could also exempt polytheists who have not met the one God. In short, the sword verse applies to a very limited set of people.

Even before the verse are qualifiers. If polytheists have acted in good faith and not supported enemies, they are not to be killed. The Koran instructs Muslims to make and keep alliances with polytheists if they honor the alliance themselves. Sura 9, the war sura, starts with four months of cessation of hostilities mandated for polytheists to freely travel. The Muslim is required to protect non-Muslims requesting it and to stand by any covenant with them. The Koran details acceptable times for battle against pagans: if they violate a covenant, or if they attack first.[551] The 'sword verse,' which does not mention a sword, is simply not a command for all-out war against non-Muslims.

The invocation to martyrdom applies only to the battlefield. It was meant to incite a ferocity and willingness to die in the soldier. It's an ordinary tactic of any general, using honor or heaven as reward of a valiant death.

In the 1950s, Sayyid Qutb reversed the defensive jihad. Before being executed by the Egyptian government, he said war should be taken into the world and offensive war is a part of jihad. Though generally disregarded among Muslims, the idea gets enormous media airplay. It is associated as a typical sentiment, which it is not.

A hundred Muslim scholars wrote the Pope, criticizing him for a 2006 statement. The term holy war, they say, does not exist in Islam – jihad means 'struggle in the way of God.'[552] Holy war actually refers to the Christian term Crusade. It stems from Judaism. "I have commanded my dedicated soldiers, warriors eager and bold, to carry out my anger…The Lord of Hosts musters an army for battle. They come, the Lord and instruments of his wrath, to destroy the land."[553]

Arabic countries almost exclusively define jihad as 'divine duty or worship,' though a minority of non-Arab Muslims thinks of it as military duty. Jihad holds an ethical and positive connotation for all Muslims. Almost none associate it with terrorist acts. It means endeavoring to live in moral certitude, fulfilling the needs of one's family, working for social justice, overcoming the scourge of drugs, and promoting education. If it comes to war, the Koran is clear. "Fight in the way of God with those who fight you, but aggress not. God loves not the aggressors."[554]

The third jihad is for social justice, Safi claims, to 'affirm the humanity of us all.' The average Muslim objects to both the extremist who kills and the Western capitalist who accumulates super-wealth while billions starve. He objects to the senseless consumption of resources. He objects to the death of each innocent child in Western military actions. This last is the jihad of Palestine.

A principle Arab complaint is the Israeli occupation. In 1948, Palestine lost four-fifths of its land with the creation of Israel. It has since lost another 50%. (See figure 20, next page.) 750,000 Palestinians became homeless in the creation. Almost all Palestinians are born and will die never leaving the remaining land under the longest military occupation on Earth – 60 years.

They can be put under house arrest without notice or cause. During the 1985 intifada – war of liberation – there are videos of

Israeli soldiers breaking the bones of civilians with rocks. Palestinians live with ubiquituous roadblocks, unable to move around in their fragmenting country. Fatima Abad Rabo was in labor, trying to get through a checkpoint to the hospital. The soldiers rifle-butted the husband and sent them home. Trying again, they were again refused. The baby died. There are hundreds, even thousands, of these stories – all documented. When the Israeli military is active, children cannot go to school, ambulances can't pass checkpoints, and curfews are brutally enforced.

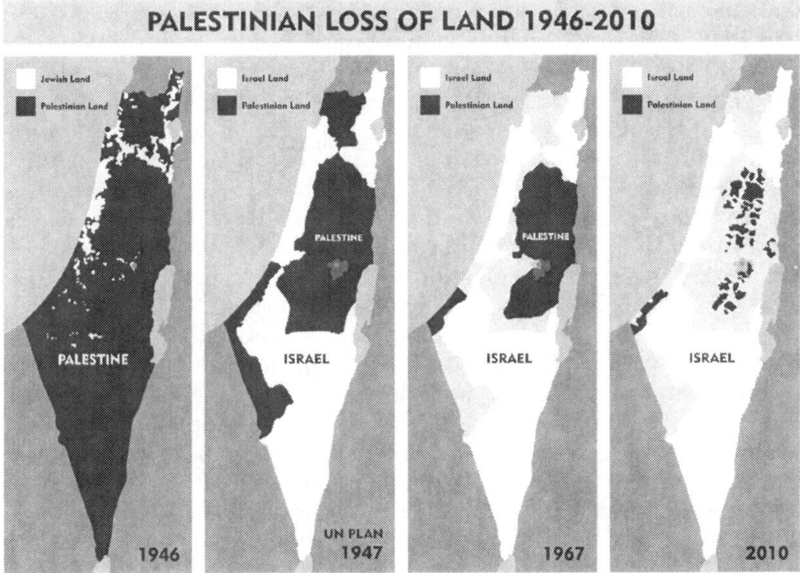

Figure 20: *Occupation Magazine* (Jan. 2005).

The Israeli settlements, walled fortresses really, are illegal under international law – no one disputes this, they ignore it. Opulent communities surrounded by poverty, they consume 80% of water for 5% of the people – green lawns in the desert. Most Palestinians lack running water. In a typical story, one woman's house was destroyed and land stolen – her family had lived there for 900 years. Highways to the settlements are for Israeli use only. In order to cross, long lines of Palestinians wait hours, sometimes days, for 2 or 3 Jewish settlers to drive past.

Waffan al-Ali was the first female suicide bomber ever. Before her attack, the ambulance driver said she had seen too many people "shot in the head, stomachs shot out, or babies forced to be born at checkpoints." Large numbers of Palestinian children suffer from anxiety and sleep disorders. Almost everyone has had a family member die in an Israeli prison or attack.[555]

Though there were disagreements, true hatred between Jews and Arabs only arose after the Israeli occupation of Palestine. With no indigenous anti-Semitic lore, the Arabs imported the bogus Protocols of the Elders of Zion around 1950.

The Tanakh God ordered his people to take the Holy Land. "If they worship a different God, put them all to the sword." Other justifications include the persecution of Jews by Hitler and the need for a Jewish state. But a claim based on a 3,000-year-old text, critics say, is questionable at best. And the remedy for persecution cannot possibly be more persecution.

The commitment to taking the Holy Land for Israel is called Zionism. Zionists, critics say, have a dark history. Irgun, Lehi, Hagadah, Palmach, the Jewish Defense League and five other groups are counted as 'Jewish terrorists.' Before becoming Prime Minister, Yitzak Shamir led the Stern Gang – a terrorist assassin organization granted general amnesty in 1949. Ariel Sharon was implicated in a 1983 terrorist action – 890 Palestinians died. Under the 'war on terror' rubric, Israel gets carte blanche to attack Palestine, but counter attacks are 'terrorism.'

Israel receives $3 billion/year in US aid, more than any other nation on the planet. They receive the highest grade of weaponry – unavailable to all other nations. They are the fourth largest military power in the world and have nuclear weapons. With US backing, Israel "offered 10% of what used to be Palestine," Israeli historian Ilan Pappe says of the failed 2000 accords. "The Israelis are talking about a 'stateless state' with no genuine sovereignty, with no independent foreign or political policies, with no proper capital, and at the mercy of the Israeli security services and policy."[556]

"The Land of Israel, [Palestine] was the birthplace of the Jewish people," the Jewish Declaration of Independence reads. "Here their spiritual, religious and political identity was shaped. Here they first attained to statehood, created cultural values of national and universal significance and gave to the world the eternal Book of Books." Zionism claims Palestine for the Jewish people. Not all of them want it.

Holocaust survivors were the first to reject it. Eli Weisel, who endured Dachau, spoke against Zionist occupation in his Nobel Prize speech. "I swear never to be silent. Wherever and whenever human beings endure suffering, we must take sides. Silence encourages the tormentor, never the victim." A number of Hasidic rabbis oppose the Jewish state of Israel on religious grounds. The International Jewish anti-Zionist Network wants "the dismantling of Israeli apartheid, the return of Palestinian refugees, and the ending of the Israeli colonization of historic Palestine." More than 500 soldiers have refused to serve in the occupation – facing criminal penalties. Dr. Hajo Meyer, an Auschwitz survivor, speaks publicly against Zionism. For his efforts, the 86-year-old is shouted at, threatened, and sent hate mail. Professor Pappe said, "there is an orchestrated campaign to silence the talk of giving young Palestinians hope instead of despair." Israelite Rami el-Hannan's daughter was killed in a suicide attack. He blames the occupation. "The suicide bomber was a victim the same as my little girl." Gush Salom, an Israeli group, claims the Zionist government is "committing war crimes on a daily basis." There are at 5 other global and uncountable local Jewish organizations opposing Zionism. Anti-Zionism, they claim, is not anti-Semitism – it is the opposite.

There is no denying Palestinian political violence. Since 1990, Palestinians have killed 800 Israelis. Most were civilians. If that classifies these as terrorist attacks, then Israel should be judged by the same measure. Between 1946 and 1950, the Muslim population of Palestine dropped from a million to 100,000. A number of massacres occurred, with small villages wiped out. This has been happening, with periods of calm, for 60 years. The 1982 Sabra and Shatila camps saw the murder of 3,000 people – almost half were children. In 1994, a school bus was deliberately blown up. The 1996 Qanah massacre destroyed a refugee shelter.[557] In 2008, 1,400 Gazans fell to Isreali guns, including 326 children. 8 Israelis died from the rocket attacks. In March, 2008, a lone Arab gunman died after killing 8 Israeli civilians. Israel killed 107 Palestinians in response – mostly civilians. There are hundreds more incidents. It is not anti-Semitism, Jewish critics claim, to oppose genocide in Palestine.

Terrorism is a real issue between Israel and Palestine, but what about the rest of the world? "More people have died in the bathtub than of terrorism," the former governor of Minnesota said. Most Americans agree with the underlying sentiment, rating it below 10th as a serious problem facing America.

To wage a 'war on terror,' or any abstraction, one had better understand it. Otherwise, the 'war' will make it worse. It's dangerous to characterize individuals in movements. It always misses the point. Not striking the heart in battle, the enemy is wounded and becomes more dangerous. It is a type of Sun Tzu's death ground – without escape or surrender, men fight their hardest. The highest strategy is taking whole. Capturing without battle is a perfect victory. Proper understanding of Islamic terrorism will end it.

First off, it's far from the only flavor. According to *al'Ahram Weekly*, the Zionist doctrine of Chabad regards non-Jews as subhuman. Particular to extremist Orthodox Judaism, it seeks to enslave, murder, or exterminate all non-Jews in Palestine. Baruch Goldstein was a Jewish extremist who murdered 29 Palestinians worshiping in the West Bank. He was lionized by many in the Jewish community. In a sense, he is an unofficial saint.

Hundreds of non-Muslim organizations have been labeled terrorists – Aum Shinrikyo, the Front for Liberation of Quebec, and Irgun. This Jewish terrorist organization struck the King David Hotel in 1949. It was called 'the worst terrorist attack of the 20th Century.' The Tamil Tigers surpass all others in suicide attacks.

Most Muslim attacks come from lands occupied by the US – Iraq had no suicide attacks before the war, and fundamentalist giants Iran and Sudan have never had one. In 4 years, Lebanon had 41 suicide attacks. When forces pulled out, no further attacks occurred. Every terrorist organization has the same political, non-religious goal: "to compel a modern democracy to withdraw military forces from the territory that the terrorists view as their homeland."[558] Terrorism is political, not religious.

15 of the 19 hijackers came from Saudi Arabia – where troops are stationed. They did cocaine, drank, and went to topless bars. They were not fundamentalists. The proscriptions against suicide in the Koran are overwhelming – if you take your own life, you will suffer in hell for eternity. Would a fanatical believer risk that on a theological nicety? Suicide bombers are political protestors, not religious. In 1998, a declaration of the World Islamic Front for Jihad against the Jews and the Crusaders objected to 1) occupation of Saudi Arabia, theft of resources, threats against neighbors, and use of Saudi Arabia as a spearhead, 2) attempt to repeat aggressions against Iraq, 3) support of Israel to the detriment of the Palestinians.

Anti-terrorism in Islam goes back to Mohammed. The Khawarij were the first apostates of Islam. Though their religious conduct was exemplary, the Prophet (it is said) expelled them. They practiced terrorism and felt themselves to be Muslims, but, according to tradition and jurisprudence, they were not. Islam forbids killing innocents. Likewise for taking arms against the state, although communal measures for addressing despotism are actually mandated. The hadith predicted these non-Muslim pretenders would arise in every age.

People fuzzily link fatwas with terrorist orders, but a fatwa is not a command – it is a religious opinion. Any Muslim can issue one; any Muslim can ignore one. Ayatollah Khomeini issued his fatwa in 1989 to kill Salman Rushdie. This is a bandied incident among anti-Islamic ideologues. But the Islamic response is ignored. "Saudi Arabia's ulamas rejected it, many Iranian intellectuals were embarrassed, and it was condemned as counter to Islam by all but one of the 49 Islamic conference states."[559] There was no united Islamic force focused on one man. It was a lone Islamic cleric in power acting unilaterally.

A 2010 fatwa was issued by hundreds of Imams. By the Koran, terrorism is a 'blasphemous act', "the opinion unanimously held by all the scholars ... in the 1400 years of Islamic history ... no forbidden action can ever become a virtuous and lawful deed due to goodness of intention."[560]

In 1992 an Algerian party became popular. The military pulled a coup and took the government. This was celebrated as a victory for democracy in the West. Muslims saw this as a hypocritical double-standard. The GIA, an Islamic group, rebelled. Thousands of innocents were killed. It came out that the military went on rampages and blamed the GIA. It's a common phenomenon in war – the false-flag attack. Heinous events are blamed on the opponent.

More than a billion people now believes 9/11 was such an event. For better or worse, such voices are being taken with increasing seriousness. 100 million Americans agree the official story was "a big fabrication."[561] 9/11 Commission Chair Lee Hamilton said, "the 9/11 commission was set up to fail." The FBI's most wanted page features bin Laden, but he is not wanted for the attack – "we have no hard evidence linking bin Laden to 9/11," FBI spokesman Rex Tomb said.[562] "We've never made the case," Dick Cheney said, "that somehow Osama Bin Laden was directly involved in 9/11."[563]

In scientific polling, the global average is only 46% who still believe al Qaeda was behind the attacks. Lt. Colonel Bob Bowman – fighter pilot, NASA physicist and congressional candidate, Major General Albert Stubblebine, and hundreds of other US military officers have signed petitions and issued statements disputing the official account. The former head of Russian armed forces, former President of Italy, Japanese senators, a dozen EU parliamentarians, Defense Ministers of Germany and Canada are a small sampling of prominent 9/11 skeptics. 10 US legislators and more than half of the 9/11 Commission believe there was a cover-up, even calling it "a national scandal."[564] Bill Doyle, head of the Coalition of 9/11

Families, said 50% of the families think 9/11 was 'an inside job.' "This is not a fringe phenomenon," *Time* magazine said as early as 2006, "It is a mainstream political reality."[565]

A common question is why no one has come forward. The answer is – they have. FBI translator Sibel Edmonds was placed under a gag order for 6 years on punishment of imprisonment. Her testimony, purged from the 9/11 Commission report, would "implicate people at the highest level," one senator said. She agreed to violate the gag order if major media would interview her, but none offered. The gag order expired and she went public with her knowledge – Osama bin Laden was a CIA asset as of September 11, 2001.

Top Secret Military Specialist April Gallop had a court case in April, 2011.[566] The case named Cheney and Rumsfeld as co-conspirators in the destruction of the World Trade Center. Ms. Gallop was working at the Pentagon on 9/11 and involved in an explosion seven minutes before the airline struck. She claims that if the official story were true, she would be dead.* Judge Walker (a first cousin of George Bush), threw the case out and fined her $15,000.[567]

Official government evidence is now sealed – in 2009, 9/11 information was placed off-limits from Freedom of Information requests without explanation. But too much lies in the public domain already. Probably the most critical piece of data is the collapse of World Trade Center 7. The BBC reported the collapse of the building at 4:54 pm, but it didn't actually fall until 5:20. The 47-story building dropped straight down in 6.5 seconds. In its original 2005 report, the National Institute of Standards and Technology did not mention it. In 2008, it investigated the event and finally explained the official version: due to thermal expansion, a steel girder on column 79 broke loose, leading to simultaneous failure of the other 82 steel columns. Collapse, they say, was inevitable.

"The story that a few columns can cause synchronized collapse is nonsense," said controlled demolition expert Tom Sullivan.[568] "This is controlled demolition," said Danny Jowenko, owner of the largest Dutch demolition company. "Absolutely, it's been imploded."[569] Thousands of experts have made strong statements that the building could not have fallen the way NIST said. "The fires were not hot enough to cause the steel to soften and the building to collapse," said Scott Grainger, a 25-year veteran in fire protection. "The government has destroyed much of the evidence."[570]

---

* See whistleblowers.com for names of 16 other intelligence and military professionals whose testimony was refused by the 911 Commission.

1,400 certified architects and engineers have signed a petition – the explanation violates the laws of physics. Among their claims: no other steel framed building has collapsed from fire. NIST's confirmation of free-fall collapse voids the entire support structure of the building – which is impossible. Pools of molten metal, testified by numerous clean-up crews on video, were flatly denied. Leader Richard Gage has 11 points of comparison with a known controlled demolition. The evidence needs to be seen for proper analysis and it can be, online, at the Architects and Engineers for 9/11 Truth website.* The NIST material is not recommended for counter opinions as the documents are unreadably opaque. Better sources are pastor Chris Mohr, magazine editor Michael Shermer, and the skeptics James Randi forum, but the critical element is a willingness to present and analyze the numerous videos of collapse. Too many sites ignore this evidence, including *Popular Mechanics*.

Perhaps it's impossible – many believe 'the government would never do such a thing,' or that they're too incompetent. But Richard Nixon disagrees, "the Warren Commission was the greatest hoax ever pulled on the American public."[571] Even US National Security Adviser Zbigniew Brzezinski told the Senate "the war on terror is a mythical historical narrative."[572]

Naomi Wolf says it's a blueprint for totalitarianism.[573] Chilean dictator Augusto Pinochet faked documents to increase the threat of the armed insurgents – people were scared and let him dismantle the democracy. Stalin raised alarms about spooky 'sleeper cells.' Hitler hyped a terrorist threat from Communists and created a 'Department of Homeland Security.' Both initiated military tribunals and secret prisons – now inglorious parts of the American system. Mussolini hatched a paramilitary force to scare civilians. We now have numerous private military contractors such as Blackwater. Every society that does this has turned it on their own citizens, Wolf contends. In a fascist shift, a terror threat is used to shut down democracy. The oppression and torture begins with a marginalized group – Islam is the fall guy for the creation of the security state.

Warrantless searches are legitimized. The president has the power to send in the National Guard, declare an emergency and martial law over the objections of state governors. Congress has no authority. Closing borders, creating travel restrictions, and applying these to critics has become normal. For example, two old ladies who run an anti-war newsletter are suspected terrorists. So is Robert Murphy, the foremost constitutional

* 'Blueprint for Truth: the Architecture of Destruction' is the title. It is also available on youtube.

scholar. He made the No Fly List after a speech critical of the security apparatus. Dissent – the guardian of democracy – is termed treason. The rule of law is subverted. A closed society is not overtly militarized. It appears unchanged – Hitler even held elections. The judiciary and Congress exist, but they are controlled. The press, academia, and all other trappings of normal society are there. It looks the same, but feels different. As Thomas Jefferson said, "the price of liberty is eternal vigilance."

Clash of Civilization

If we do fall, let it be said that we tried, right to the end, to hold to The Way of Peace.
—Hopi Chief Dan Eveham

Before the Nazis came to the northern Romanian town of Sighet, a Jew returned. He told his story of being abducted and luckily surviving a mass murder by the Nazis. He warned. He was ignored. All the town's Jews were captured and most died in concentration camps.[574] Today, we have a similar situation. Conspiracy theorists, peak-oil doom-and-gloomers, the Armageddon fringe – we ignore them. Perhaps they are wrong, perhaps right. Their numbers grow. Their voices increase. Our common sentiment is not to listen. Such ideas disturb our tranquility. Our blessed way of life cannot end. It's impossible. But all societies fall apart – where went the Romans, the Aztecs, the Nazis? Ours will not endure forever. At some point, it will fail. If societies end as they existed, then ours will end in fire and velocity, in a prayer to science. Our headlong rush of speed will be a karmic fulfillment.

It is both spiritual axiom and obvious truth that our lives can end at any moment. Death will not be delayed. So it is with civilizations. There was no desire to write this picture of a world on fire. The intent was a positive book, but this was the evident truth. There is nothing so special about our way of life that it must extend past our lives. Different voices tell us that powerful change is in the air. The sentiment is going mainstream. We may be at the end of a historical age. Though frightening, it is good to remember that destruction is also creation. Humanity need not be a prisoner of its habits. We can overcome the age-old vices of war, greed and deceit. Though only possible through collective will, it is the sum of individual acts that make it so. A teaspoon of courage multiplies like a living thing. We can face difficult truths with a compassionate and wise outlook, be decent human beings, and always maintain a joyful mind. Even if some millenarianism happens – as both atheists and the faithful seem to feel is inevitable.

"Ultimately, the struggle of the fundamentalists is against two enemies, secularism and modernism," Bernard Lewis wrote when he coined the term 'Clash of Civilizations.' Sometimes an apologist for Islam, sometimes an enemy, Lewis fails to see, or at least mention, the political anger of Middle Easterners. He confuses Arabs for all Muslims. And he simplifies the causality to a sound bite – "a surely historic reaction of an ancient rival against our Judeo-Christian heritage, our secular present, and the worldwide expansion of both."[575] Modernity and secularism, Lewis finds, are good but a bit pushy – it's really the Others' fault, and the Clash of Civilizations is frighteningly real.

Samuel Huntington wrote a better-developed thesis promoting the idea. It had many causal factors and interlinks of 8 different civilizations, from China and Latin America to Islam and the West. China, apparently, is due to establish regional hegemony and ally with Islam. The response is contra the global hegemonic values of capitalism and Western-style democracy. Russia will connect with Iran, and by extension, China, in opposition to the US. Religious sentiment will inflame it with adherents who think their way is the only way and God is on their side. He has good points and sensibly sees religion as an enhancement effect, rather than the primary driver. But he failed to note Western political manipulations in his analysis that "Islam has bloody borders."[576]

His actual argument was criticized on a number of fronts: It favored the Western system, civilizations are not distinct entities, diversity exists in all cultures, Islam is not monolithic, interpenetration and change are primary and inescapable aspects of cultures, and Islam is not a central anything.

Unfortunately, even Huntington's biased thesis has been cannibalized. All that remains is the wicked Muslims who hate freedom – the Clash of Civilizations looming down on a poorly defended West. The historical roots of 'us versus them' are supposed to be all informing, but as usual, it is less than a half-truth. Islam, Christianity and Judaism are not cosmic enemies even within their own histories.

The first interaction was an act of friendship and protection. Mohammed's early followers fled Mecca and were protected by Christians. This is the proper relation – mutual protectors.[577] From the Koran – "nearest among in love to the believers are those who say: 'we are Christians.'"[578] When Mohammed took Mecca, he erased all Kaaba pictures except Jesus and Mary. Islam is not hostile to all other traditions. "Oh, humanity, truly we made you into nations and tribes that you might know each other."[579]

The companions – the first Caliphs – are important as example. 18 years after Mohammed's death, the Muslims captured Jerusalem. When Umar was invited to pray after taking Jerusalem at the Church of the Holy Sepulchre, he demurred. His followers would insist on building a mosque where the first Islamic ruler prayed and he did not want Islam to have a conflict with Christianity. They made a huge mistake, though.

Perhaps it was a deliberate insult, but 52 years after the conquest, Muslims built the politico-religious lightning rod called the Dome of the Rock. On this holiest of spots, God had unfolded the world, made Adam, and taken his seat. There, Abraham prepared to sacrifice Isaac and Mohammed ascended to heaven on a winged horse. It was also the site of the Second Temple, destroyed by Rome in 70 ce. And it is where the Israelites have long wanted to build the Third.

The Clash of Civilizations CliffsNotes version pits the West against Islam. The idea is absurd. A religion cannot battle a geographical region. Such shorthand is dangerous in the extreme – many people die. When a people validate global war, they should know the reasons at a very deep level. All hidden causes – oil, war profiteering, and power-lust, for example – should be brought out and discussed. In Eisenhower's final address, he warned against the dangers of a military-industrial complex infiltrating and controlling the government, leading to wasteful and terrible violence.

The Islam-Western predicament highlights a recurrent historical theme – colonizers attempt to create a 'liberator/reformer' image that is never the truth. Trying to salvage the image as it falls apart and meets resistance, they only make it worse and worse until it is no longer tenable – "war in the name of peace is still war."[580]

The eleventh-century Crusades against Islam were a holy war. The nation of Islam had taken enormous territory and threatened Christendom. The Crusades were partially defensive, but they included a host of other reasons, including the corruption and venality of political leaders. But in the end, they were a holy war – a Crusade. "This crusade, this war on terror is going to take a while," George Bush said. The 43rd president declared a holy war on an abstraction. When anyone says terrorism these days, it points to one group of people. It's not necessary to say who that is – everyone knows. Us against them – a divided, apocalyptic world.

But division cannot offer salvation. "The idea, promulgated … on both sides," Reza Aslan warns, "of a cosmic battle between Islam and Christianity will become a self-fulfilling prophecy … This is not a clash of civilizations, and if we insist on framing it that way we will reap the whirlwhind. … the whole concept of an apocalyptic … clash is that both the evangelicals and the jihadists use it to to justify their actions, and as long as we persist in casting every Muslim as the enemy we will be dragged further and further into that struggle."[581]

Micheal Baigent traces out an uneasy collusion between world religions as a recent phenomenon. Each has a different endgame. Predictably, every religion sees heathens and apostates either dead or a member of their fold. The war will be glorious and it is pre-ordained by God. Billions believe in this. From such a state, we would be foolish to hope for a good ending.

But perhaps the truth is not so clear that it is merely a batch of delusional religious fools. After all, the Clash of Civilizations is nothing but a secular Armageddon. Truth lies in the middle. Maybe it is just the way humanity operates. Give a species the concept 'future' and they will blow it up in all haste. Or less precisely, we know that for every beginning there is an end. As our world came to be, so it will cease, in fire or ice. Humanity will see its final hour. Thus Armageddon is neither delusional, because it will happen, nor predestined, because it will not happen in the way or for the reasons that these various groups think.

With such a varied background of ideology, civilization may be subconsciously bringing itself to that brink. People could be so fascinated that the collective urge is pushing in that direction. The idea that war is necessary for defense becomes self-evident tautology – enemies are suddenly everywhere. We divide and think hatred is the way. Deep cultural beliefs become world truths. War is inevitable. This is what the ancient prophets saw. They were less prophets, under this tutelage, than sociologists. The more insightful saw the cycle and its coming. Therefore they could issue legitimate 'prophecies' accurately predicting the vast sweep of civilization.

It's been predicted before. Johann Bengel, in the 1730s, claimed that the end of the world would arrive in 1836. Ronald Reagan believed the conditions were in place for Armageddon. In 1984, a group of church leaders called for a conference to get Reagan to back away from the concept. "The church leaders who called the news conference warned, 'A religious doctrine, the ideology of a nuclear Armageddon, has entered our nation's political arena. The ideology identifies our nation's enemies with the enemies of God. Because the religious leaders who promote this ideology believe that the destruction of these enemies is decreed in Scripture, they conclude that *reconciliation with America's adversaries is ultimately futile.*"[582]

Never mind that the most popular president in fifty years subscribed to biblical mythology and listened to ideologues who believed the USSR was a biblical demon called Magog. He felt nuclear war with the Soviets was inevitable. It didn't happen, but it still could with another Magog. Islam is being groomed for the role, but China would suffice. And Russia still has plenty of atomic missiles.

At any rate, the Western culture of Armageddon requires three criteria to be fulfilled. The Jewish people must regroup in the land of Israel. This happened in 1948. The taking of the Temple Mount, which happened in 1967, is the second. The third is the rebuilding of the Temple of Solomon on that site.

This has not occurred for two reasons. First, the Dome of the Rock is already there. The nation of Islam is not well-disposed to the destruction of one its most sacred sites. Secondly, from the Bible – "Speak unto the children of Israel, that they bring thee a red heifer without spot, wherein is no blemish, and upon which never came yoke." The animal is invalidated under a number of conditions, such as two black hairs or cesarean birth. There is a serious project underway to breed this red heifer. A ritual sacrifice, cremation and anointment of the animal is required to cleanse a person from 'the touch of death.' These purified people can then rebuild the Temple. After that, the battle at Armageddon (Megiddo) in Israel can begin.[583]

The great concern about political 'Armageddonists' is that they don't value this world. They believe it is a sacrifice meant to be destroyed when Jesus (or the 12th Imam) returns. Thus it can be plundered, looted, and ultimately destroyed. Almost half the US congress supports fundamentalist groups with Armageddon ideologies.

Where most Armageddonists fear it, the awful reality is that sectors of all three monotheistic religions (and even some atheists) desire Armageddon. These ill-defined groups are 'destined' to battle each other. They are caught in this crucible of wanting the same beginning because each believes they will emerge victorious in the end. It has created an underworld of bizarre alliances. The CIA created the Afghan Mujahideen in the 1980s to battle the Soviet Union. The group later morphed into al-Qaeda. Jews and Christians have allied to create the conditions for the Temple on the Mount. Islam and Christianity both claim Jesus will take part on their side in the battle, while his own Jewish ancestors deny it. No peaceful solution seems possible even to the initial conditions for Armageddon. And the mythology, of course, entails global war.

But perhaps there is hope. A more elevated insight into Armageddon comes from Hopi prophecies of Peace. The 'native' Armageddon claim that there will come a time of world turbulence. Humanity will face a choice – evolve or suffer catastrophic change. The evolution is merely to choose the way of peace. The Hopi word *koyaanisqatsi* means an unbalanced civilization, a human condition requiring a different path. The essential point is that man cannot make arbitrary laws and enforce them at gunpoint. To do so violates the natural order, leading to a global suicide.

The Hopi prophesied a 'gourd full of ashes' – nuclear technology, perhaps – rendering the land uninhabitable.* Also predicted were guns (weapons of thunder), railroads (snakes of iron), electricity (land criss-crossed by spider webs), roads (rivers of stone), oil spills (sea turning black and many creatures dying), hippies (long-haired youth learning Indian ways), and the final sign – the US Skylab falling (dwelling place in the heavens that shall fall with a crash). This signals Armageddon is imminent. People become disgusted with the busyness of modern life and the corruption of leaders. The leaders attack each other and general mayhem goes global. The worse the inequality between haves and have-nots, the worse the violence will be. The more people turn to ways of peace, the less it will be. In the end, everything could be destroyed, but if only one person remains who believes in the ancient way of peace, then Earth will be saved and experience a time of great renewal. "Ancient cultures are being annihilated," Chief Dan Evehama wrote,

> Our people's lands are being taken from them, leaving them no place to call their own. This is happening because many have given up or manipulated their original spiritual teachings. The Way of Life was given to all people. It is not being honored. Because of this great sickness – greed, which infects every land and country – simple people are losing what they have kept for thousands of years.
>
> Now we must look upon each other as brothers and sisters. Wars only bring more wars, and never peace. Only by joining together in a Spiritual Peace with love in our hearts for one another, love in our hearts for the Great Spirit and Mother Earth, shall we be saved from the terrible Purification Day which is just ahead.

* The atomic bomb is arguably envisioned in the Bible, where people's skin melts before they fall to the ground.

> We have been charged to pray for you and all life on Earth, never forgetting anything or anyone in our ceremonials. Our prayer is to have a good happy life, plenty of soft gentle rain for abundant crops. We pray for Earth to live in peace and leave a beautiful world to the children yet to come. We know you have good hearts but good hearts are not enough.
>
> Hotevilla is the last holy consecrated, undisturbed traditional Native American sacred shrine to the Creator. As the prophecy says, this sacred shrine must keep its spiritual pathways open. This village is the spiritual vortex for the Hopi to guide the many awakening Native Americans and other true hearts home to their own unique culture.
>
> Where is the freedom which you all fight for and sacrifice your children for? Is it only the Indian people who have lost, or are all Americans losing the very thing which you originally came here to find? We don't share the freedom of the press, because what gets into the papers is what the government wants people to believe, not what is really happening.
>
> So as our prophecy says; then it must be up to the people with good pure hearts that will not be afraid to help us to fulfill our destiny in peace for this world. We now stand at a cross-road whether to lead ourselves in Everlasting-Life or total destruction. We believe that human beings spiritual power through prayer is so strong it decides life on Earth. If we do fall, let it be said that we tried, right up to the end, to hold fast to The Way of Peace.
>
> Our prayers for peace meet yours as the sun rises and sets. May the Great Spirit guide you safely into The Way of Love, Peace, and Freedom. May the holy ancestors of Love and Light keep you safe in your land and homes. Pray for God to give you something important to do in this great work, which lies ahead of us all, to bring peace on earth.[584]

We have a choice: we can trust this type of man, who brings corn out of the dry sand where science has tried and failed, with wisdom written in the lines of his face, with compassion and love evident in every word, or we can trust an atheist who says nothing more profound than 'religion poisons everything.'

Transcending Faith

In order to close the issue of spiritual atheism, a few topics need addressing. First, we must see if God exists. After a number of 'proofs' on both sides, we eventually have to conclude that belief in God is essentially a personal issue. You can, of course, never prove a negative, and definitive proof of God in the positive sense is unavailable. Logic as well, cannot prove anything. Many logical formulations are demonstrably false. Logic can only disprove things which are self-contradictory or in contradiction to an established truth. Logic can, however, give us guidelines to reject conceptions of God that make no sense. It can also hone in on the necessary attributes of God in the world we have. This is handled in the section 'The Concealment,' so named because God is hidden.

The next section addresses the many questions around morality. The division between relative and absolute morality appears as a sort of fiction – it is both in a sense. Morality must be rooted in cause and effect, else it is meaningless. If we flip this, then the cause-and-effect status of the world is morality. Since causality is inescapable, so is morality, but it has many ways to manifest. People have a choice, and without a choice, morality is meaningless. Morality is thus relative in that we have a choice and can take differing moral frameworks, but absolute in that sense that some moral framework is inevitable.

The concluding section lays out an interpretation of the Buddhist path. God has no place in this path – it is a solitary adventure. The Buddha was a man who worked on his mind and elevated it to the highest level. Taking his understanding, he taught what he saw – there is no self to anything, all is impermanent, and compassion is the ideal way to proceed. It is difficult to attain this wisdom, so diligence, sincerity, and an excellent example are essential. The wisdom is all-inclusive – no area of existence is beyond it. So, we must apply it to all areas of our lives fully in order to attain a greater understanding. It is beyond logical and even conceptual formulations, but these can help to cut away false views.

This whole part is called Transcending Faith. In order to attain this kind of path, we must get past faith in God, faith in Buddha, faith in science. We are really on our own and must walk this path alone. Faith, in the negative sense of neediness and being less than other, is an enormous obstruction. We can still be guided by good faith: faith that we can better ourselves significantly and faith that there might be someone a little wiser (or a lot wiser) who can show us the way. Without the first, we have an impoverished mind – the great poison of modern life. Without the second, we have arrogance – the great poison of atheism. Too many people think they are unworthy; too many atheists think they are better than others.

The Concealment

Making mistake after mistake, I walk an unmistaken path.
—Khenpo Tsultrim

The fundamental issue of atheism is simple – does God exist? There are many different ways to approach the question. Most people posit God as an absolute reality. This begs the question – what God? To put it in debatable form – what are the characteristics of God? Many imprecise spiritualists claim to believe in God, but this god is not anthropomorphic, not the creator of the universe per se, and typically not sentient. A carefully spiritual person would not use the term 'God' for their beliefs – it only clouds the issue. They believe in some higher power, animating spirit, essential reality, or transcendent sphere. They do not believe in God – the term is pre-loaded with many connotations these people do not want – inescapable masculinity for example.

One can be atheistic and spiritual. The higher essence is without any self. Further, the essence is all-pervasive, suffusing space, rocks, people, and bugs, thus not super-ordinate. It is an abstraction to logical mind, hence non-existent. It is directly perceivable to intuitive mind – which has no conception of existence or not. There is something more, says the spiritualist, but it is not God.

To discuss God, we should remove interfering ideas from the word. God is, at minimum, a conscious entity above and beyond humans. God is free, powerful, and capable of influencing our lives directly. According to Maimonides, God is the creator and guide of everything, a unique unity free from all material properties, the first and the last, and the only valid object of prayer. God knows all deeds and thoughts, rewards the faithful, and punishes transgressors. Given this, if God is not seen, it is his choice. That is the key point for and against God.

Atheists use logical constructs to 'disprove' God, as if God were subordinate to logic. The paradox of the omnipotent, omniscient God asks the question: if God is omniscient, he knows the future, so how can he then use his omnipotence to alter the future? That would make his omniscience wrong. The paradox is fairly easy to resolve. God uses his omnipotence to solve it. (Or there are many futures or no pre-ordained future.) Human inability to understand does not invalidate the solution. If human lack of understanding constituted disproof of something, then the Earth would not have revolved around the sun until the time of Copernicus. The paradox really says: if God can see the future, but then change his mind about what he says, then why can't humans explain that? The answer is because they can't.

Another version of the God paradox asks if God could create a weight so heavy that he couldn't lift it. Or could he create a puzzle so difficult that he can't solve it. This is more difficult because if you say he can, then he is not omnipotent either way. The real disproof is against omnipotence, which seems impossible, but one might say that being all-powerful, God can simply create a situation beyond the paradox. Omnipotence cannot be restricted by a meager thought puzzle.

However, omnipotence cannot exist. To be omnipotent means to be able to control every single facet of the entire universe. That is the meaning of all-powerful. Anything less is not omnipotence. To be omniscient means to know every single thing, every electron spin, in the entire universe. If an entity can control and perceive every single factor in the universe, then in fact, that being is every single thing in the universe. For God to be all-knowing and all-powerful, he must be indistinguishable from the universe. The argument might be that external control is possible, but not *total* external control. You can control a person's actions, but only to a limited extent can you control their thoughts. From the outside, their heart rate cannot be controlled, the efficiency of their liver function, the rate of toenail growth, the position of every atom. That can only be through a union with those things.

Of course, a counter-argument might be that God has set them all freely in motion and can exert control when he wishes. However, if he is omnipotent, then he can control it all simultaneously. He can reverse the spin of every electron in the universe at once. (An interesting thought game for a physicist!) To exercise that power, he would have to be inseparable from each quantum particle. But inseparability from all turns him into everything, which is meaningless. To say trite formulations such as 'God is everything,' is merely to babble nonsense. Is God then, a child-raping serial killer? Or a mass-murdering dictator, or a torturer? Is God both people who hate each other intensely, and thus insane? Is your neighborhood atheist God, disbelieving in himself?

Recently, a popular book used the 747 argument to 'disprove' God. The argument is flawed. First, it was originally used by an atheist to prove that a mechanistic origin of life is almost impossible – like a tornado assembling a 747 from scrap. The revised postulate – any creator must be *more complex than the creation* – has no proof. The simple water molecule, for example, creates quite complex forms called snowflakes. The arguer is an avid proponent of evolution and evolution exactly violates his required rules. A less complex thing – amino acids – lead to single strands of DNA, then viruses, then to single, then multi-cellular life forms, eventually leading to jelly fish, lungfish, and mammals. The standard is inconsistent – evolution is allowed to proceed from less to more complex but God is not.

There are many arguments around the existence of God. According to Augustine, everything is a mystic experience. The world is interpretable as symbols. Red is the blood of Christ, thorns the agonies from Satan. God is found in this symbolic world.

There are 'proofs' God's existence would leave traces upon the universe and those traces cannot be found. The cosmological argument may have a fatal defect – the simple-minded assertion that God is everywhere and everything, thus reducing him to nothing. But these are pointless. All logical, rhetorical proofs for or against can be countered with more sophistry. The principle argument against the existence of God is the empirically direct one. If he exists, where is he? The hidden God is a pernicious argument.

In the end, no human can prove God. Only God can prove God. There are only four possibilities – he does not care, he has forgotten us, he is hiding (at least from the faithless), or he does not exist. One and two can be ruled out – an omniscient, loving God would care and remember. They amount to non-existence for all practical human purposes and no one is arguing that is the case anyway. Christians argue he is hidden from the unfaithful. But one argument disallows this – theodical destruction of faith.

Theodicy is the big problem for most thoughtful Christians. How could a benevolent, all-powerful God allow evil? It has brought many fine theologians low. They have given up God. It's a shame and indicates a lack of the creatively spiritual. Such mundane mystifications as 'the Lord works in strange ways' are not necessary, but the question should be addressed. First is the difference between omnipotence and use of it. Power is most impressive in its restraint. Removing the question of whether God can prevent evil, the remaining problem is why would he allow it? The simple answer is 'humans have free will.' But it fails to satisfy. It gives no further purpose to the exercise of free will. We need a more meaningful answer. To get that, we need a more meaningful question – where are we headed?

God wants us to mature. Under a strict set of rules, that will not happen. A grown-up does not rely on his parents. It's even become common to cut off parental assistance, at least in the West. A parent who does this believes they are helping their child become self-reliant, confident, less self-centered, and independent. Removing himself from the picture, God forces us to do the same. Taking the idea further, God seeks an equal – somebody to meet him on his own terms. This idea is on offer in Genesis – humans could not eat of the second fruit because they would become like Gods themselves. Extending it further, humanity is perhaps one of ten billion experiments in the cosmos. Having done the math, he knows that some life somewhere in the universe will transcend its limitations. Some species will meet God through their own means. It's how they become worthy of doing so. The method by which it happens will surprise even God.

The argument is full of justifications, but if somebody wants to salvage a faith under assault, it might work. It does require that humanity become one experiment, rather than God's primary work. But for someone wrestling with theodicy, the leap should not be that far.

At any rate, all such proofs for God have a desperate, almost needy quality. The atheist disproofs are blundering straw men, based on the need to disprove. It becomes almost hateful. The logics on both sides are weak, the arguments easily defeated, and only the eggheads care. The experiment to prove or disprove God by reason failed. There is only one proof of God that could create any substantial logic for his existence. He should show himself.

One of the great things about God is his frenetic early activities. He wrestled Jacob, parted the Red Sea, flooded the world, got angry at rivers and seas, used empires to punish Israel, strolled in the garden conversing, swore vengeance, hated the Edomites, and culminated by sending his son to be tortured and killed by Romans. Afterwards, he disappeared from human history. The rest of the religious record is written as acts of the Church. For 2,000 years, he hasn't done anything. If we disallow him sending Jesus, it's much longer. God has disappeared.

Defining God, we must look at what is possible and what is not. It is not possible that we have a God that makes itself clearly and obviously known. Otherwise, there would be no doubt to

God's existence. Atheism would be impossible short of insanity. If God wished, he could simply create miracles or appear in the sky. Therefore, we are left with a God who must be hidden. It may not be rational to analyze the motives of God, but why is he hiding? This is the fundamental question of the Christian, Muslim, or Jewish concept of God. The claim is that he is testing our faith. Why would he test our faith so intensely as to make us deny our senses in order to believe? He gave us a logical mind that perceives no God. Many Christians will say there is no evidence for God and evade the debate on that basis. That doesn't fit, because we were created by God. Therefore that tool, that ability, was also created by him.

The old logic makes sense – if God gave us curiosity and intellect to search the world, then hid, what does he expect? Why should we believe in him when he provided us with faulty tools to do so? He is playing an indecent game with human longing. People want to know truth and he, by the Christian creed, expects us to believe in him on faith. He should have done a better job in our creation. A curious seeker can't force himself to believe. Lay the blame where it belongs.

God is imaginary. If he wants to send the curious soul to hell because they are compelled to search for a place in this world and for the deep truths of the universe instead of engaging in blind faith, then so be it. But this is hardly a merciful and wise God. In the end, it is personal. Belief in God is neither a logical, epistemological, nor empirical argument – it is a personal one. He cannot be proved or disproved. And for most atheists, that is disproof enough. If God was real, it would be obvious to all.

Morality

Because this is present, that will arise. Because that was born, this is being born.

—the mantra of dependent origination*

Moral relativism is one of the great bug-a-boos of modern philosophy – morality is either absolute or relative. Apparently, it is impossible to make the leap across the divided gradient between absolute and relative. According to relativity, we can choose any moral vantage we wish. Lying, killing, theft and hatred – nothing can force a person to reject these and confirm them as inherently unethical. From the other viewpoint, morality

* *Om ye dharma hetu prabhava hetum tesham tathagatho hyavadat tesham cha yo nirodha evam vadi mahashramanah svaha* in Sanskrit.

rules with an iron fist. The absolute sees morality as relative manifestation – the pigment from which all colors appear.

Such gross moral formulations as 'Thou shalt not kill/steal/lie' or its humanist echo 'killing/stealing/lying is wrong' may be too concrete. They don't seem to be especially moral formulations in any event. Nor even remotely absolute. Who would not steal food to save their child's life? Is it a moral or immoral act? If it is morally correct to kill someone before they kill many others – given that as the only possible action – then killing is not wrong as an absolute. It can only be wrong in certain circumstances.

But why should it be more wrong to kill a human than a mosquito? Both are merely creatures trying to extend their lifespan. These types of arguments are quite useful to moral relativism. That is because the Ten Commandments/humanist posits are relative phrasings. They target individualized actions. It is impossible to turn a relative prohibition such as 'killing is wrong' into an absolute moral law.

A subtler, wider net is needed to understand morality. It is neither relative nor absolute, yet somehow both. Morality is an inescapable fact to those trapped in the dream of life, yet an illusion from the absolute reality.

Causes, in other words, have effects. What we do, if repeated enough, is what we become. This is not to say that Fate is pre-ordained, but that we each create our own fate, bit by bit. One inch at a time, we hack a path from the formless jungle. That path tells us what our moral base is – and some moral base is inevitable.

A simple, but profound philosophical consequence of relativity is that all things are a matter of perspective. Any vantage point is as valid as another. If we take the proper perspective, then morality is absolute. It is not absolute in the sense of commandments written on a tablet with a throbbing glow. It is absolute in the sense that we cannot escape.

It is in the nature of life to seek to continue that existence in some form or another. Maybe that is the Darwinian force of species extension. Maybe it is the 'selfish gene.' Maybe it is the desire to continue one's own existence. If our actions indicate our true moral stance, then self-preservation is our morality. This inescapable morality is absolute to the relative being, relative to the absolute. It is absolute in the sense that, if we lack it, we cease to exist. It is relative in the sense that we can cease to exist.

Is there a happier view? Borrowing the tool of fuzzy logic can get at the moral law of consequences. If we are kind to others, they are more likely to be kind to us. If we are cruel, they tend to fear us or despise us. If we save another's life, they are generally grateful. If we murder their family, generally they are not. If we make them suffer, they will hate us. If we alleviate their suffering, they will be thankful, at least for a time. A bold and generous outlook engenders a bold and generous life. A fearful outlook makes us stay inside and draw the shades. If we are hungry, we should eat. If we eat when we are not hungry, we will become obese.

The morality here is that we must respect the rules of cause and effect. One can say these are not moral laws, but if one is obese to the point of handicap, then the person becomes society's burden – a moral argument. Or if the glutton is indifferent to starvation.

If we do not 'nurture strength of spirit to shield us from sudden misfortune,' then when negative consequences strike us, we are brought low. Though some blithe souls might not notice or may in any event be virtually immune to all but the most severe of consequences, the rest of us are less fortunate. The common man must earn his happiness. Find that search for happiness, and you understand morality.

Moral relativism is such an empty phrase as to have no meaning. What, after all, does moral mean? What does relative mean? Define these terms a certain way and you will have one answer. Under different definitions, another answer emerges. This is the peeled and oiled egg of philosophy. It can't be grasped without destroying it. Reality, or its moral dimension, is a matter of perspective. That does not imply the meaninglessness that moral absolutists love to claim. If you want meaning, then take a moral position that demands it.

The question arises: 'Does meaning exist in the ultimate sense?' No. Neither is it non-existent. It cannot be said either way. But if you meet souls with mastery of the spirit, they are joyful. And many will tell you that appearance is an illusion. 'You can,' they say, 'be happy without the existence of happiness. In fact,' our master leans forward with a wink, 'it is the only way.' The link to happiness is the key to ethics.

From the ultimate, morality must be relative. If it were not, then how could it meet the relative? Change is the definition of the relative. The ultimate is that which is beyond all relative notions. It is the unchanging. As soon as something enters the relative and makes contact, it has changed. Contact can only be made through the relative. How does the absolute make some change in the relative without being changed in itself? How can that which never changes meet that which is only change? There is no mechanism for the greater to move the lesser, for as it does, it must itself move and thus become relative. Any truly existent absolute cannot encounter the relative world – no specific absolute morality can exist.

Morality cannot be absolute because it is not universally applied in all situations in the same way. If for example someone overeats, but lacks certain digestive bacteria, they will not gain weight. But somehow the vast mechanism of cause and effect forces the perceiving entity to examine its free will and make choices. These choices have consequences. To ignore those consequences entraps one more thoroughly in the effects. To ignore the argument that actions have consequences is a moral position with several tenets. First, one cannot be bothered. Second, the universe is meaningless.

All actions taken with the belief in free will are moral statements. In this sense morality is absolute. The overweight person who eats another cookie makes the moral statement that immediate gratification supersedes other benefits. The stockbroker who deceives his clients, generating profits on their losses, makes a host of moral statements. The person who goes for a walk instead of watching television, or the person who watches TV and feels guilty that they didn't go for a walk, both make moral statements. Actions have consequences. We are forced to act. Therefore, morality is absolute from the relative perspective. We cannot evade the consequences. If we choose to ignore the consequences, we have taken a moral position that the consequences are unimportant, too frightening, overwhelming or any of a host of possibilities.

Those who ignore the consequences the most become low criminals. Apparently, substantially more prison inmates profess a belief in God than are atheists. The argument implied by the New Atheism is a red herring – the atheist is more moral than the religious person. This is the error of mistaken causality. All it proves is that a higher percentage of convicts believe in God than do not. What percentage is vegetarian? Or wears boxers? Or a victim of child abuse? Or a homosexual? Or near-sighted? Criminals are more religious because they come from a religious society, not because religion has made them criminals. The causal claim is laughable. Were these people raised in a secular society, they would probably have been atheists. They would have been as unconcerned with this early-programmed belief as with the early programmed belief in God. No one can say whether they would have committed the same crimes or not. A lack of concern with consequences, both outer and inner, makes a person immoral – and a 'criminal.'

All morality must be based on choice. A choiceless morality is not a morality at all. It is like breathing. You must do so or die. You cannot choose to directly stop breathing. You must use an indirect method, such as a bullet or rope. A more accurate, but difficult analogy is consciousness. To act at all requires consciousness. There is no choice. Therefore it is an absolute. Without consciousness, we do not exist as a person. Our consciousness is our world in toto. It is all of our experience. We may have subconscious impulses, desires, and beliefs, but if they do not come into consciousness, we do not experience them.

Therefore, morality is relative. The very notion of morality implies a choice between various acts and opinions. If there is a choice, it cannot be absolute. The absolute is not a choice, it simply is. But any choice implies a moral position, if a subtle one – there are no totally neutral acts, for every action performed is many others left undone. An action performed says it is somehow acceptable to perform. All actions leave a trace. All actions invoke some moral stance.* This is inescapable. Therefore, morality is absolute.

That you are what you repeatedly do is a moral principle. The underlying text is that we must pay attention to what we are becoming. Inexorably, as the gambler needs to risk and win money again, as the torturer's sadism grows with each victim, as the alcoholic reaches for each new drink, as the severely depressed might sleep their sorrows and lives away, as the anorexic torments herself over a body image, as the politician consolidates power, never finding enough, always paranoid over its loss, as the Buddhist monk clings to peace, longing to end suffering, as the atheist struggles to force a scientific worldview onto society, as a mother loves her children, so each of us has our moral imperative, the thing which drives us into becoming what we are and thinking it is right, thinking it is the way to live. Or into feeling ashamed because we think it is wrong and cannot stop. The complex and vast mechanism of drives and dictates pushes here and there when we know we shouldn't and yet still we do. This is the tyranny of morality, its absoluteness: that what we do again and again, we become.

It is the false cage of existence. We think morality is relative, but the truth is, any specific moral formulation is relative. If we choose to engage in acts of kindness and classical virtue, we become a kind and virtuous person. If we engage in depravity and cruelty, we become a depraved and cruel soul. If a man bundles himself in his work, peering through a microscope at

---

* Even if not all actions do so, some definitely will, so the consequent still applies. To engage in life requires decisions of morality.

the smallest things imaginable, then the world he ignores will make him an ignorant man. If day in and day out, money is our god, then greed and want will be our handmaidens and we will have no friends we trust. For no matter how much we have, the desire for more cannot be satiated.

This is why we have the promise of spiritual realization – to break free of these relative chains. We can move from being a relative being looking at the absolute cage of morality to the absolute itself, helping others caught in their relative cage. That is the religion of Buddha.

Conclusion – the Path of Awakening

Good and bad, happy and sad, all thoughts vanish into emptiness like the imprint of a bird in the sky.
—Sadhana of Mahamudra

Spirituality is the essence of religion and science before they split into separate camps. The Church actually founded scientific inquiry. As images of God, the logic went, we were given rationality to understand his creation. The focus of science without the force of the heart is empty. Meaning comes from tense desire. It is not innate in anything, yet it is there like the oak tree in an acorn. Planted and watered, it will grow. But the fruits of success can be stolen if there is no conviction beyond mere cartography of the world. The outlook of spirituality is to see truth and its task is to nurture goodness. Rationality needs intuition.

Likewise, faith without clarity is idiot devotion. The mass mind can be harnessed for corruption, personal gain, and even war. Without clear and fearless insight, demagoguery rules. The religious man falls prey to these vulgarities, but the spiritual sees through them.

Orthodoxy is the technology used for this mass control. In the move to orthodoxy, the individual path is lost. Dogma destroys. This is the critique from the Gnostics. If religion fails to nurture the spiritual, it becomes politics. If the spiritual eschews all religious approach, then it excludes the mass of humanity – higher practitioners do not need religion per se.

Despite its tendency to corruption and control, religion holds good qualities. Devotion is the foremost. It is the seed of the spiritual experience. Without devotion to one's chosen field, whether science or business, Christianity or Buddhism, one will walk away, become corrupted or lose heart. Honest devotion is the bellwether for any tradition's genuineness. The scientist devoted to truth is far less open to fraud than the scientist devoted to status. Devotion must have eyes. Blind devotion leads to Jim Jones and automatic acceptance of CDC studies. The blind devotee overlooks the priest's molestation or the egoistic Nobel Prize aspiration. Groupthink rules. One does not know what one is truly devoted to. It is a vague idea – skeptical inquiry, grace, liberation, or a historical figure such as Buddha or Darwin, Christ or Newton.

A tradition can be judged by its followers. Early Christians died horribly, and willingly, for their beliefs. They were amazing for hundreds of years, and then they weren't. Spiritual conviction is not a vice; it is a virtue. But when a tradition becomes dominant in society, the purity suffers. Corruption seizes control. Where there is power, debased men will take it. For this reason, all traditions – science, religion, art – must remain vigilant. The majority of Christians, Jews, Muslims, Buddhists, and atheists have not. All traditions have degraded as a result. Spirituality is neither weak nor unaware. It sees the indestructible basic goodness of all life, but does not ignore the depravity of human deeds. Though beneath everything is perfect purity, it often manifests as utter corruption. Even the bravest tradition can do so if the scales are unbalanced. Rigidity is the mark of corruption – it assaults freedom.

Thus, it makes sense to seek out a religion with no rules. That is why many people choose Buddhism – no fixed dogma, just guidelines. Be a better person each day. Strive for wisdom. These are probably the closest one finds to Buddhist requirements. The two are connected. Wisdom is subtly disposed toward 'virtue.' Most anyone would pick out the same words in the following list as associated with wisdom: love, generosity, revenge, forgiveness, murder, hate, torture, and patience. There is no mystery. Being virtuous points the mind at wisdom; being wise unleashes powerful virtue. Wisdom is joyful – it is not sad. It is naturally kind, but not bounded by anything. Virtue does not own wisdom. Nor is wisdom aligned with order or chaos. It is ultimate freedom. It is not cruel, but can only be accomplished by truth. It is beyond words.

Fixed rules and dogma are anathema to Buddhism. It's funny to speak of a religion that eschews rules. Of course, there are guiding principles, but each person has a higher level to strive for. Cause no harm and benefit others are essential directives. But even these conflict. One being's benefit may be another's loss. When a cow dies, it can feed many. It is impossible to engage the world and never cause harm. They are really two different styles.

The first – cause no harm – seeks personal liberation by retreating from the world. The second seeks benefit for others by advancing into the world. The first are *pratyekabuddhas*, the solitary realizers and the second are the *bodhisattvas*, the awakening beings. The bodhisattva path involves study of the science – called the view – but the activity is an intuitive response. Intuition knows right action without confusion. For rational analysis to determine these actions is impossible. Even when possible, it cannot operate quickly enough. Moment by moment, rationality will make mistakes. But bringing a finely developed equanimity and realization that nothing has an essence makes all action proper. The skill transcends relative reality.

It would be nice to say that the religion of Buddhism begins where the science leaves off, or that some seamless integration exists. But the two are really the same. It is impossible to have truth in a religion without any science or the heart in the science without any religion. Meaning includes what is seen and what is felt, truth and love, apparent beauty and essential goodness. The religion of Buddha is compassion – understanding the goodness of others.

The path is to step away from the fire of the world and settle all turmoil in one's being. The means is contained in the science. Religion is the direct seeing of the science – the non-existence of self. Having softened the ego sufficiently, the practitioner can make the next step – the vow to help others. In the 11th century, Shantideva wrote the most popular form of the Bodhisattva vow:

As earth and fire, wind and rain ceaselessly nourish limitless beings, so may I become their provision to the ends of space until all find peace. Today I take birth in the Buddha-family – now am I a child of the Buddhas. From this moment, I will make the supreme effort to fulfill this way. I will never degrade the faultless lineage of this family. As a blind man might stumble on a diamond in a pile of trash, so has the awakening heart of compassion been born in me. This supreme nectar ends death; the precious Bodhicitta is the final treasure, curing the poverty of all beings. It is the tree of sanctuary for beings weary of wandering the endless tracks of existence. It is the medicine for every suffering, the bridge over misery, the ascending moon of awareness that dispels the dark ignorance. For those caught in the perpetual storm of rebirth, it is the steady throne of happiness. At the feet of the Awakened Ones, I invite all beings to this feast.

All wisdom traditions have a technique for compassion – the great spiritual figures actively try to take away the pain of the world and return peace. That is the aching beauty of the Christ story, a noble myth at its heart. Paul's Jesus could even be seen as more real than we are. He could be a manifestation of great wisdom brought about by the power of mind. He would be illusory, but not imaginary. In other words, Paul's Jesus appeared to certain beings, a genuine manifestation of wisdom without physical reality behind it. Paul's vision was real.

This Jesus taught a method of exchanging happiness for others' pain. In his crucifixion, he suffers for the liberation of others. But Christians have lost the meaning of this act – it is an example of how to be, a profound teaching on creating a better world. In order to help, each of us could give a measure of happiness and take on a measure of suffering willingly, not as a martyr, but as a mother – without complaint or need for recognition, but out of love alone. We could emulate the aspects of Christ that care for others – all others, not just wealthy, not just elites, not just Christians – and we could strive to overcome hatred. If everyone really worked for that effort – this would be a beautiful world. Religion is just that simple. The wider the circle of care, the deeper the love within the circle, the more genuine is the spiritual ground. Just be a good person. Not trivial good, not self-righteously good, not tribally good, not smugly good, not 'it benefits me' good, but simply good. This broken-hearted goodness cares for everyone.

But for compassion, wisdom is necessary. Without it, a well-meaning person will cause damage. He might want to inflict the faceless bureaucracy of a welfare state. But such mandatory compassion is an oxymoron. The recipient becomes dependent on the state, the bureaucrat is merely doing their job, and the taxed citizen has no choice. No one gains the benefit of a personal compassion. The situation leads to general resentment by almost all parties. One cannot enforce compassion. It is a personal matter, unique to each heart, not a government policy.

Of course, religion is always politics, but politics is not always bad. In this case, it is the commitment to humanity, in fact to all that lives. It is the willingness to involve oneself in the world's suffering in order to help. It includes the ugly aspect of politics. Being clean and pure is an unaffordable luxury. Kindness may be rewarded with scorn, love with hate, years of effort with a blunt instant of futile destruction, but it is the path itself that matters. Motivation is key.

To walk the path, the practitioner must release stale ego manifestations, any internal aspect of mind causing pain to oneself or others. This uncovers the selfless nature within. This essential nature, empty of concept, suffuses all beings. It is what we really are. When goodness meets another, they are seen to be identical. Goodness knows itself. When a person can rest in their goodness, become it, it is simpler to see past the interference. It becomes easy to not only forgive others their neuroses, but to love them for the pain they feel.

Thousands of dharma texts have been written, millions of teachings given. All say the same – inside each of us is unlimited compassion, love, joy, and equanimity. It is who we are. Nobody can escape their essence. The religion of Buddhism is to recognize and nurture that essence in every being.

There are many ways to speak of the religion of Buddhism – ritual, cultural, historical, or following the example of the Buddha. But this bodhisattva path seems the heart of it all. The bodhisattva is a scientist to himself, a religious figure to others – a spiritual union.

Religion is a social construct, unnecessary for the higher student. But it is necessary for the ordinary one. Realized beings hold the path open for us. We perceive this as the religious aspect, but for them it is an outstretched hand. It is a finger pointing at the truth, but not truth itself. This finger is the doctrine – the teachings. But it is just as much the ritual.

Buddhism does have ritual aspects, but no particular ritual is indispensable. Contemplation of not-self, taking refuge, and meditation – these are important to Buddhism, but irrelevant to the higher truth beyond it. It is an important goal to leave religion behind. As Dzongsar Khyentse Rinpoche said, "ultimately, you have to get rid of Buddhism."[585] The practitioner stuck on ritual is ultimately blocked, while one who loses the ritual meaning wastes his time. Someone who feels the form is the key is controlled by the form – it has become solid, a 'truth' in itself. If the form is in control, the practitioner is not free. Rituals are not useless, however – far from it. Meditative ritual holds the mind in a higher view, purifies negative habits by loosening the mind, and reshapes awareness by strengthening the bond to awakening.

The meditative approach offers a much-needed quality to our society – a slowing down, an unwinding of the speed that now towers over our lives. One master calls this speed a form of aggression. It attempts to dominate, to be busy, to get everything done, and to maintain control. But control is an illusion – in the end we die. The speed attempts to run down the reality of death – to overcome the insubstantiality of the self. Trying to fortify the self through religious means is called 'spiritual materialism.'

Trungpa Rinpoche, in coining the term, applied it to East and West. When people pray for a football team, a new car, the attainment of a profound state, or special spiritual powers, they are practicing spiritual materialism. When people invent haphazard spiritual technique without rules, form, or view, it is typically spiritual materialism. The marketplace is wide, including Catholic indulgences, priestly sanctions, God's blessing as wealth, and bogus healing techniques. Any time spirituality slips from concern for others and insight about the truth of groundlessness, anytime it aggrandizes the self, there is spiritual materialism. Its worst forms control others, legitimize war, and plunder the downtrodden. Secular humanists are not immune – often they are the worst.

At any rate, the slowing down is an important first approach to peace, but here most people mistake the path for the goal. Initially, meditation slows the mind, allowing a clear, stable focus. This naturally brings peace – agitation must subside for stable focus to exist. Attention cannot be fragmented. But this skill is not truly stable. Though it can be held indefinitely in skilled meditation, it fails in engagement with the world.

Spirituality is 'self-existing healthiness' in everyone. Meditation helps us get out of our own way. We must make friends with ourselves, accept our neurosis without judgment. It's a paradox – we really don't get it because there's nothing to get, but we can tap into that unceasing instant of nowness. We can be blazingly present with no fixed notion of that. Then we become haunted by the depth of reality, by its vivid emptiness. But it's not in the style of New Age witchcraft. The Dorje Dradul said, "Don't expect supernormal magic of any kind on the spiritual path."[586]

Skillful meditation can take one far. With tremendous effort, it is possible to see the voidness of self and phenomena. When the mind perceives this as normal reality, peace is much closer to hand, a part of the being, and at long last indestructible. Over time, the diligent practitioner is disturbed by fewer and fewer things, and ultimately, by nothing at all.

The most difficult, highest path of all is to 'keep one eye on the absolute nature.' This practice of bare attention joins the ever-present display of existence to the timeless truth of wisdom. The unity of this indestructible wisdom mind with suffusing compassion is spirituality. It cannot be defined. *Things are not as they seem,* Buddha said, *nor are they otherwise.*

End Notes

[1] Bryan Appleyard, *Understanding the Present: An Alternative History of Science* (New York: Tauris Parke, 2004), preface.
[2] Garland E. Allen, "Is a New Eugenics Afoot?" *Science* 294 (2001): 5540.
[3] F. William Engdahl, *Seeds of Destruction: The Hidden Agenda of Genetic Manipulation* (Montreal: Global Research, 2007), p. 65.
[4] Karl Popper, *The Logic of Scientific Discovery* (New York: Harper, 1965), Section 1.
[5] *Dangerous Knowledge*, BBC documentary.
[6] Michael Polanyi, 'Transcendence and Self-transcendence,' *Soundings* 53:1 (1970): 88–94.
[7] http://www.springerlink.com/content/q14v337661412040/
[8] Arthur Zajonc (ed.), *New Physics and Cosmology: dialogues with the Dalai Lama* (Oxford University Press, 2004), p. 119.
[9] http://particleadventure.org/hadrons.html
[10] John Moffat, *Reinventing Gravity* (Thomas Allen Publishers, 2008), p. 151.
[11] F. Nicastro *et al.*, 'The Far-ultraviolet signature of the "missing" baryons in the Local Group of Galaxies,' *Nature* 421 (2003): 719–721.
[12] *Ibid.*
[13] Edwin Hubble, *The Observational Approach to Cosmology* (Oxford: Clarendon Press, 1937).
[14] T. Van Flandern, 'Big Bang: Top 30 Problems,' *Meta Research Bulletin* 11 (2002).
[15] Moffat *op. cit.*, pp. 94–6.
[16] Martin Rees, *Before the Beginning* (New York: Basic Books, 1998), p. 185.
[17] 'Cosmic Inflation,' Wikipedia.
[18] 'Big Bang's afterglow fails intergalactic shadow test,' *Physorg* (Sep. 1, 2006).
[19] http://www.wired.com/science/space/news/2007/11/big_bang
[20] John Mather and John Boslough, *The Very First Light: the true inside story of the scientific journey back to the dawn of the universe* (New York: Basic Books, 1996), p. 252.
[21] D. N. Spergel *et al.*, 'First Year Wilkinson Microwave Anisotropy Probe (WMAP) Observations: Determination of Cosmological Parameters,' arXiv:astro-ph/0302209 (2003).
[22] R. Scranton *et al.*, 'Physical Evidence for Dark Energy,' arXiv:astrop-ph/0307335 (2003).
[23] Edward Wright, 'Inflation,' *Cosmology Tutorial*, http://www.astro.ucla.edu/~wright/cosmolog.htm.
[24] S. Arbabi-Bidgoli and V. Muller, 'Void scaling and void profiles in CDM models,' arXiv:astrop-ph/0111581 (2001).
[25] Eric J. Lerner, 'Two world systems revisited: a comparison of plasma cosmology and the Big Bang,' http://bigbangneverhappened.org/p27.htm.
[26] A. L. Camp, 'Summary of Big Bang Creation Story' (2006), theoutlet.us/SummaryofBig-BangCreationStory.pdf.
[27] A. Zee, *Fearful Symmetry: the search for beauty in modern physics* (Macmillan, 1986).
[28] Moffat *op. cit.*, p. 199.
[29] Lerner *op. cit.*
[30] Eric J. Lerner, *The Big Bang Never Happened* (Random House, 1991), Ch. 1.
[31] http://www.lifesci.sussex.ac.uk/home/John_Gribbin/
[32] Ilya Prigogine, *Order out of Chaos: Man's new dialogue with nature* (Shambhala, 1984), p. 299.
[33] *Ibid.*, p. 292.
[34] *Ibid.*, p. 128.

[35] Lerner *op. cit.*, Ch. 7.
[36] *Ibid.*, Ch. 1.
[37] Zajonc *op. cit.*, p. 191.
[38] *Ibid.*, p. 90.
[39] http://emptywheel.firedoglake.com/2010/01/08/gruber-did-not-disclose-conflict-to-the-wapo/
[40] Above cases from Horace Freeland Judson, *The Great Betrayal: Fraud in Science* (Harcourt, 2004), Ch. 2.
[41] 'NIH Science busters get new assignment,' *Science Services* (Oct. 16, 1993).
[42] Judson *op. cit.*, Ch. 3-4.
[43] *Ibid.*, Ch. 5.
[44] http://www.naturalnews.com/030557_psychiatry_fraud.html
[45] D. Rennie *et al.*, 'Dealing with Research Misconduct in the United Kingdom,' *British Medical Journal* 316 (1998): 1726.
[46] R. Horton, 'The Hidden Research Paper,' *JAMA* 287 (2002).
[47] R. L. Engler *et al.*, 'Misrepresentation and Responsibility in Medical Research,' *New England Journal of Medicine* 317:22 (1987): 1383–89.
[48] J. Lehrer, 'The Truth Wears Off,' *New Yorker* (Dec. 13, 2010).
[49] Judson *op. cit.*, pp. 9-42.
[50] S. Lock, 'Lessons from the Pearce Affair: Handling Scientific Fraud,' *BMJ* 310 (1995): 1547–48.
[51] S. Lange, 'Questions of Scientific Responsibility: the Baltimore Case,' *Journal of Ethics and Behavior* 3:1 (1993): 3–72.
[52] Judson *op. cit.*, pp. 229-30.
[53] D. Fanelli, 'How Many Scientists Fabricate and Falsify Research? A Systematic Review and Meta-Analysis of Survey Data,' *PLoS ONE* 4:5 (2009): e5738.
[54] B. C. Martinson, M. S. Anderson and R. de Vries, 'Scientists behaving badly,' *Nature* 435 (2005): 737–738.
[55] http://www.whale.to/v/cantekin.html
[56] S. Eastwood, P. Derish, E. Leash and S. Ordway, 'Ethical issues in biomedical research: Perceptions and practices of postdoctoral research fellows responding to a survey,' *Science and Engineering Ethics* 2 (1996): 89–114.
[57] J. Ranstam, M. Buyse, S. L. George, S. Evans, N. L. Geller, *et al.*, 'Fraud in medical research: An international survey of biostatisticians,' *Controlled Clinical Trials* 21 (2000): 415–427.
[58] M. S. Anderson, B. C. Martinson, and R. De Vries, 'Normative dissonance in science: results from a national survey of US scientists,' *Journal of Empirical Research on Human Research Ethics* 2 (2007): 3–14.
[59] J. E. Bekelman, Y. Li, C. P. Gross, 'Scope and impact of financial conflicts of interest in biomedical research: A systematic review,' *Journal of the American Medical Association* 289 (2003): 454–465.
[60] S. Sismondo, 'Pharmaceutical company funding and its consequences: a qualitative systematic review,' *Contemporary Clinical Trials* 29 (2008): 109–113.
[61] P. Woolff, 'Deception in Scientific Research,' *Jurimetrics Journal* 29 (1998).
[62] Fanelli *op. cit.*
[63] U. Neill, 'Stop Misbehaving!' *Journal of Clinical Investigations* 116:7 (2006): 1740.
[64] Bertrand Russell, *The Scientific Outlook* (London: George Allen & Unwin, 1931), p. 256.
[65] http://articles.mercola.com/sites/articles/archive/2004/07/07/healthcare-death-part-one.aspx
[66] D. L. Rosenhan, 'On being sane in insane places,' *Science* 179 (1973).
[67] J. Boivin *et al.*, 'Incidence of Second Cancers in Patients Treated for Hodgkin's Disease,' *JNCI* 87:10 (1995): 732–741.
[68] www.naturalnews.com/023689_chemotherapy_cancer_disease.html

---

[69] Eva Jablonka and Marion J. Lamb, *Evolution in Four Dimensions: Genetic, Epigenetic, Behavioral, and Symbolic Variation in the History of Life* (MIT Press, 2006), p. 67.
[70] D. L. Barlett & J. B. Steele, 'Deadly Medicine,' *Vanity Fair* (Jan. 2011).
[71] 'Study Finds Traces of Drugs in Drinking Water in 24 Major U.S. Regions,' Associated Press (Mar. 10, 2008).
[72] Mike Stobbe, 'Fluoride's reputation gets a little spotty,' Associated Press (Jan. 8, 2011).
[73] K. Stade, 'Radiation Exposure Debate Rages Inside EPA,' *Public Employees for Environmental Responsibility* (Apr. 5, 2011), http://www.peer.org/news/news_id.php?row_id=1325.
[74]http://www.medhelp.org/posts/Current-Events---/At-least-the-US-is-testing-their-milkhow-is-this-for-messed-up/show/1501154
[75] David Kirby, *Evidence of Harm* (St. Martin's Press, 2005), p. 326.
[76] 'Mercury and Medicine: Taking Unnecessary Risks,' Committee on Government Reform report (May 2003).
[77] J. Warkany and D. M. Hubbard, 'Acrodynia and Mercury,' *Journal of Pediatrics* 42:3 (1953).
[78] J. A. Lowe, *et al.*, 'Mercury Poisoning Associated with High Dose,' *Liver Transplantation Surgery* 2:6 (1996).
[79] Kirby *op. cit.*, p. 50
[80] US Dept. of Health, Education, and Welfare, 'Mercury Containing Drug Products for Topical Anti-microbial Over-the-Counter Human Use: Establishment of a Monograph,' *Federal Register* 47 (1982): 436–442.
[81] Kirby *op. cit.*, p. 83.
[82] Peter Patriarca, Director of Viral Products. Internal FDA email to Martin Meyers, National Vaccine Office of the CDA (Jun. 29, 1999).
[83] E. Fombonne, 'Is there an Epidemic of Autism?' *Pediatrics* 107:2 (2001): 411–2.
[84] F. Lorscheider, 'How Mercury causes brain neuron degeneration,' *Neuro-report* 12 (2001).
[85] W. S. Slikker, 'Developmental Neurotoxicity of Therapeutics: survey of novel recent findings,' *Neurotoxicology* 1:2 (2000): 250.
[86] T. M. Burbacher, *et al.*, 'Comparison of Blood and Brain Mercury Levels in Infant Monkeys exposed to Vaccines containing thimerosal,' *Environmental Health Perspectives* 113:8 (2005):1015–21.
[87] Kirby *op. cit.*, p. 164.
[88] 'Infant exposure to thimerosal containing vaccines and risk thereof,' CDC (May 2000), cited in *Evidence of Harm.*
[89] Kirby *op. cit.*
[90] L. Hewitson, *et al.*, 'Pediatric vaccines influence primate behaviour, and Amygdala Growth and Opioid Ligand Binding,' http://www.ageofautism.com/2008/05/pediatric-vacci.html.
[91] M. Bauman and K. Nelson, 'Thimerosal and Autism?' *Pediatrics* 111:3 (2003): 674–79.
[92] http://www.healing-arts.org/children/cdc.htm
[93] P. Stehr-Green, 'Autism and Thimerosal containing vaccines: lack of consistent evidence for an association,' *American Journal of Preventitive Medicine* 25:2 (2003): 101–6.
[94] Robert Kennedy, Jr., 'Central Figure in CDC Vaccine Cover-Up Absconds with $2M,' *Huffington Post* (Mar. 11, 2010).
[95] Kirby *op. cit.*, pp. 407, 326.
[96] Mark Blaxill, 'The Governance Problem: summary of highlights of scientific review of safety datalink information,' *Schafer Autism Report* (May 2001).
[97] David Ayoub, 'Global Vaccine Agenda: Mercury and Autism,' YouTube.
[98] Press Release, Office of Representative Dave Weldon (2004).

[99] Ayoub *op. cit.*
[100] Kirby *op. cit.*, p. 401.
[101] M. E. Pichichero *et al.*, 'Mercury Concentrations, metabolism and infant receiving vaccines containing Thimerosal,' *Lancet* 360:9347 (2022): 1737–41.
[102] S. G. Gilbert and K. S. Grant-Webster, 'Neurobehavorial effects of developmental methylmercury exposure,' *Environmental Health Perspectives* 103 Suppl 6 (1995): 135–142.
[103] FDA Science Board, 'FDA Science and Mission at Risk: Report of the Subcommittee on Science and Technology' (Nov. 2007).
[104] Robert Kennedy, Jr., 'Deadly Immunity,' *Rolling Stone* (Jun. 20, 2005).
[105] Representative Dave Weldon, memo to the CDC, subject: 'VSD data access by Dr. Geier' (Nov. 6, 2003), cited in Kirby *op cit.*, p. 397.
[106] 'Summary Statistics: Thimerosal Study,' CDC National Immunization Program. No Date. http://autismactionnetwork.org/science.html
[107] M. Levin, ''91 Memo Warned of Mercury in Shots,' *LA Times* (Feb 8, 2005).
[108] *Infowars.com* (Aug. 18, 2009).
[109] Ludwig Fleck, *Genesis and Development of a Scientific Fact* (University of Chicago Press, 1979 [1935]).
[110] *Ibid.*, p. 27.
[111] *Ibid.*, pp. 59–60.
[112] *Ibid.*, p. 74.
[113] *Ibid.*, p. 50
[114] *Ibid.*, p. 121.
[115] http://www.wearechangechicago.com/we-are-change-chicago-member-assaulted-and-arrested-on-false-charges-for-questioning-dr-oz-about-vaccines.html
[116] Neil Z. Miller, 'More than 2000 vaccinated babies died: The cost of doing business,' *NaturalNews* (Mar. 24, 2011).
[117] Eileen Dannemann, 'CDC allegedly falsifies reports--ignoring up to 3,587 Miscarriages from H1N1 Vaccine,' National Coalition of Women press release (Oct. 28, 2010).
[118] *The Health Century*, Blackwell WGBH, PBS.
[119] http://www.vaclib.org/basic/quotes.htm
[120] *Physicians' Desk Reference 2003* (Thomson, 2002).
[121] John Baron, *The Life of Edward Jenner*, Vol. II (1838), p. 304, cited in Eleanor McBean, *The Poisoned Needle* (1957).
[122] *History of inoculation and vaccination*, p. 6, cited in McBean.
[123] McBean *op. cit.*
[124] *Ibid.*
[125] *Morbidity and Mortality Weekly Report* 59(05): 125–129 (2010).
[126] www.thinktwice.com
[127] Archie Kalokerinos, *Every Second Child* (Keats, 1981).
[128] Neil Z. Miller, '7 reasons schools should not mandate vaccines,' *NaturalNews* (Jul. 14, 2011).
[129] www.shirleys-wellness-cafe.com
[130] Kirby *op. cit.*, p.406
[131] Jennifer Margulis, 'The Vaccine debate,' *Mothering* magazine (Jul. 2009).
[132] J. Gordon, 'Commentary: Parents should not be legally liable for refusing to vaccinate their children,' *Michigan Law Review* 107 (2009).
[133] Dan Vergano, 'Who's Teaching the Doctors,' *USA Today* (Mar. 9, 2000).
[134] *Money Talks: Profits over Patient Safety*, documentary (2006).
[135] David Burd, 'A cure for US AIDS: Travel to Canada,' *RethinkingAids* (April 12, 2010).
[136] Judson *op. cit.*, p. 322
[137] San Francisco AIDS conference, 1990.

[138] 'Modern Trends in Human Leukemia VI,' *Haematology and Blood Transfusion* 29 (1985), p. 1, quoted in C. Farber, 'Fatal distraction,' *Spin* magazine (June 1992).
[139] Celia Farber, 'Out of Control: Aids and the Corruption of Medical Science,' *Harpers* (Mar. 2006).
[140] NYU Medical Center, interview with Robert Gallo by James M. Scutero (Nov. 11, 1993).
[141] http://www.duesberg.com/about/pdpolicyrep.html
[142] Rebecca Culshaw, *Science Sold Out: Does HIV really cause AIDS, p. 14* (North Atlantic Books, 2007).
[143] 'Durbin Declaration' (2000).
[144] Harvey Bialy, *Oncogenes, Aneuploidy, and AIDS: A Scientific Life and Times of Peter H. Duesberg* (North Atlantic Books, 2004).
[145] Culshaw *op. cit.*, p. 19.
[146] *Ibid.*, pp. 20–21.
[147] *Ibid.*, p. 24.
[148] Z. Grossman, 'Pathogenesis of HIV infection,' *Nature Medicine* 12 (2006), pp. 289–95.
[149] Farber *op. cit.*
[150] Peter Duesberg, 'AIDS acquired by drug consumption and other non-contagious risk factors,' *Pharmacology and Therapeutics* 55:3 (1992): 201–77.
[151] Peter Duesberg, 'Human Immunodeficiency Virus and Acquired Immunodeficiency Syndrome: Correlation but not Causation,' *Proc. Natl. Acad. Sci.* 86:3 (1989): 755–64.
[152] *The AIDS Deception*, Gary Null Films (2001).
[153] Duesberg (1989) *op. cit.*
[154] http://www.ourcivilisation.com/aids/chap6.htm
[155] *The AIDS Deception.*
[156] Hiram Caton, 'Junk Science goes Belly Up,' in *The AIDS Mirage* (1998).
[157] 'Presidential AIDS Advisory Panel Report: A synthesis report of the deliberations by the panel of experts invited by the President of the Republic of South Africa, the Honourable Mr Thabo Mbeki,' (Mar. 2001), p. 42.
[158] Henry H. Bauer, *The Origin, Persistence and Failings of HIV/AIDS Theory* (McFarland, 2007).
[159] 'HIV and breastfeeding again,' (Feb. 13, 2008), http://wp.me/p8Qhq-1t.
[160] N. S. Padian, S. C. Shiboski, S. O. Glass, and E. Vittinghoff, 'Heterosexual transmission of human immunodeficiency virus (HIV) in Northern California: results from a ten-year study,' *American Journal of Epidemiology* 146 (1997): 350–7.
[161] 'Condoms and HIV: What everyone knows is once again wrong,' (Feb. 10, 2008), http://wp.me/p8Qhq-1r.
[162] Duesberg (1989) *op. cit.*
[163] globalatlas.who.int/globalatlas/dataQuery/default.asp
[164] Roche Diagnostic Systems, Inc., Amplicor HIV-1 Monitor Test Kit (June 1996).
[165] 'Everyone reacts positive on the ELISA test for AIDS,' *Continuum* 5:5 (Winter 1998/9): 8–10.
[166] Darin Brown, 'Why owners of AB+ canines need not be concerned,' *You Bet Your Life* (Sept. 27, 2006), http://barnesworld.blogs.com/barnes_world/2006/09/darin_brown_exp.html.
[167] F. Barrè-Sinoussi, *et al.*, 'Isolation of a T-lymphotropic retrovirus from a patient at risk for acquired immune deficiency syndrome (AIDS),' *Science* 220:4599 (1983): 868–71.
[168] D. Gisselquist, *et al.*, 'HIV infections in sub-Saharan Africa not explained by sexual or vertical transmission,' *Int J STD AIDS* 13 (2002): 657–666.
[169] Sheryl Gay Stolberg, 'For retired chimps a life of leisure,' *New York Times* (Jan. 7, 2003).
[170] Culsha *op. cit.*, p. 37.

[171] *The AIDS Deception*.
[172] Duesberg (1992) *op. cit*.
[173] Culshaw *op. cit.*, p. 45.
[174] http://www.naturalnews.com/026531_fraud_doctors_doctor.html
[175] J. Lauritsen, *Poison by Prescription: the AZT story* (Pagan Press, 1990).
[176] Culshaw *op. cit.*, p. 49.
[177] 'Presidential AIDS Advisory Panel Report,' *op. cit.*, p. 58.
[178] Marcia Angell, *The Truth about the Drug Companies: How They Deceive Us and What to Do About It* (Random House, 2004).
[179] David Rasnick, *The AIDS Deception*.
[180] www.liamscheff.com
[181] Farber (2006) *op. cit.*
[182] Amanda Bennett and Anita Sharpe, 'AIDS Fight Is Skewed By Federal Campaign Exaggerating Risks,' *The Wall Street Journal* (May 1, 1996).
[183] David Rasnick, 'Conspiracy indeed!' *British Medical Journal* Rapid Response (Apr. 18, 2003).
[184] Oswald Hanfling, *Logical Positivism* (Routledge History of Philosophy, 2003), p. 193.
[185] Popper, *The Logic of Scientific Discovery*.
[186] *Ibid.*, Section 4.
[187] *Ibid.*, Introduction.
[188] *Ibid.*, Section 12.
[189] *Ibid.*, Section 30.
[190] *Ibid.*, Section 4.
[191] *Ibid.*, Section 3.
[192] Address on Max Planck's 60th birthday.
[193] Popper *op. cit.*, Section 10.
[194] *Ibid.*, Section 83.
[195] *Ibid.*, Section 78.
[196] *Ibid.*, Section 6, 'Falsifiability as a criterion of demarcation.'
[197] *Ibid.*, Section 24.
[198] *Ibid.*, Section 79.
[199] *Ibid.*, Section 85.
[200] Jerry Coyne, *Why Evolution is True* (Viking Press, 2009), Ch. 1.
[201] *Ibid.*, back cover.
[202] *Ibid.*, p. 228.
[203] Richard Dawkins, *The Greatest Show on Earth: The Evidence for Evolution* (Free Press, 2009), pp. 8–9.
[204] Richard Dawkins, *The Selfish Gene* (Oxford University Press, 2006 [1976]), p. 146.
[205] *Ibid.*, pp. 90, 96.
[206] *Ibid.*, p. 88.
[207] *Ibid.*, p. 58.
[208] *Ibid.*, p. 88.
[209] *Ibid.*, p. 89.
[210] Dawkins, *Greatest Show*, p. 214.
[211] Jablonka & Lamb *op. cit.*, p. 28.
[212] Theodosius Dobzhansky, *Genetics and origin of species* (Columbia University Press, 1937), cited in Jablonka & Lamb *op. cit.*, p. 29.
[213] Coyne *op. cit.*, Introduction.
[214] *Ibid.*, p. 166.
[215] Altenberg Conference, 2008.
[216] Richard Milton, 'Darwinism – The forbidden subject,' Alternative Science website (1996).
[217] Jablonka & Lamb *op. cit.*, p. 62.

[218] Jerry Fodor and Massimo Piattelli-Palmarini, *What Darwin Got Wrong* (Farrar, Strauss, & Giroux, 2010), p. 104.
[219] S. J. Gould and R. C. Lewontin, 'The Spandrels of San Marco and the Panglossian Paradigm: a critique of the adaptationist programme,' *Proceedings of the Royal Society of London. Series B. Biological Sciences* 205 (1979): 581–98, cited in *ibid.*, p. 98.
[220] Fodor *op. cit.*, p. 126.
[221] Walter J. Remine, *The Biotic Message: Evolution Versus Message Theory* (Saint Paul Science, 1993).
[222] Fodor *op. cit.*, p. 71.
[223] *Ibid.*, p. 40.
[224] M. J. West-Eberhard, 'Developmental plasticity-origin of species difference,' *PNAS* 102 Suppl 1 (2005): 6543–49.
[225] Kauffman, 1993, cited in Fodor *op. cit.*, p. 475.
[226] 'Charles Darwin's tree of life is 'wrong and misleading', claim scientists,' *Telegraph* (Jan. 22, 2009).
[227] M. A. Bedau, 'Weak Emergence,' (1997) in James Tomberlin (ed.), *Philosophical Perspectives: Mind, Causation, and World*, vol. 11 (Oxford: Blackwell Publishers, 1997), pp. 375–399.
[228] M. Ridley, 'Modern Darwins,' *National Geographic* (Feb. 2009).
[229] C. Tabin, 'What is Evo-Devo,' PBS Nova (Oct. 26, 2009).
[230] Jablonka & Lamb *op. cit.*, p. 67.
[231] J. A. Shapiro (1999), cited in Jablonka & Lamb *op. cit.*, p. 71.
[232] Dawkins (2009) *op. cit.*, p. 216.
[233] Jablonka & Lamb *op. cit.*, Ch. 3.
[234] *Ibid.*, p. 153.
[235] Hugh Ross, quoted in A. L. Camp, 'Summary of Big Bang Creation Story' (2006).
[236] Jablonka & Lamb *op. cit.*, p. 130.
[237] *Ibid.*, p. 322.
[238] Francis Collins, *The Language of God: A Scientist Presents Evidence for Belief* (Free Press, 2006), preface.
[239] Kenneth R. Miller, *Finding Darwin's God: A Scientist's Search for Common Ground Between God and Evolution* (Harper Collins, 1999), p. 287.
[240] G. Wald, 'Life and Mind in the Universe,' *International Journal of Quantum Chemistry* 26 Suppl 11 (1984): 1–15.
[241] *Atom: the illusion of Reality*, BBC documentary.
[242] Thomas Kuhn, *The Structure of Scientific Revolutions* (University of Chicago Press, 1962).
[243] Max Planck, *Scientific Autobiography and Other Papers*, pp. 33–4, cited in *ibid.*
[244] CNA, *National Security and the Threat of Climate Change*' (April 2007), http://www.cna.org/reports/climate.
[245] http://www.climatedepot.com/a/6767/Green-Guru-James-Lovelock-Admits-the-Obvious-Everybody-might-be-wrong-Climate-change-may-not-happen-as-fast-as-we-thought-and-we-may-have-1000-years-to-sort-it-out.
[246] Senator O. G. Hatch, 'UN climate scientists speak out on global warming,' Senate Minority Report (Sept. 12, 2009).
[247] F. Seitz, 'A major Deception on Global Warming,' *Wall Street Journal* (June 12, 1996).
[248] S. Schneider, 'Don't Bet All Environmental Changes Will Be Beneficial,' *APS News* 5:8 (1996).
[249] 'No consensus on IPCC's level of ignorance,' BBC News (Nov. 13, 2007).
[250] 'Bitten by the IPCC,' *National Post* (Mar. 23, 2007).
[251] 'Physician, Heal Thyself,' *Climate Resistance* (Dec. 28, 2007).

[252] M. Hulme and M. Mahony, 'Climate Change: what do we know about the IPCC?' *Progress in Physical Geography* (2010), p. 10.
[253] US Senate Committee on Environment and Public Works, 'Inhofe Floor Speech On Global Warming: 2007 – Global Warming Alarmism Reaches A Tipping Point' (Oct. 26, 2007).
[254] 'AMS survey of weathercasters on climate change,' ABC-33 (Nov. 15, 2009).
[255] R. Lindzen, 'Climate Science: Is It Currently Designed To Answer Questions?' arXiv:0809.3762v3 (2008).
[256] P. H. Gleick *et al.*, 'Climate Change and the Integrity of Science,' *Science* 328:5979 (2010): 689–90.
[257] Petition to the council of the American Physical Society, 2010.
[258] http://climatedepot.com/a/1096/Execute-Skeptics-Shock-Call-To-Action-At-what-point-do-we-jail-or-execute-global-warming-deniers--Shouldnt-we-start-punishing-them-now
[259] misterkel.blogspot.com
[260] http://www.theglobeandmail.com/commentary/please-remain-calm-the-earth-will-heal-itself/article1389062/
[261] http://en.wikipedia.org/wiki/Scientists_opposing_the_mainstream_scientific_assessment_of_global_warming
[262] www.uoguelph.ca/~rmckitri/research/WegmanReport.pdf.
[263] J. L. Daly, 'Hockey Stick: a New Low in Climate Science' (2000), http://www.john-daly.com/hockey/hockey.htm.
[264] Briffa *et al.* (2002), quoted in www.climateaudit.info/pdf/mcintyre-heartland_2010.pdf.
[265] Appleyard *op. cit.*
[266] Corbett Report, Interview with Richard Lindzen (Nov. 22, 2010).
[267] K. Guy, 'Don't Buy Hype about Global Warming,' *Sun-Sentinel* (Sept. 11, 2011).
[268] Corbett Report #134.
[269] Hatch, Senate Minority Report *op. cit.*
[270] J. Stokes, 'Over 4.5 Billion people could die from Global Warming-related causes by 2012,' *The Canadian* (2007).
[271] W. Reilly, 'UN calls Climate Debate Over,' *UPI* (May 10, 2007).
[272] H. Collins *et al.*, 'Experiments with interactional expertise,' *Studies in History and Philosophy of Science Part A* 37 (2006): 656–74.
[273] E. Knoll, 'The Communities of Scientists and Journal Peer Review,' *JAMA* 263:10 (1990): 1330–32.
[274] Judson, *The Great Betrayal: Fraud in Science* (Harcourt, 2004), p. 257.
[275] 'Peer Review and the Acceptance of New Scientific Ideas,' *Sense About Science* (2004).
[276] T. Jefferson *et al.*, 'Effects of Editorial Peer Review: a Systematic Review,' *JAMA* 287:21 (2002a): 2784–6.
[277] T. Jefferson *et al.*, 'Measuring the quality of editorial peer review,' *JAMA* 287:21 (2002b): 2786–90.
[278] Judson *op. cit.*, Introduction.
[279] *Ibid.*, Ch. 6.
[280] E. Wager and T. Jefferson, 'The Shortcomings of Peer Review,' *Learned Publications* 14 (2001): 257–63.
[281] Jefferson *et al.* (2002a) *op. cit.*
[282] M. Hojat *et al.*, 'Impartial judgment by the "gatekeepers" of science: fallibility and accountability in the peer review process,' *Adv Health Sci Educ Theory Pract* 8 (2003): 75–96.
[283] R. A. Deyo *et al.*, 'The messenger under attack–intimidation of researchers by special-interest groups,' *NEJM* 336 (1997): 1176–1180.
[284] S. Lock, 'Does editorial peer review work?' *Ann Intern Med* 121:1 (1994): 60–1.

[285] R. Smith, 'Peer review: a flawed process at the heart of science and journals,' *JRSM* 99:4 (2006): 178–182.
[286] F. Godlee *et al.*, 'Effect on the quality of peer review of blinding reviewers and asking them to sign their reports: a randomized controlled trial,' *JAMA* 280:3 (1998): 237–240.
[287]S. Cole, 'Chance and consensus in peer review,' *Science* 214:4523 (1981): 881–6.
[288]http://brain.oxfordjournals.org/cgi/content/abstract/123/9/1964?ijkey=afcda51e07c50ab3e08af83318b3e152fcfd020c&keytype2=tf_ipsecsha
[289] L. Bornmann, 'Scientific Peer Review: Analysis of Peer Review Process,' *Human Architecture* 1:2 (2008): 23–38.
[290] Collins *et al. op. cit.*
[291] M. E. Lloyd, 'Gender factors in reviewer recommendations for manuscript publication,' *J Appl Behav Anal* 23:4 (1990): 539–543.
[292] D. F. Horrobin, 'The Philosophical Basis of Peer Review and the Suppression of Innovation,' *JAMA* 263:10 (1990): 1438–41.
[293] Quoted in Horrobin *op. cit.*
[294] Collins *et al. op. cit.*
[295] H. H. Bauer, 'Science in the 21st century: knowledge monopolies and research cartels,' *J. Sci. Explor.* 18 (2004): 643–660.
[296] T. Gold, 'New Ideas in Science,' *J. Sci. Explor.* 3:2 (1989): 103–12.
[297] Michael Talbot, *The Holographic Universe* (Harper Collins, 1991), p. 47.
[298] *Ibid.*, p. 50.
[299] David Bohm, *Wholeness and the Implicate Order* (Ark Paperbacks, 1983), xv.
[300] *Ibid.*, p. 11.
[301] *Ibid.*, p. 35.
[302] 'Physics of the Mind: Holographic Realities,' New Dimensions Radio (Apr. 30, 1991).
[303] Bohm *op. cit.*
[304] J. Achterberg *et al.*, 'A possible relationship between cancer, mental retardation and mental disorders,' *Social Science & Medicine. Part A: Medical Psychology & Medical Sociology* 12 (1978): 135–39.
[305] B. Klopfer, 'Psychological Variables in Cancer,' *Journal of Projective Techniques* 21:4 (1957): 331–40.
[306] R. Restack, 'People with Multiple Minds,' *Science Digest* 92 (June 1984): p. 76.
[307] Talbot *op. cit.*, p. 103.
[308] *Ibid.*, p. 104.
[309] *Ibid.*, p. 106.
[310] *National Geographic* 129 (1966), p. 58, cited in Talbot, p. 104.
[311] *Scientific American* 216 (1967), p. 104, cited in Talbot, p. 104.
[312] David Hume, *An Enquiry Concerning Human Understanding* (1748), Section X: 'Of Miracles.'
[313] Princeton Engineering Anomalies Research, Robert Jahn biography, http://www.princeton.edu/~pear/jahn.html.
[314] Talbot *op. cit.*, p. 199.
[315] Quoted in Talbot *op. cit.*, p. 199.
[316] *Ibid.*, p. 200.
[317] *Ibid.*, p. 219.
[318] *Ibid.*, p. 264.
[319] *Ibid.*, p. 265.
[320] *Ibid.*, p. 271.
[321] Rupert Sheldrake, *Dogs That Know When Their Owners Are Coming Home* (Crown Publishers, 1999).
[322] *Ibid.*, p. 248.
[323] M. W. Wagner and M. Monnet, 'Attitudes of college professors toward extrasensory perception,' *Zetetic Scholar* 5 (1979): 7–16.

[324] Ken Wilbur, *Quantum Questions: Mystical Writings of the World's Great Physicists* (Shambhala, 1981), James Jeans section.
[325] *Ibid.*, Pauling section.
[326] *Ibid.*, Eddington section.
[327] *Ibid.*, Schroedinger section.
[328] *Ibid.*, de Broglie section.
[329] *Ibid.*, Heisenberg section.
[330] *Ibid.*, Introduction.
[331] Prigogine *op. cit.*, p. 32.
[332] G. W. F Hegel, *Philosophy of Mind. Encyclopedia of the Philosophical Sciences* (Oxford: Clarendon Press, 1971 [1817]), trans. William Wallace, p. 174.
[333] Khenpo Tsultrim Gyamtso, *Progressive Stages of Meditation on Emptiness* (Longchen, 1986), Ch. 2.
[334] Popper *op. cit.*, Section 12.
[335] L.Q. English, 'On the 'Emptiness' of particles in condensed matter physics,' in *Foundations of Science* 12 (2006): 155–71.
[336] C. Sagan, 'Wonder and Skepticism,' *Skeptical Enquirer* 19:1 (1995).
[337] Marcello Truzzi, 'On Pseudo-Skepticism,' *Zetetic Scholar* 12–13 (1987).
[338] T. Halwes, 'The Myth of the Magical Scientific Method,' dharma-haven.org.
[339] Quoted in L. Barnett, *Life* 7:9, International Edition (24 October 1949), p.58. Letter to his brother, Frank.
[340] Trungpa Rinpoche, 'The Ultimate Truth Is Fearless,' the Opening Ceremony of the Karma Dzong Meditation Center (Feb. 25, 1972).
[341] Wilbur *op. cit.*, Eddington section.
[342] Appleyard *op. cit.*, p. 234.
[343] Manly Palmer Hall, 'Living in the Light of Value.' Lecture in *Philosophy of Value*, manlyhallway.com.
[344] Appleyard *op. cit.*, p. 214.
[345] Jack Miles, *God: a Biography* (Vintage, 1995).
[346] *Ibid.*, p. 16.
[347] Genesis 12:1.
[348] Exodus 22:29.
[349] Deuteronomy 13:15.
[350] II Samuel 12:9–10.
[351] I Kings 9:3.
[352] II Samuel 7:8–14.
[353] Deut. 29:21–24.
[354] Miles *op. cit.*, Ch. 8.
[355] Psalm 137:9.
[356] Psalms 139.
[357] II Kings 23.
[358] Isaiah 44:6, 45:5.
[359] Joshua 23:26.
[360] Exodus 22:11.
[361] William W. Hallo and J.J.A. van Dijk, *The Exaltation of Inanna.* Yale Near Eastern Researches 3 (Yale University Press, 1968), pp. 7–8.
[362] Exodus 6.
[363] Robert Wright, *The Evolution of God* (Little, Brown, and Co., 2009), Ch. 5.
[364] *Ibid.*, Ch. 7.
[365] Patrick D. Miller, *The Religion of Ancient* Israel. Library of Ancient Israel (Westminster John Knox Press, 2000).
[366] Miles *op. cit.*, Ch. 10.
[367] Ezekiel 20:25.
[368] Job 40:2.
[369] Job 42:2–6.

[370] Job 13:15–16, 23.
[371] Miles *op. cit.*, p. 325.
[372] Deuteronomy 7:1–4.
[373] Nehemiah 10:40.
[374] II Chronicles 36.
[375] Matthew 6:19, John 6:27, Luke 6:30, Mark 10:21, Luke 20:35, Luke 12:51, Matthew 10:35, Matthew 6:5.
[376] Matthew 27:24-5.
[377] Luke 6:1–4
[378] Bart Ehrman, *Misquoting Jesus: The Story Behind Who Changed the Bible and Why* (HaperOne, 2007), p. 152.
[379] Luke 22:20.
[380] Bart Ehrman, 'The Neglect of First-born in New Testament Studies,' Presidential Lecture, Society of Biblical Literature (Mar. 1997).
[381] John 13:36, 14:5, 16:5.
[382] Bart Ehrman, *Jesus Interrupted: Revealing the Hidden Contradictions in the Bible (And Why We Don't Know About Them)* (HarperOne, 2009), Chs. 3–4.
[383] John 8:42–44.
[384] Ehrman (2009) *op. cit.*, Ch. 2.
[385] Isaiah 7:14.
[386] Mark 16:8.
[387] John 21:24.
[388] Mark 13:26–7.
[389] Luke 12:40.
[390] Matthew 10:28.
[391] Matthew 5:17–20.
[392] Romans 6:5–8.
[393] John Shelby Spong, *Liberating the Gospels: Reading the Bible with Jewish Eyes* (HarperOne, 1997).
[394] Gospel of Philip.
[395] Matthew 2:23. Kenneth Humphreys, *Jesus Never Existed*, jesusneverexisted.com.
[396] Judges 13:5.
[397] Matthew 4:25.
[398] Luke 12:1.
[399] Justin Martyr, 'Dialogue with Trypho,' 8:6.
[400] The Octavius of Minucius Felix, Ch.23.
[401] I Corinthians 15:11–12.
[402] I Corinthians 11:23–6.
[403] James 2:8.
[404] Helmut Koester, *Ancient Christian Gospels* (Continuum International Publishing Group, 1990), p. 64.
[405] II Corinthians 5:5.
[406] Corinthians 15:3–4.
[407] E.g., Mark 13.
[408] II Corinthians 6:3.
[409] I Corinthians 15:5–7.
[410] Hebrews 8:4.
[411] Earl Doherty, *The Jesus Puzzle: Did Christianity Begin with a Mythical Christ* (Canadian Humanist Publications, 1999), p. 94.
[412] II Corinthians 12:2–4.
[413] I Corinthians 2:8.
[414] Ephesians 3:9–10.
[415] Ephesians 6:12.
[416] Hebrews 8:2, 9:11.

[417] Ascension of Isaiah 9:13–17.
[418] Proverbs 8.
[419] M. T. Wright, *The New Testament and the People of God* (Fortress Press, 1992), p. 284–5.
[420] Doherty *op. cit.*, p. 159.
[421] Luke 17:34–5
[422] Mark 2:27.
[423] Mark 3:1–6.
[424] Isaiah 35:5 and Matthew 11:4–5.
[425] II Kings 4:42–4.
[426] Doherty *op. cit.*, p. 243.
[427] *Ibid.*, Ch. 23.
[428] *Ibid.*, Ch. 10.
[429] http://en.wikipedia.org/wiki/Chariton
[430] Luke 22:10.
[431] Gospel of Thomas.
[432] *Ibid.*
[433] John 14:6.
[434] I Clement 41:3.
[435] On the Origin of the World 103:11–20.
[436] Tripartite Tractate.
[437] Elaine Pagels, *The Gnostic Gospels* (Vintage, 1989), p. 33.
[438] The Gospel of Philip 53:24–24.
[439] Book of Thomas the Contender 138:17–18.
[440] Treatise on Resurrection.
[441] Mark 4:11.
[442] Apocalypse of Peter 76:27–34.
[443] Simon Magus.
[444] Hippolytus, Refutation of all Heresies 6.18.
[445] Romans 16:7.
[446] The Thunder, Perfect Mind 13:16.
[447] Hypostasis of the Arkons 94.21–95.7.
[448] Mark 4:10–12.
[449] Gospel of Philip 71:35–72:4
[450] Pagels *op. cit.*, p. 120.
[451] Teachings of Silvanus 88:24–92:12.
[452] Gospel of Truth 28:16.
[453] Gospel of Truth 29:8–30:12.
[454] The Thunder, Perfect Mind.
[455] Hippolytus 6.17.
[456] Trimorphic Protennoia (Three Shaped Thought).
[457] Thomas 37:20-35.
[458] Interpretation of the Knowledge 17:21–7.
[459] Irenaeus, Against all Heresies I.5.4, quoted in Pagels *op. cit.*, p. 124.
[460] Gospel of Truth 17:10-16.
[461] Allogenes.
[462] Testimony of Truth 44:2.
[463] Dialogue of the Savior 134:1–22.
[464] Silvanus 85:24–106:14.
[465] Gospel of Thomas 32:19–33:5.
[466] Pagels *op. cit.*
[467] D. Dennett and L. LaScola, 'Preachers who are not Believers,' Center for Cognitive Studies (March 15, 2010).
[468] David Kinnaman and Gabe Lyons, *Unchristian: What a new Generation really thinks* (Baker, 2007), p. 123.

[469] *Ibid.*
[470] *Ibid.*, p. 155.
[471] Jonathan Edwards, 'The Excellency of Christ,' 1839 Sermon.
[472] Chris Hedges, *American Fascists* (Free Press, 2006).
[473] E. Heubeck, 'The Integration Theory and Practice: A Program for New Traditionalist Movement,' Free Congress Foundation (2001).
[474] Al Dager, *Vengeance Is Ours: The Church In Dominion* (Sword Publishers, 1990).
[475] S. Leslie, 'Dominionism and the Rise of Christian Imperialism,' Discernment Ministries (Dec. 2005).
[476] *Ibid.*
[477] C. Peter Wagner, Global Link Newsletter (Nov. 1, 2005), quoted in *ibid.*
[478] Jay Grimstead, COR Steering Council letter (May 1993), quoted in *ibid.*
[479] Rick Joyner, 'Taking the Land' (Nov. 29, 2005), quoted in *ibid.*
[480] Michael Baigent, *Racing Toward Armageddon: The Three Great Religions and the Plot to End the World* (HarperOne, 2009).
[481] Michael Weinstein, *With God on Our Side: One Man's War Against an Evangelical Coup in America's Military* (St. Martin's Griffin Press, 2008), p. 201.
[482] *Ibid.*, p. 203.
[483] *Ibid.*, p. 208.
[484] Hope Taylor, 'December 15th, President Bush and Iraq,' quoted in Leslie *op cit.*
[485] Alexander Nemets and Tomas Torda. 'Council for National Policy Conference, Part 1,' Newsmax Archives (May 9, 2002).
[486] S. Posner, 'Secret Society: Just Who is the Council for National Policy and why isn't it paying taxes?' AlterNet (Mar. 1, 2005).
[487] Paul and Phillip Collins, 'Deep Politics of God: The CNP, Dominionism, Ted Haggard Scandal,' ConspiracyArchive (Feb. 27, 2007).
[488] Leslie *op. cit.*
[489] Bob Jones & Paul Keith Davis, 'Shepherd's Rod 2004' (Oct. 7, 2003), quoted in *ibid.*
[490] David Chilton, *Productive Christians in an Age of Guilt Manipulators* (Tyler, TX: Institute for Christian Economics, 1981), p. 61.
[491] *Invisible Children*, documentary (2008).
[492] Ecclesiastes 3:19–21.
[493] Koran 4:171.
[494] Sachiko Murata and William Chittick, *The Vision of Islam* (Paragon House, 1994), p133.
[495] Koran 28:88.
[496] Murata & Chittick *op. cit.*, pp. 260–4.
[497] Koran 2:115.
[498] Murata & Chittick *op. cit.*, p. 37.
[499] *Ibid.*, p. 267.
[500] Carl W. Ernst, *The Shambhala Guide to Sufism* (Shambhala, 1997).
[501] Barbara Metcalf, *Moral Conduct and Authority: The Place of Adab in South Asian Islam* (University of California Press, 1984), p. 10.
[502] Koran 21:96, 27:82.
[503] Murata & Chittick *op. cit.*, pp. 193–236.
[504] Koran 22:7.
[505] Koran 14:48, 27:88, 81:1–14.
[506] Koran 21:69.
[507] Koran 8:33.
[508] Murata & Chittick *op. cit.*, p. 328.
[509] Ed Hotaling, *Islam without Illusions: Its Past, Its Present, and Its Challenge for the Future* (Syracuse University Press, 2003).
[510] *Ibid.*, Ch. 1.

[511] Karen Armstrong, *Mohammed: A Prophet for Our Time* (Modern Library, 2007), p. 73.
[512] Ernst *op. cit.*, Introduction.
[513] Karen Armstrong, *Islam: A Short History* (Modern Library, 2002), pp. 125-7.
[514] *Ibid.*, Ch. 7.
[515] Farid Esack, Anna Ghonim, and Javed Memon , 'Progressive Islam: a definition and declaration,' http://ihsan-net.blogspot.ca/2004/12/progressive-islam-view-from-october.html
[516] Gallup Poll responses, quoted in John Esposito, *Who Speaks for Islam?: What a Billion Muslims Really Think* (Gallup Press, 2008), p. 26.
[517] *Ibid.*
[518] *Ibid.*
[519] Ebrahim Moosa, 'The Debts and Burdens of Critical Islam,' in *Progressive Muslims: On Justice, Gender and Pluralism*, ed. Omid Safi (Oxford: Oneworld, 2003).
[520] Abdullahi An-Na'im, 'Political Islam in National Politics and International Relations,' in *The Secularization of the World: Resurgent Religion and World Politics* ed. Peter L. Berger (Eerdmans, 2000), p. 117.
[521] Samuel Huntington, *The Clash of Civilizations and Remaking of World Order* (Simon & Schuster, 2011), p. 215.
[522] Armstrong (2002) *op. cit.*, p. 15.
[523] Omid Safi, *Progressive Muslims: On Justice, Gender, and Pluralism* (OneWorld, 2003), p. 88.
[524] *Ibid.*, p. 89.
[525] 911trafficking.com
[526] Murata & Chittick *op. cit.*, pp. 332–5.
[527] Khaled Abou El Fadl, 'The Ugly Modern and the Modern Ugly: Reclaiming the Beautiful in Islam,' in Safi *op. cit.*
[528] *Ibid.*, p. 59.
[529] Armstrong (2002) *op. cit.*, Ch. 5.
[530] Ahmad S. Moussalli, 'Islamic Democracy and Pluralism,' in Safi *op. cit.*, p. 286.
[531] Esposito *op. cit.*, Introduction.
[532] http://www.sistersinislam.org.my/news.php?item.255.8
[533] Mohammad Omar Farooq, 'On Apostasy and Islam: 100+ Notable Islamic Voices affirming Freedom of Faith,' http://apostasyandislam.blogspot.ca/.
[534] Esposito *op. cit.*, p. 107.
[535] *Ibid.*, Ch. 4.
[536] Sadiyaa Shaikh, 'Transforming Feminism: Islam, Women and Gender Justice,' in Safi *op. cit.*, pp. 152–3.
[537] Tazim R. Kassam, 'On being a scholar of Islam: risks and responsibilities,' in Safi *op. cit.*
[538] Farid Esack, 'In Search of Progressive Islam beyond 911,' in Safi *op. cit.*, p. 85.
[539] Naeem Jeenah quoted in Esack, *ibid.*
[540] Esposito *op. cit.*, Ch. 5.
[541] *Ibid.*, Ch. 6.
[542] Yossef Bodansky, *Bin Laden: The Man who declared War on America* (Prima Lifestyles, 2001), p. 3.
[543] Koran 5:32.
[544] Esposito *op. cit.*, p. 164.
[545] Michael Bonner, *Jihad in Islamic History: Doctrines and Practice* (Princeton University Press, 2008).
[546] Koran 22:78
[547] Koran 43:89, 106:6.
[548] Koran 8:59–62.
[549] Koran 4:90.
[550] Koran 50:45.

[551] Koran 9:6.
[552] Open Letter to Pope Benedict XVI (2006), http://www.catholicculture.org/culture/library/view.cfm?recnum=7910.
[553] Isaiah 13:3–5.
[554] Koran 2:190.
[555] *Palestine is still the issue*, John Pilger documentary (2002).
[556] *Ibid.*
[557] http://www.voicesofpalestine.org/massacres.htm.
[558] Robert Pape, *Dying to Win: The Strategic Logic of Suicide Terrorism* (Random House, 2005).
[559] Hotaling *op. cit.*, p. 90.
[560] Shaykh-ul-Islam Dr. Muhammad Tahir-ul-Qadri, *Fatwa on Suicide bombings and terrorism* (Minhaj-ul-Quran International, 2010), pp. 36, 45.
[561] 2010 Angus Reid Public Opinion poll, http://www.angus-reid.com/polls/40260/americans-disagree-with-iranian-president-on-911-fabrication/.
[562]http://www.fbi.gov/wanted/topten/usama-bin-laden and Muckraker report (June 6, 2006).
[563] Tony Snow show (Mar. 29, 2006).
[564] http://patriotsquestion911.com/.
[565] L. Grossman, 'Why 911 Conspiracy theories won't go away,' *Time* (Sept. 3, 2006).
[566] 'Amidst Growing World Doubts About 9/11, Career Army Officer Takes Bush Administration Officials to Court April 5th Represented by the Center for 9/11 Justice,' HeraldOnline (Mar. 23, 2011).
[567] R. Ananda, 'April Gallop versus Dick Cheney: Court Dismisses 9/11 Suit against Bush Officials,' *Global Research* (Apr. 29, 2011).
[568] *9/11: Explosive Evidence Experts Speak Out*, Architects and Engineers for 9/11 Truth documentary (2011).
[569] http://www.dailypaul.com/172140/danny-jowenko-is-dead-3-days-after-sabrosky-interview-implicates-cia-mossad-in-911
[570] *9/11: Explosive Evidence Experts Speak Out.*
[571] The White House Tapes.
[572] Zbigniew Brzezinski, Senate Foreign Relations Committee testimony (Feb. 1, 2007).
[573] Naomi Wolf, *The End of America: A Letter of Warning to a Young Patriot* (Chelsea Green Publishing, 2007).
[574] Elie Wiesel, *Night* (Farrar, Strauss, Giroux, 2006), Ch. 1.
[575] Bernard Lewis, 'The Roots of Muslim Rage,' *Atlantic* (Sept. 1990).
[576]Samuel Huntington, 'Clash of Civilizations,' 1992 lecture at the American Enterprise Institute.
[577] Amir Hussain, 'Muslims, Pluralism and Interfaith Dialogue,' in Safi *op. cit.*, p. 254.
[578] Koran 5:82.
[579] Koran 49:13.
[580] Corbett Report, Episode 104.
[581] Reza Aslan, quoted in Weinstein *op. cit.*, p. 205.
[582] 'Armageddon – Group of Church Leaders Asks Candidates to Repudiate Nuclear Doomsday theory,' *Washington Post* (Oct. 24, 1984).
[583] Baigent *op. cit.*
[584] Message from Chief Dan Evehema, Hotevilla, Az. (1996).
[585] Dzongsar Khyentse Rinpoche, Mahamudra Seminar, New York Shambhala Center (2005).
[586] Dorje Dradul of Mukpo, 'Meditation and the 4th moment,', Naropa University opening talk, Boulder (1974).

Bibliography

'Amidst Growing World Doubts About 9/11, Career Army Officer Takes Bush Administration Officials to Court April 5th Represented by the Center for 9/11 Justice.' HeraldOnline (Mar. 23, 2011).

'AMS survey of weathercasters on climate change.' ABC-33 (Nov. 15, 2009).

'Armageddon – Group of Church Leaders Asks Candidates to Repudiate Nuclear Doomsday theory.' *Washington Post* (Oct. 24, 1984).

'Big Bang's afterglow fails intergalactic shadow test.' *Physorg* (Sep. 1, 2006).

'Bitten by the IPCC.' *National Post* (Mar. 23, 2007).

'Charles Darwin's tree of life is 'wrong and misleading', claim scientists.' *Telegraph* (Jan. 22, 2009).

'Condoms and HIV: What everyone knows is once again wrong.' http://wp.me/p8Qhq-1r (Feb. 10, 2008).

'Durbin Declaration' (2000).

'Everyone reacts positive on the ELISA test for AIDS.' *Continuum* 5:5 (Winter 1998/9): 8–10.

'HIV and breastfeeding again.' http://wp.me/p8Qhq-1t (Feb. 13, 2008).

'Mercury and Medicine: Taking Unnecessary Risks.' Committee on Government Reform report (May 2003).

'NIH Science busters get new assignment.' *Science Services* (Oct. 16, 1993).

'No consensus on IPCC's level of ignorance.' BBC News (Nov. 13, 2007).

'Peer Review and the Acceptance of New Scientific Ideas.' *Sense About Science* (2004).

'Physician, Heal Thyself.' *Climate Resistance* (Dec. 28, 2007).

'Physics of the Mind: Holographic Realities.' New Dimensions Radio (Apr. 30, 1991).

'Presidential AIDS Advisory Panel Report: A synthesis report of the deliberations by the panel of experts invited by the President of the Republic of South Africa, the Honourable Mr Thabo Mbeki.' Mar. 2001.

'Study Finds Traces of Drugs in Drinking Water in 24 Major U.S. Regions.' Associated Press (Mar. 10, 2008).

'Summary Statistics: Thimerosal Study.' CDC National Immunization Program. No Date. http://autismactionnetwork.org/science.html

2010 Angus Reid Public Opinion poll, http://www.angus-reid.com/polls/40260/americans-disagree-with-iranian-president-on-911-fabrication/.

9/11: Explosive Evidence Experts Speak Out, Architects and Engineers for 9/11 Truth documentary (2011).

Achterberg, J., *et al.* 'A possible relationship between cancer, mental retardation and mental disorders.' *Social Science & Medicine. Part A: Medical Psychology & Medical Sociology* 12 (1978): 135–39.

AIDS Deception, The. Gary Null Films (2001).

Allen, Garland E. 'Is a New Eugenics Afoot?' *Science* 294 (2001): 5540.

Ananda, R. 'April Gallop versus Dick Cheney: Court Dismisses 9/11 Suit against Bush Officials.' *Global Research* (Apr. 29, 2011).

Anderson, M. S., B. C. Martinson, and R. De Vries. 'Normative dissonance in science: results from a national survey of US scientists.' *Journal of Empirical Research on Human Research Ethics* 2 (2007): 3–14.

Angell, Marcia. *The Truth about the Drug Companies: How They Deceive Us and What to Do About It.* Random House, 2004.

Appleyard, Bryan. *Understanding the Present: An Alternative History of Science.* New York: Tauris Parke, 2004.

Arbabi-Bidgoli, S. and V. Muller. 'Void scaling and void profiles in CDM models.' arXiv:astrop-ph/0111581 (2001).
Armstrong, Karen. *Islam: A Short History.* Modern Library, 2002.
Armstrong, Karen. *Mohammed: A Prophet for Our Time.* Modern Library, 2007.
Atom: the illusion of Reality, BBC documentary.
Ayoub, David. 'Global Vaccine Agenda: Mercury and Autism.' YouTube.
Baigent, Michael. *Racing Toward Armageddon: The Three Great Religions and the Plot to End the World.* HarperOne, 2009.
Barlett D. L., and J. B. Steele. 'Deadly Medicine.' *Vanity Fair* (Jan. 2011).
Barnett, L. *Life* 7:9, International Edition (24 October 1949).
Barrè-Sinoussi, F., *et al.* 'Isolation of a T-lymphotropic retrovirus from a patient at risk for acquired immune deficiency syndrome (AIDS).' *Science* 220:4599 (1983): 868–71.
Bauer, H. H. 'Science in the 21st century: knowledge monopolies and research cartels.' *J. Sci. Explor.* 18 (2004): 643–660.
Bauer, Henry H. *The Origin, Persistence and Failings of HIV/AIDS Theory.* McFarland, 2007.
Bauman, M. and K. Nelson. 'Thimerosal and Autism?' *Pediatrics* 111:3 (2003): 674–79.
Bekelman, J. E., Y. Li, C. P. Gross. 'Scope and impact of financial conflicts of interest in biomedical research: A systematic review.' *Journal of the American Medical Association* 289 (2003): 454–465.
Bennett, Amanda and Anita Sharpe. 'AIDS Fight Is Skewed By Federal Campaign Exaggerating Risks.' *The Wall Street Journal* (May 1, 1996).
Berger, Peter L. (ed.). *Secularization of the World: Resurgent Religion and World Politics.* Eerdmans, 2000.
Bialy, Harvey. *Oncogenes, Aneuploidy, and AIDS: A Scientific Life and Times of Peter H. Duesberg.* North Atlantic Books, 2004.
Blaxill, Mark. 'The Governance Problem: summary of highlights of scientific review of safety datalink information.' *Schafer Autism Report* (May 2001).
Bodansky, Yossef. *Bin Laden: The Man who declared War on America.* Prima Lifestyles, 2001.
Bohm, David. *Wholeness and the Implicate Order.* Ark Paperbacks, 1983.
Boivin J., *et al.* 'Incidence of Second Cancers in Patients Treated for Hodgkin's Disease.' *JNCI* 87:10 (1995): 732–741.
Bonner, Michael. *Jihad in Islamic History: Doctrines and Practice.* Princeton University Press, 2008.
Bornmann, L. 'Scientific Peer Review: Analysis of Peer Review Process.' *Human Architecture* 1:2 (2008): 23–38.
Brown, Darin. 'Why owners of AB+ canines need not be concerned.' *You Bet Your Life* (Sept. 27, 2006), http://barnesworld.blogs.com/barnes_world/2006/09/darin_brown_exp.html.
Brzezinski, Zbigniew. Senate Foreign Relations Committee testimony (Feb. 1, 2007).
Burbacher, T. M., *et al.* 'Comparison of Blood and Brain Mercury Levels in Infant Monkeys exposed to Vaccines containing thimerosal.' *Environmental Health Perspectives* 113:8 (2005):1015–21.
Burd, David. 'A cure for US AIDS: Travel to Canada.' *RethinkingAids* (April 12, 2010).
Camp, A. L. 'Summary of Big Bang Creation Story.' theoutlet.us/SummaryofBigBangCreationStory.pdf (2006).
Caton, Hiram. *The AIDS Mirage.* 1998.
Chilton, David. *Productive Christians in an Age of Guilt Manipulators.* Tyler, TX: Institute for Christian Economics, 1981.
CNA, *National Security and the Threat of Climate Change.'* http://www.cna.org/reports/climate (April 2007).

Cole, S. 'Chance and consensus in peer review.' *Science* 214:4523 (1981): 881–6.
Collins, Francis. *The Language of God: A Scientist Presents Evidence for Belief.* Free Press, 2006. Collins, H., *et al.* 'Experiments with interactional expertise.' *Studies in History and Philosophy of Science Part A* 37 (2006): 656–74.
Collins, Paul and Phillip. 'Deep Politics of God: The CNP, Dominionism, Ted Haggard Scandal.' ConspiracyArchive (Feb. 27, 2007).
Corbett Report, Episode #104.
Corbett Report, Episode #134.
Corbett Report, Interview with Richard Lindzen (Nov. 22, 2010).
Coyne, Jerry. *Why Evolution is True.* Viking Press, 2009.
Culshaw, Rebecca. *Science Sold Out: Does HIV really cause AIDS.* North Atlantic Books, 2007.
Dager, Al. *Vengeance Is Ours: The Church In Dominion.* Sword Publishers, 1990.
Daly, J. L. 'Hockey Stick: a New Low in Climate Science' http://www.john-daly.com/hockey/hockey.htm (2000).
Dangerous Knowledge, BBC documentary.
Dannemann, Eileen. 'CDC allegedly falsifies reports--ignoring up to 3,587 Miscarriages from H1N1 Vaccine.' National Coalition of Women press release (Oct. 28, 2010).
Dawkins, Richard. *The Greatest Show on Earth: The Evidence for Evolution.* Free Press, 2009.
Dawkins, Richard. *The Selfish Gene.* Oxford University Press, 2006 (1976).
Dennett, D. and L. LaScola, 'Preachers who are not Believers.' Center for Cognitive Studies (March 15, 2010).
Deyo, R. A. *et al.* 'The messenger under attack–intimidation of researchers by special-interest groups.' *NEJM* 336 (1997): 1176–1180.
Doherty, Earl. *The Jesus Puzzle: Did Christianity Begin with a Mythical Christ.* Canadian Humanist Publications, 1999.
Dorje Dradul of Mukpo, 'Meditation and the 4th moment.' Naropa University opening talk, Boulder (1974).
Duesberg, Peter. 'AIDS acquired by drug consumption and other non-contagious risk factors.' *Pharmacology and Therapeutics* 55:3 (1992): 201–77.
Duesberg, Peter. 'Human Immunodeficiency Virus and Acquired Immunodeficiency Syndrome: Correlation but not Causation.' *Proc. Natl. Acad. Sci.* 86:3 (1989): 755–64.
Dzongsar Khyentse Rinpoche, Mahamudra Seminar, New York Shambhala Center (2005).
Eastwood, S., P. Derish, E. Leash and S. Ordway. 'Ethical issues in biomedical research: Perceptions and practices of postdoctoral research fellows responding to a survey.' *Science and Engineering Ethics* 2 (1996): 89–114.
Edwards, Jonathan. 'The Excellency of Christ.' 1839 Sermon.
Ehrman, Bart. 'The Neglect of First-born in New Testament Studies.' Presidential Lecture, Society of Biblical Literature (Mar. 1997).
Ehrman, Bart. *Jesus Interrupted: Revealing the Hidden Contradictions in the Bible (And Why We Don't Know About Them).* HarperOne, 2009.
Ehrman, Bart. *Misquoting Jesus: The Story Behind Who Changed the Bible and Why.* HaperOne, 2007.
Engdahl, F. William. *Seeds of Destruction: The Hidden Agenda of Genetic Manipulation.* Montreal: Global Research, 2007.
Engler, R. L., *et al.* 'Misrepresentation and Responsibility in Medical Research.' *New England Journal of Medicine* 317:22 (1987): 1383–89.
English, L.Q. 'On the 'Emptiness' of particles in condensed matter physics.' *Foundations of Science* 12 (2006): 155–71.
Ernst, Carl W. *The Shambhala Guide to Sufism.* Shambhala, 1997.
Esack, Farid, Anna Ghonim, and Javed Memon , 'Progressive Islam: a definition and declaration.' http://ihsan-net.blogspot.ca/2004/12/progressive-islam-view-from-october.html

Esposito, John. *Who Speaks for Islam?: What a Billion Muslims Really Think.* Gallup Press, 2008.
Evehema, Chief Dan. Hotevilla, Az. (1996).
Fanelli, D. 'How Many Scientists Fabricate and Falsify Research? A Systematic Review and Meta-Analysis of Survey Data.' *PLoS ONE* 4:5 (2009): e5738.
Farber, C. 'Fatal distraction.' *Spin* magazine (June 1992).
Farber, C. 'Out of Control: Aids and the Corruption of Medical Science.' *Harpers* (Mar. 2006).
Farooq, Mohammad Omar. 'On Apostasy and Islam: 100+ Notable Islamic Voices affirming Freedom of Faith.' http://apostasyandislam.blogspot.ca/.
FDA Science Board. 'FDA Science and Mission at Risk: Report of the Subcommittee on Science and Technology' (Nov. 2007).
Fleck, Ludwig. *Genesis and Development of a Scientific Fact.* University of Chicago Press, 1979 (1935).
Fodor, Jerry and Massimo Piattelli-Palmarini, *What Darwin Got Wrong.* Farrar, Strauss, & Giroux, 2010.
Fombonne, E. 'Is there an Epidemic of Autism?' *Pediatrics* 107:2 (2001): 411–2.
Gilbert, S. G. and K. S. Grant-Webster. 'Neurobehavorial effects of developmental methylmercury exposure.' *Environmental Health Perspectives* 103 Suppl 6 (1995): 135–142.
Gisselquist, D., *et al*. 'HIV infections in sub-Saharan Africa not explained by sexual or vertical transmission.' *Int J STD AIDS* 13 (2002): 657–666.
Gleick, P. H., *et al*. 'Climate Change and the Integrity of Science.' *Science* 328:5979 (2010): 689–90.
Godlee, F., *et al*. 'Effect on the quality of peer review of blinding reviewers and asking them to sign their reports: a randomized controlled trial.' *JAMA* 280:3 (1998): 237–240.
Gold, T. 'New Ideas in Science.' *J. Sci. Explor*. 3:2 (1989): 103–12.
Gordon, J. 'Commentary: Parents should not be legally liable for refusing to vaccinate their children.' *Michigan Law Review* 107 (2009).
Grossman, L. 'Why 911 Conspiracy theories won't go away.' *Time* (Sept. 3, 2006).
Grossman, Z. 'Pathogenesis of HIV infection.' *Nature Medicine* 12 (2006): 289–95.
Guy, K. 'Don't Buy Hype about Global Warming.' *Sun-Sentinel* (Sept. 11, 2011).
Gyamtso, Khenpo Tsultrim. *Progressive Stages of Meditation on Emptiness.* Longchen, 1986.
Hall, Manly Palmer. 'Living in the Light of Value.' Lecture in *Philosophy of Value,* manlyhallway.com.
Hallo, William W. and J.J.A. van Dijk, *The Exaltation of Inanna.* Yale Near Eastern Researches 3. Yale University Press, 1968.
Halwes, T. 'The Myth of the Magical Scientific Method.' dharma-haven.org.
Hanfling, Oswald. *Logical Positivism.* Routledge History of Philosophy, 2003.
Hatch, Senator O. G. 'UN climate scientists speak out on global warming.' Senate Minority Report (Sept. 12, 2009).
Health Century, The. Blackwell WGBH, PBS.
Hedges, Chris. *American Fascists.* Free Press, 2006.
Hegel, G. W. F. *Philosophy of Mind. Encyclopedia of the Philosophical Sciences.* Oxford: Clarendon Press, 1971 (1817), trans. William Wallace.
Heubeck, E. 'The Integration Theory and Practice: A Program for New Traditionalist Movement.' Free Congress Foundation (2001).
Hewitson, L., *et al*. 'Pediatric vaccines influence primate behaviour, and Amygdala Growth and Opioid Ligand Binding.' http://www.ageofautism.com/2008/05/pediatric-vacci.html.
Hojat, M., *et al*. 'Impartial judgment by the "gatekeepers" of science: fallibility and accountability in the peer review process.' *Adv Health Sci Educ Theory Pract* 8 (2003): 75–96.
Horrobin, D. F. 'The Philosophical Basis of Peer Review and the Suppression of Innovation.' *JAMA* 263:10 (1990): 1438–41.

Horton, R. 'The Hidden Research Paper.' *JAMA* 287 (2002).
Hotaling, Ed. *Islam without Illusions: Its Past, Its Present, and Its Challenge for the Future.* Syracuse University Press, 2003.
Hubble, Edwin. *The Observational Approach to Cosmology.* Oxford: Clarendon Press, 1937.
Hulme, M. and M. Mahony, 'Climate Change: what do we know about the IPCC?' *Progress in Physical Geography* (2010), p. 10.
Hume, David. *An Enquiry Concerning Human Understanding.* 1748.
Huntington, Samuel. 'Clash of Civilizations.' 1992 lecture at the American Enterprise Institute.
Huntington, Samuel. *The Clash of Civilizations and Remaking of World Order.* Simon & Schuster, 2011.
Invisible Children, documentary (2008).
Jablonka, Eva and Marion J. Lamb, *Evolution in Four Dimensions: Genetic, Epigenetic, Behavioral, and Symbolic Variation in the History of Life.* MIT Press, 2006.
Jefferson, T., *et al.* 'Effects of Editorial Peer Review: a Systematic Review.' *JAMA* 287:21 (2002a): 2784–6.
Jefferson, T., *et al.* 'Measuring the quality of editorial peer review.' *JAMA* 287:21 (2002b): 2786–90.
Judson, Horace Freeland. *The Great Betrayal: Fraud in Science.* Harcourt, 2004.
Kalokerinos, Archie. *Every Second Child.* Keats, 1981.
Kennedy, Jr., Robert. 'Central Figure in CDC Vaccine Cover-Up Absconds with $2M.' *Huffington Post* (Mar. 11, 2010).
Kennedy, Jr., Robert. 'Deadly Immunity.' *Rolling Stone* (Jun. 20, 2005).
Kinnaman, David and Gabe Lyons. *Unchristian: What a new Generation really thinks.* Baker, 2007.
Kirby, David. *Evidence of Harm.* St. Martin's Press, 2005.
Klopfer, B. 'Psychological Variables in Cancer.' *Journal of Projective Techniques* 21:4 (1957): 331–40.
Knoll, E. 'The Communities of Scientists and Journal Peer Review.' *JAMA* 263:10 (1990): 1330–32.
Koester, Helmut. *Ancient Christian Gospels.* Continuum International Publishing Group, 1990.
Kuhn, Thomas *The Structure of Scientific Revolutions.* University of Chicago Press, 1962.
Lange, S. 'Questions of Scientific Responsibility: the Baltimore Case.' *Journal of Ethics and Behavior* 3:1 (1993): 3–72.
Lauritsen, J. *Poison by Prescription: The AZT story.* Pagan Press, 1990.
Lehrer, J. 'The Truth Wears Off.' *New Yorker* (Dec. 13, 2010).
Lerner, Eric J. 'Two world systems revisited: a comparison of plasma cosmology and the Big Bang.' http://bigbangneverhappened.org/p27.htm.
Lerner, Eric J. *The Big Bang Never Happened.* Random House, 1991.
Leslie, S. 'Dominionism and the Rise of Christian Imperialism.' Discernment Ministries (Dec. 2005).
Levin, M. ''91 Memo Warned of Mercury in Shots.' *LA Times* (Feb 8, 2005).
Lewis, Bernard. 'The Roots of Muslim Rage.' *Atlantic* (Sept. 1990).
Lindzen, R. 'Climate Science: Is It Currently Designed To Answer Questions?' arXiv:0809.3762v3 (2008).
Lloyd, M. E. 'Gender factors in reviewer recommendations for manuscript publication.' *J Appl Behav Anal* 23:4 (1990): 539–543.
Lock, S. 'Does editorial peer review work?' *Ann Intern Med* 121:1 (1994): 60–1.
Lock, S. 'Lessons from the Pearce Affair: Handling Scientific Fraud.' *BMJ* 310 (1995): 1547–48.
Lorscheider, F. 'How Mercury causes brain neuron degeneration.' *Neuro-report* 12 (2001).
Lowe, J. A., *et al.* 'Mercury Poisoning Associated with High Dose.' *Liver Transplantation Surgery* 2:6 (1996).

Margulis, Jennifer. 'The Vaccine debate.' *Mothering* magazine (Jul. 2009).
Martinson, B. C., M. S. Anderson and R. de Vries. 'Scientists behaving badly.' *Nature* 435 (2005): 737–738.
Mather, John and John Boslough. *The Very First Light: the true inside story of the scientific journey back to the dawn of the universe.* New York: Basic Books, 1996.
McBean, Eleanor. *The Poisoned Needle.* 1957.
Metcalf, Barbara. *Moral Conduct and Authority: The Place of Adab in South Asian Islam.* University of California Press, 1984.
Miles, Jack. *God: a Biography.* Vintage, 1995.
Miller, Kenneth R. *Finding Darwin's God: A Scientist's Search for Common Ground Between God and Evolution.* Harper Collins, 1999.
Miller, Neil Z. '7 reasons schools should not mandate vaccines.' *NaturalNews* (Jul. 14, 2011).
Miller, Neil Z. 'More than 2000 vaccinated babies died: The cost of doing business.' *NaturalNews* (Mar. 24, 2011).
Miller, Patrick D. *The Religion of Ancient* Israel. Library of Ancient Israel. Westminster John Knox Press, 2000.
Milton, Richard. 'Darwinism – The forbidden subject.' Alternative Science website (1996).
Moffat, John. *Reinventing Gravity.* Thomas Allen Publishers, 2008.
Money Talks: Profits over Patient Safety, documentary (2006).
Morbidity and Mortality Weekly Report 59(05): 125-129 (Feb. 12, 2010).
Murata, Sachiko and William Chittick. *The Vision of Islam.* Paragon House, 1994.
Neill, U. 'Stop Misbehaving!' *Journal of Clinical Investigations* 116:7 (2006): 1740.
Nemets, Alexander and Tomas Torda. 'Council for National Policy Conference, Part 1.' Newsmax Archives (May 9, 2002).
Nicastro, F., *et al.* 'The Far-ultraviolet signature of the "missing" baryons in the Local Group of Galaxies.' *Nature* 421 (2003): 719–721.
NYU Medical Center, interview with Robert Gallo by James M. Scutero (Nov. 11, 1993).
Open Letter to Pope Benedict XVI (2006), http://www.catholicculture.org/culture/library/view.cfm?recnum=7910.
Padian, N. S., S. C. Shiboski, S. O. Glass, and E. Vittinghoff. 'Heterosexual transmission of human immunodeficiency virus (HIV) in Northern California: results from a ten-year study.' *American Journal of Epidemiology* 146 (1997): 350–7.
Pagels, Elaine. *The Gnostic Gospels.* Vintage, 1989.
Palestine is still the issue, John Pilger documentary (2002).
Pape, Robert. *Dying to Win: The Strategic Logic of Suicide Terrorism.* Random House, 2005.
Patriarca, Peter, Director of Viral Products. Internal FDA email to Martin Meyers, National Vaccine Office of the CDA (Jun. 29, 1999).
Petition to the council of the American Physical Society, 2010.
Physicians' Desk Reference 2003. Thomson, 2002.
Pichichero, M. E., *et al.* 'Mercury Concentrations, metabolism and infant receiving vaccines containing Thimerosal.' *Lancet* 360:9347 (2022): 1737–41.
Polanyi, Michael. 'Transcendence and Self-transcendence.' *Soundings* 53:1 (1970): 88–94.
Popper, Karl. *The Logic of Scientific Discovery.* New York: Harper, 1965.
Posner, S. 'Secret Society: Just Who is the Council for National Policy and why isn't it paying taxes?' AlterNet (Mar. 1, 2005).
Press Release, Office of Representative Dave Weldon (2004).
Prigogine, Ilya. *Order out of Chaos: Man's new dialogue with nature.* Shambhala, 1984.
Princeton Engineering Anomalies Research, Robert Jahn biography, http://www.princeton.edu/~pear/jahn.html.

Ranstam, J., M. Buyse, S. L. George, S. Evans, N. L. Geller, *et al.* 'Fraud in medical research: An international survey of biostatisticians.' *Controlled Clinical Trials* 21 (2000): 415–427.
Rasnick, David. 'Conspiracy indeed!' *British Medical Journal* Rapid Response (Apr. 18, 2003).
Rasnick, David. *The AIDS Deception.*
Rees, Martin. *Before the Beginning.* New York: Basic Books, 1998. Rennie, D. *et al.* 'Dealing with Research Misconduct in the United Kingdom.' *British Medical Journal* 316 (1998): 1726.
Reilly, W. 'UN calls Climate Debate Over.' *UPI* (May 10, 2007).
Remine, Walter J. *The Biotic Message: Evolution Versus Message Theory.* Saint Paul Science, 1993.
Restack, R. 'People with Multiple Minds.' *Science Digest* 92 (June 1984): p. 76.
Ridley, M. 'Modern Darwins.' *National Geographic* (Feb. 2009).
Rinpoche, Trungpa. 'The Ultimate Truth Is Fearless.' Opening Ceremony of the Karma Dzong Meditation Center (Feb. 25, 1972).
Roche Diagnostic Systems, Inc., Amplicor HIV-1 Monitor Test Kit (June 1996).
Rosenhan, D. L. 'On being sane in insane places.' *Science* 179 (1973).
Russell, Bertrand. *The Scientific Outlook.* London: George Allen & Unwin, 1931.
Safi, Omid (ed.). *Progressive Muslims: On Justice, Gender and Pluralism.* Oxford: Oneworld, 2003.
Safi, Omid. *Progressive Muslims: On Justice, Gender, and Pluralism.* OneWorld, 2003.
Sagan, C. 'Wonder and Skepticism.' *Skeptical Enquirer* 19:1 (1995).
Schneider, S. 'Don't Bet All Environmental Changes Will Be Beneficial.' *APS News* 5:8 (1996).
Scranton, R., *et al.* 'Physical Evidence for Dark Energy.' arXiv:astrop-ph/0307335 (2003).
Seitz, F. 'A major Deception on Global Warming.' *Wall Street Journal* (June 12, 1996).
Sheldrake, Rupert. *Dogs That Know When Their Owners Are Coming Home.* Crown Publishers, 1999.
Sismondo, S. 'Pharmaceutical company funding and its consequences: a qualitative systematic review.' *Contemporary Clinical Trials* 29 (2008): 109–113.
Slikker, W. S. 'Developmental Neurotoxicity of Therapeutics: survey of novel recent findings.' *Neurotoxicology* 1:2 (2000): 250.
Smith, R. 'Peer review: a flawed process at the heart of science and journals.' *JRSM* 99:4 (2006): 178–182.
Spergel, D. N., *et al.* 'First Year Wilkinson Microwave Anisotropy Probe (WMAP) Observations: Determination of Cosmological Parameters.' arXiv:astro-ph/0302209 (2003).
Spong, John Shelby. *Liberating the Gospels: Reading the Bible with Jewish Eyes.* HarperOne, 1997.
Stade, K. 'Radiation Exposure Debate Rages Inside EPA.' *Public Employees for Environmental Responsibility* (Apr. 5, 2011), http://www.peer.org/news/news_id.php?row_id=1325.
Stehr-Green, P. 'Autism and Thimerosal containing vaccines: lack of consistent evidence for an association.' *American Journal of Preventitive Medicine* 25:2 (2003): 101–6.
Stobbe, Mike. 'Fluoride's reputation gets a little spotty.' Associated Press (Jan. 8, 2011).
Stokes, J. 'Over 4.5 Billion people could die from Global Warming-related causes by 2012 .' *The Canadian* (2007).
Stolberg, Sheryl Gay. 'For retired chimps a life of leisure.' *New York Times* (Jan. 7, 2003).
Tabin, C. 'What is Evo-Devo.' PBS Nova (Oct. 26, 2009).

Tahir-ul-Qadri, Shaykh-ul-Islam Dr. Muhammad. *Fatwa on Suicide bombings and terrorism*. Minhaj-ul-Quran International, 2010.
Talbot, Michael. *The Holographic Universe*. Harper Collins, 1991.
Tomberlin, James (ed.). *Philosophical Perspectives: Mind, Causation, and World*, vol. 11 (Oxford: Blackwell Publishers, 1997).
Tony Snow show (Mar. 29, 2006).
Truzzi, Marcello. 'On Pseudo-Skepticism.' *Zetetic Scholar* 12–13 (1987).
US Dept. of Health, Education, and Welfare. 'Mercury Containing Drug Products for Topical Anti-microbial Over-the-Counter Human Use: Establishment of a Monograph.' *Federal Register* 47 (1982): 436–442.
US Senate Committee on Environment and Public Works, 'Inhofe Floor Speech On Global Warming: 2007 – Global Warming Alarmism Reaches A Tipping Point' (Oct. 26, 2007).
Van Flandern, T. 'Big Bang: Top 30 Problems.' *Meta Research Bulletin* 11 (2002).
Vergano, Dan. 'Who's Teaching the Doctors.' *USA Today* (Mar. 9, 2000).
Wager, E. and T. Jefferson, 'The Shortcomings of Peer Review.' *Learned Publications* 14 (2001): 257–63.
Wagner, M. W. and M. Monnet. 'Attitudes of college professors toward extrasensory perception.' *Zetetic Scholar* 5 (1979): 7–16.
Wald, G. 'Life and Mind in the Universe.' *International Journal of Quantum Chemistry* 26 Suppl 11 (1984): 1–15.
Warkany, J. and D. M. Hubbard. 'Acrodynia and Mercury.' *Journal of Pediatrics* 42:3 (1953).
Weinstein, Michael. *With God on Our Side: One Man's War Against an Evangelical Coup in America's Military*. St. Martin's Griffin Press, 2008.
West-Eberhard, M. J. 'Developmental plasticity-origin of species difference.' *PNAS* 102 Suppl 1 (2005): 6543–49.
Wiesel, Elie. *Night*. Farrar, Strauss, Giroux, 2006.
Wilbur, Ken. *Quantum Questions: Mystical Writings of the World's Great Physicists*. Shambhala, 1981.
Wolf, Naomi. *The End of America: A Letter of Warning to a Young Patriot*. Chelsea Green Publishing, 2007.
Woolff, P. 'Deception in Scientific Research.' *Jurimetrics Journal* 29 (1998).
Wright, Edward. 'Inflation.' *Cosmology Tutorial*, http://www.astro.ucla.edu/~wright/cosmolog.htm.
Wright, M. T. *The New Testament and the People of God*. Fortress Press, 1992.
Wright, Robert *The Evolution of God*. Little, Brown, and Co., 2009.
Zajonc, Arthur (ed.). *New Physics and Cosmology: dialogues with the Dalai Lama*. Oxford University Press, 2004.
Zee, A. *Fearful Symmetry: the search for beauty in modern physics*. Macmillan, 1986.